E Pluribus Unum?

E Pluribus Unum?

Contemporary and Historical Perspectives on Immigrant Political Incorporation

Gary Gerstle and John Mollenkopf

Editors

Russell Sage Foundation • New York

The Russell Sage Foundation

The Russell Sage Foundation, one of the oldest of America's general purpose foundations, was established in 1907 by Mrs. Margaret Olivia Sage for "the improvement of social and living conditions in the United States." The Foundation seeks to fulfill this mandate by fostering the development and dissemination of knowledge about the country's political, social, and economic problems. While the Foundation endeavors to assure the accuracy and objectivity of each book it publishes, the conclusions and interpretations in Russell Sage Foundation publications are those of the authors and not of the Foundation, its Trustees, or its staff. Publication by Russell Sage, therefore, does not imply Foundation endorsement.

Library of Congress Cataloging-in-Publication Data

E pluribus unum? : contemporary and historical perspectives on immigrant political incorporation / Gary Gerstle and John Mollenkopf, editors.
p. cm.
Includes bibliographical references and index.
ISBN 0-87154-306-0
1. Immigrants—United States—History. 2. United States—Emigration and immigration—History. 3. Americanization—History. I. Gerstle, Gary, 1954–
II. Mollenkopf, John H., 1946–
JV6450 .P58 2001
325.73—dc21   2001041780

Text design by Suzanne Nichols

RUSSELL SAGE FOUNDATION
112 East 64th Street, New York, New York 10021
10 9 8 7 6 5 4 3 2 1

To John Higham and Martin Shefter,
who walked these paths before us

—— Contents ——

Contributors   ix

Acknowledgments   xi

Introduction   The Political Incorporation of Immigrants,
               Then and Now   1
               Gary Gerstle and John Mollenkopf

PART I   THE POLITICS OF IMMIGRANT
               INCORPORATION

Chapter 1   Beyond the Boss: Immigration and American
               Political Culture from 1880 to 1940   33
               Evelyn Savidge Sterne

Chapter 2   Building America, One Person at a Time:
               Naturalization and Political Behavior of the
               Naturalized in Contemporary American Politics   67
               Louis DeSipio

PART II   IMMIGRANTS AND AMERICAN CIVIC
               CULTURE

Chapter 3   Sea Change in the Civic Culture in the 1960s   109
               Philip Gleason

Chapter 4   Making Americans: Immigration Meets Race   143
               Desmond King

PART III   TRANSNATIONALISM AND THE
               POLITICAL BEHAVIOR OF IMMIGRANTS

Chapter 5   Immigrants, Transnationalism, and Ethnicization:
               A Comparison of This Great Wave and the Last   175
               Ewa Morawska

Chapter 6   On the Political Participation of Transnational
             Migrants: Old Practices and New Trends   213
             Luis Eduardo Guarnizo

PART IV   *IMMIGRANTS AND THE AMERICAN
           STATE*

Chapter 7   Policing Boundaries: Migration, Citizenship, and
             the State   267
             T. Alexander Aleinikoff

Chapter 8   Historical Patterns of Immigrant Status and
             Incorporation in the United States   292
             Reed Ueda

PART V   *IMMIGRANTS, SCHOOLS, AND
           POLITICAL SOCIALIZATION*

Chapter 9   School for Citizens: The Politics of Civic
             Education from 1790 to 1990   331
             David Tyack

Chapter 10   Public Education, Immigrants, and Racialization:
             The Contemporary Americanization Project   371
             Laurie Olsen

Index   413

—— Contributors ——

Gary Gerstle is professor of history and director of the Center for Historical Studies at the University of Maryland.

John Mollenkopf is professor of political science and sociology and director of the Center for Urban Research at the City University of New York Graduate Center.

T. Alexander Aleinikoff is a professor at the Georgetown University Law Center and a senior associate at the Migration Policy Institute.

Louis DeSipio is associate professor of political science and director of the Latina-Latino Studies Program at the University of Illinois at Urbana-Champaign.

Philip Gleason is professor emeritus of history at the University of Notre Dame.

Luis Eduardo Guarnizo is associate professor of sociology at the Department of Human and Community Development at the University of California, Davis.

Desmond King is professor of politics and fellow of St. John's College, University of Oxford.

Ewa Morawska is professor of sociology and history at the University of Pennsylvania.

Laurie Olsen is executive director of California Tomorrow in Oakland, California.

Evelyn Savidge Sterne is assistant professor of history at the University of Rhode Island.

David Tyack is Vida Jacks Professor of Education and professor emeritus of history at Stanford University.

Reed Ueda is professor of history at Tufts University.

―― Acknowledgments ――

I N PUTTING TOGETHER this book, we have assembled a number of
debts that we would like to acknowledge here. Our greatest
debt, and it is a very large one indeed, is to the Social Science
Research Council and, in particular, to its Committee on International Migration, chaired by Charles Hirschmann and directed by
Josh DeWind. The committee invited us to participate in its major
conference on international migration in Sanibel, Florida, in 1996.
Immediately after Sanibel, the committee organized a Historical
Comparisons Working Group and authorized it to develop work-
shops on themes that had interested Sanibel conference partici-
pants but had not received sufficient attention there. Out of that
working group, chaired by Nancy Foner and consisting of Richard
Alba, Josh DeWind, Joel Perlmann, George Sanchez, Joe Trotter,
Mary Waters, and the two of us, came the idea for a workshop on
questions of immigrant political incorporation, past and present.
That workshop, funded by the SSRC and occurring in Santa Fe,
New Mexico, in May 1997, formed the foundation for the current
book. The Santa Fe gathering would not have been possible but
for the generosity of the SSRC, its commitment to developing new
literature on migration and immigrants, and the expertise of its
staff, committees and working groups. We would like to thank, in
particular: Josh DeWind, who gave us critical help with every aspect of the workshop, from the largest intellectual matters to the
smallest administrative details; Nancy Foner, whose enthusiasm
and intellectual guidance were indispensable; and members of the
Historical Comparisons Working Group, who made invaluable
contributions to the workshop design. Christian Fuersich, program
assistant for the Committee on International Migration, was always
available to help with innumerable administrative chores and

helped us to solve the tricky logistical problems that any conference, even a comparatively small one such as ours, generates. We
would also like to thank Christian's successors, Sara Pasko, Walter
Miller, and Veda Truesdale, who have helped us in numerous
ways to turn the workshop papers into a book.

Most of the authors included in this volume offered the first
drafts of their essays at the Santa Fe workshop. In addition to our
authors, the workshop included a number of scholars who offered
commentary on the papers and, through their particular interven-
tions and reflections on the workshop as a whole, added a great
deal to our enterprise. We would like to thank them all: Josh
DeWind, Paula Fass, Nancy Foner, David Guttierez, Ira Katznelson, Paula McClain, Terence McDonald, Joel Perlmann, Nina Glick
Schiller, Joseph Stewart, Margaret Weir, and Aristide Zolberg.

We have been impressed with the professionalism, expertise,
and thoroughness of the publications wing of the Russell Sage
Foundation and feel fortunate to have placed our book in their
care. We would like to thank, in particular, David Haproff and
Suzanne Nichols, the past and current directors of publications at
Russell Sage, as well as our production editor, Emily Chang, our
copyeditor, Katherine Kimball, and other members of the publications staff.

Finally, we would like to thank our authors. They, after all,
have done the lion's share of the work for this volume and they
have responded diligently and with good cheer to the two rounds
of revisions requested by us and then to a third round requested
by the publisher. We thank them for their efforts and we hope that
they will be proud, as are we, to be contributors to this volume.

Gary Gerstle
John Mollenkopf

June 2001

—— Introduction ——

The Political Incorporation of Immigrants, Then and Now

Gary Gerstle and John Mollenkopf

I N THE HALF century between 1881 and 1930, 27.6 million immigrants arrived on our shores, mostly from eastern, central, and
southern Europe. Although as many as a third of some groups
ultimately returned to their countries of origin, those who stayed
had an enormous impact on a national population that stood at
only 50 million in 1880. In the peak decade of this influx, between
1901 and 1910, newly arriving immigrants alone boosted the nation's population by 10.4 percent and accounted for more than
half the population growth in many of the cities where they settled. To distinguish them from earlier English, Scottish, Irish, German, and Scandinavian immigrants, commentators of that period
called them "the new immigrants."

Now, at the dawn of the twenty-first century, another great
migration is once more reshaping America. Since Congress liberalized the immigration laws in 1965, more than 20 million immigrants have arrived from Latin America, the Caribbean, and Asia.[1]
Although these new "new immigrants" make up a smaller share of
a much larger national population (totaling 194 million in 1965),
they, too, are having a pervasive impact on America, just as arriving in a new society is reshaping the lives of these newcomers
and their children. Owing to declining fertility rates among the
native born, these new "new immigrants" make up more than 30
percent of the overall national population growth. Because immigrants are concentrating in certain places, from which natives

1

have tended to move away, the substantial national impact is magnified in the "gateway cities" in which they have settled. In places like New York, Los Angeles, Miami, and San Francisco, immigrants and their children comprise more than half the total population (Mollenkopf, Olson, and Ross forthcoming; Gerstle 2000).

Now, as then, incorporating this massive body of immigrants into American society is a central challenge for our civic and political institutions. This process goes to the core of who we are as a people and as a nation. It is also deeply intertwined with the many struggles over the status of involuntary Americans, particularly Native Americans, African Americans, Hispanic Americans in the parts of the United States ceded from Mexico, and Puerto Ricans. Because the nature of modern America has largely been determined by the interaction of immigration, urbanization, and industrialization, understanding the interplay of these factors has been a focal concern of historians, political scientists, and sociologists. Scholars from these disciplines, as well as economic historians and historically oriented geographers, have produced an enormous body of work on the turn-of-the-century migration. Those who study the current immigration have not yet produced an equal body of work, but they are well on their way. To say the least, what immigrant absorption means for America and what living in America means for immigrants and their children are now, as they were eighty years ago, highly charged topics commanding the attention not only of scholars but of federal commissions, the National Academy of Sciences, journalists, and broad public opinion, as well.

Although the absorption of these two great waves of immigration have been critical episodes in the nation-building process and have stimulated much social research, surprisingly little effort has been devoted to the systematic study of how these two eras resemble or differ from each other. Few historians of the past great wave of migration have addressed the current one, and only a few social scientists studying the current migration have formally compared it with the previous one, though they approach the current wave with many, often unexamined, assumptions about the last. (For exceptions, see Foner 2000; Min 1999; Shanahan and Olzak 1999; Morawska 1990; and Morawska and Spohn 1997.) Far too little dialogue has taken place about the lessons historians and social scientists can learn from each other or about how juxtaposing the two waves can help us expand our ability to theorize and understand either the specific processes of immigrant incorporation or the larger story of American national development. Instead of embracing the lessons of historiography, contemporary social scientists often rely on stereotypes, even caricatures, of what historians have come to believe and prefer to think of the new "new immigration" as distinctive. For their part, historians have not risen to the challenge of applying the lessons they learned from the earlier wave to the current one.

This volume aims to correct two aspects of this situation: First, it engages historians and social scientists in a dialogue about how each group thinks about immigrant political incorporation and what they can learn from each other. Second, it sets the stage for the more systematic comparative study of what Rogers Smith (2001) has called "the politics of people-building" in these two eras. The result, we hope, is at least modest progress on both fronts. Readers of this volume will see some of the lessons that social scientists should have learned from historians but did not. They will also see how the distinctively new ways in which contemporary social scientists see the current situation may be of value to historians as they go about their work. Finally, the juxtaposition of the two approaches allows us to ask how the similarities and differences between these two periods may help both disciplines to transcend the time-boundedness of their perspectives.

SIMILARITIES AND DIFFERENCES IN THE OLD AND NEW "NEW IMMIGRANTS"

The arrival of 28 million foreign-born people from 1880 to 1930 drove the net foreign-born population of the United States from 6.7 million to 14 million, or from 9.7 percent to 14.7 percent of the total. Three-quarters came from Europe, particularly Italy (4.6 million), Austria-Hungary (4.1 million), Russia and Poland (3.7 million), and Germany (2.9 million), but this wave of immigration also planted seeds that would germinate in the contemporary period, with 148,000 arriving from China, 926,000 from Mexico, and

368,000 from the Caribbean (Gibson and Lennon 1999). Although these new foreign residents spread across the country, different groups tended to cluster in different places, particularly in large, rapidly growing cities like Boston, New York, Chicago, Pittsburgh, Milwaukee, St. Louis, and San Francisco. New immigrants provided half the population growth in these cities at the turn of the century.

By 1930, immigrants and their children made up half to three-quarters of the populations of these and other northern and western cities. They provided the labor force for rapidly growing manufacturing, construction, warehousing, and other blue-collar sectors, leading to the formation of a white, ethnic, urban working class. Nationality, gender, and industry interacted to create new ethnic divisions of labor that provided the foundation for post–World War I developments—the Polish autoworkers of Detroit, the Italian construction workers of Chicago, and the Jewish garment workers of New York.

Legal restrictions on immigration adopted in 1924 and after, the Great Depression of 1929 to 1941, and World War II (1941 to 1945) dramatically cut the number of new foreign arrivals. Between 1930 and 1965, only 5.5 million immigrants arrived, mostly post–World War II displaced persons. As the previous generation of immigrants aged and passed away, the number and share of foreign-born residents in the U.S. population gradually diminished, bottoming out at 10.3 million persons and 5.4 percent of the population in 1960. At the same time, their children, the "old second generation," became an increasingly large share of the population as the U.S. economy was growing steadily, income inequality declining, and the median family income rising substantially in real terms.

These circumstances produced steady upward mobility for the (white) native-born children of the immigrants who arrived from 1880 to 1930 compared either with their parents or, because they were starting on the whole from a lower base, with the native born (Alba 1990; Waters 1990; Card, DiNardo, and Estes 1999). The resumption of sustained national economic growth after the onset of World War II created many new economic opportunities for these immigrant children. It also created new demands for unskilled labor in northern and western cities, which was met not by renewed European immigration but through the northward and westward migration of African Americans from the southern states, later augmented by Puerto Rican migration to New York City and, to a lesser degree, Chicago, and by Mexican migration to San Antonio, Los Angeles, and other emerging cities of the Southwest. The children of the earlier immigrants generally stood in front of these minority groups in the ethnic queue of the labor market. Their upward mobility gradually blurred the formerly sharp distinctions between native white Protestants and young adult children of Catholic and Jewish immigrants. Meanwhile, the appearance of comparatively disadvantaged native minority groups alongside these white ethnics made the distinction between whites and blacks (and other native minority groups) the central social cleavage in northern metropolitan areas.

With major revision in the rules governing immigration in 1965, however, the seemingly fixed nature of racial difference as the central division in urban society once more began to change as the number of immigrants arriving in the United States and the net foreign-born population began to grow again. Twenty million foreign-born persons have been legally admitted since 1965, and several million more have arrived without documentation. This surge caused the net foreign-born population to rebound to 28.4 million, or 10.4 percent of the population, by 2000.[2] In contrast with the previous wave, only 3.2 million of these later immigrants came from Europe. Most came from Mexico (4.5 million), the Caribbean (3.4 million), other parts of Latin America (2.4 million), and Asia (6.9 million, primarily from China, the Philippines, Korea, Vietnam, and India). Even more so than before, the foreign-born population is concentrated in a relatively few "gateway" cities. More than a third of the national total are located in the Los Angeles and New York metropolitan areas alone, with another fifth in Miami, Houston, Chicago, San Francisco, and Boston. Mexican factory workers, Chinese restaurant workers, West Indian nurses, and Korean grocers have added new layers to the ethnic division of labor in these places.

These two waves of immigration share powerful similarities but also have sharp differences. Both waves ended up in disproportionately urban destinations; both inserted new national-origin groups into an established ethnic division of labor (that is, distinctive ethnic concentrations within the lattice of industries and occupations) in these urban areas; and both set up complicated new patterns of competition and synergy with previous immigrant and native populations. In both waves, groups clustered in certain neighborhoods, giving them a specific ethnic character, but these neighborhoods nonetheless remained diverse in their composition, requiring groups to interact with one another. The trajectories of each group reflected the opportunities and barriers afforded by the places they arrived at and the time they arrived as well as the strategies, resources, and burdens each group brought to bear on them. Each wave of groups faced established elites, interests, and institutions that feared they might destabilize prevailing political arrangements but that also sought to use the new immigrants to advance their own agendas. Both waves arrived in the United States at times of rapid economic transformation and growing income and wealth inequality (in part stimulated by their arrival at the bottom of the social hierarchy). Both sought to organize collective political and economic action that would span the ethnic and cultural boundaries created by differing national origins. All experienced religious or racial discrimination. Even the European immigrants of the first wave and their descendants had to fight hard to win acceptance for their Catholic and Jewish religions and to gain recognition that they were "white" and not members of "inferior" Slavic, Italian, and Jewish races.

Although these two great waves of immigration experienced broadly similar processes, the specific contexts of origin and reception are starkly different, or so it would seem from the twenty-first-century vantage point. In 1880, the United States was still recovering from the Civil War. The North was largely white and Protestant (though Irish and German Catholics had already made their marks on northern cities and had been important participants in the Union army). The northern cities were entering a period of sustained economic growth and transformation that would begin with steam, rail, and small manufacturing and culminate in electricity, the automobile, air travel, corporate capitalism, and mass consumption. Turn-of-the-century immigration was a central stimulant to this transformation. If we can judge by Olivier Zunz's (1982) seminal study of Detroit, immigrants were segregated by ethnicity and integrated by class at the beginning of this process but more integrated by ethnicity and segregated by class at the end of it.

The immigrants entering this economic vortex often succeeded in increasing their real household earnings over time, but this took far longer for most groups than is often recognized. Not until the 1940s and 1950s, sixty to seventy years after the new immigrants began arriving, could their descendants point with some assurance to their groups' economic and social progress. They secured this progress not just by working diligently at their jobs but also by struggling through a major economic crisis and political transformation, the Great Depression and the New Deal. Their votes made the Democratic Party dominant in national politics, and their support was critical in building a state willing to regulate capitalism and promote political incorporation among immigrants and other outsiders. This process nationalized the urban political machines that had earlier mobilized their votes and promoted blue-collar white ethnic interests, including strong labor unions, social protections of various sorts, and an end to religious discrimination. By the 1940s and 1950s, these cultural and political struggles had yielded real progress across the immigrant generations in economic, social, and political terms.

A less visible source of this progress may have been the constriction of immigrant flows—first by World War I, then by restrictive national quotas enacted in 1924, and finally by the Depression and World War II. These factors dramatically slowed the arrival of new immigrant workers, who, it was feared, might have weakened the labor market position of their predecessors and extended their cultural contact with the old country. The 1924 quotas, which were meant principally to stop southern and eastern European immigrants (and to reinforce bans on Asian immigrants) on the grounds that they were of racially inferior stock, angered those European immigrants already here and impelled them to organize, to become naturalized, and to vote. Many became convinced that economic and social progress would come only through political and social conflict. They were also eager to shed their racial stigmatization either by civil rights campaigns to overturn all racial distinctions or by becoming "white" themselves.

Although only time will tell, the picture after 1965 seems to be quite different. Instead of settling in prosperous industrial cities, most new "new immigrants" have found themselves in urban areas that have been undergoing a tumultuous racial transition and uncertain economic change. This shift has been especially rapid in the blue-collar activities that absorbed so many in the earlier immigrant wave. Where urban economies have been prospering, they have done so largely on the basis of advanced corporate services, nonprofit social services, and government employment (as well as high technology in southern California). The immigrant groups with large numbers of professionals among their ranks, such as Koreans, Indians, and Filipinos, have experienced remarkable social mobility in these contexts. Most recent immigrants, however, have lacked the education or skills required for success in the new economy.

The previous wave of immigrants had also been poorly educated, but in this respect they did not much differ from the native population of their time, nor were credential requirements for good jobs nearly so high as they are today. Although both immigrant waves were ethnically diverse, the current one is largely non-European, so native whites are prone to classify its members as nonwhites alongside African Americans, even as immigrants have increasingly competed with blacks for jobs and political influence. Moreover, as blue-collar work in central cities has declined, so have the traditional institutions of immigrant political incorporation, including political party organizations, labor unions, and the Catholic Church.

Finally, today's immigrants enter a more culturally relaxed, multicultural, and perhaps less prejudiced society, in which the black struggle for justice has ended many aspects of institutionalized discrimination against nonwhites. In the mid-1990s, the political environment did become hostile toward immigrants, as anti-immigrant groups sought to reduce the flow of new migrants, restrict immigrants' contact with or allegiance to their nations of origin, and penalize those who did not become American citizens or learn English quickly. This anti-immigrant reaction appears not to have taken hold, however, serving mainly to stimulate higher levels of naturalization and political mobilization among immigrants themselves. Meanwhile, America seems to be tolerating the spreading practice of holding dual citizenships. No looming international geopolitical cataclysm seems likely to prompt native-born

Americans to force immigrants to choose between their allegiances, although one could always emerge (with China, for example) with little notice.

Echoes of the past immigrant wave can be found in the desire of many contemporary immigrants, even nonwhite ones, to distance themselves socially and politically from African Americans and to become if not white then at least "not black." Competition between the new immigrants and their children and the black political establishment in many areas may strengthen this color line within the nonwhite population and reinscribe the nation's oldest and most invidious racial distinction—between black and nonblack—on twenty-first-century metropolitan society. On the other hand, it is equally possible that the colored character of the current immigration will scramble old racial distinctions, even to the point of removing race as a defining characteristic of America.

In short, the systematic comparison of political incorporation of the great eras of immigration at the end of the nineteenth and twentieth centuries has much to teach us about American national development. How much will future generations care about an entity called America? In our increasingly globalized age, will national identities and incorporation into national polities cease to have so much salience, while immigrant affiliation becomes far more open ended and voluntary than in the past? It is hard to know. Nevertheless, we cannot turn our backs. It is incumbent upon us as scholars and citizens to make sense of where we have been and where we are going.

DISCIPLINARY PERSPECTIVES

One might well argue that sociology and political science were both founded in the United States on the study of immigrant incorporation. Certainly, those who established the Chicago school of sociology used that city as a laboratory for understanding processes of neighborhood change, ethnic succession, and urban transformation. Survey research and social research were initially prompted by concern for the living conditions of immigrants. The early works of political science also dealt with big-city bosses, the reform of municipal administration, and the ethnic base of politics. Indeed, even Robert Dahl's classic 1961 work of political science, *Who Governs? Democracy and Power in an American City,* tells the story of how ethnic succession intertwined with urban political modernization in New Haven.

The early work in these social science disciplines produced a "received wisdom" based on the apparent success of the first and second generations of immigrants between the 1930s and the 1960s. It held that they experienced "straight-line assimilation," to the point where the contemporary descendants of white immigrants, at least, can choose their "ethnic options." As social scientists turn their attention to the current wave of migration, however, they are less likely to think that this "received wisdom" applies. They see, instead, the possibility of "segmented assimilation" and downward mobility for many immigrant groups, especially those most likely to be classified as racially nonwhite (Portes and Zhou 1993; Gans 1992). They worry about a systematic exclusion of current immigrants from politics and the ways in which local institutions work against incorporation rather than promote it, as, in their view, historians have argued in the past.

Much of the best historical scholarship questions whether the "received wisdom" was ever adequate for its time, much less for today. Although some contemporary social scientists paint a positive picture of the urban machines, for example, historians see them in a far less flattering light. Contemporary social scientists seem to think historians have concluded that assimilation worked in a fairly straightforward fashion, whereas contemporary historical scholarship describes the contested nature of this process, the price that groups paid to achieve material gains, and the ways in which reality departed from its democratic image (Gerstle 1999). The time is ripe, therefore, to take careful stock of what the best strands of both kinds of scholarship are saying and how they can learn from each other.

A full-scale comparison of immigration past and present is too big an undertaking to be accomplished in a single volume. Our task here is more modest and more focused: to inquire into the manner in which immigrants, either voluntarily or involuntarily, became or are becoming part of the American polity. We approach this task by looking at institutions—political parties, the state, labor unions, voluntary associations, and schools—that are thought to be important to political incorporation and by asking how they have done—or failed to do—their work in defining the boundaries of the American nation, extending or restricting access to citizenship and civil rights, and formulating processes of inclusion and exclusion. We also look at how the political cultures that immigrants encountered in America and those that they brought with them, or to which they remain linked, influence the trajectories of political inclusion or exclusion. We ask how institutional processes and cultural dispositions have shaped the process of becoming American—or not—and how immigrants articulate their political and cultural aspirations.

This book is organized into five parts. Each part consists of a pair of essays, one by a historian (in one case, by a historically minded sociologist) and one by a social scientist (in one case, by a legal scholar), offering different perspectives on the assigned theme. In some parts, the essays reflect methodological and conceptual divergences between history and the social sciences; in others, the differences are less disciplinary than interpretive or ideological. In all cases, we think the scholarly pairings generate a lively interchange of ideas and enrich our understanding of the story of immigrant political incorporation, past and present.

THE POLITICS OF IMMIGRANT INCORPORATION

The "political boss" and the "party machine" hold special places in historical thinking about the modes of political incorporation dominant a hundred years ago. Many historical accounts depict the bosses as crooked but indispensable caretakers of urban immigrant masses whom no one else would help to adapt to their new circumstances. Just how important were bosses and their political machines to immigrant political incorporation? Did institutions such as unions, churches, and other kinds of voluntary associations play more important, if less appreciated, roles? Given that political parties seem weak and incapable of fulfilling these functions today, what critical institutions of incorporation, if any, have taken their place?

Evelyn Savidge Sterne assesses the myth of the "boss" in her wide-ranging and illuminating "Beyond the Boss: Immigration and American Political Culture from 1880 to 1940." She argues that political machines were undoubtedly an important feature of the immigrant landscape, though neither as dominant nor as empowering of immigrants as some scholars have thought. Indeed, Sterne argues, labor unions, civic associations, and the Catholic Church were as important to immigrant political incorporation as the political machine—perhaps even more so. So, too, was the Great Depression, an economic crisis that created opportunities for political reorganization and new spaces for participation by newcomers. The absence of strong political machines today may not hinder contemporary immigrant political incorporation, as is sometimes thought, especially where labor unions and civic associations organize immigrant communities. Sterne points out, however, that political incorporation can take a long time—fifty years in the case of the old "new immigrants"—and depends not just on the efforts of political leaders and the immigrants themselves but also on events, such as economic depressions, that throw prevailing political structures into disarray and create opportunities for new forms of political mobilization.

Are the institutions Sterne writes about available to immigrants today? Louis DeSipio's meticulous "Building America, One Person at a Time: Naturalization and Political Behavior of the Naturalized in Contemporary American Politics" argues that they are not. While noting the rising number of immigrants who have naturalized in the 1990s, DeSipio's central finding is that relatively few of these recently naturalized are politically active, at least as measured by their willingness to vote. The reason, he suggests, lies in an American political system whose institutions and rules have, since the 1950s, discouraged the participation of the poorer and less educated elements of the American electorate. He underscores the decline of political parties (and their machines) as one factor and the increasing professionalization of civic associations, with the attendant atrophy of their grassroots appeal, as another. Even the 1965 Voting Rights Act, passed to encourage minority participation in American politics, has, ironically, worked in the opposite direction by creating safe districts in which minority representatives, once elected, encounter little opposition and thus see little point in galvanizing the electorate or mobilizing new voters (such as the recently naturalized). If the recent immigrants are becoming incorporated into something called America, DeSipio makes clear, they are not doing so through partisan political institutions or processes.

DeSipio paints a sobering picture of immigrant political disinterest and alienation. Nevertheless, his analysis, in combination with Sterne's, suggests that some institutions and events may still be capable of altering this situation. First, the organization of immigrant workers into labor unions that is currently under way in certain immigrant metropolises, such as Los Angeles, suggests that it may yet be possible to resuscitate one institution that, in the past, has been central to immigrant political mobilization. Sterne's analysis also reminds us of how long it took the "new immigrants" of the previous era to make their mark on American politics, an effect accomplished only when an economic crisis weakened the dominant political arrangements. From this perspective, a full evaluation of the current immigrant situation may not be possible for another twenty to thirty years. We have to be alert, too, to how dramatic changes in economic well-being or public policy can affect immigrants' relationship with their polity. Nevertheless, DeSipio's analysis ably documents the obstacles to immigrant political mobilization and incorporation that currently prevail in American society.

IMMIGRANTS AND AMERICAN CIVIC CULTURE

Civic culture is a second important arena for immigrant political incorporation. A popular argument, powerfully set forth by Philip Gleason in "Sea Change in the Civic Culture of the 1960s," holds that traditional civic culture, dominant through the mid-1960s, attracted immigrants with a promise of equality, liberty, and individual opportunity. To participate in this culture, immigrants had to sacrifice some of their ethnic distinctiveness and repudiate group claims—for example, demanding special treatment from the state because of their group's alleged accomplishments or victimization. If they were willing to forgo these claims, they would be accorded the same status as old-stock Americans. Gleason does not deny the persistent gap between this ideal civic culture, which he calls, following Gunnar Myrdal, the American Creed, and its actual application to American life, but he argues that it "nonetheless has been brought closer to full realization over the course of the years," making America an exceptionally free and democratic society.

According to Gleason, this civic culture fell apart in the 1960s, diminished by the conflict and disillusionment surrounding the civil rights revolution and the war in Vietnam. In its place arose a new political culture, less optimistic than the old and more willing to acknowledge group claims by oppressed minorities. This has altered the political climate, giving immigrants much less reason to join the mainstream and much more encouragement for maintaining their linguistic and cultural separateness. As a result, Gleason suggests, America has been less successful since the 1960s in incorporating new immigrants into its polity and in convincing them of the value of the American Creed. If such circumstances persist, Gleason implies, America will not only lose its capacity to absorb newcomers but will also diminish the very freedom and democracy that have long been this country's hallmark.

Desmond King disputes this line of interpretation in his provocative "Making Americans: Immigration Meets Race." He rejects the notion that the American Creed of liberal universalism was ever a dominant ideology in the United States or that we can understand American history as gradually realizing the creed's ideals. Focusing on the period from 1880 to 1930, he demonstrates an intensifying discrimination against eastern and southern European immigrants, Chinese immigrants, Native Americans, and African Americans that undermines the argument that liberal ideals were predominant. Drawing on the work of Rogers Smith, he insists that American national identity was, from the country's very beginning, constructed on the exclusion from the polity and from metaphorical representations of the nation (such as in Westerns and other movies) of groups marked as savage, racially inferior, or non-Protestant. From his perspective, it is wrong to view the 1960s as a fall from the golden age of American liberal universalism, for that golden age never existed. The 1960s should be seen instead as one more in an ongoing series of negotiations through which Americans have attempted to uproot old, and stubborn, problems of racial discrimination and exclusion.

TRANSNATIONALISM AND THE POLITICAL BEHAVIOR OF IMMIGRANTS

Implicit in the arguments put forward by DeSipio and Gleason is the suggestion that the forces of social and political incorporation are weaker now than they were at the turn of the past century. Either the allure of becoming American or the pressure to become so has atrophied—perhaps both. Whereas DeSipio and Gleason focus on factors internal to the United States to explain this phenomenon, another group of scholars focuses on external factors, especially globalization. This latter group claims that today's immigrants are far more international or "transnational" than previous immigrants and thus are much less willing to embrace one nation's culture or polity. To contemporary immigration scholars, this emergent "transnationalism" means that immigrants are so immersed in the cultures of two countries—their country of origin and their country of residence—that they belong to neither but find reason to cultivate national loyalties to both. Transnational ties diminish immigrant loyalty to the United States, thereby retarding, even halting, their political incorporation.

The success of this argument would seem to depend a great deal on whether transnationalism is in fact a phenomenon distinctively new. Its advocates claim that it is. But is this the case? In a sophisticated paper, "Immigrants, Transnationalism, and Ethnicization: A Comparison of This Great Wave and the Last," Ewa Morawska argues that the immigrants of the period from 1880 to 1940 possessed far deeper transnational loyalties than is generally realized. As many as 30 to 40 percent of the southern and eastern Europeans who arrived at the turn of the twentieth century returned home, and many traveled back and forth across the Atlantic. Those who did not kept in close touch with their relatives and friends in the old country through letters and newspapers. Virtually all of those European immigrants, whether they stayed or returned home, constructed complex identities that drew on both the Old World and New World cultures, a culturally syncretic, even transnational, process that historians now label "ethnicization." In view of the prevalence and durability of transatlantic ties that historians have demonstrated, Morawska urges scholars of contemporary migration to abandon their presumption that earlier waves of immigration can be understood in terms of a rupture with the old country and "straight-line assimilation" into American society.

Morawska does not believe that the new transnationalism is simply a carbon copy of the old, however. She stresses the greater diversity of peoples and backgrounds discernible in the current immigration and the consequent variation in the forms of ethnicization and transnationalism. Morawska calls on scholars to examine these differences, past and present, in a systematic way. The transnationalisms of the two periods also differ because of what Morawska sees as a decline of the nationalist ideal. Neither the immigrants nor the natives of today regard the nation, or "la patria," according to Morawska, as the "primordial, morally imperative, and exclusive symbolic community" it was once thought to be. Across a wide range of societies, many individuals and groups no longer feel the nationalist imperative that earlier generations experienced. The nation-states in which they reside are often willing to acknowledge forms of religious, ethnic, regional, or gender belonging that are not only independent of the nationalist ideal but may actually corrode it. Most remarkable, perhaps, is that nation-states seem increasingly willing to recognize the legitimacy of dual citizenship and thus to accept the possibility that other nation-states might have equal or greater claims on their citizens. This official tolerance of dual, even competing, loyalties, Morawska points out, would have been unimaginable fifty or one hundred years ago; its existence would seem to have important consequences for both the processes and content of immigrant political incorporation.

Luis Eduardo Guarnizo, in "On the Political Participation of Transnational Migrants: Old Practices and New Trends," picks up Morawska's challenge in his intensive case study of transnational political practices among Dominican and Colombian migrants to New York and Salvadoran immigrants in Los Angeles. While acknowledging that transnational political activity was an important process in the past, he argues that it has taken on distinctive new forms, not simply because international travel and communications are now cheaper and faster but also because neither sending-country states nor the United States are forcing immigrants to choose one national membership or the other. To the contrary, having spent many years thinking of emigrants as traitors to the national cause, sending-country states are now actively encouraging dual citizenship, and the U.S. government no longer seems to level any sanctions against this practice. Retaining membership in the polity of the sending state is no longer mutually exclusive with becoming an American citizen or engaging in political action in the United States as a resident alien. Instead, some sending states now want their emigrants to play formal political roles both "there" and "here."

Guarnizo distinguishes between the "transnationalism from below" discussed by many contemporary scholars and the "transnationalism from above" most of interest to him. The former describes the tendency of immigrants to retain ties to their home villages, maintaining transnational families and kinship networks and investing in communal facilities back in the villages, such as schools, health clinics, or power plants. Guarnizo joins those who take the view, however, that the most important aspect of transnational political activity is efforts by sending countries to construct a "deterritorialized state" that will retain the loyalties of emigrants, keep them under political control, and use them to advance sending-state interests. He documents this position by a close look at three groups in two cities. As he notes, every major Dominican political party has an office in Washington Heights (the Dominican neighborhood of northern Manhattan), where Dominican presidential candidates campaign and raise funds. Indeed, former Dominican president Leonel Fernández lived for many years in Washington Heights and retains his green card. In 1997, the Dominican Congress granted Dominicans living abroad the right to vote in Dominican presidential elections, starting in 2002. This close connection with home-country politics is not inconsistent, Guarnizo points out, with a high level of involvement in New York City politics, including the election of Dominicans to seats on the city council and in the state assembly. Similarly, Colombians living abroad have been able to vote in that country's national elections since 1961, and the Colombian government has established a program to provide services to and promote Colombian identity among its emigrants in the United States and has sought to use them as a lobby in support of U.S. aid to Colombia.

Finally, the Salvadoran governing party, Arena, has made a major effort since 1992 to gain support among Salvadorans in Los Angeles. While Arena has not yet made much headway there, Guarnizo sees its activities as fundamentally similar to the efforts of the more successful Dominican and Colombian governments to control their emigrants and to organize them as a political resource within the United States. He expects this to be a relatively permanent feature of immigrant politics in the United States, and likely to make this immigrant wave's road to political incorporation different from that of the last.

IMMIGRANTS AND THE AMERICAN STATE

Until recently, scholars of contemporary immigration have shown little interest in the state's role in shaping the immigrant experience. They have depicted the state as irrelevant or at best secondary to the economic and social forces that impel international migration. Yet as T. Alexander Aleinikoff and Reed Ueda show, the state deeply structures the immigrant experience. It establishes and guards borders, determines the volume and character of immigrants allowed in, decrees categories of legal status, and controls access to citizenship, voting, and eligibility for publicly sponsored services. It possesses a fundamental interest in defining a polity compatible with its aims and in determining the role that immigrants and their children should play in it.

In "Policing Boundaries: Migration, Citizenship, and the State," Aleinikoff offers us a bold conceptual piece on how to think about the state's role in shaping access of immigrants to American society and determining the terms under which they can claim membership in the American polity. He first stresses the need to see the American state as a complex series of institutions ranging from the local to the national and from the legislative to the administrative. Sometimes the different parts work in concert with one another, sometimes not; sometimes the state responds to the interests of the society, or the most powerful factions within it, while at other times it responds to internally generated bureaucratic imperatives. But it is wrong, Aleinikoff argues, to view the state simply as a jumble of clashing interests and bureaucracies, for certain fundamental beliefs have long guided the American state's immigration policy: a commitment, since the 1860s, to jus soli (citizenship on the basis of birthplace as opposed to parentage, race, or national origin); a reluctance to strip any man of his citizenship (the state, for many years, refused to extend this protection to women); and a commitment to granting most constitutionally guaranteed rights to all residents of the United States, even immigrants and noncitizens. The Supreme Court set forth these policies in a series of judicial decisions that, in the Court's eyes, made good on principles set forth in the U.S. Constitution. In the process, the Court made itself an indispensable player in the American state and in shaping the experience of immigrants in American society.

In Aleinikoff's eyes, the Court's constitutional interpretations made possible a largely liberal immigration system, especially when compared with those of other nations. In at least two critical areas, however—regulation of immigration and naturalization—the Supreme Court turned its power over to the Congress, to the point of renouncing its right of judicial review, thus creating opportunities for illiberal legislation. The Congress alone, the Court decided, could determine how many immigrants to allow into the United States, from which social categories (men, women, family relatives, unskilled laborers, professionals, political radicals, paupers, prostitutes), and from which foreign lands (northwestern Europe, southeastern Europe, Africa, Asia, Latin America). The Congress possessed the same power to decide whom to admit to citizenship and under what terms. The Court ruled that these powers were inherent to the United States as a sovereign state in an international system of states in which, as with foreign policy, no domestic court could interfere.

What this meant in practice is the subject of "Historical Patterns of Immigrant Status and Incorporation in the United States," Reed Ueda's authoritative survey of the immigration, citizenship, discrimination, and antidiscrimination policies enacted by the U.S. Congress from 1789 to the present. Like Aleinikoff, Ueda notes the many liberal policies emanating from the American state, especially in the nineteenth century, which made the United States more open to immigrants and more committed to their quick political incorporation than almost any other nation in the world. Ueda's stress on the openness of American society resembles Philip Gleason's emphasis on liberal universalism as the dominant American creed. Ueda's story of the late nineteenth and twentieth centuries diverges from Gleason's account, however, while buttressing Desmond King's. Beginning in the 1880s with the Chinese Exclusion Act and culminating in the 1924 Immigration Restriction Act, which reduced immigration from eastern and southern Europe to a trickle and barred eastern and southern Asian immigrants altogether, the United States repeatedly violated liberal universalism in order to recast itself as a racially superior and homogeneous society of western European, or "Nordic," stock. The ethnic and racial composition of American society today would be far different had those restrictive laws not been imposed to keep out millions of "undesirables." The impact of those laws shows the state's extraordinary ability to determine the contours of American society.

Ueda does not end his account with restriction, for he stresses that American law was reversed as the civil rights movement built pressure to pass the Hart-Celler Immigration Act, a "revolutionary new law" that, he argues, abolished the racially charged notions that had underwritten the nation's immigration regime for nearly half a century. That 1965 law revived mass immigration and the tenet that America does not discriminate on the basis of race, creed, or ethnicity. Still, Ueda finds traces of the racially motivated 1920s immigration-restriction system in the new system of "regulatory state pluralism" that seeks, through affirmative action and related policies, to bestow entitlements and opportunities on disadvantaged racial minorities. While he understands how these policies emerged logically from a past suffused with racial discrimination, Ueda, like Gleason, criticizes their effects as inimical to the best aspect of the American heritage—the tradition of liberal individualism. For Ueda, ironically and controversially, the United States in 2001 is still not as open and free a society for immigrants as it was in the nineteenth century, largely owing to the regulatory powers exercised by the state.

IMMIGRANTS, SCHOOLS, AND POLITICAL SOCIALIZATION

The historical mythology surrounding immigrant incorporation invariably assigns a key role to the public schools. Here the children of past immigrants allegedly learned English, civic ideals, and cultural mores. The schools traditionally melted the many into one by providing the tools and incentive necessary to participate in civic life. As long as the schools did this work, immigrants were effectively socialized and incorporated. Now that they no longer do, the incorporation of immigrants has become a more perilous and uncertain project.

The final section of the book interrogates this mythology by asking what role schools have historically played in civic education and what role they play now. In "School for Citizens: The Politics of Civic Education from 1790 to 1990," David Tyack offers a masterful synthesis of two hundred years of civic education. Tyack makes clear that he is focusing on what public educators wanted to impart to students in the classroom, not on how, or if, the lessons transformed the students. He identifies five distinct periods of civic education, stretching from the 1790s to the 1990s, during which the emphasis on transmitting republican and American values—liberty, independence, order, individual rights and duties, patriotism—remained fairly constant even as the pedagogies meant to deliver these values changed over time. Educators in the early national period (1790s to 1830s) worried about securing support for the republican idea of government itself, whereas those in the common-school era (1840s to 1880s) focused on creating a common national culture to counteract growing differences in ethnicity, language, and religion among the American population. Concern about immigrants and their capacity to become responsible citizens intensified in the turn-of-the-century period (1880s to 1920s), leading to coercive Americanization campaigns meant to impose a harsh uniformity on the children of strange-speaking and strangely-costumed newcomers.

Tyack's view of the harshness of this period corresponds closely to the views of Desmond King and Reed Ueda, but Tyack sees the effect of that period ebbing sooner. Progressive education, Tyack argues, made strides in the 1930s and 1940s, inaugurating a fourth period of civic education, which insisted on ethnic, religious, and then racial equality as pillars of citizenship instruction. Most educators of the time did not encourage group difference, as later educators would; to the contrary, they continued to insist on unifying all Americans around republican and patriotic ideals. In Tyack's eyes, however, progressive educators did a great deal to encourage ethnic, religious, and racial tolerance.

For Tyack, this period, stretching from the 1930s through the 1960s, forms a golden age of citizenship instruction, especially because it helped to prepare for the civil rights movement of the 1960s and the inclusion of blacks as equal citizens. In this sense, his argument draws close to that of Philip Gleason. Just as Gleason's golden age was upended by the unanticipated radicalization and group balkanization of the 1960s, so too, is Tyack's. An emphasis on group rights and multiculturalism overtook the earlier celebration of America as an experiment in liberty in which every individual has a chance to get ahead. Tyack is not sure, however, that this major shift in educational emphasis (the fifth period of civic education, from the 1970s to the 1990s) has made much difference in what American schoolchildren actually learn about their country and how they conceive of their relationship to it. Indeed, he finds comfort in the idea that arguments about multiculturalism keep alive the idea that "political education matter[s] to the whole society." His greatest concern is that a new discourse on schooling as a form of human capital for individual economic advancement in the global marketplace is replacing the old discourse that education should teach Americans about their common political inheritance and prepare them to be responsible citizens. Thus, our moment is a perilous one as schoolchildren, native born and immigrant alike, are no longer being taught that they live in a society of democratic promise that will flourish only if they learn their rights and embrace their duties.

Laurie Olsen's essay, "Public Education, Immigrants, and Racialization: The Contemporary Americanization Project," could not be more different from Tyack's. In place of a sweeping history of civic education, she offers us a case study of one California high school in the 1990s. Instead of focusing on the intentions of educators, Olsen relates the experience of schoolchildren. In her chronicle, told largely from the children's viewpoint, civic ideals remain relevant to the school experience, although in a diminished form: civic education seems to have become synonymous with learning English. Immigrant schoolchildren experience their lack of proficiency in English keenly and are eager to learn more in order to become American. Becoming American, however, as they quickly learn from the school's "hidden curriculum," does not entail learning about democracy, opportunity, or civic rights or duties; rather, it involves learning the importance of racial distinctions in the school and in American society at large. Peer societies in the school organize themselves largely around race—Americans (white), blacks, Latinos—and the newcomers are really outcasts or invisible until they, too, acquire a racial identity. Many of the immigrant children are Asian, and therefore they do not have easy access to any of the existing racial categories. They must create a new racial identity for themselves based either on their national origin or on a pan-Asian identity forged out of national groups that, in Asia, possess little sense of commonality. They must then negotiate their place in the racial hierarchy—higher than blacks? Equal to Mexicans? Lower than whites?

Olsen ably renders the complexity of this process and the trepidation it stirs up in the immigrant children. She demonstrates the dominance of a teenage racial system that students feel they cannot escape and that teachers are either too busy or too powerless to mitigate. Olsen raises questions parallel to Tyack's about whether the multicultural and bilingual policies of the past quarter century have made much difference in the experience of schoolchildren. Ethnic and racial equality in this high school seems a distant, even receding, dream. Programs such as those teaching English as a second language, meant to ease immigrants' transition into American society, seem to have created as many problems as they have solved. At the conclusion of her essay, Olsen wonders whether America's democratic promise matters at all in this school or elsewhere among America's youth. Olsen shows us political incorporation at work, but it is incorporation not into a democratic polity but rather into a harsh racial hierarchy.

FUTURE DIRECTIONS FOR RESEARCH

The pairing of historical and contemporary perspectives across these five dimensions of immigrant political incorporation suggests a host of new directions for future research. It demonstrates how much we have yet to learn about the immigrant experience, how much we might gain by comparing the present with the past, and how important it is for historians and social scientists to come together to conduct joint inquiries. Evelyn Sterne's historical chapter points us toward the systematic study of how contemporary voluntary institutions in immigrant communities shape immigrant access to local political systems. Such a study must go beyond examining how local party organizations selectively organize the immigrant and second-generation vote to inquire as well into the roles of churches, fraternal organizations, community centers, women's groups, and labor unions. Until that has been done, too little will be known about the various dimensions along which immigrants are or are not becoming incorporated into American political life. From Louis DeSipio, historians should learn that their almost universal assumption that the high rates of naturalization among immigrants in the 1920s led to high levels of immigrant political activity in the 1930s may not be warranted. Certainly, it is imperative that some historians focus on the link (or lack of one) between naturalization and political mobilization in the 1920s and 1930s. Ewa Morawska and Desmond King issue a similar kind of admonition about a key assumption that often informs the work of social scientists—namely, that immigrants of the past assimilated rather quickly and unproblematically into the American polity.

Laurie Olsen presents a grim picture of the immigrant experience in today's public schools, but ultimately, we can only assess the current situation through historical comparison. Olsen's essay makes clear the need for historical studies of the "hidden curriculum" of racial and ethnic sorting that past generations of schoolchildren have experienced and how this shaped their Americanization and incorporation. One can certainly imagine, on the basis of Desmond King's essay, that rigid systems of racial and ethnic sorting pervaded urban high schools in the first, second, and third decade of the past century, powerfully affecting the immigrant and ethnic populations of those years. Some scholars, such as Paula Fass, have done such studies, but more historical work of this sort needs to be written. Adopting a historical perspective also warns against imputing too much importance to any case study until it is located in the proper context: were these systems of racial and ethnic sorting worse at certain historical moments than at others—during the years of peak migration, for example, or times of economic hardship? Did their influence lessen during the period that David Tyack and Philip Gleason see as the golden years of civic culture (1930s to the 1960s)? How do we assess their influence in private schools, especially parochial institutions? And how did these systems of sorting interact with other influences on schoolchildren emanating from home, work, religious institutions, neighborhoods, and mass culture?

Simply providing a historical context, of course, is not going to give us all the answers we seek. Indeed, historians are sometimes too quick to historicize or periodize without sufficiently developing the conceptual implications of what they are doing. Take the golden era of civic culture referred to by Tyack and Gleason. How are we to reconcile their claims for the special character of this era with the fact, stressed by King and Ueda, that these years were marked by a highly restrictive and racially discriminatory system of immigrant regulation (1924 to 1965)? One path of resolution is simply to determine which group of scholars has the stronger argument or the better evidence. Perhaps it makes more sense, however, to adopt the approach suggested by Alexander Aleinikoff: to recognize that the American state possesses both liberal and antiliberal tendencies and that both can influence public policy, either sequentially or simultaneously. Thus, it may have been the case that American civic culture and the political incorporation of immigrants made significant advances even as a set of discriminatory immigration laws sharply restricted access to this civic polity and culture. If this was indeed the case, we need to inquire into how these seemingly contradictory phenomena coexisted, and in particular, to ask whether the contradictions generated conflict and instability or whether they functioned to support each other. Historical research can help us provide some answers, but that research must itself be guided by theoretical and conceptual frameworks that will help us to understand how nations function, how states operate, how civic cultures advance. And, in this regard, social scientists and political theorists have much to teach historians.

Taken as a totality, these essays teach us several basic lessons. The first is that social science often rests on unexamined assumptions both about the current context (which a historical perspective might suggest is actually quite contingent) and about what historians have said about the past (assuming unproblematic straight-line assimilation where historical research shows struggle, selective incorporation, and ambiguity). Similarly, historians have not yet taken on the challenge of studying the current era of immigration in contrast with immigration at the turn of the past century nor that of theorizing the continuities and discontinuities between these eras. All the essays in this volume, in their own ways, suggest ideas about how to go about these tasks.

The second basic lesson is that the thorough incorporation of first-generation immigrants into local and national political processes has been the relatively rare exception, not the rule, in the United States. More typical are various forms of exclusion, subordination, and co-optation. This stands to reason because political establishments, whatever their ethnic or class composition or ideological leanings, benefit little from mobilizing and empowering marginal groups. Only under certain circumstances, such as a breakdown of the dominant coalition or a crisis of its capacity to govern combined with rapid demographic and economic changes that may undermine its social base, will some part of the political establishment find it to its advantage to mobilize emerging nationality groups. Even then, these groups may be required to sacrifice certain important goals or political positions in order to be allowed admittance (Shefter 1994).

If the pace of immigrant political incorporation is slow in the first generation, it picks up in the second. Our third lesson is that the children of the post-1965 immigrants, the second generation, are likely to have a greater impact on American politics than their parents, just as the children of the migrants from 1880 to 1920 provided the social base for the New Deal in the 1930s. We should think of immigration not simply as one wave that washes in and through the polity but rather as a series of generational waves, with the second having different political characteristics from the first. Naturalized immigrants may be relatively few and uninvolved in the process of Americanization; immigrant children born here will grow up as citizens and will play the central role in the process of "ethnicization" described by Ewa Morawska. We must carefully examine the circumstances under which successive immigrant generations have come of political age, both in the past and now.

The fourth lesson that these essays teach us is that what seems

solid now may melt and then evaporate when historical circumstances change. We tend to read developments of the 1990s as
defining the overall character of post-1965 era of immigration; but
it could be argued that the 1990s were, rather, a fluid period in
terms of Americanization, incorporation, racialization, social mobility, and transnationalism. We will not really know how these
processes turn out for another twenty to thirty years. Thus, for
example, while one can certainly argue, as several of our authors
do, that the decline in civic culture and political parties has wor-
sened the current prospects for immigrant political incorporation,
one must also be alert to less visible processes that might, in the
right set of circumstances, strengthen civic culture and invigorate a
"politics of inclusion" in immigrant communities.

An appreciation for fluidity and contingency is also useful
when analyzing the manner in which the international system of
nation states shapes the immigrant experience. Luis Guarnizo
makes the important point that this system is now more open to
multiple and transnational forms of citizenship (and individual
rights) than in the past. This was often not the case for previous
immigrants, as Americans of German or Japanese descent are particularly aware: U.S. involvement in international conflict can have
major consequences for what is demanded of those whose national loyalty is suspect. If the current situation is novel, however,
it may be less fixed than transnationalists tend to assume. It is not
hard to imagine the international system becoming less peaceful
and open or to imagine circumstances under which long-settled
Americans might press Mexican Americans, Chinese Americans, or
Muslim Americans to demonstrate their loyalty to America. Historical perspectives on matters of immigrant political incorporation
suggest that we must heighten our sensitivity to key assumptions
about the current context. These assumptions must be made visible, and a way for testing their validity should be built into our
research designs.

Finally, these essays teach us that states are important both in
determining the volume and destinations of migrants within the
international system and in shaping the speed and character of
political incorporation of migrants into the societies in which they
have settled. The American state, as Alexander Aleinikoff reminds
us, comprises a complex series of institutions that do not always

work in concert with each other. Nevertheless, it is possible to identify the major political tendencies of that state and to demonstrate how they impact on immigrants in particular eras of the past and present. The essays by Evelyn Sterne, David Tyack, and Laurie Olsen remind us that key encounters between this "state" and immigrants often occur at a local level, in public schools run by municipal school boards, and thus that any theory about the American state must address its federal character and the devolution of important powers onto independent local authorities.

These essays, as we have tried to show, stimulate a great deal of thought. Because the rate of immigration into the United States shows no signs of slowing, and because the children of the post-1965 immigrants are becoming an increasing share of the native-born population, the question of whether and how they will be incorporated into our political system will loom ever larger. Other advanced societies, not just fellow settler-states like Canada and Australia but also European states and even Japan, are experiencing similar trends. Thus the issue of immigration has not just national but also global significance.

NOTES

1. These figures are drawn from U.S. Immigration and Naturalization Service 2000b, tables 1 and 2, and U.S. Bureau of the Census 2000b.
2. Editors' calculation based on data from U.S. Bureau of the Census 2000a. In addition, 15 million people had two foreign-born parents, accounting for 5.4 percent of the U.S. population, while another 13 million, or 4.3 percent of the population, had one foreign-born parent. Almost 90 percent of the foreign born arrived after 1964, but only about 60 percent of the second generation are children of the new "new immigrants," the remainder being the aging "old second generation."

REFERENCES

Alba, Richard D. 1990. *Ethnic Identity: The Transformation of White America*. New Haven: Yale University Press.

Card, David, John DiNardo, and Eugena Estes. 1999. "The More Things Change: Immigrants and the Children of Immigrants in the 1940s, the 1970s, and the 1990s." In *Issues in the Economics of Immigration,* edited by George W. Borjas. Cambridge, Mass.: National Bureau of Economic Research.

Dahl, Robert Alan. 1961. *Who Governs? Democracy and Power in an American City.* New Haven: Yale University Press.

Fass, Paula. 1989. *Outside In: Minorities and the Transformation of American Education.* New York: Oxford University Press.

Foner, Nancy. 2000. *From Ellis Island to JFK: New York's Two Great Waves of Immigration.* New Haven: Yale University Press.

Gans, Herbert. 1992. "Second-Generation Decline: Scenarios for the Economic and Ethnic Futures of the Post-1965 American Immigrants." *Ethnic and Racial Studies* 15(2): 173–93.

Gerstle, Gary. 1999. "Liberty, Coercion, and the Making of Americans." In *The Handbook of International Migration: The American Experience,* edited by Charles Hirschmann, Philip Kasinitz, and Josh DeWind. New York: Russell Sage Foundation.

———. 2000. "Immigration and Ethnicity in the American Century." In *Perspectives on Modern America: Making Sense of the Twentieth Century,* edited by Havard Sitkoff. New York: Oxford University Press.

Gibson, Campbell, and Emily Lennon. 1999. "Historical Census Statistics on the Foreign-Born Population of the United States: 1850 to 1990." Working Paper 29. Washington: U.S. Bureau of the Census, Population Division.

Min, Pyong Gap. 1999. "A Comparison of Post-1965 and Turn-of-the-Century Immigrants in Intergenerational Mobility and Cultural Transmission." *Journal of American Ethnic History* 18(3): 65–85.

Mollenkopf, John, David Olson, and Timothy Ross. Forthcoming. "Immigrant Political Participation in New York and Los Angeles." In *Governing Cities,* edited by Michael Jones-Correa. New York: Russell Sage Foundation.

Morawska, Ewa. 1990. "The Sociology and Historiography of Immigration." In *Immigration Reconsidered,* edited by Virginia Yans-McLaughlin. New York: Oxford University Press.

Morawska, Ewa, and Willfried Spohn. 1997. "Moving Europeans in the Globalizing World: Contemporary Migrations in a Historical-Comparative Perspective, 1955–1994 Versus 1870–1914." In *Global History and Migration,* edited by Wang Gungwu. Boulder, Colo.: Westview.

Portes, Alejandro, and Min Zhou. 1993. "The New Second Generation: Segmented Assimilation and Its Variants." *Annals of the American Academy of Political and Social Science* 530:74–97.

Shanahan, Suzanne, and Susan Olzak. 1999. "The Effects of Immigrant Diversity and Ethnic Competition on Collective Conflict in Urban America, 1869–1924 and 1965–1993." *Journal of American Ethnic History* 18(3): 40–64.

Shefter, Martin. 1994. "Political Incorporation and Political Extrusion: Party Politics and Social Forces in Postwar New York." In *Political Parties and the State: The American Historical Experience,* edited by Martin Shefter. Princeton, N.J.: Princeton University Press.

Smith, Rogers M. 2001. "Citizenship and the Politics of People-Building." *Citizenship Studies* 530(5): 73–79.

U.S. Department of Commerce. U.S. Bureau of the Census. 2000a. *Current Population Survey: Annual Demographic Supplement.* Washington: U.S. Government Printing Office (March).

———. 2000b. *Statistical Abstract of the United States, 1999.* Washington: U.S. Government Printing Office.

U.S. Immigration and Naturalization Service. 2000. *Statistical Yearbook of the Immigration and Naturalization Service, 1998.* Washington: U.S. Government Printing Office.

Waters, Mary C. 1990. *Ethnic Options: Choosing Identities in America.* Berkeley: University of California Press.

Zunz, Olivier. 1982. *The Changing Face of Inequality: Urbanization, Industrial Development, and Immigrants in Detroit, 1880–1920.* Chicago: University of Chicago Press.

—— Part I ——

The Politics of Immigrant Incorporation

— Chapter 1 —

Beyond the Boss: Immigration and American Political Culture from 1880 to 1940

Evelyn Savidge Sterne

> For decades, Skeffington had made himself among the most accessible of public figures, and he had made a ritual of receiving the public in his home. Promptly at 9:45 each morning he held court, and all who came to him were ultimately received. . . . He had no high opinion of the intelligence of the electorate, but experience had taught him that it quite adequately grasped the fact that all successful political activity was based on *quid pro quo*. In the light of benefits to be conferred, he thought it unlikely that those who came to him this morning would consider themselves as uncommitted on election day. . . . The sensible man helped to perpetuate in office the leader from whom he was able to secure assistance.
>
> —Edwin O'Connor, *The Last Hurrah*

IN HIS AFFECTIONATE portrait of the fictional Frank Skeffington, loosely based on Boston boss James Curley, the novelist Edwin O'Connor captures a popular and enduring historical image. Well into the 1970s, scholars assumed that the urban machine was *the* vehicle through which new Americans became politically active during the immigration-heavy decades of the late nineteenth and early twentieth centuries. According to this reasoning, bosses like O'Connor's Skeffington made themselves indispensable to ethnic neighborhood life through a combination of material assistance, symbolic recognition, and community involvement. In return, grateful immigrants delivered up their votes. It was a neat symbiotic relationship that simultaneously kept the machine in power, provided new Americans with needed services, and incorporated them into the polity.

In the 1980s, however, historians and political scientists began to question the power of the political machine. Newer evidence prompted them to doubt its centrality to urban politics and its ability to provide for voters. Scholars began to search for alternative modes of incorporation, and many looked to the labor union. As another highly visible institution representing ethnic working people, the union was a logical choice. Moreover, as a self-made organization the union satisfied the new social historians' desire to find agency in ethnic working-class life.

It has taken a surprisingly long time for scholars to recognize that in focusing on unions and machines, they have targeted only those immigrants who possessed the prerequisites to be active voters or organized workers. Without dismissing the importance of these institutions as politicizing agents, we need to recognize that they do not tell the whole story. For many of America's newcomers, the path to the polity led not through the machine headquarters or the union hall but rather through a network of civic associations. It was through local institutions such as women's clubs and men's mutual aid societies that many immigrants sought to influence, directly or indirectly, electoral politics and the state. Places of worship and especially Roman Catholic churches—nominally, at least, the religious home of most "new" immigrants— were particularly valuable as sites where members formed solidarities and raised challenges.

To understand ethnic politics between 1880 and 1940, the period associated with the "new" immigration, we need to consider machines, unions, and civic associations as alternative yet mutually reinforcing modes of incorporation. Mid-nineteenth-century politics had been relatively open to foreign-born voters, but by the end of the century a host of structural obstacles, ranging from voting restrictions to high rates of remigration, impeded the ability and the will of immigrants to engage in public life. New Americans had to find creative ways to enter the polity at a time when it was inaccessible to many of them, as well as to native-born women and people of color. That said, it is important to note that the incorporation of "old" and "new" immigrants differed in degree rather than in kind. In the earlier period, too, parties or machines, unions, and civic institutions had all helped to bring immigrants into public life. In the new period, however, workers' and ethnic associations became more critical as political parties grew less welcoming. It was not until the 1920s and 1930s that legal and demographic changes toppled many of these electoral barriers, and cultural skirmishes and economic crises gave foreign-born Americans vital reasons to engage in politics. At that point immigrants and ethnics who had been mobilizing through a variety of institutions formally entered the polity, as voters.

OLD IMMIGRANTS, NEW IMMIGRANTS, AND NEW BARRIERS

It is generally accepted that the "new" immigrants—hailing from Asia, Mexico, and southern and eastern Europe and arriving between about 1890 and 1924—confronted electoral obstacles that the "old" immigrants—the mid-nineteenth-century stream from Ireland, Germany, and Scandinavia—had not. To be sure, there were certain similarities between the two. Members of both waves confronted the problems of citizenship, language, lack of experience with democratic politics, and the more immediate priority of economic survival. Both were motivated to become political to protect their financial interests and their cultural imperatives. Finally, immigrants in both periods entered public life through a complex organizational landscape that encompassed party machinery, unions, ethnic networks, and civic associations.

Nonetheless, the old immigrants had advantages that reflected both their cultural equipment and the nation they entered. The Irish spoke English and had a long tradition of organizing against the British (Emmons 1989, 37–39; Gerber 1989, 333–35). The Germans had less political experience but were able to apply their skills in organizing guilds and "Vereine" (associations) to civic life in the United States (Gerber 1989, 332–33). Scandinavians, for their part, enjoyed a cultural kinship with the nation's Anglo-Saxon Protestant founders and thus were welcomed into the Republican Party. Economics motivated various groups to become involved in American public life, albeit in different ways. Whereas the Irish entered politics to gain access to the good jobs denied them in the private sector, the more prosperous Germans became involved in city affairs to have a say in the levying of taxes and the provision of services that affected their homes and businesses (Gerber 1989, 364–70).

Perhaps the most critical factor in the incorporation of older immigrants was the relatively open nature of the polity they encountered. The decades following the American Revolution witnessed a steady expansion of the suffrage for solvent white men (even as it contracted for nonwhites and the underclass). By the 1850s, just six of the thirty-one states retained tax-paying requirements for voting (Keyssar 2000, chapter 2). Some western states, such as Illinois, even allowed aliens to vote in hope of stimulating settlement (Gjerde 1997, 38). This worked to the advantage of the Germans and Scandinavians, who tended to settle in these regions. The one glaring exception to this pattern was Rhode Island, which until 1888 barred immigrants from voting unless they owned real estate. As the first state to industrialize and thereby attract a substantial immigrant population, Rhode Island harbored particular concerns about foreign-born voters (Sterne 1999, 23–24, 34–35, 66).

Not only could most nineteenth-century immigrants vote, outside of Rhode Island, but they also entered a vibrant and accessible political culture. The "second-party system" that arose in the 1840s was characterized by intense partisanship (fomented by an active party press), frequent elections, more patronage incentives (resulting from a growth in city services and bureaucracies), and a street-based mass politics that encouraged voters to join uniformed marching companies and attend parades punctuated by music and cannon fire (Gerber 1989, 321–24, 337–40; McGerr 1986, chapter 2). Some scholars have dissented from this view, arguing that this "spectacular" political culture was carefully managed from above and exaggerated by a partisan press (Altschuler and Blumin 1997). Although it is important not to overstate the democratic nature of the mid-nineteenth-century polity, it is difficult to deny that the politics of this era generated a certain excitement and engagement among native-born and foreign-born citizens alike. In Buffalo, for example, Democrats bearing torches and accompanied by bands and fireworks would march through Irish and German neighborhoods during election season (Gerber 1989, 339). In many towns and cities, immigrants had their own campaign clubs (McGerr 1986, 23–24).

Organizing styles and political issues also served to draw in new citizens. Because "parties organized voters where they lived," the ethnic neighborhood was a distinct political unit in which new Americans mobilized behind their own leaders and through their own networks (Gerber 1989, 327). Living at a time when municipal government was more active and autonomous than it would be in the next century, immigrants organized around tangible local issues that they could affect (Gerber 1989, 328). Moreover, the later nineteenth century was characterized by a divisive cultural politics that focused on such hot-button questions as temperance, public education, and woman suffrage. These issues mobilized ethnic voters (albeit on different sides) to defend their cultural prerogatives and their views of the appropriate relationship between state and society. Thus many immigrants first entered public life to defend an ethnic separatism, only to become politically active Americans (Fuchs 1995, 26–30; Gjerde 1997, chapters 9–10). Even those seeking to isolate themselves in rural western communities found it impossible to be "hermetically sealed" (Gjerde 1997, 229). By the end of the nineteenth century, "old" immigrants had become sufficiently integrated into the political mainstream to elect compatriots as mayors and governors in the regions where they congregated (Kantowicz 1980, 807–11).

Thanks to personal characteristics and changes in America's electoral culture, political prospects were considerably dimmer for the new immigrants. Far fewer of them spoke English, and more were culturally marginalized because they were not Protestants and did not fit current definitions of "whiteness" (Higham 1969, chapter 6). More of them remained poor, having arrived at a time when land supplies had contracted, the nation was industrializing, and most jobs available to them were dangerous and poorly paid. Finally, a much higher proportion of these immigrants did not become citizens or voters because they planned to remigrate, in part because of the growing ease and affordability of overseas travel.[1] Asian Americans could not become citizens even if they wanted to, having been denied that right by the Naturalization Act of 1870.

The new immigrants also had the misfortune to arrive just as politics in the United States was undergoing a transition that did not bode well for popular engagement. Between the Gilded Age and the 1920s, American politics shifted from a rowdy, partisan, street-based electoral culture to a distant and bureaucratic style of campaigning that made politics less interesting and less accessible (McGerr 1986). Another problem was that the "old" immigrants, most notably the Irish, were entrenched within the major-party system and reluctant to share their hard-won power with new arrivals. At the same time, "progressive" reforms replaced a partisan, ward-level system with professionalized and centralized municipal administrations. Not only did this remove some of the excitement from politics, but it also hurt ethnic voters and candidates who could wield power on a local level but were disadvantaged in citywide contests. In Boston, the result was a new interest-group politics dominated by middle-class civic associations (Connolly 1998, chapter 4).

Perhaps the greatest obstacle of all was the denial of access to the vote. The new immigration coincided with a period of sharp and deliberate electoral contraction. In response to emancipation and industrialization as well as mass immigration, communities across the country obstructed access to the polls through taxes, literacy tests, property requirements, residency rules, early poll closings, Asian exclusion laws, and stricter naturalization procedures—as well as the older tradition of gender restrictions (Keyssar 2000, chapter 5). Intensifying the problem were complicated registration requirements designed to stymie the rank-and-file elector. These new rules combined with reduced party competition, and a resulting decline in popular interest, to seriously depress voter turnout after the turn of the twentieth century (Piven and Cloward 1989, chapters 3–4).

The result was that the new immigrants were far less well positioned than their earlier counterparts to become incorporated into American politics. Not only were they put at a disadvantage personally, but they also entered an electoral culture whose structure and style discouraged mass participation. These immigrants had to find creative ways to engage with public life. They turned to party machines, unions, and civic associations.

IMMIGRANTS AS VOTERS: THE MACHINE

The urban machine provided the most direct link to electoral politics for those newcomers who were willing and able to become voters. At first vilified by contemporaries and scholars, in time the political machine was recognized as providing useful services and able to turn immigrants into active citizens, albeit for selfish motives. This alliance, it was assumed, provided benefits to needy recipients even as it obstructed "progressive" reform—until the federal government stepped in as an alternative service provider in the 1930s. Recently, however, scholars have begun to question whether machines were ever as powerful as had been assumed. The question we need to evaluate, then, is just how central were machines in incorporating immigrants into American politics.

The earliest commentators on the political machine were reform-minded contemporaries who saw the institution as a scourge on American life. In the popular image, the boss was a demagogue, often an Irish Democrat, who manipulated the votes of a dangerous and unassimilated class of immigrants. According to James Bryce, who in 1889 articulated one of the earliest critiques, the machine preyed on voters who lacked patriotism, civic duty, and "experience in self-government" (Bryce 1893, 1: 651). For them, politics was "simply a mode of making a livelihood or a fortune" (Bryce 1893, 1: 640). Sixteen years later, muckraker Lincoln Steffens expanded on this sorry tale. In an exposé of Rhode Island titled "A State for Sale," Steffens deplored the rampant vote-buying through which the local Republican machine remained in power. Local politics, he charged, was "grounded on the lowest layer of corruption that I have found thus far—the bribery of voters with cash at the polls" (Steffens 1905, 338). Steffens did not blame this corruption on mercenary ethnics alone. Here and in his larger work, *The Shame of the Cities*, he noted that American business owners too were selling their votes in exchange for contracts and franchises (Steffens [1903] 1966).

The portrait that emerged from these critiques was that machines were immoral and inefficient institutions that fostered urban corruption through an unholy alliance with unscrupulous business interests and uneducated immigrants. The pursuit of self-interest was the motive for all parties. The solution proposed was the progressive campaign to replace partisan leaders with trained civil servants who would bring honesty and efficiency to municipal government. Missing from this interpretation was any sense that machines might fill a useful or even a necessary function in city life or that bosses might serve their constituents better than reformers would (Allswang 1986, 15).

By the 1930s, however, scholars had gained a grudging appreciation of the machine as proto–welfare state. They came to acknowledge that urban bosses generally were more skilled than reformers in understanding and meeting the needs of urban immigrants. Writing in 1935, J. T. Salter saw the machine as serving as an "intermediary between the citizen and the state" by helping immigrants to find jobs, secure relief, and negotiate their problems with the law (Salter 1935, 18). Robert K. Merton later distinguished between the machine's "manifest functions" (corruption and inefficiency) and its "latent functions" (provision of jobs and assistance and mediation among various socioeconomic groups) (Merton 1957, 60–66). Through this distinction, it became possible simultaneously to condemn the machines for their excesses and commend them for their contributions.

The result was a lasting recognition of the machine's productive roles in urban ethnic life. Scholars came to accept that, before the rise of industrial unionism and the welfare state, the machine provided immigrants with assistance unavailable from other sources. New York's Tammany Hall created jobs for thousands of supporters as inspectors, commissioners, police officers, and construction workers. It operated its own welfare system by purchasing coal for the poor and providing food baskets for widows, and it even filled a social role by sponsoring weekend outings such as clambakes (Allswang 1986, chapters 2–3). No less critical was the cultural recognition that the machine offered new Americans. Nominating ethnic candidates was only the most obvious way in which bosses demonstrated their respect. Whereas progressive reformers encouraged newcomers to adopt "American" ways by doing away with drinking and Sunday recreation, machine politicians embraced ethnic community life by attending weddings, funerals, and festivals and competing to give the most lavish donations. Tammany Hall also appealed to ethnic voters by lobbying for state aid to parochial schools and for the designation of Columbus Day as a legal holiday (Allswang 1986; Hofstadter 1955, 182–84).

Bosses understood their constituents not only because they tended to share their ethnoreligious heritage but also because they were accessible. Like O'Connor's Skeffington, who received callers at his home every morning, Tammany Hall's Charles Francis Murphy stationed himself at a Second Avenue lamppost every evening without fail (Allswang 1986, 69). Practices like these enabled machine politicians to grasp the problems and priorities of their constituents. At the same time, these encounters enabled immigrants to develop a personal and tangible connection to a government that otherwise seemed remote and unfriendly.

Whether material or symbolic, machine assistance came with a price. Holders of patronage jobs were expected to donate a portion of their wages to the machine, thus funding its expensive outreach operations. The fictional Skeffington, for example, "installed a system of tithes. . . . Each party worker who had been given employment by the party gave to the party, in return, a modest proportion of his annual earnings" (O'Connor 1956, 157). Beneficiaries also were expected to become naturalized, often with the machine's assistance, and to vote for machine candidates. New York's Boss Murphy kept detailed records on his constituents. If an elector had not cast his ballot by 3:00 P.M. on election day, Murphy sent a party worker to his home or workplace to encourage him to vote (Allswang 1986, 69). Although such activities clearly were motivated by self-interest, their by-product was to bring immigrants into public life as citizens and voters.

By about 1945, however, changes in the political landscape had rendered the machine redundant. It is widely assumed that this peculiarly American institution had largely disappeared by the end of World War II. According to the "last hurrah" thesis popularized by O'Connor's novel, the New Deal killed the machine by usurping its role as a social service agency. The 1930s also witnessed the rise of industrial unions, through which many ethnic workers were able to secure benefits for themselves. Moreover,

second- and third-generation immigrants tended to be more prosperous, better assimilated, and thus less receptive to boss appeal
than their parents and grandparents had been (Allswang 1986, 30–
31). Some scholars, of course, have argued that certain machines
benefited from the New Deal by using the dispensation of federal
funds to retain voter loyalties (Erie 1988, 224–25; Luconi 1996;
Stave 1970). Chicago's Daley machine, a particularly stalwart organization, lasted well into the 1970s. The general consensus, however, is that the golden age of machine politics had ended by the
start of World War II.

The theme that emerges from this later and more nuanced
portrait is reciprocity rather than exploitation. While the machine
used immigrants to secure votes, immigrants used the machine to
obtain jobs, advocacy, and recognition. No longer seen as ignorant and manipulable, immigrants now appeared as savvy actors
who worked with urban bosses out of rational choice rather than
coercion. Bosses, for their part, emerged less as antireform de-
mons than as practical politicians who understood and addressed
their constituents' needs. It was no coincidence that this sympathetic and even sentimental portrait emerged at the very moment
that the machine was in decline. Once the boss was no longer a
major player in urban life, it became possible for scholars to regard him more indulgently. Observers like O'Connor, writing in
the 1950s, could look back with nostalgia to the colorful, kindly,
and approachable boss in an age in which politics was becoming
less personal and more remote (Allswang 1986, 29).

It is only recently that scholars have begun to debunk the machine again, this time by questioning whether it ever enjoyed as
loud a hurrah as had been assumed. One study finds that between
1870 and 1945, supposedly the golden age of the boss, more than
one-third of major American cities were free of political machines
in any given year. Moreover, it was less common for one "dominant" machine to control city politics than for a series of "fac-
tional" machines to compete for control (Brown and Halaby 1987,
597–99). Certainly there were potentates, like Providence's
Charles "Boss" Brayton, who controlled city and state government
with an iron fist, but more common was the small-time boss competing with his rivals in the urban political marketplace. Strained
by limited resources, bosses like these often were unable or unwilling to provide expensive jobs and services (Erie 1988; Eth-

ington 1994; McDonald 1986). Some responded by awarding their benefits selectively. This often meant that Irish American bosses kept the meaty perks for their compatriots—or, as in Rhode Island, a Yankee boss pandered to Italian and French Canadian voters turned off by the state's weak and Irish-dominated Democratic Party. Bosses did not necessarily serve even their supporters very well, however, as many patronage positions were dead-end jobs (Erie 1988, 89–90).

Moreover, a number of ethnic leaders mobilized against machines rather than around them. Challenging the dominance of the dichotomy between Yankee reformer and ethnic machine, James Connolly finds that Jewish, Italian, and even Irish leaders in Progressive Era Boston seized on antiboss sentiment to mobilize their communities, overcome internal divisions, and, in the case of the Irish, distance themselves from machine corruption (Connolly 1998, chapter 2). In this reading, opposition to the machine became a rallying point for new Americans. All in all, the message that emerges from these various critiques is that the machine was far less powerful than it seemed as an institution that incorporated immigrants into American politics.

Furthermore, we need to remember that machines formed relationships only with that minority of immigrants who were eligible to vote and interested in casting ballots. Certainly, by providing tempting perks bosses could lure to the polls newcomers who might otherwise have remained at home. Yet fewer than half of the nation's immigrants became citizens in the first decades of the twentieth century.[2] Because of the various personal and structural barriers discussed earlier, a still smaller minority took advantage of the citizen's right to cast a ballot. As we have seen, many bosses lacked the resources to overcome these obstacles. The machine, though a colorful and undeniably important factor in turn-of-the-century urban America, was by no means the only institution through which immigrants became politically incorporated.

IMMIGRANTS AS ORGANIZED WORKERS: THE UNION

It was in concert with other mobilizing institutions, among them unions, that political machines helped to turn immigrants into engaged citizens and active voters. According to the standard interpretation, the Knights of Labor sought to forge an inclusive and politically engaged union, only to be co-opted by reformers and crushed by the post-Haymarket backlash. The American Federation of Labor (AFL), the story goes, responded by taking the safer course of a narrow and apolitical "business" unionism, while the short-lived Industrial Workers of the World (IWW) drew its members (many of them new immigrants) into left-wing politics. It was not until the rise of the Congress of Industrial Organizations (CIO) in the 1930s that unionists once again reached out to the broader working class and forged a productive and lasting relationship with the state. More recently, however, historians have complicated this story by suggesting that the AFL was more politically active and the CIO less transformative than we have assumed. To evaluate this debate is to develop a deeper perspective on just how useful unions were in bringing immigrants into American politics.

The Knights of Labor was the first broadly based union that offered a political vehicle to the nation's newcomers. Open to almost all "producers," this was the first union to which immigrants (other than the Chinese) had access regardless of gender, skill level, and country of origin. As members, they formed part of an organization that saw politics as a supplement to workplace reform. Although the Knights of Labor was ambivalent about electoral strategies and envisioned only a limited role for the state, it did recognize that working people could make a difference in public affairs (Fink 1983, chapter 2). The union's innovative strategies were at once its signal strength and its fatal flaw. Political involvement subjected members to co-optation by a conservative and bureaucratic state (Fink 1983, 34–35) and attacks by a business-state alliance (Voss 1993, chapters 7–8), and inclusiveness fostered internal divisions that often followed ethnic lines (Oestreicher 1986). Crippled by these various problems and felled by the antiunion reaction that followed the Haymarket riot of 1886, the union fell apart in the 1890s just as the "new" immigration was picking up steam.

New Americans who were active in the Knights of Labor would have left the Noble and Holy Order with conflicting lessons about politics. On the one hand, many of them had received a civic education, become active in the electoral arena, and learned that it was possible for ordinary citizens to make their voices heard. On the other hand, they also realized how stacked the winner-take-all electoral system was against grassroots challenges, how risky and expensive those challenges were, and how difficult it was for the multiethnic working class to unite and achieve change within a generally unsympathetic state (Montgomery 1993; Oestreicher 1988, 1269–72).

A number of scholars see the demise of the Knights of Labor as marking the end of a golden period in working-class politics (Shefter 1986; Voss 1993). The Gilded Age had presented a moment of possibility, as workers experimented with a variety of tactics and pursued bold visions for overturning capitalism or at least making it more humane—not only through the Knights of Labor but also through socialism and the Greenback Labor Party. After 1886, however, a counteroffensive mounted by business and government forced workers to choose between greater militancy and an accommodationist policy focused on the protection of skilled workers. By the 1890s, a broad range of working-class strategies had narrowed to two vehicles, the trade union and the party machine, which neatly divided the goals of economic and political action (Katznelson 1981; Shefter 1986). The AFL became the mouthpiece for trade unionists and, it is widely assumed, decided to play it safe: rejecting the inclusive and political approach of its predecessor, the new federation restricted its ranks to craft workers, its vision to the immediate issues of wages and hours, and its strategy to economic tactics such as strikes.

Gwendolyn Mink (1986) argues that tensions between "old" and "new" immigrants were the key to this shift. The new immigrants, she notes, had the misfortune to arrive when the nation was mired in its worst depression to date and employers were launching an antiunion offensive. The AFL responded with a defensive strategy. Viewing new immigrants as competitors for pieces of a limited economic pie, it restricted its membership to skilled workers, who tended to be male and "old-stock." Fearing the government as a rival for the loyalties of working people, it blocked state efforts to forge a direct relationship with workers by providing workplace protections and social insurance. The result was that the recognized voice of American labor was an institution representing a tiny minority of the working class and reluctant to invoke the power of the state, other than to restrict immigration and protect unions. Those working people who were politically active split between the two major parties, "old" immigrants and their unions voting Democratic (with minor legislative gains as their reward) and "new" immigrants supporting a Republican Party that discouraged them from voting and largely ignored their needs. Old immigrants thus formed part of a conservative labor movement that discouraged independent politics and the pursuit of state benefits. New immigrants remained unorganized and politically immobilized. In Mink's interpretation, the AFL served neither group well.

A number of historians have challenged this critical reading by rejecting the assumption that the AFL avoided politics and focused on bread-and-butter goals. In his study of labor politics in Gilded Age Chicago, Richard Schneirov disagrees that a visionary Knights of Labor was replaced by a conservative and apolitical AFL. Instead, he demonstrates, in its early years the AFL encouraged the state to regulate sweatshops and take over public utilities, reached out to unskilled workers, and saw better wages and hours as the foundations for a broader vision (Schneirov 1998, chapter 12). By the late 1890s, Chicago unions not only had won concessions from the Democrats but also had reoriented politics toward a new liberalism that broke with laissez-faire and placed labor's demands on the public agenda (Schneirov, chapter 13, conclusion). Rather than rejecting politics, "Chicago labor was politicized to its core" (Schneirov, 356).

Julie Greene's study of the national AFL suggests that the federation became only more political during the Progressive Era. Beginning with a policy of lobbying for laws that would ensure a limited role for the state in the workplace, by 1906 the AFL had shifted to direct involvement in congressional and presidential campaigns. The union was pushed in this direction by rank-and-file political engagement, the growth of the federal state, the open-shop offensive of the National Association of Manufacturers, and the Democrats' decision to reach out to working-class voters at a time when turnout was declining (Greene 1998, chapters 2–5). Responding to the leadership's new strategy, the International Typographers' Union organized California workers behind William Jennings Bryan's 1908 presidential bid, and the railroad brotherhoods and United Mine Workers campaigned for Woodrow Wilson in 1916—to name only a few examples (Greene 1998, 165, 262, 265, 267). Although rank-and-file unionists often resisted centralized directives about politics, the AFL did help to elect Democratic majorities and to place working-class issues on the national agenda. In fact, the union succeeded almost too well. With the enactment of such laws as the 1916 Adamson Act (which granted railroad workers an eight-hour day), President Wilson moved beyond Samuel Gompers' vision of a limited role for the state and forged a direct relationship with workers, one not mediated by the AFL (Greene 1998, chapter 8). The relevance of Greene's argument here is that the AFL not only brought unionists of "old" immigrant stock into a productive relationship with the state but also, unwittingly, forged a bond between unorganized newer immigrants and the Democratic Party.

The story of Progressive Era union politics becomes even more vibrant and complicated when we shift our lens from the nation to the locality. In his study of San Francisco building-trades workers, Michael Kazin finds that for many AFL unions "no separation existed between economic and political activity" (Kazin 1987, 277). San Francisco locals sponsored political debates, bankrolled independent labor parties, and endorsed candidates. During elections, unionists formed booster clubs, and their business agents distributed campaign buttons as they made their rounds. Union legislative agendas, moreover, went beyond Asian exclusion and union protection to include tax reform, antitrust laws, and public ownership of utilities—issues that could appeal to the broader working class. These activities, Kazin finds, were a natural outgrowth of union membership. "Whether they lived in Sydney, Winnipeg, or Chicago, skilled workers tended to thrust themselves into politics behind their growing unions" (Kazin 1987, 282). Furthermore, though there were moments when AFL workers promoted their interests at the expense of the unorganized and vulnerable, there were others, such as the effort to organize municipal laborers, when they reached out to the unskilled. It is clear that AFL unions could be electoral vehicles for old immigrants, and it is possible that they prompted newer immigrants to engage with politics, too.

According to Joseph McCartin, World War I only intensified

the relationship between organized labor, individual workers, and the state. Labor gained control of wartime regulatory agencies such as the National War Labor Board, won government protection for unions, and placed industrial democracy on the national agenda (McCartin 1997, chapters 2–3). It was a common joke in Washington, D.C., that "Gompers had a key to the back door of the White House" (McCartin 1997, 80). At the same time individual workers, many of them new immigrants who had previously had little contact with the state, seized on wartime rhetoric to assert their rights as industrial citizens and used the new regulatory agencies to claim those rights. As immigrant John Cemka testified at one National War Labor Board hearing, they wished to "live as Americans ought to live" (McCartin 1997, 111). Although these gains for labor were reversed amid the reaction of the postwar period, they set the stage for the 1930s. Challenging David Montgomery's (1987) more pessimistic argument that the war brought on the "fall of the house of labor," McCartin argues that the war laid down valuable precedents for the New Deal by legitimating the concept of industrial democracy, creating a relationship between labor and the Democrats, and giving rank-and-file workers a tantalizing taste of workplace justice (McCartin 1997, chapter 9).

The standard interpretation of the decades that followed holds that after the lull of the open-shop, laissez-faire 1920s, workers used the CIO to empower themselves in politics and the workplace during and after the New Deal. According to Lizabeth Cohen (1990), by the 1930s workers were beginning to come together across ethnic lines on the basis of their shared experiences as partakers of mass culture and victims of the Depression. Some, like the French Canadians of Woonsocket, Rhode Island, formed independent unions to defend their economic security and their cultural autonomy (Gerstle 1989). More joined the CIO, inspired by its militancy, its inclusive "industrial" strategy, and its "culture of unity," which provided a network of shared institutions such as a newspaper, a radio show, ladies' auxiliaries, family socials, and multiethnic cultural events (Cohen 1990, chapter 8).

Membership in the CIO and political engagement were mutually reinforcing. Pressure from frustrated workers prompted Congress to pass the Wagner Act in 1935, which in turn fostered the growth of the CIO. Gratitude for Wagner (as well as the Social

Security and Fair Labor Standards Acts) turned many ethnic workers into loyal Democrats; and their cohesion in the CIO and its
political arm, Labor's Non-Partisan League, made labor a force to
be reckoned with (Fraser 1989, 70–71). In fact, "the relationship
between the 'second New Deal' and the 'new unionism' was organic" (Fraser 1989, 68). All in all, this interpretation sees the rise
of the CIO as critical to the politicization of the ethnic working
class in the 1930s.

In recent years, numerous studies have challenged the assumption that the new labor federation had a progressive and politically transformative effect on the American working class. Some
scholars depict the CIO as a conservative, bureaucratic institution
that sought to control rather than inspire the rank and file (Faue
1991; Lynd 1996). Others complain that the CIO exhibited an initial militancy later dampened by an unfortunate but probably unavoidable partnership with the Democrats. According to this interpretation, the CIO sacrificed its exuberant dreams of industrial
democracy on the altar of wages and stability by entering into an
ill-fated relationship with the state (Brody 1993, chapter 4; Dubofsky 1994; Fraser 1989, 76–78; Harris 1982; Lichtenstein and
Harris 1993; Tomlins 1985). This in turn prompted union leaders
to reject a partnership with the left, a position cemented during
the McCarthy era.

Although the CIO may have discouraged rank-and-file militancy and left-wing activism, it still brought its membership into a
closer relationship with the state. Unionists—many of them immigrants or ethnics—now voted Democratic at the urging of CIO
leaders, out of their own gratitude for the economic security secured in part through the party's support, and out of a new sense
that their votes mattered. It also is likely that becoming political as
workers prompted unionists to become political as ethnics or
members of religious communities, coming to the polls to promote their cultural priorities as well as their economic interests.
The CIO, then, was an undeniable watershed in the political incorporation of the nation's immigrants. More generally, it seems
safe to assume that being a member of any union—the Knights of
Labor, the AFL, the IWW, or the CIO—could be an intensely politicizing experience.

Yet we must remember that even as unions became more inclusive, only a minority of the nation's immigrants were organized workers. The Wagner Act, after all, did not protect occupations such as domestic service in which many immigrant women labored. When American union membership peaked in the 1950s, only about 35 percent of the nonagricultural workforce was organized—and this percentage has been falling ever since. Taken together, unions and party machines did politicize a significant proportion of immigrants between 1880 and 1940. Because those immigrants were overwhelmingly male and of older stock, however, we need to look elsewhere to round out the story. Although the influence of machines and unions cannot be dismissed, we need to look at civic associations to understand how other immigrants entered and influenced electoral politics.

IMMIGRANTS AS COMMUNITY ACTIVISTS: CIVIC ASSOCIATIONS

During this period when machines and unions were off limits to many immigrants, community institutions offered an indirect yet effective political entrée. Settlement houses, ethnic associations, neighborhood networks, and most of all places of worship served as places in which newcomers discussed problems, formed solidarities, developed leadership skills, and raised challenges. These institutions were open to people barred from unions or electoral politics by gender, language, citizenship, or occupation. Moreover, even immigrants who had access to other resources may have felt more comfortable in these local organizations, which were situated in their neighborhoods and often run by their compatriots. It was through these institutions that many immigrants became aware of the problems and possibilities of American politics and from them that they stepped into the electoral arena. Churches, fraternal orders, and other ethnic institutions had helped to mobilize older immigrants as well, but these organizations became even more important in an age when electoral politics was less accessible.

Settlement houses, a staple of turn-of-the-century urban America, could politicize the people they served. These community centers served a function comparable to that of party machines, even though they acted on different motives. The settlement house typically provided immigrants with needed services, such as job referrals and health care, in hope that they would rise out of poverty and enter the American mainstream. Although some clients rejected the settlements' assimilationist imperatives, others recognized the advantages of becoming citizens and English speakers, and with the settlements' help they overcame these initial barriers to becoming voters. Moreover, immigrants no doubt used settlement houses as community spaces where they assembled and discussed problems, another important precursor to political activity. Historians have noted that settlement work vaulted administrators like Jane Addams into public life by making them aware of social problems and eager to find solutions. Largely overlooked has been the likelihood that these institutions politicized their clients as well, often in ways the settlement workers did not anticipate.

If settlement houses were run by outsiders for immigrants, a host of self-generated community institutions served the same purpose of easing the transition to American life and in many cases to American politics. Ethnic social clubs and fraternal orders helped to politicize both old and new immigrants. In 1876, a contemporary reported that Chicago Germans used their extensive network of reading rooms, music halls, and gymnasiums to "discuss the political situations." The Workingmen's Party of the United States drew on these ethnic networks to organize German Socialists (Schneirov 1998, 81). Nineteenth-century Irish political clubs were established in "grog shops and by street gangs and in volunteer fire companies" (Fuchs 1995, 44). The Irish in Chicago, as well as their counterparts in Butte, Montana, were drawn into local politics through their Land Leagues—a good example of how homeland nationalism could inspire political engagement in the adopted country (Emmons 1989, chapters 9–10; Schneirov 1998, chapter 5). In New England, ethnic newspapers such as the *Gazzetta del Massachusetts* (Connolly 1998, 57–59) and *L'Eco del Rhode Island* fostered an Italian American political identity. Although the ethnic press did not offer a physical site where potential voters congregated, it did help to create a political community.

Mutual aid societies also played a politicizing role. In an age before people had access to employer- or state-funded social insurance, immigrants formed associations that paid for funerals and helped members to survive periods of illness and unemployment, as well as organizing street festivals and family gatherings (Emmons 1989, 103–21; Smith 1985, chapter 4). In many cases, these institutions acted as bridges between the neighborhood and the polity. The Sons of Italy, for example, encouraged members to Americanize even as they preserved elements of their native culture. As Luigi Cipolla of the Rhode Island chapter put it, "Our main object is to impress upon the unnaturalized that there are obligations they cannot overlook. . . . It is their duty to remain here, keep their savings in the country, build homes, and assume the responsibilities of American citizenship" (*Providence Journal,* December 21, 1919: 5). Some immigrants went further and used their self-help groups as lobbying agencies. In Butte, Irish fraternal orders such as the Ancient Order of Hibernians protested discrimination and provided aspiring officeholders with receptive forums and ready-made constituencies (Emmons 1989, 112, 114–16).

Female immigrants rarely belonged to mutual aid societies (Smith 1985, 127–28). Instead, they formed their own networks of assistance and solidarity and used these networks to become political actors. During the late nineteenth and early twentieth centuries, native-born middle-class women took advantage of a "separate spheres" mentality to carve out political roles. Capitalizing on their duties as moral guardians, they transformed themselves from private homemakers to "social housekeepers" and won themselves a voice in public affairs (Baker 1984). Immigrant women too used traditional gender roles and networks to develop nontraditional public roles. Middle-class Latinas in Tampa, Florida, organized clubs, nurseries, and health clinics. After 1920, they used these voluntarist strategies in tandem with their newfound right to vote to work for political reform and economic justice (Hewitt 1993).

Working-class immigrant women, generally lacking the time or the resources to form clubs, relied on informal networks that were equally politicizing. While husbands and sons congregated in saloons, wives and daughters exchanged stories and recipes in markets and on street corners. More fundamentally, they shared in a daily struggle for survival that united women of diverse ethnic backgrounds into circles of mutual assistance that blurred distinctions between public and private. When a community crisis arose, they used these networks to convey information and rally support (Cameron 1993). In 1902, Jewish housewives in New York City organized a successful three-week boycott of kosher butchers in response to a steep price increase (Hyman 1980). Their counterparts in Boston formed the West End Mothers' Club, which organized boycotts and marches and lobbied for state price-control laws (Connolly 1998, 65). In 1912, housewives and wage-earning women in Lawrence, Massachusetts, employed female networks to initiate and sustain the successful "Bread and Roses" textile strike (Cameron 1993).

This type of community activism was an unconventional but effective way to influence politics and a critical one for newcomers who lacked access to unions and the vote. Foreign-born women like the kosher boycotters "were not apolitical. They simply expressed their political concerns in a different, less historically accessible arena—the neighborhood" (Hyman 1980, 93). Neighborhood-based strikes and boycotts did not influence electoral politics directly, in the sense of affecting the outcome of elections, but did have an indirect effect by bringing important questions to the attention of politicians and reformers. Moreover, these crowd-based activities awakened in participants a broader sense of injustice and an empowering sense of capability.

Although each of these community institutions served in its own way to mobilize immigrants, none could rival the Catholic Church in the size of its constituency or the extent of its resources. For the nation's overwhelmingly Catholic immigrant population, the church was the only organization of which anyone could be a member regardless of gender, occupation, citizenship, or country of birth (Orsi 1985, xv). Moreover, no other organization dished out a comparable menu of services. Dioceses operated orphanages, hospitals, and working-girls' homes as well as parochial schools. Individual parishes, for their part, offered charitable assistance in the form of food baskets and affordable heating and cooking fuel. Parishes also provided libraries and gymnasiums, ran classes in English and domestic science, and sponsored day nurseries and summer camps. Parishioners could participate in a dizzying array of lay activities that ranged from debating clubs and study groups to bands and sports teams to mother's societies and women's clubs. Finally, parishes were social centers where people attended concerts, costume parties, and lawn festivals. In all of these ways, the church offered a community amid the alienation of urban life (Dolan 1992, 204; Emmons 1989, 97; Salvatore forthcoming; Sterne 1999, 161–62; Sterne 2000, 157–59). It functioned "both as a mini-city and as a macro-family" (Kane 1994, 112).

The church's ostensible functions were to provide spiritual sustenance, material relief, and social fellowship, yet it acted less overtly but quite powerfully as an alternative political space. The very act of building a church, frequently at lay initiative, united communities and provided many immigrants with their "first New World experience of large-scale collective action" (Tentler 1997, 138). Moreover, church architecture itself was a powerful political statement, claiming urban space and signifying to outsiders that Catholics were a growing constituency in city life. Rhode Island's triennial Holy Name parade—which by the 1920s attracted more than thirty-five thousand marchers and one hundred thousand spectators—sent a similar message by demonstrating Catholic strength and solidarity (Sterne 2000, 159–61). Inside parishes, an extensive network of activities provided forums in which members learned to be organizers and speakers. In 1923, a team from the Italian Church of the Holy Ghost in Providence beat a Boston congregation in a debate over the League of Nations. The *Visitor,* Rhode Island's Catholic weekly, proudly attributed the victory to the popularity of the Holy Ghost Lyceum, whose weekly lecture series "turns out orators and debaters as a Ford factory does Fords" (*Providence Visitor,* May 11, 1923: 3).

Many immigrants used their parishes as springboards from which they became active in the larger community. It was at church that many Catholics developed opinions, skills, and solidarities; these in turn encouraged them to speak out on matters of importance, and to speak with the moral authority that religion provided. Sometimes the connection between religion and politics was philosophical or symbolic. Irish and German Catholics in the late-nineteenth-century Midwest entered politics to resist Protestant "moral reform" movements such as temperance. These initiatives violated Catholics "corporatist" worldview, which was informed by a particularistic religious tradition and held that independent churches and families, rather than a strong state, were the keys to social order (Gjerde 1997, chapters 9–10). Italian Americans in the twentieth-century Northeast employed patron-saint street festivals, such as the popular Festa della Madonna del Carmine, to challenge an Americanism rooted in Anglo-Saxon Protestantism. Using a complex iconography that blended sacred and secular, old world and new, participants asserted their civic fitness by sending the message that they could be Italian, American, and Catholic at the same time (Sterne 1999, 1–2).

At other times the link between religion and politics was more tangible. In nineteenth-century Buffalo, struggles within congregations (often erupting when parishioners sought to assert control over priests) "were breeding grounds for democratic citizenship" (Gerber 1989, 323–24). More generally, parish life was "a principal source of the skills and values that . . . political action required. Immigrants honed their political skills in the parish as well as the local machine" (Tentler 1997, 40). By the 1920s, middle-class Irish Catholics in Providence were putting these skills to work and using their lay organizations to coordinate political campaigns, rally against discrimination, and lobby for workplace legislation and against immigration restriction. The local chapter of the National Council of Catholic Men conducted naturalization and voter registration drives. In all of these ways, Catholic immigrants made the transition from private devotion to public activism (Sterne 1999, chapter 5; Sterne 2000, 162, 164–73).

These benefits were particularly critical for immigrant women, most of whom lacked access to formal institutions such as unions and parties but could justify parish activity as consistent with their roles as family nurturers and spiritual leaders. They also could become active outside the church by invoking their roles as homemakers and Catholics, in an immigrant version of domestic feminism (Kane 1994, chapters 5–6; Sterne 2000, 163–64). In Progressive Era Boston, middle-class Irish women formed a League of Catholic Women that sponsored lectures, conducted social work, and urged members to be active in public affairs (Connolly 1998, 72–74). In 1920s Providence, women's clubs campaigned against the Equal Rights Amendment, registered voters, conducted immigrant outreach, and lobbied for church- and family-friendly legislation (Sterne 2000, 169–71).

The Catholic Church thus functioned in a Habermasian sense as "a sphere which mediates between society and state," an arena in which information was exchanged and public opinion developed (Habermas 1974, 50; Habermas 1995). Moreover, it was an immensely popular arena by virtue of its resources and accessibility. Of course church attendance varied widely among and even within ethnic groups, with attendance typically higher among the Irish and French Canadians and lower among the Italians, for example (Abramson 1971; Vecoli 1969). Certainly some immigrants remained apathetic or fiercely anticlerical, but many others—even those who lacked a strong sense of faith—recognized the church as a community center and an organizational base. It was through their parishes, then, that many new Americans became active citizens and voters.

The immigrant church nonetheless remains on the margins of American political historiography. Scholars have long recognized that religion, as a belief system and an institutional structure, sustained the struggles of African Americans during and after slavery (Higginbotham 1993; Morris 1984; Raboteau 1978). More recently, historians have acknowledged that Protestantism had a central if ambiguous influence on antebellum labor activism (Schantz 2000; Sutton 1998; Lazerow 1995; Murphy 1992). They have been slower, however, to apply these lessons to the study of twentieth-century ethnic and working-class history. Modern American labor historians tend to dismiss the church as being a negative influence that discouraged members from "radical" or "political" forms of activism.

To be sure, it was not unproblematic for immigrants to become political through their parishes or indeed through other civic associations. The Catholic Church encouraged women to resist initiatives such as birth control and the Equal Rights Amendment, reforms that could have benefited them. Catholics who entered politics through the church did so under the aegis of a hierarchical institution that sought to control and moderate their activism. Similar charges may be leveled at other civic institutions. Women's clubs and ethnic mutual aid societies were run by middle-class leaders who may have marginalized working-class immigrants and sought recognition and respectability rather than more immediate economic goals. Settlement houses were administered by educated women who mixed social service with a strong and often offensive dash of ethnocentrism. Furthermore, it was by no means a certainty that immigrants who sought assistance through these networks would enter politics. Nonetheless, it is undeniable that civic associations were institutions through which members could acquire political skills and engage in public life, sometimes in ways of which their religious or secular leaders disapproved. These institutions form a largely untold chapter in the story of immigrant political incorporation.

IMMIGRANTS AND ELECTORAL POLITICS: BREAKTHROUGHS

Civic associations mingled with machines and unions in the complex landscape of immigrant politics. It was by working in tandem, consciously or otherwise, that these institutions provided an education and a venue for new Americans in the late nineteenth and early twentieth centuries. By the 1920s, many immigrants were either involved in or on the margins of electoral politics. A series of demographic, legal, and economic shifts then made politics more accessible, more attractive, and more critical.

World War I initiated this series of changes. An intensive and sometimes coercive assimilation campaign convinced many new Americans that they were full-fledged Americans and deserved to be treated as such. Like the nation's African Americans, those immigrants who served in the armed forces found it galling to return from a crusade to "make the world safe for democracy" to a form of second-class citizenship. After the armistice was signed, the culture wars of the "tribal twenties" revived the Ku Klux Klan, instituted harsh new immigration restrictions, and fueled the Prohibition battle (Higham 1969, chapter 10). Enraged and alarmed by these assaults on their cultural prerogatives and their civic fitness, many immigrants become active citizens in defense of their rights, just as their forebears had done in the late nineteenth century. Moreover, more of them had access to the ballot, thanks to the Nineteenth Amendment, the coming of age of second- and third-generation immigrants, and the dissolution of biased voting restrictions such as Rhode Island's municipal property requirement

(Andersen 1979; Lubell 1952, 28–29).[3] At the same time, the John-son-Reed Act of 1924 reduced the flow of immigrants and encouraged aliens to become citizens and engage with American life, now that they no longer had the option of commuting between the old world and the new.[4] By the late 1920s, then, there were fewer immigrants and more U.S.-born "ethnics" with a political voice and a reason to use it.

Scholars agree that these developments set the stage for the mobilization of immigrants and ethnics between 1928 and 1936. When Al Smith ran for president in 1928, he gave these voters a reason to come to the polls (Key 1952, 164–66). As a Catholic of immigrant, working-class origins, he was the first presidential contender with whom ethnic Americans felt kinship. Moreover, a vote for "Alcohol Al" was a vote against the immensely unpopular and nativist Eighteenth Amendment. When Smith made a campaign stop in Providence, one voter attended the rally bearing a placard that read, "Remember November 6—BEER!" (White 1983, 64).

The onset of the Great Depression the following year cemented this budding relationship between immigrants and electoral politics. Although churches and mutual aid societies tried to rise to the occasion, they were incapable alone of providing for a population of which 25 percent—and in some communities as much as one-half—was unemployed. In Chicago and across the country, many turned to the union and the state for those protections and benefits previously provided by employers or, more often, by ethnic institutions (Cohen 1990, 218–38). In Washington they found a chief executive who, with some prodding, was willing to accept responsibility for the social welfare through such programs as the Wagner Act, the Works Progress Administration, and the Social Security Act.

Moreover, despite his patrician origins Franklin D. Roosevelt was a chief executive with whom Americans felt connected. Coming into voters' living rooms through his fireside chats, sending his wife into the coal mines to talk with workers, and inspiring Americans through his own victory over polio, Roosevelt forged a personal relationship with voters who previously had felt distant from their elected officers. This relationship was visible in the framed portraits of the president in ethnic and working-class homes, in the affectionate nicknames—FDR and ER—with which voters addressed the First Couple, and in the letters that Americans sent to the White House (McElvaine 1993, chapter 5). As one writer puts it, "I've always thought of F.D.R. as my personal friend" (McElvaine 1983, 223).

In short, by the late 1930s more immigrants could vote, more had good reason to vote, and more had a sense that their votes mattered. Although the final incentives were the crisis of the Great Depression and the personal appeal of Smith and Roosevelt, the "realignment" of 1928 to 1936 was not a sudden change (Gamm 1986). The Democrats, V. O. Key argues, "recruited potential converts who had been accumulating under the effects of long-term demographic trends and were awaiting political activation" (Key 1952, 166). More than demographics had been at work, however. For decades, immigrants had been mobilized slowly but steadily through party machines, unions, and civic associations. All three of these institutions had nudged them into politics by urging them to become citizens, encouraging them to lobby and campaign, or teaching them to assert themselves in less formal, community-based ways. All three organizations remained active in the 1930s, to varying degrees. Machines admittedly were on the wane, yet some, as we have seen, remained active by dispensing federal welfare funds. Although some ethnic voters were disappointed by the failure of their churches and aid societies to get them through the economic crisis, they did not abandon these community institutions. In Providence, for example, the church remained central to ethnic community life as relief provider, social center, and organizing site (Sterne 1999, 324–35). It was unions and the Democratic Party, however, that now took the lead in incorporating new Americans into electoral politics.

These voters transformed American politics by forging a "New Deal" coalition that kept the Democrats in control of the nation almost without interruption through 1968, and elected an Irish Catholic president in 1960. They also transformed policy by forcing lawmakers to build on the New Deal legacy by protecting more workers and improving on America's new welfare state. Finally, this mobilization transformed ethnic communities by turning immigrants into active citizens with the ability to influence elections and make demands of the state.

Two caveats are necessary, however. One is that the revolution of the 1930s was incomplete. The ethnic mobilization left out Asian immigrants, who until 1952 were barred from becoming naturalized. Among the entire American population, never since 1900 have more than two-thirds of eligible voters cast ballots in a presidential election (Piven and Cloward 1989, 54, 125, 161). In recent years, turnout has been closer to 50 percent. Political participation is particularly low among foreign-born voters. As Louis DeSipio demonstrates in chapter 2 of this volume, even though naturalization is rising, immigrants remain politically marginalized.

The second caveat is that the opening up of electoral politics in the 1930s did not necessarily undermine nontraditional vehicles of incorporation. Just as women continued to influence politics through voluntarist strategies after they had won the right to vote (Chafe 1991, chapter 2; Cott 1987, chapter 3; Hewitt 1993, 216), so it makes sense that immigrants continued to work through civic institutions even after it became easier for them to join unions and cast ballots. The vote is not, after all, the only marker of political engagement (Baker 1997, 898). The encouraging conclusion is that even today, when voter turnout and union membership are declining and many immigrants remain disconnected from electoral politics, civic associations—in concert with unions and political parties—hold potential to bring new Americans into public life. To consider these three modes of incorporation, then, can help us not only to understand the past but also to engage the question of how immigrants become politically active in the present.

NOTES

1. One study finds that between 1908 and 1923, 35 percent of all immigrants returned home. The remigration rate was more than 50 percent for southern Italians and a number of eastern European ethnic groups but much lower for members of old immigrant groups: 22 percent for Scandinavians, 18 percent for Germans, and a low 11 percent for the Irish. There are no comparable statistics for the nineteenth century, although what data are available suggest that "old" immigrants were less likely to return home then, too. Between 13 and 23 percent of

Germans remigrated from 1884 to 1892, and just 10 percent of all postfamine Irish immigrants returned home (Wyman 1993, 10–12).

2. In 1910 and 1920, respectively, 45.6 and 48.7 percent of immigrants were citizens (Ueda 1980, 747).

3. As mentioned earlier, in 1888 Rhode Island overturned the rule that immigrants must own real estate in order to vote. Until 1928, however, the state continued to require that all urban voters own personal property worth at least $134 in order to vote in city elections. This rule was clearly biased against workers and immigrants (Sterne 1999, 303–4).

4. Between 1920 and 1930, the proportion of immigrants who were naturalized rose from 48.7 to 58.8 percent. By 1950, that number had risen to 67.9 percent (Ueda 1980, 747).

REFERENCES

Abramson, Harold J. 1971. "Ethnic Diversity Within Catholicism: A Comparative Analysis of Contemporary and Historical Religion." *Journal of Social History* 4(4): 359–88.

Allswang, John M. 1986. *Bosses, Machines, and Urban Voters.* 2d ed. Baltimore: Johns Hopkins University Press.

Altschuler, Glenn C., and Stuart M. Blumin. 1997. "Limits of Political Engagement in Antebellum America: A New Look at the Golden Age of Participatory Democracy." *Journal of American History* 84(3): 855–85.

Andersen, Kristi. 1979. *The Creation of a Democratic Majority, 1928–1936.* Chicago: University of Chicago Press.

Baker, Jean H. 1997. "Politics, Paradigms, and Public Culture." *Journal of American History* 84(3): 894–99.

Baker, Paula. 1984. "The Domestication of Politics: Women and American Political Society, 1780–1920." *American Historical Review* 89(3): 620–47.

Brody, David. 1993. *Workers in Industrial America: Essays on the Twentieth-Century Struggle.* 2d ed. New York: Oxford University Press.

Brown, M. Craig, and Charles N. Halaby. 1987. "Machine Politics in America, 1870–1945." *Journal of Interdisciplinary History* 17(3): 587–612.

Bryce, James. 1893. *The American Commonwealth.* 3d ed. 2 vols. New York: Macmillan.

Cameron, Ardis. 1993. *Radicals of the Worst Sort: Laboring Women in*

Lawrence, Massachusetts, 1860–1912. Chicago: University of Illinois Press.

Chafe, William H. 1991. *The Paradox of Change: American Women in the Twentieth Century.* New York: Oxford University Press.

Cohen, Lizabeth. 1990. *Making a New Deal: Industrial Workers in Chicago, 1919–1939.* New York: Cambridge University Press.

Connolly, James J. 1998. *The Triumph of Ethnic Progressivism: Urban Political Culture in Boston, 1900–1925.* Cambridge, Mass.: Harvard University Press.

Cott, Nancy. 1987. *The Grounding of Modern Feminism.* New Haven: Yale University Press.

Dolan, Jay P. 1992. *The American Catholic Experience: A History from Colonial Times to the Present.* Notre Dame: University of Notre Dame Press.

Dubofsky, Melvyn. 1994. *The State and Labor in Modern America.* Chapel Hill: University of North Carolina Press.

Emmons, David M. 1989. *The Butte Irish: Class and Ethnicity in an American Mining Town, 1875–1925.* Chicago: University of Illinois Press.

Erie, Steven P. 1988. *Rainbow's End: Irish-Americans and the Dilemmas of Urban Machine Politics, 1840–1985.* Berkeley: University of California Press.

Ethington, Philip J. 1994. *The Public City: The Political Construction of Urban Life in San Francisco, 1850–1900.* New York: Cambridge University Press.

Faue, Elizabeth. 1991. *Community of Suffering and Struggle: Women, Men, and the Labor Movement in Minneapolis, 1915–1945.* Chapel Hill: University of North Carolina Press.

Fink, Leon. 1983. *Workingmen's Democracy: The Knights of Labor and American Politics.* Chicago: University of Illinois Press.

Fraser, Steve. 1989. "The 'Labor Question.'" In *The Rise and Fall of the New Deal Order, 1930–1980,* edited by Steve Fraser and Gary Gerstle. Princeton: Princeton University Press.

Fuchs, Lawrence H. 1995. *The American Kaleidoscope: Race, Ethnicity, and the Civic Culture.* 2d ed. Hanover, N.H.: Wesleyan University Press.

Gamm, Gerald H. 1986. *The Making of New Deal Democrats: Voting Behavior and Realignment in Boston, 1920–1940.* Chicago: University of Chicago Press.

Gerber, David A. 1989. *The Making of an American Pluralism: Buffalo, New York, 1825–1860.* Chicago: University of Illinois Press.

Gerstle, Gary. 1989. *Working-Class Americanism: The Politics of Labor in a Textile City, 1914–1960.* New York: Cambridge University Press.

Gjerde, Jon. 1997. *The Minds of the West: Ethnocultural Evolution in the Rural Middle West, 1830–1917.* Chapel Hill: University of North Carolina Press.

Greene, Julie. 1998. *Pure and Simple Politics: The American Federation of Labor and Political Activism, 1881–1917.* New York: Cambridge University Press.

Habermas, Jürgen. 1974. "The Public Sphere." *New German Critique* 1(3): 49–55.

———. 1995. *The Structural Transformation of the Public Sphere: An Inquiry into a Category of Bourgeois Society.* Translated by Thomas Burger, with Frederick Lawrence. 7th ed. Cambridge, Mass.: MIT University Press.

Harris, Howell John. 1982. *The Right to Manage: Industrial Relations Policies of American Business in the 1940s.* Madison: University of Wisconsin Press.

Hewitt, Nancy A. 1993. "In Pursuit of Power: The Political Economy of Women's Activism in Twentieth-Century Tampa." In *Visible Women: New Essays on American Activism,* edited by Nancy A. Hewitt and Suzanne Lebsock. Urbana, Ill.: University of Illinois Press.

Higginbotham, Evelyn Brooks. 1993. *Righteous Discontent: The Women's Movement in the Black Baptist Church, 1880–1920.* Cambridge, Mass.: Harvard University Press.

Higham, John. 1969. *Strangers in the Land: Patterns of American Nativism, 1860–1925.* 8th ed. New York: Atheneum.

Hofstadter, Richard. 1955. *The Age of Reform: From Bryan to F.D.R.* New York: Knopf.

Hyman, Paula. 1980. "Immigrant Women and Consumer Protest: The New York City Kosher Meat Boycott of 1902." *American Jewish History* 70(1): 91–105.

Kane, Paula M. 1994. *Separatism and Subculture: Boston Catholicism, 1900–1920.* Chapel Hill: University of North Carolina Press.

Kantowicz, Edward R. 1980. "Politics." In *Harvard Encyclopedia of American Ethnic Groups,* edited by Stephan Thernstrom, Ann Orlov, and Oscar Handlin. Cambridge, Mass.: Harvard University Press, Belknap Press.

Katznelson, Ira. 1981. *City Trenches: Urban Politics and the Patterning of Class in the United States.* Chicago: University of Chicago Press.

Kazin, Michael. 1987. *Barons of Labor: The San Francisco Building Trades and Union Power in the Progressive Era.* Chicago: University of Illinois Press.

Key, V. O., Jr. 1952. "The Future of the Democratic Party." *Virginia Quarterly Review* 28(2): 161–75.

Keyssar, Alexander. 2000. *The Right to Vote: The Contested History of Democracy in the United States.* New York: Basic Books.

Lazerow, Jama. 1995. *Religion and the Working Class in Antebellum America.* Washington, D.C.: Smithsonian Institution Press.

Lichtenstein, Nelson, and Howell John Harris. 1993. *Industrial Democracy in America: The Ambiguous Promise.* New York: Cambridge University Press.

Lubell, Samuel. 1952. *The Future of American Politics.* 2d ed. New York: Harper and Brothers.

Luconi, Stefano. 1996. "Machine Politics and the Consolidation of the Roosevelt Majority: The Case of Italian Americans in Pittsburgh and Philadelphia." *Journal of American Ethnic History* 15(2): 32–59.

Lynd, Staughton. 1996. *"We Are All Leaders": The Alternative Unionism of the Early 1930s.* Urbana, Ill.: University of Illinois Press.

McCartin, Joseph A. 1997. *Labor's Great War: The Struggle for Industrial Democracy and the Origins of Modern American Labor Relations, 1912–1921.* Chapel Hill: University of North Carolina Press.

McDonald, Terrence J. 1986. *The Parameters of Urban Fiscal Policy: Socioeconomic Change and Political Culture in San Francisco, 1860–1906.* Berkeley: University of California Press.

McElvaine, Robert S., ed. 1983. *Down and Out in the Great Depression: Letters from the "Forgotten Man."* Chapel Hill: University of North Carolina Press.

———. 1993. *The Great Depression: America, 1929–1941.* 2d ed. New York: New York Times Books.

McGerr, Michael. 1986. *The Decline of Popular Politics: The American North, 1865–1928.* New York: Oxford University Press.

Merton, Robert K. 1957. *Social Theory and Social Structure.* New York: Free Press.

Mink, Gwendolyn. 1986. *Old Labor and New Immigrants in American Political Development: Union, Party, and State, 1875–1920.* Ithaca, N.Y.: Cornell University Press.

Montgomery, David. 1987. *The Fall of the House of Labor: The Workplace, the State, and American Labor Activism, 1865–1925.* New York: Cambridge University Press.

———. 1993. *Citizen Worker: The Experience of Workers in the United States with Democracy and the Free Market During the Nineteenth Century.* New York: Cambridge University Press.

Morris, Aldon D. 1984. *The Origins of the Civil Rights Movement: Black Communities Organizing for Change.* New York: Macmillan.

Murphy, Teresa Anne. 1992. *Ten Hours' Labor: Religion, Reform, and Gender in Early New England.* Ithaca, N.Y.: Cornell University Press.

O'Connor, Edwin. 1956. *The Last Hurrah*. Boston: Little, Brown.

Oestreicher, Richard. 1986. *Solidarity and Fragmentation: Working People and Class Consciousness in Detroit, 1875–1900*. Urbana, Ill.: University of Illinois Press.

———. 1988. "Urban Working-Class Political Behavior and Theories of American Electoral Politics." *Journal of American History* 74(4): 1257–86.

Orsi, Robert A. 1985. *The Madonna of 115th Street: Faith and Community in Italian Harlem, 1880–1950*. New Haven: Yale University Press.

Piven, Frances Fox, and Richard A. Cloward. 1989. *Why Americans Don't Vote*. 2d ed. New York: Pantheon Books.

Raboteau, Albert. 1978. *Slave Religion: The "Invisible Institution" in the Antebellum South*. New York: Oxford University Press.

Salter, J. T. 1935. *Boss Rule: Portraits in City Politics*. New York: McGraw-Hill.

Salvatore, Nick. Forthcoming. "Faith in Context: Three Catholic Parishes in Chicago, 1860–1940." In *Religion and the City,* edited by Virginia L. Brereton and Mark Wilhelm.

Schantz, Mark S. 2000. *Piety in Providence: Class Dimensions of Religious Experience in Antebellum Rhode Island*. Ithaca, N.Y.: Cornell University Press.

Schneirov, Richard. 1998. *Labor and Urban Politics: Class Conflict and the Origins of Modern Liberalism in Chicago, 1864–1897*. Chicago: University of Illinois Press.

Shefter, Martin. 1986. "Trade Unions and Political Machines: The Organization and Disorganization of the Working Class in the Late Nineteenth Century." In *Working-Class Formation: Nineteenth-Century Patterns in Western Europe and the United States,* edited by Ira Katznelson and Aristide R. Zolberg. Princeton: Princeton University Press.

Smith, Judith E. 1985. *Family Connections: A History of Italian and Jewish Immigrant Lives in Providence, Rhode Island, 1900–1940*. Albany, N.Y.: State University of New York Press.

Stave, Bruce M. 1970. *The New Deal and the Last Hurrah: Pittsburgh Machine Politics*. Pittsburgh: University of Pittsburgh Press.

Steffens, Lincoln. 1905. "Rhode Island: A State for Sale." *McClure's Magazine* 24(4): 337–53.

———. 1966. *The Shame of the Cities*. 1903. New York: Hill and Wang.

Sterne, Evelyn. 1999. "All Americans: The Politics of Citizenship in Providence." Ph.D. diss., Duke University.

———. 2000. "Bringing Religion into Working-Class History: Parish, Public, and Politics in Providence, 1890–1930." *Social Science History* 24(1): 149–82.

Sutton, William R. 1998. *Journeymen for Jesus: Evangelical Artisans Confront Capitalism in Jacksonian Baltimore*. University Park, Pa.: Pennsylvania State University Press.

Tentler, Leslie Woodcock. 1997. "Present at the Creation: Working-Class Catholics in the United States." In *American Exceptionalism? U.S. Working-Class Formation in an International Context*, edited by Rick Halpern and Jonathan Morris. New York: St. Martin's Press.

Tomlins, Christopher. 1985. *The State and the Unions: Labor Relations, Law, and the Organized Labor Movement in America, 1880–1960*. New York: Cambridge University Press.

Ueda, Reed. 1980. "Naturalization and Citizenship." In *Harvard Encyclopedia of American Ethnic Groups*, edited by Stephan Thernstrom, Ann Orlov, and Oscar Handlin. Cambridge, Mass.: Harvard University Press, Belknap Press.

Vecoli, Rudolph J. 1969. "Prelates and Peasants: Italian Immigrants and the Catholic Church." *Journal of Social History* 2(3): 217–68.

Voss, Kim. 1993. *The Making of American Exceptionalism: The Knights of Labor and Class Formation in the Nineteenth Century*. Ithaca, N.Y.: Cornell University Press.

White, John K. 1983. "Alfred E. Smith's Rhode Island Revolution: The Election of 1928." *Rhode Island History* 42(2): 56–66.

Wyman, Mark. 1993. *Round-Trip to America: The Immigrants Return to Europe, 1880–1930*. Ithaca, N.Y.: Cornell University Press.

—— Chapter 2 ——

Building America, One Person at a Time: Naturalization and Political Behavior of the Naturalized in Contemporary American Politics

Louis DeSipio

NATURALIZATION AND THE rights of the naturalized have become fodder for the national political debate in a way that they had not for many years. In the 1996 presidential campaign, for example, the Republicans accused President Bill Clinton of spurring an increase in the numbers of newly naturalized citizens and allowing the naturalization of ineligible applicants in an effort to boost the Democratic vote. In another twist, the legality of some of the controversial funds collected by the Clinton campaign and the Democratic National Committee from "foreign" sources hinged on whether the immigrant contributors were U.S. citizens or permanent residents. Representative Bob Dornan (R-Calif.) blamed his defeat on the votes of unnaturalized immigrants for his opponent Loretta Sánchez. In an unlikely alliance, the California secretary of state and the Immigration and Naturalization Service (INS) promised to investigate the citizenship status of voters in the district. The 1996, 1998, and 2000 elections have seen leaders of ethnic communities make new claims on the impact of their communities' votes based largely on expectations for the votes of the

TABLE 2.1 **Naturalizations, by Decade and Various Years**

Decade or Year	Naturalizations
1907 to 1910	111,738
1911 to 1920	1,128,972
1921 to 1930	1,773,185
1931 to 1940	1,518,464
1941 to 1950	1,987,028
1951 to 1960	1,189,949
1961 to 1970	1,120,263
1971 to 1980	1,464,772
1981 to 1990	2,214,265
1991 to 2000	5,671,994
1991	308,058
1992	240,252
1993	314,681
1994	434,107
1995	488,088
1996	1,044,689
1997	598,225
1998	473,152
1999	872,427
2000	898,315

Source: U.S. Immigration and Naturalization Service 1999b, 2001a, 2001b.

newly naturalized. National and local candidates in each of these elections have changed their behaviors to reach not just ethnic voters but naturalized voters, as well.

The new electoral prominence of naturalization followed an increase in immigrant interest in becoming U.S. citizens. In 1996, more than 1 million immigrants became U.S. citizens in a single year. During the 1990s, more than 5 million immigrants were naturalized, a number greater than in the three prior decades combined (see table 2.1).

On the surface, this combination of increasing demand for naturalization and growing electoral awareness of the votes of naturalized citizens might indicate a return to the group-based political incorporation of immigrants that characterized earlier periods of American immigration history (Erie 1988; chapter 1, this volume). Despite the surface similarities between the charges of the

1996 campaign and this earlier model of immigrant incorporation, however, the contemporary model for immigrant political incorporation is quite different. By the end of the twentieth century, the process of immigrant political adaptation occurred primarily at the individual level. More important, at the beginning of the twenty-first century the political world of immigrants, like the political world of U.S.-born citizens, offers greater opportunities to individuals with more education, higher earnings, and greater age. Finally, the infrastructure of ethnic-community-based institutions that facilitated naturalization in earlier eras is largely absent in today's immigrant communities. In sum, the contemporary process of immigrant political adaptation has not only shifted from a group focus to an individual focus, but it has also incorporated the class and education bias that shapes political participation more generally in American society (Verba and Nie 1972; Wolfinger and Rosenstone 1980; Verba, Schlozman, and Brady 1995).

JOINING THE POLITY THROUGH NATURALIZATION

Contrary to popular assumptions, many immigrants never become naturalized citizens. In 1990, for example, just 8 million of the 19.8 million foreign-born residents of the United States had been naturalized (U.S. Bureau of the Census 1993). Not all of the nonnaturalized immigrants were eligible for citizenship. Approximately 3.25 million had immigrated in the previous five years and, thus, were not yet eligible for naturalization. Between 2 million and 3 million were undocumented immigrants. Another 2 million had attained legal status in the previous year under the 1986 Immigration Reform and Control Act and would not be eligible for citizenship until 1993. Even with these caveats, however, it is clear that many citizenship-eligible immigrants do not naturalize (DeSipio 1996b, particularly appendix 2).

These numbers are imprecise because there are no comprehensive data sources on immigrants to the United States. This absence of data makes it difficult to answer not only the relatively simple question of how many immigrants eligible to do so have naturalized but also the analytically more complicated question of what distinguishes immigrants who naturalize from those who do not.

The INS keeps no records of what happens to immigrants once they arrive in the United States. Thus all estimates of naturalization rates based on immigration data underestimate true naturalization rates by failing to account for immigrants who have emigrated from the United States or have died. Similarly, estimates based on census data both overestimate and underestimate naturalization rates. The census makes no distinction between documented and undocumented immigrants, so its pool of "immigrants" is often much larger than the pool of citizenship-eligible immigrants, even when recent legal immigrants are subtracted from the pool. Hence, estimates based on census data underestimate the share of the eligible who are naturalized. Census data generally undercount hard-to-reach populations, however, including immigrants. The count, then, of 19.8 million foreign-born residents in 1990 underestimates the true number of foreign-born residents.

A final source of data on the immigrant and naturalization-eligible population is survey data. Again, these data have weaknesses. Most specifically, no single survey encompasses all contemporary immigrants. Instead, the national survey data that do exist on immigrants focus on just one of the major immigrant populations—Latinos.

Despite their weaknesses, survey data offer the first important insight about naturalization-eligible immigrants—that it is inaccurate to separate them into just two categories—denizen and citizen. A 1988 survey of Latino immigrants eligible for naturalization (the National Latino Immigrant Survey) indicates that among Latinos, approximately one-third of eligible immigrants have naturalized, one-third are not interested in becoming U.S. citizens, and one-third have begun to naturalize but have not yet succeeded in their efforts (Pachon and DeSipio 1994). Although no comparable data exist for other immigrant ethnic groups, I would hypothesize that immigrants from other parts of the world—particularly Asia and Europe—have higher shares of the immigrant population who have naturalized and fewer who have begun but not completed the process. I have no basis to estimate the share of immigrants from other parts of the world who are not interested in naturalization.

Census data do not offer the same level of precision as the National Latino Immigrant Survey, and there are no comparable survey data for other immigrant populations. Census data do, however, offer a simpler measure of the share of immigrants who have naturalized. Table 2.2 presents two measures of naturalization rates, in addition to the numbers of immigrants by country of origin. The second column in the table presents raw naturalization rates for all immigrants to the United States from the region or country, and the third column narrows the field to only those immigrants who immigrated from 1980 to 1990.[1] As immigrants from different parts of the world have different immigration histories and vastly different average lengths of residence, the raw naturalization rates falsely compare immigrants from regions that sent the bulk of their immigrants in the 1960s and before with those from regions that have sent the majority of their immigrants more recently. Thus, the naturalization rates among post-1980 immigrants offer a better foundation for comparison. Even among these post-1980 immigrants, however, the naturalization rate varies by region and by country.

DISTINGUISHING DENIZENS FROM CITIZENS

What, then, distinguishes immigrants who naturalize from those who do not? As a brief analysis of the data presented in table 2.2 indicates, the most consistently salient characteristic is length of residence. Across all immigrant populations and periods of immigration, the immigrants with longer residency in the United States are more likely to naturalize than those with shorter periods of residence (Gavit 1922; U.S. Immigration and Naturalization Service 1999b, table 53).

That said, the speed of naturalization varies by nationality and by region of origin. Although these variations traditionally show consistency across regions—with Asian immigrants naturalizing the fastest and immigrants from the Americas naturalizing the slowest—the patterns are now in flux. Over the decade under study, the average immigrant who naturalized from Asia waited approximately seven years after immigrating, the average European immigrant nine to ten years, and the average immigrant from Latin America and the Caribbean twelve to fourteen years. Tradi-

TABLE 2.2 **Naturalization Rates for Various Regions and Countries of Origin, 1990**

Region and Country	Former Nationals Residing in United States	Naturalization Rate (Percentage)	
		All Immigrants	Immigrants from 1980 to 1990
Africa	363,819	34.1	15.4
Asia	4,979,037	40.8	17.4
China	529,837	44.1	15.7
India	450,406	34.9	13.4
Japan	290,128	28.2	3.2
Korea	568,397	40.6	14.9
Philippines	912,674	53.9	25.9
Vietnam	543,262	42.7	26.6
Europe	4,016,678	64.7	13.6
Germany	711,829	71.9	12.0
Italy	580,592	75.8	20.5
Poland	388,328	62.4	17.5
United Kingdom	640,145	49.6	7.1
Soviet Union	333,725	58.9	16.9
North America	8,124,257	29.3	12.5
Canada	744,830	54.1	7.7
Caribbean	1,938,348	39.7	15.1
Cuba	736,971	51.0	14.8
Dominican Republic	347,858	27.6	14.0
Jamaica	334,140	38.4	17.2
Central America	1,133,978	20.7	9.8
El Savador	465,433	15.4	10.1
Mexico	4,298,014	22.6	12.7
Oceania	104,145	34.0	12.6
South America	1,037,497	30.8	11.7
Colombia	286,124	29.0	11.2
Total	19,767,316	40.5	14.4

Source: U.S. Bureau of the Census 1993.
Note: Table lists only regions or countries of which at least 250,000 former nationals were residing in the United States in 1990.

tionally, the immigrant groups with the longest wait between immigration and naturalization have been nationals of the two countries that border the United States—Mexico and Canada. Among Mexicans and Canadians who naturalized from 1980 to 1990, the average wait was fifteen to sixteen years. Data for the most recent year with available data (1997) show a narrowing of these differences, with Asian, European, and Mexican immigrants who naturalized having waited approximately eight years (U.S. Immigration and Naturalization Service 1999b, table 53). Some nationalities continued to wait much longer periods—immigrants from the Caribbean who naturalized in 1997 had waited fifteen years before doing so, and Canadian immigrants more than twenty-one years. This change in 1997 over long-established patterns reflects a change in the composition of the pool of naturalization applicants and is, I believe, related to the method in which the INS records the year of immigration for those who were legalized under the Immigration Reform and Control Act. Although nationality may influence some of this variation, other factors seem to play a much greater role in determining who will naturalize and who will not.

Scholars have identified several clusters of factors that explain these diverse rates of naturalization—sociodemographic characteristics, attitudinal and associational variables, immigration and settlement characteristics, and inconsistent bureaucratic treatment. It should be noted that these clusters overlap. Although some analysts do examine just one of the clusters, most people who have looked at naturalization in any depth cast their net more widely. Each cluster reflects a major source of data on naturalizing citizens, and their shortcomings reflect what is missing from those data sets.

Of these clusters, sociodemographic characteristics of immigrants are the most studied. Such factors as income, white-collar employment, professional status, home ownership, years of schooling, and English-language ability explain some of the differences that influence the likelihood of naturalization (Barkan and Khokolov 1980; Portes and Mozo 1985; Jasso and Rosenzweig 1990; Yang 1994; DeSipio 1996b). The married are more likely to naturalize than the unmarried, and women more likely than men. Immigrants who arrived as young children are more likely to naturalize than are those who arrived here as teenagers or adults.

These demographic characteristics partially explain the more rapid naturalization rates of Asian immigrants and the slower rates among Latino immigrants. On average, Asian immigrants are more likely to exhibit the traits that predict successful naturalization. Latinos, on the other hand, are more likely to have low wage jobs, low levels of formal education, and weaker English skills—all factors that discourage naturalization.

Analysts examining sociodemographic characteristics of immigrants generally rely on INS or Census Bureau data sets. Because the INS does not collect follow-up data on immigrants after the time of immigration, analysis of their data is frequently limited to characteristics at the time of immigration and cannot account for settlement experiences in the United States. Census data do allow measurement of sociodemographic characteristics after immigration, but they cannot include such formal measures as the type of visa on which the immigrant entered the United States. Neither INS nor census data include attitudinal measures.

A second stream of the scholarship looks at attitudinal and associational variables, such as roots in the United States, attitude toward life in the United States, and social identification as an American (García 1981; Portes and Curtis 1987). These are found to be positive predictors of naturalization. Immigrants who associate mostly with noncitizens are less likely to naturalize (DeSipio 1996a). Immigrant community attitudes also influence naturalization. Michael Jones-Correa (1998) finds that an "ideology of return" to the home country discourages naturalization. For the most part, studies of this type examine survey data, which permit a more detailed examination of immigrants' experiences once they arrive in the United States and the relationship of these experiences to the naturalization decision. The weakness with survey data, however, is that there is no comparative data on immigrants from all parts of the world. Often, the attitudinal surveys examine small subsets of the immigrant population and are geographically bound to just one city. To date, there are just two such national surveys, and both of these focus on Latinos.

A third set of predictive variables concerns immigration and settlement experiences. Among the findings of this scholarship are that immigrants who entered as refugees and skilled workers are more likely than other immigrants to naturalize (Jasso and Rosenzweig 1990). Immigrants who left their native countries for political reasons (whatever the formal source of the immigrant visa) are also more likely to naturalize than those who migrated for other reasons (Portes and Mozo 1985; Jasso and Rosenzweig 1990). This scholarship has also generated a curious counterintuitive finding: the higher the home country's gross national product, the lower the likelihood of naturalization (Yang 1994). This analysis combines government data sources with survey data. Again, the limitation on the survey data limits the comparative utility of these studies.

Scholars of naturalization have also examined whether, controlling for a variety of factors, national or regional origin continues to have a predictive value in distinguishing immigrants who naturalize from those who do not. The answer would appear to be yes, though the absence of comparative data reduces the utility of these findings. Guillermina Jasso and Mark Rosenzweig (1990) find that immigrants from Mexico are less likely, on average, to naturalize than nationals of other countries who send large numbers of immigrants, controlling for other immigration-related factors. Alejandro Portes and Rafael Mozo (1985) find, similarly, that immigrants from Canada and Mexico are less likely to naturalize than nationals of other countries, controlling for sociodemographic factors. Finally, in earlier research (DeSipio 1996b), I have found that among Latinos, Cubans and Dominicans are more likely than Mexicans to begin the naturalization process and, once they begin the process, to become U.S. citizens (controlling for sociodemographic, associational, and immigration-related factors).

That some nationalities continue to have a higher or lower likelihood of naturalizing should not obscure the larger finding. The likelihood of naturalization increases for individuals with more education and higher incomes and for older immigrants. These traits are reinforced by certain characteristics at the time of immigration. People who immigrate at younger ages are more likely to naturalize: younger immigrants have more exposure to American society and customs and also more exposure to American education. The likelihood of naturalization is also shaped by U.S. immigration law: immigrants who migrate for political reasons are also more likely to naturalize. Because there is no comprehensive survey data on immigrant naturalization, it is not possi-

ble to say how these factors interact nor to assess their relative
influence on naturalization, controlling for the impact of all other
factors. That said, differences between individual immigrants account for part of the gap between immigrant attachment to the
United States and successful naturalization more than nationality
differences. Each of the factors discussed so far varies from individual to individual. Thus, whereas naturalization has historically
been awarded or denied as much because of nationality as because of individual characteristics, in recent times it has come to
be very much a function of an individual relationship with the
state.

The final influence on who naturalizes and who does not explains in part the increased likelihood of naturalization among the
educated and the socially advantaged. It also explains the large
number of immigrants who have actively pursued naturalization
but have not been able to achieve their goals. That is the administration of the naturalization program. Naturalization administration
is highly decentralized, which results in differential treatment of
applicants from one INS district office to another. The impact of
this administrative inconsistency is difficult to measure precisely,
but it has two consequences for immigrants pursuing naturalization. First, immigrants from different countries and regions experience different administrative denial rates (DeSipio and Pachon
1992). This may, in part, reflect different immigrant skill and education levels, but it also reflects variation in office practice. Overall, applicants from Latin America, the Spanish- and English-
speaking Caribbean, and Africa have higher-than-average denial
rates. Furthermore, the rates of unsuccessful applications are
higher than average in some INS offices than in others. Offices at
the high end of the spectrum for administrative denials—those in
Miami, Newark, and San Jose—and the low end—those in Boston
and Denver—have a sufficient mix of immigrants that immigrant
characteristics alone can not explain the variation. The variety of
experiences of individual naturalization applicants who go before
the INS may, in turn, lead to confusion in immigrant populations
that could discourage some interested immigrants from seeking
naturalization.

In sum, naturalization is far from automatic among immigrants
interested in becoming U.S. citizens. The likelihood of naturalization is shaped by individual characteristics, and the factors that

predict naturalization also influence eventual participation in American politics. Thus those who naturalize should be most likely to participate in politics. This connection between naturalization and political engagement does not appear, however, at least among Latinos who have naturalized.

CHANGING INCENTIVES TO NATURALIZE

Beginning in 1993, the costs of denizenship began to increase and the psychic costs of naturalization for immigrants from some countries began to decline (for a more detailed discussion of these factors, see DeSipio 1996a). The consequence was a dramatic increase in immigrant interest in naturalization over the last decade of the twentieth century (see table 2.1). I trace this surge in interest to 1993. Although it may appear not to have occurred until 1995 or even 1996, this lag reflects more about INS processing delays than about the patterns of applications. Instead, I suggest, demand for naturalization began to increase in 1993. By 1996, the number of naturalizations had roughly tripled the average levels before the surge in demand. Naturalizations at this level are unprecedented in the ninety-year history of federal control of naturalization.

Why did immigrants suddenly seek naturalization at such high levels? First, the United States and at least one of the states— California—began to change a long-standing pattern in the treatment of denizens (DeSipio 1996a). Before 1994, permanent residents, and particularly permanent residents with the five years of residence required to make them eligible for U.S. citizenship, had most of the rights and eligibility for programmatic benefits as did citizens. Beginning with California's Proposition 187 and then with the Personal Responsibility and Work Opportunity Reconciliation Act of 1996 (Welfare Reform Bill), legislatures began to deny immigrants and their households social welfare benefits (DeSipio and de la Garza 1998, chapter 4). Although relatively few immigrants use these benefit programs (at least relative to their economic status), many heard the anti-immigrant message of these legislative changes and more actively pursued naturalization.

A second change also altered the incentive structure of naturalization. Several immigrant-sending countries have sought to reduce the psychic costs to émigrés seeking to become U.S. citizens (Aleinikoff 2000; Jones-Correa 2000). This new approach takes a variety of forms, but all seek to reshape the relationship between the sending country and the émigré. Colombia, for example, encourages dual citizenship and seeks to maintain an ongoing relationship with the U.S.-born children of its U.S.-naturalized émigrés. Mexico has not gone as far as Colombia in establishing a new relationship with its émigrés but promotes a dual nationality that allows for full economic, though not political, rights. It has also promised an easy renaturalization to nationals who become U.S. citizens but later decide to return to Mexico to live permanently. The Mexican case is particularly important both because of the numbers of its émigrés in the United States and because its attitude was traditionally one of disdain toward émigrés who sought U.S. citizenship (de la Garza 1997). The goal of these policies is to create an interest group in the United States that is sensitive to the needs of the sending country.

A third change in the incentive structure has been less instrumental. Beginning in 1993, the INS required that immigrants with aging immigrant identification cards ("green cards") replace their cards. For many long-term residents (who had developed English-language skills), the procedure and cost of replacing the aging cards was significantly less complicated or expensive than naturalizing. Because the new green cards will have to be replaced every ten years, the utility of naturalization increased.

A fourth change in the mid-1990s affected the pool of eligible immigrants. One of the three components of the Immigration Reform and Control Act was the program to legalize long-term undocumented residents of the United States. Approximately 2 million immigrants who had resided in the United States as undocumented aliens since before 1982 earned permanent resident status through this program. Another 1 million agricultural laborers who had shorter periods of undocumented residence also earned legalized status. They began to be eligible for naturalization in late 1993. Thus at the same time that the incentive structure of naturalization was changing and the INS created a bureaucratic incentive to naturalize, the pool of eligible immigrants was growing quite dramatically, by as many as 3 million.

This increase was notable for two reasons. First, it was much larger than any comparable annual increase: in an average year, between 550,000 and 750,000 immigrants attain naturalization eligibility (some of these are children and can only naturalize if their parents do so). Second, the legalization recipients have long periods of U.S. residence; all have resided in the United States since at least 1982. Furthermore, to obtain legalized status they had either to demonstrate a knowledge of the English language, U.S. history, and civics comparable to what is asked of naturalizing citizens or to take classes to meet these objectives. Thus they are now, a few years later, further along in the process of adapting to U.S. life and better prepared than most newly naturalization-eligible immigrants. They, of course, join the 550,000 to 750,000 immigrants from five years before who begin to become eligible for naturalization each year.

The presence of these newly legalized immigrants in the naturalization pool explains the changes in the length of time between immigration and naturalization in 1996 noted earlier. For each national-origin group with large numbers of legalization recipients, 1990 served as the year of immigration for many of the immigrants who naturalized in 1996. The INS records the year that legalization was granted as the year of immigration (or, more specifically, adjustment of status to that of permanent resident). Thus, many of these 1990 immigrants are legalization beneficiaries who in fact migrated before 1982.

A fifth change in the incentive structure to naturalize was a by-product of the 1996 Antiterrorism and Effective Death Penalty Act. Among other provisions, this federal crime bill raised the likelihood that permanent residents who had committed crimes in the United States either would be deported or would be barred from reentering the United States after a voluntary departure. Anecdotal evidence indicates that some permanent-resident parents, fearing that their minor children might later become involved in gang activity, have been naturalizing to protect them from application of these provisions. Both before and after the passage of the law, permanent residents convicted of felonies were ineligible to naturalize.

Finally, the INS periodically spurred a surge in demand by raising or threatening to raise the fee for naturalization. This goal was achieved in January 1999, when the fee was increased from $95 to $225. Before this increase and several prior efforts, applications increased dramatically in the months preceding the increase or proposed increase.

In addition to the approximate tripling of citizenship applications, what is the impact of these changes in incentive on the propensity to naturalize? Again, no data presently exist with which to analyze the experiences of immigrants who have recently naturalized. I suspect that the changed incentive structure has moved many more previously disinterested immigrants to apply for naturalization. Presumably, some immigrants who had begun but not completed naturalization before 1993 experienced sufficient incentive to complete their efforts. In sum, then, I would expect that the post-1993 naturalization applicants show fewer individual differences than those who naturalized before 1993.

It is important to note, though, that even with higher numbers of immigrants becoming U.S. citizens, since 1993 no more than half of the eligible pool of long-term immigrants have become citizens. Admittedly, a higher share of these noncitizens are made up of immigrants who do not want to pursue U.S. citizenship. The pool of citizenship-eligible immigrants, however, is likely to continue to include many who have expressed an interest in naturalizing and some who have initiated the process in some way. Their numbers are reinforced by the 550,000 to 750,000 immigrants who reach their fifth year of permanent residence each year. In other words, a large untapped pool of citizenship-eligible immigrants remains who have not yet pursued naturalization.

At the end of the decade, new applications for naturalization began to decline. If present trends continue, there will be no more than 500,000 new applications for citizenship in 2001 (U.S. Immigration and Naturalization Service 2001a). Although this represents a considerable decline from the mid-decade highs, this number still exceeds the numbers of applications from earlier in the decade. Again, however, it reinforces the pattern of a slowly growing pool of the naturalization-eligible population who are either not interested in citizenship or are interested but are not yet mobilized to proceed toward U.S. citizenship.

POLITICAL BEHAVIOR OF THE NATURALIZED

It has long been assumed that the naturalized engage in politics at higher levels than comparably situated U.S.-born citizens. There is

a logic behind this assumption as well as a specific historical circumstance that may explain its origin. Among contemporary immigrants, however, these claims have no empirical foundation. On
the contrary, in contemporary elections, most empirical studies indicate that naturalized citizens register and vote at rates lower
than comparably situated U.S.-born citizens.

The historical origin of the claims of high levels of political
activity among the naturalized is the last period of higher-than-
routine immigrant interest in naturalization—the 1920s and the
early 1930s (see chapter 1, this volume).[2] Scholarly work from this
era speaks of the energetic involvement of naturalized citizens in
politics, particularly in local politics, and of their influence in
some elections. These claims are for the most part not empirically
substantiated in the scholarly analysis of this era, but the assertion
is made widely enough to have become accepted as a truism
(some more recent studies have attempted to look at the political
behaviors of the naturalized and their children from this era with
greater methodological rigor; see Andersen 1979 and Gamm
1986).

When the analysts from the 1920s and the 1930s sought to
examine the question of why naturalized citizens of the period
were disproportionately active in politics, they used the following
logic, again without any proof: Naturalizing citizens develop a
more complete understanding of U.S. politics through the requirements of the naturalization process. With this greater knowledge,
they take the responsibilities of democracy more seriously, and
they participate more. In this period, their added participation was
spurred by the ethnically charged 1928 presidential election, with
Democrat Al Smith's Catholicism and support for a repeal of Prohibition, and by the Great Depression and the beginnings of the
New Deal in the 1932 and 1936 elections. This unique historical
period—covering the three national elections from 1928 to 1936—
created an environment in which the naturalized (and their children) did have a particularly strong and cohesive political voice.
The economic difficulties of the day were important to them, and
they were able to develop alliances with other disaffected groups
to form the coalition that would later support President Franklin
D. Roosevelt and the Democrats for a political generation.

Whether or not the naturalized participated in politics at high levels in the 1920s and the 1930s, the same assertions are made about today's immigrants. Again, however, there is little substantiation for these claims. What is offered is anecdotal evidence from specific elections. Often, however, these examples do not distinguish between the political behaviors of the naturalized and their U.S.-born coethnics. Furthermore, they do not measure the combined impact of the immigrant ethnic vote.

A recent example of this sort of claim is the 1996 congressional election in California. Many commentators attributed Loretta Sánchez's victory over Robert Dornan to the votes of Latino immigrants. Implicitly, Dornan made this claim with his charge that Sánchez (and a Latino community–based organization, Hermandad Mexicana) had "stolen" the election by manipulating the votes of naturalizing (but not yet naturalized) Latinos. Undeniably, many people in the district are Latino (the district was drawn under the provisions of the 1965 Voting Rights Act to create a majority-minority district). It is equally certain that many of these Latino residents of the district were not U.S. citizens. The claim of Latino influence on the outcome of this race has two weaknesses, however. First, Latinos—regardless of nativity—made up no more than 30 percent of the voters in the district (and probably closer to 25 percent). Thus, though they may well have overwhelmingly supported Sánchez, Latino voters alone are not responsible for her victory. Second, at least 60 percent of these Latino voters had voted in previous congressional elections. Thus, if they were naturalized voters, they were not recent entrants into electoral politics. In sum, these anecdotal claims often collapse upon even the simplest investigation.

Several recent studies have tapped survey data (often collected for other purposes) to compare the political behaviors of U.S.-born and foreign-born ethnics. In an earlier study, for example, I measured four forms of political activity—involvement in community organizations, parental involvement in the schools, voter registration, and voting—to compare the political behavior of naturalized and native-born Mexican Americans and Cuban Americans (DeSipio 1996c).[3] Across each of these four types of political activity, bivariate comparisons indicated that the native born and the naturalized had comparable levels of activity. When variations did appear, the native born usually exhibited higher levels of participation.

When I examined these differences using multivariate models that looked not just at the source of citizenship but also at standard sociodemographic predictors of participation, I found that when naturalization status did prove to be statistically significant, it was a *negative* predictor of political activity. The two political activities for which naturalization proved to be a significant, negative predictor of political activity in the multivariate models were the two that related to voting—voter registration and voting in one of the four elections immediately preceding the survey (including both presidential and local elections). In both of these models, the standard sociodemographic measures that broadly predict political activity among American adults had a greater impact on the dependent variable than did source of citizenship. The sociodemographic measures included in the models were years of education and degrees earned, income, labor force participation, and age. I also included two variables unique to immigrant ethnic populations—national origin and language used at home (neither of which proved to be significant). Source of citizenship proved to be insignificant for two other types of political activity—membership in community organizations and parental involvement in the schools.

Analysis of the Current Population Survey's data on registration and voting in the 1996 elections largely tells the same story (Bass and Casper 1999).[4] Controlling for sociodemographic characteristics, foreign-born citizens were found to be one-third less likely to register and one-quarter less likely to vote than the native born. Interestingly, naturalized citizens from Latin America were somewhat more likely to report having registered to vote than immigrants from other parts of the world, though these national-origin differences were not statistically significant.

These national findings are largely reinforced by four studies of immigrant ethnic populations in specific cities—New York, Los Angeles, and Miami—that rely on both survey data and ecological inference. The first of these city-level studies measures voting among six immigrant ethnic populations in New York City elections (Levitt and Olson 1996). This study examines electoral districts with high concentrations of Dominican, Jamaican, Chinese, Italian, Russian, and Ecuadorian immigrants in five elections in the early 1990s. The authors find that in the districts with high concentrations of five of the six ethnic populations (all but Russians), the rate of voter turnout was lower than the citywide average. Chinese-dominated electoral districts turn out at the lowest rates, just 73 percent of the average for the city. Although this study does not adequately account for the interaction between sociodemographic characteristics and nationality characteristics, it reinforces the finding that the naturalized participate at lower rates than the native born.

John Mollenkopf, David Olson, and Tim Ross (forthcoming) extend this study to look at immigrant neighborhoods in New York and Los Angeles. These neighborhoods are home to both first- and second-generation immigrants. Although they indicate that structural and electoral factors explain some of the variation within each city, their consistent finding is that voters in neighborhoods with high concentrations of immigrants are *less* likely to turn out than those in neighborhoods without such concentrations.

In New York, Mollenkopf, Olson, and Ross find that predicted turnout for the 1996 presidential election declined by about 1 percent for each 10 percentage-point increase in foreign-born population. In Los Angeles, a 10 percentage-point increase in foreign-born population decreases turnout by 2 percent. The authors find some variation among ethnic groups: In New York, West Indians and Dominicans are more likely to vote than native-born citizens. Chinese, Italians, and Russians, on the other hand, are less likely to vote. In Los Angeles, Salvadorans, Mexicans, and Filipinos were less likely to turn out than voters in native-born ethnic neighborhoods.

These findings are reinforced by a second New York–based study. Lorraine Minnite, Jennifer Holdaway, and Ronald Hayduk (1999), reporting on a 1997 telephone survey of 1,662 adults, find that self-reported voting rates in the 1994 and 1996 elections varied by nativity in a statistically significant manner, controlling for sociodemographic and institutional factors. As with the other studies, they find that the native born are more likely to participate than the foreign born. Minnite, Holdaway, and Hayduk's particular contribution comes from their examination of both a presidential and nonpresidential election. The gap between the native and foreign born was greater in the nonpresidential election year under study.

Kevin Hill and Dario Moreno (1996) analyze the Cuban respondents to the Latino National Political Survey, most of whom reside in Florida. They examine three subsets of this population—immigrants who migrated before they were ten years of age, immigrants who migrated after they had turned ten, and U.S.-born Cubans (who are almost all native-born children of immigrants). They test which of these subsets is most likely to participate in seven nonelectoral political activities. Overall, the second generation are less likely to undertake these activities than the migrants who arrived after the age of ten. In a regression model, however, percentage of life spent in the United States proves a significant and positive predictor of undertaking these activities, suggesting that the relative youth of the second generation may be dampening their political activity relative to their immigrant parents.

Without a national immigrant voting survey that is broadly inclusive in terms of immigrant ethnic populations and verifies self-reported registration and voting, the results of these disparate studies must suffice in answering the question of the likelihood of voting among immigrants. To the extent that these populations are representative of the naturalized citizen population broadly, however, the data indicate that the naturalized will not have a disproportionate political voice. In fact, they will have less of a voice than comparably situated U.S.-born citizens. Although they are a privileged subset of the immigrant population, the naturalized are more likely than the population as a whole to have the sociodemographic characteristics that are usually associated with political marginalization. In the past, these demographic traits were overcome, at least for some immigrant ethnic groups, by political socialization and mobilization targeted by the political machines and by ethnic leaders. This was the very role of the machine for privileged immigrant ethnic groups, at least early in its existence. In today's high-technology politics, in contrast, there is no comparable agent for most immigrants. The independent and negative impact of naturalization on registration and voting indicates that naturalized citizens experience a political distance that is a function not simply of their economic and educational disadvantages but also of their lack of political socialization.

STRUCTURING THE POLITICAL ENVIRONMENT OF THE NATURALIZED

Clearly, these data on the political behavior of the naturalized are very limited. They do not present a comprehensive picture of the political lives of naturalized U.S. citizens. Instead, they examine components of the naturalized. More important, perhaps, they describe immigrants who naturalized before the current surge in interest in naturalization. I turn now to the political environment that today's naturalizing citizens join, examining it from three dimensions—the political-institutional dynamics of voter mobilization and demobilization in the nation as a whole and in the areas in which many new immigrants reside, immigrant ethnic community leaders' efforts to create an "ethnic" politics, and the structural opportunities and barriers created by U.S. society through the Voting Rights Act. Each of these factors shapes the opportunities for political socialization of the voluntary citizens.

Institutions and Incorporation

The naturalized are not isolated from currents that shape the opportunity for participation among all U.S. citizens. Rather, laws and political institutions play an important role in shaping political behavior among all potential electorates. I include in this discussion not only national political influences, of which all citizens are a part, but also state and, particularly, local politics and local political environments. Certainly, Thomas "Tip" O'Neill's observation that "all politics is local" applies to all Americans. Arguably, it is more important for voluntary citizens because it is with local government and local political actors that they are likely to have the most contact, and it is around service delivery issues that they are most likely to become involved in politics.

The national political laws and institutions that shape the likelihood of participation on the part of naturalized citizens are both formal and informal. The formal structure of voting regulation in the United States has been one of decentralization. For most of the nation's history, the federal government has delegated the regulation of voting to the states, and the states have used this power both to include and to exclude. At the turn of the century, for example, many states used their authority over voting to include the nonnaturalized in the vote (Rosberg 1977; Raskin 1993). The more common pattern, however, has been to create barriers that exclude many from participation or make it more difficult for some to participate. From the gender and property-holding requirements of the early nineteenth century to registration requirements of the twentieth century, states have created barriers to participation, particularly for those individuals who had fewer skills and lower incentive to participate. This traditional pattern of state and local regulation of voting faced a major challenge with the passage of the Voting Rights Act of 1965. Although the act protects the voting rights of some immigrant ethnic populations as a group, it does not provide a means to overcome the costs of participation that make it less likely that potential voters of younger ages with lower-than-average incomes and education will participate (Wolfinger and Rosenstone 1980). Naturalized citizens disproportionately fall into these categories of likely nonparticipants (DeSipio 1996b).

Another national political institution that shapes the political incorporation of the naturalized is the political party. In the late nineteenth century, parties mobilized new voters in order to be competitive. Among the beneficiaries of this party-focused mobilization were the newly naturalized. Beginning at the turn of the century, this mobilization became more selective, and the parties supported legal changes that initiated the process of electoral demobilization that continues today.

With few exceptions, today's parties no longer take an active role in mobilizing new electorates. Instead, their mobilization efforts increasingly focus on mobilizing likely participants at election time. Aided by technology, this is taken to extremes, with parties limiting their efforts to individuals who have, for example, voted in four of the last four elections. Rhetorically, the parties do retain a commitment to bringing new citizens into their folds to build their coalitions, but these efforts focus primarily on electoral and candidate message and do not involve registration and get-out-the-vote efforts (see, for example, Guy Gugliotta, "Democrats Hope to Translate Latino Distrust of GOP into Votes," *Washington Post*, January 5, 1998; Michael Totty, "GOP Sees El Paso as Test of Its Appeal to Hispanics," *Wall Street Journal* [Texas edition], January 7, 1998). Equally important, the parties have made only limited efforts to promote naturalization in immigrant communities. Other mediating institutions have taken on some of the traditional roles of the parties in the twentieth century, such as the media and interest groups, but neither of these institutions has sought to mobilize the newly naturalized (with the possible exception of the ethnic media).

In terms of both institutions and laws, a more important focus for examining the process of immigrant political incorporation is states and localities. Immigrant political incorporation has long been a function of cities and local political institutions (Muller 1993). At the height of the last wave of immigration at the turn of the century, some immigrants were actively recruited to the political process through urban machines and ethnic organizations (Erie 1988; chapter 1, this volume). Other immigrants, however, were not actively recruited and more often were neglected, to become politically involved only when national politics convulsed in the period from 1928—with Al Smith's presidential campaign, the introduction of Smith's Catholicism into the national political debate, and the efforts associated with the Smith campaign to repeal Prohibition—to 1932 and 1936, with the Depression and establishment of the Democratic Party coalition that included European ethnic populations in its core membership (Andersen 1979; Gamm 1986; Cohen 1990; chapter 1, this volume).

Among today's immigrants and naturalized citizens, the primary point of contact with government and political institutions is located at the state and local level. The services that these naturalized citizens tap—education, sanitation, parks and recreation, transportation, public health, and social welfare—are services delivered primarily or exclusively by states and localities. It is these local governments and local political orders, often unconsciously, that train new citizens in how to participate and what to expect of American government and politics. The political incorporation of contemporary immigrants, then, cannot be separated from the political environments of the areas in which they reside, primarily urban areas and primarily on the coasts (DeSipio 2000).

These localities have taken a slightly more proactive role than has the federal government in encouraging naturalization among immigrants (a notable difference from the role of municipal governments in the second and third decades of the twentieth century; see chapter 1, this volume). In the modern era, several cities and states created public agencies to facilitate naturalization; others funded private agencies to provide naturalization assistance. Although these efforts emerged in response to the same pressures that spurred the surge in naturalization in the 1990s (and rapidly disappeared as those pressures diminished), they helped overcome the bureaucratic barriers that deter many interested immigrants from pursuing naturalization. These public institutions, however, cannot take a role in making voters of the newly naturalized.

Local political and civic institutions could take on this role, but for the most part they have not. State and local political parties generally follow the lead of the national parties and target their mobilization efforts at likely voters around election time. In part, this failure to take a more active role in mobilizing new citizens into electoral politics is a function of increasing noncompetitiveness in many elections in the United States, particularly local elections (Browning, Marshall, and Tabb 1997). Recent mayoral races in New York, Los Angeles, Miami, and Houston—all cities with sizable immigrant and naturalized populations—did see partisan competition, but in all cases the races themselves were not particularly competitive.

The laws of one state—California—deserve special note in this discussion. California receives approximately one-quarter of all new immigrants to the United States each year (U.S. Immigration and Naturalization Service 1999b, table 17). As a result, its laws and political culture are particularly important to the question of the political incorporation of the naturalized. More so than in other states, the law in California creates an environment in which any potential impact of partisanship will be dampened. All local races in the state are nonpartisan. Between 1998 and 2000, state legislative and congressional races followed a limited form of nonpartisanship in which the two candidates with the highest number of votes in the primary faced each other in the general election. Campaigns in California are expensive, perhaps more so than in other states, requiring extensive fundraising and dependent on paid media. Although there is no research that examines the impact of this nonpartisanship, paid-media dependence, and expense on the mobilization of newly naturalized citizens in California, these factors further reduce the incentive for parties to reach out to potential new electorates.

The dearth of mobilization in immigrant ethnic communities has been well documented. Perhaps the most comprehensive study examined immigrant point-of-entry communities in five immigrant-receiving cities—New York, Los Angeles, Houston, Chicago, and Miami. Although the focus of this study was solely on Latino communities, its findings are instructive (de la Garza, Menchaca, and DeSipio 1994). During the 1990 general election, Latinos in only one of these cities—Miami—saw any mobilization by political institutions. In the others, particularly in New York and Houston, there was virtually no effort to inform, mobilize, or turn out Latino voters. Latino elites were somewhat more active than political and electoral institutions, but they too took little interest in drawing out the Latino vote. As the electoral environment is currently structured, there is minimal incentive to reach out to communities such as these that have little history of participation.

A final set of institutions that have traditionally played a role in facilitating immigrant naturalization and political socialization are the ethnic and civic organizations located in immigrant ethnic communities. In chapter 1 of this volume, for example, Evelyn Sterne identifies the importance of mutual aid societies, church groups, women's organizations, and settlement houses in promoting naturalization among immigrants in the second and third decades of the twentieth century. Although these organizations, or their contemporary equivalents, remain in many immigrant communities, they play a much weaker role in immigrant civic and political adaptation than they have in the past. The reasons for this are several. Perhaps, most important, few immigrants perceive an attachment to or membership in community-based voluntary organizations (de la Garza with Lu 1999). Many of the community-based organizations that do remain do not invest in developing a broad membership (Skerry 1993). Instead, they are professionally managed and depend on government and philanthropic assistance to operate. They undoubtedly provide important and needed services to immigrants (including, in some cases, assistance with naturalization). By the nature of their organization and funding, however, they cannot actively promote political engagement among immigrants and naturalized citizens. The staff and management, who shape the direction of many of the community-based organizations that do exist in immigrant communities, are often native born (Pardo 1998). Finally, immigrants, like the population as a whole, have declining levels of civic engagement (Skocpol and Fiorina 1999). The impact of this society-wide decline in civic engagement has particular implications for immigrant ethnic populations, but there has been little scholarly study of its impact on them.

In sum, both national and local institutions reinforce a pattern of demobilization that has characterized U.S. politics since the 1950s. Although legal and institutional barriers shape participation for all U.S. citizens, arguably they have a particular influence on the newly naturalized. First, the newly naturalized are more likely than the population as a whole to have the demographic characteristics that predict lower levels of electoral participation. Second, many of the newly naturalized have lower levels of political socialization in U.S. politics. Socialization can help to overcome the barriers created by demobilization, registration requirements, and nonpartisanship. Finally, the newly naturalized are geographically concentrated in areas that are more likely to be the most demobilized—specifically, urban areas with low levels of electoral competition and California—which, on top of noncompetitive elections, has diminished the incentive for parties to mobilize new electorates. Thus, the first factor shaping political incorporation of naturalized citizens is the laws and institutions that shape electoral participation for all in the United States.

Immigrants and Ethnic Politics

Despite the rapid increase in naturalization, the naturalized are a minority of Latino voters. Among Asian American voters, the majority may be naturalized, though the absence of concrete data make it harder to ascertain the nativity of voters. Despite these differences, in both of these large immigrant ethnic populations the community leaders, such as elected officials and heads of major community and national organizations, are more likely to be native born than naturalized. For the foreseeable future, this pattern will remain.

The influence of immigrants and naturalized citizens on ethnic politics is twofold. First, immigration provides the numbers on which ethnic leaders are able to make claims on U.S. political institutions. Although Asian and Latino populations would be increasing even if immigration were to stop, the dramatic growth of these populations is a function of immigration, and it is the dramatic growth that allows demands to be made. Second, the public policy needs of the naturalized in settling in and adapting to American society have broadened the range of ethnic politics by shifting the community leaders' attention from the politics of civil rights to a politics that combines civil rights with the protection of the rights of immigrants to programmatic benefits (DeSipio and de la Garza 1999). This shifting focus became evident at the national level for the first time in the 1996 campaign and reflects a major change in the meaning of ethnic politics in the United States (DeSipio, de la Garza, and Setzler 1999).

The claims of ethnic leaders on American society would ring more hollow without the numbers generated by immigration. Over the past decade, legal immigration has swelled the population of the United States by between 750,000 and 1,000,000 annually. Undocumented immigrants add another 200,000 to 300,000 each year. Approximately 80 percent of these immigrants are Latino or Asian. Without this engine of growth, the validity and urgency of the claims made by ethnic leaders would decline. Although ethnic leaders do not always acknowledge that the electoral influence they represent is more potential than real, the importance of immigration to the Latino and Asian American claim on American politics and its institutions cannot be underestimated (de la Garza 1996).

The scholarship on contemporary ethnic politics in the United States is recent. Although ethnicity has been an increasing focus of scholarly attention in political science, the study of ethnic politics among contemporary ethnic groups in the United States is still very much in its infancy. As a result, fundamental questions such as what share of the politically active population is made up of naturalizing citizens cannot be answered. The existing scholarship has paid more attention to such questions as the composition of panethnic politics (that is, Latino and Asian American politics) as against politics based on national origin (Espiritu 1992; de la Garza et al. 1992; Fox 1996), ethnic (particularly Latino) participation in national electoral politics (de la Garza and DeSipio 1992, 1996, 1999), and ethnic participation in state and local electoral politics and in organizational politics (Uhlaner, Cain, and Kiewet 1989; Jackson and Preston 1991; Hardy-Fanta 1993; de la Garza, Menchaca, and DeSipio 1994; Jones-Correa 1998). Scholars have examined the reasons for low levels of ethnic participation in politics more than what ethnic voters have accomplished (DeSipio 1996b; DeSipio, de la Garza, and Setzler 1999). Finally, Latinos have received much more scholarly attention from political scientists than have Asian Americans, and virtually nothing has been written on the political behaviors of naturalized citizens from other parts of the world. Until very recently, case studies have dominated the literature.

Beginning in the mid-1990s, the content of ethnic politics began to change. Again, California's Proposition 187 offers a good starting point for this change. In 1994, an off-year election, Latinos in California voted at levels that exceeded their turnout in the previous presidential election (there are no comparable data for Asian Americans). The Latino turnout, though unprecedented, did not shape the outcome of the election. In the face of overwhelming Latino opposition, Proposition 187 passed because of an increase in the non-Latino white vote and the Anglo community's support for the proposition at levels comparable to the Latino opposition. In defeat, however, the agenda of Latino ethnic politics and, to a less dramatic degree, Asian American ethnic politics expanded. Defending the rights of immigrants and seeking to ensure that the government would take a role in providing for their settlement in the United States took on a greater part in the meaning of ethnic politics.

The new concern for immigrants' rights appeared in the 1996 elections and took various forms (DeSipio and de la Garza 1999). One of the major events of the campaign season from the perspective of Latino organizations and elites was the October 1996 march on Washington. The march did not come anywhere near to matching its model, the 1995 African American Million Man March, at the mass level. Nevertheless, it was a target for organizing in the election year and received some press attention. Many senior Latino elected officials spoke to marchers as part of the official program. The rhetoric at the march reflected the new, post–Proposition 187 ethnic politics. Immigrants' rights, condemnations of the provisions of the welfare reform bill that deny benefits to permanent residents, and calls for increased naturalization dominated more traditional discussions of civil rights. These messages had been part of Latino discourse throughout the campaign—including a more muted form at the Democratic national convention—but were most explicit at the march.

This added focus for Latino ethnic politics seems to have had an impact at the ballot box, though it was muted because of low turnout. In the 1996 election, for the first time since the 1960s, it is accurate to speak of a Latino vote. Cuban Americans abandoned their traditional Republican partisanship to split their votes evenly between Clinton and Dole. Polling data indicate that the impetus for this switch was Cuban American concerns of Republican anti-immigrant rhetoric. Among non-Cuban Latinos, support for Clinton and the Democrats rose by approximately 10 percent over 1992 levels (to approximately 75 percent). Again, the best available explanation for this switch was Mexican American and Puerto Rican concern about Republican attitudes toward the rights of immigrants. This support came despite Clinton's signature on the welfare reform and immigration reform bills. His support for these bills, even as he noted that the welfare reform bill would "hurt legal immigrants," was less vitriolic than that of a vocal element in the Republican Party. Thus, Latinos were inclined to vote for Clinton in spite of his support for the welfare reform bill.

The Latino voice was somewhat muted by what appears to be only a slight increase in Latino turnout (DeSipio, de la Garza, and Setzler 1999). Despite claims from within the Latino community of a vast increase in turnout, what data exist indicate only a modest increase over 1992 levels, despite a dramatic growth in the adult population of Latino citizens (turnout among the electorate as a whole declined by about 9 percent). Thus, Latinos moved more solidly to the Democrats, in partial response to concerns about the rights of immigrants, but did not mobilize at new levels.

A bare majority of Asian American voters also supported Clinton, a switch from 1992, when the majority supported the Republicans. The Asian American electorate is more heterogeneous than Latinos, and there are no comparable polling data on Asian American national-origin groups. Yet the movement of the Asian American vote in the same direction as the Latino vote indicates that similar concerns about the rights of immigrants influenced this community as well. Clearly, Asian Americans were also influenced by the efforts in California to reshape the rights of immigrants (Proposition 187) and access of ethnic and racial minorities to affirmative action programs (Proposition 209).

The changes in the significance and importance of ethnic politics are, however, subject to limits. At the local level, Latino and Asian American identities are not as easy to sustain. The status of Chicago as the one multiple-Latino city (with Mexican Americans and Puerto Ricans) is now being challenged. Puerto Ricans still dominate New York Latino politics, but the Dominican community increasingly challenges this domination. Although these two populations share many public policy needs, they compete for local resources. This competition places gains in national Latino politics in danger. Soon, the Salvadoran population of Los Angeles will be in a similar position to challenge the dominance within the Latino community of its Mexican American population.

The Asian American identity has always been more heterogeneous than the Latino identity, with cleavages based on language, historical animosities, experience with discrimination in the United States, and immigration history (Espiritu 1992). At the local level, particularly in Los Angeles and northern California, the formation of successful panethnic Asian American political movement will be difficult. This potential for cleavage at the local level, during a period when national politics is incorporating the needs of immigrant settlement into ethnic politics, will be even more pronounced in the next few years as redistricting efforts force groups to organize around identity to make demands for new seats (DeSipio 1999).

Nevertheless, the broadening focus of ethnic politics in the United States to explicitly capture the settlement experience of immigrants is important for several reasons. First, it provides a receptive environment for the newly naturalizing citizens. These issues of immigrant rights are necessarily important in the households of naturalizing citizens, and community leaders are talking about these issues and organizing around them. This increases the likelihood that naturalized citizens will create political coalitions with their U.S.-born coethnics. Second, this broadening of ethnic politics to incorporate immigrants' rights reflects a sensitivity on the part of the native born. At least in the Latino community, the naturalized are a minority of voters. For these issues to prove important suggests an awareness that transcends narrow personal interest, a forward-looking politics that is more than simply a politics of short-term interest. Finally, by moving away from a narrow focus on civil rights, Latino and Asian American leaders have created the foundation for a panethnic political coalition that could unite them behind the Democratic Party at unprecedented levels. This unity faces a challenge at the local level, where competing national-origin-based interests cannot be subsumed into a panethnic identity.

The Voting Rights Act and the Structuring of Ethnic Politics in the United States

The Voting Rights Act, particularly the majority-minority districts that are drawn under it, give weight to the numbers that immigrants bring to ethnic communities and link the political needs of U.S.-born and naturalized coethnics. Although this linking of interests does not depend on it, the act has an unintended impact that may slow the process of immigrant political adaptation. The districts drawn under the its provisions are relatively safe for incumbents, reducing the likelihood of new voter mobilization. Because naturalizing immigrants need more of this mobilization than do U.S.-born voters, they pay an added price for majority-minority districts.

When originally enacted by Congress in 1965, the Voting Rights Act was designed to eliminate the formal barriers that southern states had created to obstruct the African American vote. These barriers, including outright intimidation, literacy tests, and more subtle tactics such as moving polling places the night before the election, fell rapidly, but jurisdictions quickly found other strategies to dilute the impact of the African American vote. Congress increasingly tried to guarantee a meaningful vote to African

Americans (and, after 1975, to Latinos, Asian Americans, Native Americans, and Alaskan Natives).

The search for a meaningful vote focused on a specific strategy—designing districts with a sufficient majority of votes from the targeted minority to ensure that it could elect to office the candidate of its choice. The courts usually define this "candidate of the community's choice" as a person of the same ethnic or racial group as the majority of the district's residents. As most minority communities have lower-than-average shares of the adult population who vote, the goal of creating a district that will elect a minority often requires having much more than a simple majority of residents of the district. In African American communities, district designers often seek districts that are 60 to 65 percent African American. In Latino and Asian American districts, however, a larger majority is often needed because of high shares of the populations who are not U.S. citizens.

The nature of majority-minority districting is such that noncitizens have an important role in shaping political opportunities for their citizen coethnics. Districting does not take citizenship into account. Thus noncitizens, when they are numerous enough, force the creation of minority districts (DeSipio and de la Garza 1992). In communities receiving large numbers of immigrants, then, the opportunity to elect coethnics may precede the establishment of a sizable electorate.

The residential patterns of Latinos and Asian Americans is such that these districts—whatever the level of office—include immigrants, naturalized citizens, and U.S.-born citizens. This blending of citizens and noncitizens in the same districts reinforces the linkages of the interests of these populations. Although it is rarely recognized as a benefit of district-based, majoritarian election systems (as opposed to, for example, systems of proportional representation), this combining of interests offers immigrants and naturalized citizens the opportunity to develop an awareness of U.S. politics that is shaped in an ethnic context. Certainly none of the legislative history of the Voting Rights Act indicates that Congress intended it to shape ethnic politics in the United States, but its implementation assures that districting is part of the context of contemporary ethnic politics. Clearly, ethnic electoral districts included U.S.- and foreign-born coethnics in the past as well, but it was a function of custom and political opportunism. For communities covered by the Voting Rights Act, it is now a matter of law (reinforced by custom and political opportunism).

An unintended consequence of the Voting Rights Act may be a slowing of the process of political socialization among new voters in these districts. This does not occur in a vacuum. The act's mandate of majority-minority districts, I suggest, builds on the decline of political parties and the demobilization of the electorate to reduce the likelihood that the newly naturalized and other new potential voters will be the target of electoral, candidate, or party outreach.

If districts are to be designed in such a way that Latinos and Asian Americans are elected, they have to include large numbers of people who cannot vote (larger shares than in districts that elect non-Hispanic whites and African Americans). Latinos and Asian Americans are young populations, so these districts will have higher shares of people under the age of eighteen. They also have higher shares of noncitizens, so among the adults not all are eligible to vote. Finally, they are poorer and less educated populations, so among the citizen adults, Asian American and Latino districts will have high shares of people who are less likely to vote. The ironic consequence of this confluence of characteristics among Latinos and Asian Americans in districts designed to elect them is that districts will be created with relatively few actual voters (de la Garza and DeSipio 1993). As a result, once an official is elected, he or she is less likely to face opposition and, arguably, will have less reason than other elected officials to encourage more voting or to regularly mobilize all but a minimal core of voters in elections. Thus, where political socialization used to be the responsibility of ethnic politicians, the structure of contemporary elections now discourages exactly this activity.

The ultimate impact of this circumstance is debatable. Some argue that elected officials who are minority take a special responsibility for mobilization, regardless of whether they need to do so to get reelected. Electoral data show that this hope frequently goes unrealized. Turnout in Latino congressional districts, for example, is consistently the lowest among competitive elections for Congress. Although this is a question that merits further research, it is important to observe that the newly naturalized are likely to be concentrated in majority-minority districts and, as a result, are potentially less likely to be socialized to regular electoral participation.

The Voting Rights Act, then, has contradictory but profound effects on the process of immigrant political adaptation. It fights the individualist nature of immigrant political adaptation by reinforcing group interests through the districting process. Yet, at the same time, it may serve to slow the process of naturalized citizen participation in U.S. politics by reducing the incentive for political institutions and political leaders to socialize the newly eligible.

This impact may change in coming years. A five-member Supreme Court majority has coalesced in opposition to some, but so far not all, race-sensitive districting . If the Supreme Court coalition opposed to majority-minority districting remains in place, the litigation that follows redistricting resulting from the 2000 census may well create fewer majority-minority districts and will place fewer Latinos and Asian Americans in those minority districts that are created. Because of the dramatic increases in naturalization, this is a crucial moment in which to shape the future political participation of new U.S. citizens. These new citizens were counted to create districts after the 1990 census, but by 2000, they were eligible voters (U.S. citizens) who may not yet have become part of the electoral process.

CONCLUSION

Just as many immigrants never become U.S. citizens, many naturalized citizens never become regular participants in American politics. The individualistic nature of both the decision to naturalize and the decision to vote or participate in other forms of American politics rewards well-positioned immigrants but also serves to exclude many. Participation is lower across all populations for people with lower levels of education and low incomes, characteristics that are more likely to describe the naturalized than those born in the United States. The available evidence, however, demonstrates that the naturalized are even less likely than comparably situated U.S.-born citizens to become active members of the polity. Thus the consequence of these informal barriers are amplified in the population of naturalized citizens. In the past, this has not been of great concern to analysts and policymakers because the naturalized citizens were few. If current patterns continue for the next ten years, the nation could soon be in a situation in which one in twelve adults is a naturalized citizen.

This pattern of low political participation among the naturalized raises a dilemma for the citizenship process. The formal requirements for citizenship test knowledge, not behavior. Yet the national rhetoric surrounding naturalization focuses on the behavior of good citizenship, including political involvement. This disjuncture between what the nation seems to want from its voluntary citizens and the standards that it establishes for immigrants seeking citizenship raises the likelihood that naturalized immigrants will not be able to take full advantage of their new citizenship. The turn-of-the-century model of selective group-based immigrant incorporation made more explicit the connection to the political consequences of citizenship, at least for those groups that received assistance with naturalization. Contemporary politics have not been able to develop an equivalent behavioral component to the requirements for naturalization.

In an earlier article examining the Voting Rights Act and Latino political behaviors, Rodolfo de la Garza and I suggested a second route to citizenship that supplements the current system of meeting knowledge-based standards. We proposed that each immigrant be given, at the time of immigration, a five-year nonrenewable voter registration privilege (we do not agree on whether this privilege should be limited to state and local elections or should include voting in all elections). If during this five-year period the immigrant regularly votes, we would argue, he or she has demonstrated the qualities of a good citizen and should receive U.S. citizenship after meeting the five-year residence requirement (de la Garza and DeSipio 1993). Were this proposal to be implemented (which we both recognize as politically unlikely), probably few immigrants would take advantage of it, but the opportunity to establish citizenship through the behavior of good citizenship creates an added incentive for ethnic community mobilization of immigrants and could create an ethos where the desire to join the American polity is more explicitly linked to the participation in its politics. It is that ethos of mobilization that is missing for most in today's immigrant political world.

NOTES

1. As I have indicated, the census has no means to distinguish legal from undocumented immigrants. The naturalization rates given in table 2.2 are computed by dividing the number of naturalized citizens from each country or region by the total number of immigrants. Thus, countries that have sent large numbers of undocumented immigrants will have lower naturalization rates. This might explain some of the variation within regions—for example, the United Kingdom's relatively low naturalization rates compared with other countries in Europe.

2. These experiences from the 1920s and the early 1930s are not the only historical examples of the political influence of the naturalized. Thomas Jefferson's 1800 victory in New York state has been attributed to the immigrant vote (Muller 1993, 21). Steven Erie finds that the urban machines relied on naturalization to swell voter rolls and win several elections, including the 1868 New York gubernatorial race and mayoral races in the 1870s and early 1880s (Erie 1988, 51–53).

3. There is no comparable study of Latinos more broadly or of other immigrant ethnic populations nationally.

4. Although the Current Population Survey is always subject to over-reporting (as, for that matter, are all surveys that rely on self-reporting of registration and voting), the 1996 election might have triggered higher-than-average rates of overreporting, particularly among Latino respondents (Shaw, de la Garza, and Lee 2000).

REFERENCES

Aleinikoff, T. Alexander. 2000. "Between Principles and Politics: U.S. Citizenship Policy." In *From Migrants to Citizens: Membership in a Changing World*, edited by T. Alexander Aleinikoff and Douglas Klusmeyer. Washington, D.C.: Brookings.

Andersen, Kristi. 1979. *The Creation of a Democratic Majority, 1928–1936*. Chicago: University of Chicago Press.

Barkan, Elliott R., and Nikolai Khokolov. 1980. "Socioeconomic Data as Indices of Naturalization Patterns in the United States: A Theory Revisited." *Ethnicity* 7(1): 159–90.

Bass, Loretta E., and Lynne M. Casper. 1999. "Are There Differences in Registration and Voting Behavior Between Naturalized and Native-

Born Americans?" Working Paper 28. Washington, D.C.: U.S. Census Bureau, Population Division. Accessed on June 1, 2001 at : *www. census.gov/population/www/documentation/twps0028/twps0028.html.*

Browning, Rufus, Dale Rogers Marshall, and David H. Tabb. 1997. *Racial Politics in American Cities.* New York: Longman.

Cohen, Lizabeth. 1990. *Making a New Deal: Industrial Workers in Chicago, 1919–1939.* New York: Cambridge University Press.

de la Garza, Rodolfo O. 1996. "El Cuento de los Números and Other Latino Political Myths." In *Su Voto Es Su Voz: Latino Politics in California,* edited by Aníbal Yáñez-Chavez. San Diego: Center for U.S.-Mexican Studies, University of California, San Diego.

———. 1997. "Foreign Policy Comes Home: The Domestic Consequences of the Program for Mexican Communities Living in Foreign Countries." In *Bridging the Border: Transforming Mexico-U.S. Relations,* edited by Rodolfo O. de la Garza and Jesus Velasco. Boulder, Colo.: Rowman and Littlefield.

de la Garza, Rodolfo O., with Fujia Lu. 1999. "Explorations into Latino Voluntarism." In *Nuevos Senderos: Reflections on Hispanics and Philanthropy,* edited by Diana Campoamor, William A. Díaz, and Henry A. J. Ramos. Houston: Arte Público Press.

de la Garza, Rodolfo, and Louis DeSipio. 1993. "Save the Baby, Change the Bathwater, and Scrub the Tub: Latino Electoral Participation After Twenty Years of Voting Rights Act Coverage." *Texas Law Review* 71(7): 1479–1539.

———, eds. 1992. *From Rhetoric to Reality: Latino Politics in the 1988 Elections.* Boulder, Colo.: Westview Press.

———, eds. 1996. *Ethnic Ironies: Latino Politics in the 1992 Elections.* Boulder, Colo.: Westview Press.

———, eds. 1999. *Awash in the Mainstream: Latino Politics in the 1996 Elections.* Boulder, Colo.: Westview Press.

de la Garza, Rodolfo, Louis DeSipio, F. Chris García, John A. García, and Angelo Falcón. 1992. *Latino Voices: Mexican, Puerto Rican, and Cuban Perspectives on American Politics.* Boulder, Colo.: Westview Press.

de la Garza, Rodolfo, Martha Menchaca, and Louis DeSipio, eds. 1994. *Barrio Ballots: Latino Politics in the 1990 Elections.* Boulder, Colo.: Westview Press.

DeSipio, Louis. 1996a. "After Proposition 187, the Deluge: Reforming Naturalization Administration While Making Good Citizens." *Harvard Journal of Hispanic Policy* 9: 7–24.

———. 1996b. *Counting on the Latino Vote: Latinos as a New Electorate.* Charlottesville: University Press of Virginia.

———. 1996c. "Making Citizens or Good Citizens? Naturalization as a

Predictor of Organizational and Electoral Behavior Among Latino Immigrants." *Hispanic Journal of Behavioral Sciences* 18(2): 194–213.

———. 1999. "Election? What Election? Illinois Latinos and the 1996 Elections." In *Awash in the Mainstream: Latino Politics in the 1996 Elections*, edited by Rodolfo O. de la Garza and Louis DeSipio. Boulder, Colo.: Westview Press.

———. 2000. "The Dynamo of Urban Growth: Immigration, Naturalization, and the Restructuring of Urban Politics." In *Minority Politics at the Millennium*, edited by Richard A. Keiser and Katherine Underwood. New York: Garland Publishing.

DeSipio, Louis, and Rodolfo O. de la Garza. 1992. "Making Them Us: The Political Incorporation of Immigrant and Nonimmigrant Minorities." In *Nations of Immigrants: Australia, the United States, and International Migration*, edited by Gary Freeman and James Jupp. Melbourne: Oxford University Press.

———. 1998. *Making Americans, Remaking America: Immigration and Immigrant Policy*. Boulder, Colo.: Westview Press.

———. 1999. "Beyond Civil Rights? Immigration and the Shifting Foundation of Latino Politics." Paper presented to the Center for Advanced Study, University of Illinois at Urbana-Champaign, Conference on Territories and Boundaries of Latinidad. Urbana (October 29–30).

DeSipio, Louis, Rodolfo O. de la Garza, and Mark Setzler. 1999. "Awash in the Mainstream: Latinos and the 1996 Elections." In *Awash in the Mainstream: Latino Politics in the 1996 Elections*, edited by Rodolfo O. de la Garza and Louis DeSipio. Boulder, Colo.: Westview Press.

DeSipio, Louis, and Harry Pachon. 1992. "Making Americans: Administrative Discretion and Americanization." *UCLA Chicano-Latino Law Review* 12(1): 52–66.

Erie, Steven P. 1988. *Rainbow's End: Irish Americans and the Dilemmas of Urban Machine Politics, 1840–1985*. Berkeley: University of California Press.

Espiritu, Yen Le. 1992. *Asian American Panethnicity: Bridging Institutions and Identities*. Philadelphia: Temple University Press.

Fox, Geoffrey. 1996. *Hispanic Nation: Culture, Politics, and the Constructing of Identity*. Secaucus, N.J.: Birth Lane Press.

Gamm, Gerald H. 1986. *The Making of New Deal Democrats: Voting Behavior and Realignment in Boston, 1920–1940*. Chicago: University of Chicago Press.

García, John A. 1981. "Political Integration of Mexican Immigrants: Explorations into the Naturalization Process." *International Migration Review* 15(4): 608–25.

Gavit, John Palmer. 1922. *Americans by Choice*. New York: Harper.

Hardy-Fanta, Carol. 1993. *Latina Politics/Latino Politics: Gender, Culture, and Political Participation in Boston*. Philadelphia: Temple University Press.

Hill, Kevin, and Dario Moreno. 1996. "Second-Generation Cubans." *Hispanic Journal of Behavioral Sciences* 18(2): 175–93.

Jackson, Bryan O., and Michael Preston, eds. 1991. *Racial and Ethnic Politics in California*. Berkeley, Calif.: Institute for Governmental Studies Press.

Jasso, Guillermina, and Mark R. Rosenzweig. 1990. *The New Chosen People: Immigrants in the United States*. New York: Russell Sage Foundation.

Jones-Correa, Michael. 1998. *Between Two Nations: The Political Predicament of Latinos in New York City*. Ithaca, N.Y.: Cornell University Press.

———. 2000. "Under Two Flags: Dual Nationality in Latin America and Its Consequences for the United States." Cambridge, Mass.: David Rockefeller Center for Latin American Studies, working paper series no. 99/00–3.

Levitt, Melissa, and David Olson. 1996. "Immigration and Political Incorporation: But Do They Vote?" Paper presented at the 1996 Northeastern Political Science Association Meeting. Boston (November 12–14).

Minnite, Lorraine C., Jennifer Holdaway, and Ronald Hayduk. 1999. "Political Incorporation of Immigrants in New York." Paper presented at the 1999 annual meeting of the American Political Science Association. Atlanta, Georgia (September 2–5).

Mollenkopf, John, David Olson, and Tim Ross. Forthcoming. "Immigrant Political Participation in New York and Los Angeles." In *Governing Cities*, edited by Michael Jones-Correa. New York: Russell Sage Foundation.

Muller, Thomas. 1993. *Immigrants and the American City*. New York: New York University Press.

Pachon, Harry, and Louis DeSipio. 1994. *New Americans by Choice: Political Perspectives of Latino Immigrants*. Boulder, Colo.: Westview Press.

Pardo, Mary. 1998. *Mexican American Women Activists: Identity and Resistance in Two Los Angeles Neighborhoods*. Philadelphia: Temple University Press.

Portes, Alejandro, and John Curtis. 1987. "Changing Flags: Naturalization and Its Determinants Among Mexican Immigrants." *International Migration Review* 21(2): 352–71.

Portes, Alejandro, and Rafael Mozo. 1985. "Naturalization, Registration, and Voting Patterns of Cubans and Other Ethnic Minorities: A Preliminary Analysis." In *Proceedings of the First National Conference on Citizenship and the Hispanic Community.* Washington, D.C.: National Association of Latino Elected Officials Educational Fund.

Raskin, Jamin. 1993. "Legal Aliens, Local Citizens: The Historical, Constitutional, and Theoretical Meanings of Alien Suffrage." *University of Pennsylvania Law Review* 141: 1391–470.

Rosberg, Gerald M. 1977. "Aliens and Equal Protection: Why Not the Right to Vote?" *Michigan Law Review* 75(5 and 6): 1092–1136.

Rosenstone, Steven J., and John Mark Hansen. 1993. *Mobilization, Participation, and Democracy in America.* New York: Macmillan.

Shaw, Daron, Rodolfo O. de la Garza, and Jongho Lee. 2000. "Examining Latino Turnout in 1996: A Three-State Validated Survey Approach." *American Journal of Political Science* 44(2): 332–40.

Skerry, Peter. 1993. *Mexican Americans: The Ambivalent Minority.* New York: Free Press.

Skocpol, Theda, and Morris Fiorina, eds. 1999. *Civic Engagement in American Democracy.* Washington, D.C.: Brookings.

Uhlaner, Carole, Bruce Cain, and D. Roderick Kiewet. 1989. "Political Participation of Ethnic Minorities in the 1980s." *Political Behavior* 11(3): 195–232.

U.S. Department of Commerce. U.S. Bureau of the Census. 1993. *The Foreign-Born Population, by Race, Hispanic Origin, and Citizenship, for the United States and States.* CPH-L-134. Washington: Bureau of the Census.

U.S. Immigration and Naturalization Service. Office of Policy and Planning. 1999a. *Monthly Statistical Report, September FY 1999: Year-End Report.* Washington: U.S. Immigration and Naturalization Service.

———. 1999b. *1997 Statistical Yearbook of the Immigration and Naturalization Service.* Springfield, Va.: National Technical Information Service.

———. 2000. *Monthly Statistical Report, Second Quarter, Ending March 31, 2000.* Washington: U.S. Immigration and Naturalization Service.

———. 2001a. "Statistics: Naturalization Benefits." March. Accessed June 1, 2001 at *www.ins.usdoj.gov/graphics/aboutins/statistics/msrapr01/NATZ.HTM.* Washington: U.S. Immigration and Naturalization Service.

———. 2001b. *1998 Statistical Yearbook of the Immigration and Naturalization Service.* Springfield, Va.: National Technical Information Service.

Verba, Sidney, and Norman Nie. 1972. *Participation in America: Political Democracy and Social Equality.* New York: Harper and Row.

Verba, Sidney, Kay Lehman Schlozman, and Henry E. Brady. 1995. *Voice and Equality: Civic Voluntarism in American Politics.* Cambridge, Mass.: Harvard University Press.

Wolfinger, Raymond, and Steven Rosenstone. 1980. *Who Votes?* New Haven: Yale University Press.

Yang, Philip Q. 1994. "Explaining Immigrant Naturalization." *International Migration Review* 28(3): 449–77.

—— Part II ——

Immigrants and American
Civic Culture

—— Chapter 3 ——

Sea Change in the Civic Culture in the 1960s

Philip Gleason

WRITING IN THE still-placid 1950s of eighteenth-century conditions that set the stage for the American and French Revolutions, Robert R. Palmer describes a "revolutionary situation" in terms uncannily prophetic of what was to happen in the United States in the decade following the publication of his book. By a revolutionary situation he meant

> one in which confidence in the justice or reasonableness of existing authority is undermined; where old loyalties fade, obligations are felt as impositions, laws seem arbitrary, and respect for superiors is felt as a form of humiliation; where existing sources of prestige seem undeserved, hitherto accepted forms of wealth and income seem ill-gained, and government is sensed as distant, apart from the governed and not really "representing" them. In such a situation the sense of community is lost, and the bond between social classes turns to jealousy and frustration. People of a kind formerly integrated [in the social system] begin to feel as outsiders, or those who have never been integrated begin to feel left out. . . . No community can flourish if such negative attitudes are widespread or long-lasting. The crisis is of community itself, political, economic, sociological, personal, psychological, and moral at the same time. Actual revolution need not follow, but it is in such situations that actual revolution does arise. (Palmer 1959, 21)

A revolutionary situation of this sort unquestionably developed in the United States in the 1960s. Although accompanied by considerable violence, "actual revolution" did not ensue; yet the

crisis wrought deep and lasting changes in American political, social, and cultural life (Balogh 1996; Graham 1998). The aim of this
essay is to suggest the ways that the sea change in the civic culture in the 1960s affected immigrants and their participation in
American life. Its impact on these matters is, of course, only one
aspect of the story; but because race and ethnicity were so centrally involved in the larger upheaval, our inquiry must be set in
that context.

In the generation that came of age immediately preceding the
crisis of the 1960s, the civic culture—in more popular terms, democracy, the American Creed, the American way of life—was
held to be the best on earth. Problems existed, to be sure, especially in the area of race relations, but only because Americans
were not fully living up to their national ideals. The solution prescribed was to make practical reality conform to abstract principle
by treating everyone the same way, recognizing the rights and
dignity of every individual without regard to race, creed, or color.
In the 1960s, that understanding of American civic culture was first
questioned and then widely rejected—vehemently so by many influential voices. In keeping with Palmer's diagnosis, older patterns
of social, cultural, and political authority lost their legitimacy, and
people clamored for fundamental changes in "the system." Among
the most important of the changes that resulted was the elaboration of a new understanding of the relationship of race to the civic
culture. According to this view, the traditional American values of
freedom and equality were to be achieved not by disregarding
race and treating everyone the same but by taking race and group
belonging into positive account in social policy. Although dominant among elites, this view never enjoyed majority support in the
population as a whole, and it is presently being challenged by a
reassertion of the traditional ideal of "color-blind" liberal universalism.

THE ERA OF "THE AMERICAN CREED"

Since the founding of the nation as an independent polity in the
last quarter of the eighteenth century, Americans' understanding
of themselves as a people has included both universalistic and

particularistic elements. By the former is meant the ensemble of ideals theoretically applicable to all—most notably, freedom, equality, self-government, and respect for the dignity of the individual—for which the American War of Independence was fought and which the people regarded as the fundamental basis of the nation's distinctive character. The founders' vision was future oriented—the United States, its great seal proclaims, is "Novus Ordo Seclorum," the "new order of the ages"—and the full realization of that vision was a sacred trust bequeathed to subsequent generations. This framework of ideological values and beliefs constituted the essence of American civic culture, and it underlay the earliest legislation on naturalization, which was, for its time, extremely generous in accepting newcomers as fellow citizens of the young republic (Nagel 1971; Kettner 1978; Gleason 1980; Huntington 1981).

Although abstract universal principles were the self-consciously proclaimed core of the myth of national identity, there were also more particularistic dimensions to American self-understanding—dimensions we now conceptualize as racial, ethnic, or gender related. Thus African American slaves and Native Americans were excluded from the national community from the outset; the situation of free blacks was highly ambiguous; and women did not enjoy the same rights as men. Even the liberal naturalization law of 1790 provided that only "free, white" immigrants were eligible for citizenship. Asians were later specifically excluded; and in the second quarter of the nineteenth century, Americanism was so closely linked to Protestantism that the civic status of Catholics was called into question. Powerful nativist movements emphasizing these particularistic elements in a rigidly exclusive way have arisen several times in the course of American history.

So persistent is this strain of ethnocentric particularism that some commentators now interpret the nation's record of discrimination on the basis of race, ethnicity, and gender as embodying an exclusionary ideology existing side by side with, and having the same "official" status as, the ideology of freedom, equality, and democracy traditionally held to be the basis of the nation's civic culture. In other words, America's failure to realize its noble ideals in practice is not to be understood as resulting from an inevitable gap between the affirmation of abstract ideals, which were quite novel when first introduced, and their progressive realization in a society in which older ways of thinking and acting were still deeply rooted—where, in fact, one institution of that society, slavery, flatly contradicted those ideals. Rather, according to the view expounded most fully by Rogers M. Smith (1988, 1993, 1997) and tacitly accepted by Desmond King in chapter 4 of this volume, the failure in question was not really a failure but the result of a deliberately held commitment to a national "countertradition" according to which racism, sexism, and ethnic prejudice were on a par with freedom, equality, and democracy as defining elements of American identity and civic culture.[1]

The divergence between these two interpretations has something of the character of disagreements as to whether the proverbial glass of water is half full or half empty. The countertradition version of the half-empty view of things is quite new, having been advanced only a little more than a decade ago, and it reflects, in my opinion, the sea change described in this chapter. I prefer the older half-full interpretation, according to which our civic culture rests at bottom on noble abstractions, which, though always contested and still imperfectly realized, have nonetheless been brought closer to full realization over the course of the years. True, the American people failed dismally at many points in their history to discern and act upon what now seem to us the obvious requirements of the democratic principles they so proudly proclaimed. It must be remembered, however, that the understanding of what democratic principles entail in practice has developed historically, just as our understanding of the natural world has developed historically. Indeed, controversy still exists over what freedom and equality really mean and how they are to be attained (Pole 1978; Miller and Walzer 1995). Rather than portraying "inegalitarian ideologies and institutions of ascriptive hierarchy" (Smith 1993, 549) as having coequal status with the American Creed, we might better reflect, thankfully and with due modesty, that historical experience has given us a deeper and more comprehensive understanding of our fundamental national values and what they require in practice.

Whatever its validity for earlier times, the countertradition thesis will hardly work at all for the years from World War II to the early 1960s. During that epoch the liberal universalism embodied in the national ideology was hegemonic in its sway—not, of course, in the sense that everyone agreed on how that ideology was to be understood and acted upon but rather in the sense that virtually everyone agreed that what made Americans American was their commitment to democratic values. The war itself was largely responsible for this phenomenon, which came about because totalitarianism in general and Nazism in particular posed a shocking challenge to what Americans took to calling "the democratic way of life." Carl Becker, the detached skeptic who had earlier called his fellow historians "keepers of useful myths," (Becker 1935, 247) was sufficiently aroused to reaffirm "some generalities that still glitter" (Becker 1940). His doing so illustrated a point made by Alain Locke, a prominent African American intellectual. "Democracy," Locke wrote, "has encountered a fighting antithesis, and has awakened from its considerable lethargy and decadence to a sharpened realization of its own basic values" (Locke 1942, 206). Becker and Locke were anything but voices crying in the wilderness. On the contrary, a powerful ideological revival swept the country in the late 1930s and the early 1940s—a veritable flood of books, articles, speeches, and radio broadcasts extolling democracy, along with organizational efforts to mobilize support for it, and even a rousing cantata titled "Ballad for Americans," which put the national heritage to music and which Horace Kallen (1946), the father of cultural pluralism, was still warmly recommending in 1946 (Gleason 1992, chapter 7).

The overwhelming consensus among the contributors to this national awakening was that the civic culture rested on ideas and commitment to values. It is ideas that make us a nation, James Truslow Adams assured readers of the *New York Times Magazine* ("The Ideas That Make Us a Nation," November 24, 1940: 3, 24). An Ivy League sociologist agreed: "What really stirs our hearts and minds," he asserted in a symposium on foreign influences in American life, "is our set of ideals and values. . . . In the present crisis we know with our innermost being how dear to us are our American ideals of democracy, decency, and individual freedom, our belief in free speech and in free elections and in the right to worship as we choose" (Leyburn 1952, 60). First Lady Eleanor Roosevelt was perhaps most eloquent in a passage the U.S. Office of Education quoted in a pamphlet designed for use in naturalization classes:

> We know that this country is bound together by an idea. The citizens of this country belong to many races and many creeds. They have come here and built a great Nation around the idea of democracy and freedom. . . . [The present crisis challenges us] to preserve what this country was founded to be, a land where people should have the right to life, liberty, and the pursuit of happiness, regardless of race or creed or color. We have not achieved it. We are very far from it in many ways, but we know that that is what we must achieve. (U.S. Office of Education 1942, 1)

The implications for intergroup relations of this understanding of American identity, which Mrs. Roosevelt treated as self-evident, were elaborated by a host of commentators, most influentially by Gunnar Myrdal. His monumental study, *An American Dilemma: The Negro Problem and Modern Democracy* ([1944] 1962), highlights the ideological contradiction between theory and practice—between "the American Creed" (an expression Myrdal put into general circulation) and its systematic violation in the racist attitudes of whites and their discriminatory treatment of African Americans. Myrdal also emphasizes the role of the war in reinforcing the cognitive dissonance felt by white Americans who rejected Nazi racism but allowed a racial caste system to exist in their own country.

Especially since the 1960s, Myrdal has been called naive for assuming that whites were seriously discomfited by the "dilemma" he had pointed out (Southern 1987; Jackson 1990). According to the opposing view, gains in civil rights came about through militant pressure on the part of blacks, not because whites were conscience stricken. That is true enough, but it overlooks several important aspects of Myrdal's analysis. For one thing, as he explicitly points out, blacks had already become more militant by the time he wrote, and the ideological nature of the struggle against Hitlerism served to reinforce their militancy and to undermine the moral and intellectual foundations of their racist oppressors' position. He further perceived that the discrepancy between ideal and reality made discrimination legally suspect, and he predicted that blacks would make increasing use of the courts to challenge the racial caste system. All this led Myrdal to conclude that not since Reconstruction had prospects been better for *"fundamental changes in American race relations, changes which will involve a development toward the American ideals"* (Myrdal 1962, lxi; chapter 45).

That prophetic statement surely belies the charge of naiveté, for in it Myrdal anticipates much of what was to happen in race relations over the next two decades. Throughout the civil rights (as opposed to "black power") phase of the movement, appeal to the universalist values of the American Creed was the crucial point of leverage in seeking legal redress from discrimination and in winning white support for the cause of racial justice. The fundamental premise of the struggle to end segregation and achieve integration was that black Americans should be treated no differently from anyone else; they should enjoy the same individual rights and personal dignity that the Constitution guaranteed to all Americans—without let or hindrance based on race or color.[2]

Although the most important, racism was not the only form of particularistic feeling that offended against liberal universalism in the World War II era. What we now call ethnicity was also somewhat suspect, at least in the form of "nationality," a term that carried faint but discernible political overtones. That kind of in-group feeling, if too publicly paraded by "immigrant nationalities," struck most observers as deplorably ethnocentric. After Hitler manipulated the ethnic nationalism of the Sudeten German minority in prosecuting his aggressive designs on Czechoslovakia, the term took on positively dangerous coloration. For the buildup to war in Europe showed that a disaffected national minority could be a political threat—a potentially disloyal fifth column ready to rise up from within, giving aid and comfort to an external foe that claimed to be the true spiritual homeland of the minority in question. Although actually a negligible threat, even in Europe, the fifth-column menace was taken very seriously at the time and contributed to the hysteria surrounding the wartime removal and incarceration of Japanese Americans (Wolfe 1939; Britt 1940; Ringer 1983, 853, 875, 893, 904, 905). As late as 1943, a highly respected student of intergroup relations maintained that the fifth column could "no longer be regarded as a myth" (Wirth 1943, 9).

Despite the contrary example of the Japanese American removal, in which long-standing racial hostility came together with post–Pearl Harbor panic, another dimension of the situation ruled out thinking of minority groups primarily in terms of the political threat they posed—namely, the conviction that the universalism of the American Creed demanded tolerance of diversity. For if, as the overwhelming consensus had it, we were one people by virtue of our common commitment to the abstract ideals of democracy, it followed that differences of race, creed, color, language, or national background did not make any real difference. We were "Americans All." Racial, ethnic, or cultural differences might indeed add an appealing spice of "pluralism" to the American scene, but they were implicitly understood to be superficial, merely skin deep. Loyalty, meaning wholehearted acceptance of the political system, was the only absolute essential—as the postwar "Red scare" made starkly clear—and it was a gross betrayal of that system to allow prejudice to color one's thinking or discrimination to affect one's behavior in dealing with minority groups (Gleason 1992, chapter 6).

If American minorities were to be tolerated while those in Europe had proved so serious a threat to national unity, there had to be some basic difference between them. Myrdal formulated the accepted interpretation with aphoristic pithiness: "The minority peoples of the United States are fighting for status within the larger society; the minorities of Europe are mainly fighting for independence from it" (Myrdal 1962, 50). Louis Wirth's theoretical elaboration of the minority-group concept is the key text, however, not only because it was so influential but also because it reveals so clearly how the assumptions of the democratic ideology affected American thinking on the subject of intergroup relations.

Wirth's essay, "The Problem of Minority Groups," appeared in a volume published in 1945 addressing how the social sciences could help in meeting the "world crisis." In it he defines a minority group as "a group of people who, because of their physical or cultural characteristics, are singled out from the others in the society in which they live for differential and unequal treatment and who therefore regard themselves as objects of collective discrimination" (Wirth 1945, 347). The inclusion of "unequal treatment" in this definition, as well as his subsequent discussion, left no doubt that Wirth believed minority groups were justified in regarding themselves "as objects of collective discrimination." In other words, minority groups were, by definition, victims; and the actions that made them victims—differential and unequal treatment by others in the society—violated the norms of the democratic ideology.

Although much else has changed in how we think about minorities, the elements of victimization and denial of equality have persisted, receiving, if anything, greater emphasis now than when Wirth wrote more than a half century ago. His classification of minorities, by contrast, has been forgotten, but it is even more revealing of the liberal universalism that underlay his thinking. Wirth lists four kinds of minority groups—pluralistic, assimilationist, secessionist, and militant—which represent "crucial successive stages in the life-cycle of minorities generally" (Wirth 1945, 364). Thus pluralistic minorities, which demand toleration for their distinctive existence, would normally evolve into assimilationist minorities, which seek full status for their members in the larger society; only if full status is denied are assimilationist minorities likely to become secessionist minorities, demanding economic and political autonomy as well as cultural toleration. Militant minorities are clearly a morbid deviation, for they seek not toleration or autonomy for themselves but domination over all other groups. In this manner, Wirth built into his typology a dynamic process that was shaped by the American expectation of individual assimilation of minority group members rather than the European aspiration for the collective autonomy of solidary groups.[3]

The obvious implication of Wirth's analysis is that if Americans were true to their principles, the "problem of minority groups" would disappear because minorities would no longer be subjected to the kind of "differential and unequal treatment" that risks driving them into the dangerously divisive secessionist and militant stages. Considered from this angle, the real problem was that the majority—American society as a whole—behaved so badly in this regard. How was this failure to be accounted for, especially if, as Myrdal insisted, Americans were sincerely committed to democratic principles? Looking back today, most people would probably give a one-word answer: racism. That word was still relatively new at the time, however, and had a somewhat restricted application (Banton 1988, 25–28). Because Nazism was what gave it visibility, discussions of racism in the 1940s often focused on anti-Semitism, and the word was understood to designate a systematically theorized set of beliefs about racial superiority and inferiority. The kind of generalized hostility to "the other" now called racism was, in the 1940s and 50s, called "prejudice."

Because prejudice is a psychological phenomenon having to do with attitudes held by individuals, thinking of the problem in terms of prejudice fit nicely with the individualism so deeply rooted in the American tradition. Yet that same tradition held that individuals are their own masters, able to remake themselves if they really want to do so. Some twenty-four hundred psychologists placed the imprimatur of social science on that optimistic belief: "Prejudice is a matter of attitudes, and attitudes are to a considerable extent a matter of training and information," they stated in a 1944 manifesto. "Through education and experience people can learn that their prejudiced ideas about the English, the Russians, the Japanese, Catholics, Jews, Negroes, are misleading or altogether false" (quoted in Murphy 1945, 455–56; also see Allport 1954, 477–80). Richard Rodgers and Oscar Hammerstein made the same point musically in *South Pacific*, for if, as the song has it, "you've got to be taught to hate," you could also be taught not to hate.[4] That conviction, permeating the culture, inspired, or at the very least reinforced, a mammoth educational campaign aimed at eliminating prejudice and improving race relations.

Wartime emphasis on the need for national unity played into this campaign, and the American Creed furnished both its goals and its essential content. On a more down-to-earth level, wartime population shifts, especially the movement of African Americans into northern industrial cities, made the race question a national issue for the first time.[5] The great Detroit race riot in the summer of 1943, along with mob violence against Mexican Americans in Los Angeles, dramatized the new situation and sparked an urgent drive to improve intergroup relations. Two years later, no fewer than 123 national organizations were active in the field; for several years after the war, Louis Wirth devoted most of his energies to this work through the American Council on Race Relations; and President Harry Truman educated by example in appointing the first modern civil rights commission and by desegregating the armed services (Williams 1947; Watson 1947).

On the level of formal education, attention to race and intergroup relations expanded enormously. An "intercultural educa-tion" movement, pioneered in the late 1930s, blossomed in ele-mentary and secondary schools during and immediately after the war (Montalto 1978; Vickery and Cole 1943). However, the Ameri-can Council on Education warned in 1949 that school textbooks failed to deal adequately with minority groups—a finding that was to be confirmed repeatedly in subsequent years. A dozen major college textbooks on minorities or race relations appeared in the postwar decade, along with more than a thousand scholarly books and articles; by the 1960s, more than seven hundred institutions of higher education offered courses on these subjects. The moral and ideological dimensions of this campaign were openly avowed: prejudice and discrimination are morally wrong; they violate dem-ocratic principles, and they have to be eliminated if the promise of liberty and justice for all is ever to become a reality (King 1956; Rose 1968, 9, 75–76; Harding et al. 1968).

Immigration as such did not figure in discussion of these mat-ters. The restrictions imposed in the 1920s and reaffirmed (over President Truman's veto) in 1952 had so completely cut off over-seas immigration that it seemed to belong to an almost forgotten past. Minorities derived from immigration were, of course, to be tolerated, but they were not seen as a problem (except insofar as Jews and Catholics were subject to religious prejudice) because they had already been "Americanized." That was a matter for deep satisfaction, for it meant that the civic culture of liberal universal-ism had successfully transformed a congeries of different immi-grant groups into one people. Assimilation had done its work in that area; and if American ideals were actually applied in the area of race, African Americans could also be assimilated. For though the word was never used—perhaps because it suggested the then ultrasensitive issue of interracial marriage—the goals of the civil rights and integration movement were, as Lewis M. Killian (1981, 43) later wrote, "fundamentally and unrelentingly assimilationist."

Critics at the time bemoaned "conformity," and later historians deplored the consensus mentality of the 1950s. Yet these criti-cisms—along with the complacency of the era and its fierce intol-erance of ideological deviation—testify to the fact that Americans thought well of themselves, of their record against totalitarianism, and of their social, economic, and political system. Race was the one great domestic problem, and it would be solved by making the system work for blacks as well as whites.

THE CRISIS YEARS

John F. Kennedy was a Navy veteran, formed by World War II and its aftermath, whose outlook reflected this civic culture. His being the first Catholic to win the presidency vindicated the nation's historic commitment to religious tolerance; the enthusiasm that greeted his inaugural challenge to "ask what you can do for your country," and the overwhelming response to his call for Peace Corps volunteers, demonstrated that patriotic idealism still flourished among the American people. Although racial confrontation intensified dramatically during Kennedy's brief administration, and though his horrifying assassination contributed mightily to the atmosphere of incipient crisis, the real turning point with respect to the civic culture came only in the mid-1960s.[6]

The passage of the Civil Rights Act of 1964, followed the next year by the Voting Rights Act and the Hart-Celler Immigration Act, which did away with the system of racially based national-origins quotas that dated back to the 1920s, may be taken as the high-water mark of postwar liberal universalism. The outburst of racial rioting in Watts, a black neighborhood in Los Angeles, which came within days of the passage of the Voting Rights Act, and the dramatic introduction of the "Black Power" slogan in 1966 symbolized the shift to a more radically alienated cultural temper. Large-scale American military involvement in Vietnam, which also began in 1965, generated massive protests, especially on college campuses, which became interwoven with the racial issue as the war dragged on.

The race issue and the war were basic, but other factors contributed to the "revolutionary situation" that developed in the second half of the decade: the resurgence of political radicalism in the New Left; an eruption of drug use and the rapid growth of a deeply anti-traditional and anti-rationalist counterculture; a profound upheaval in sexual mores and ideas about gender; and a spiritual tempest in the Catholic Church that left the institution shaken and its communicants disoriented. The climactic years witnessed two more shocking assassinations—of Martin Luther King Jr. and Robert F. Kennedy—and hundreds of race riots, campus disruptions, and outbursts of violence by self-styled urban guerrillas. After 1970, the continuing withdrawal of American troops from Vietnam, coupled with a kind of exhaustion from the preceding frenzy, marked the ebbing of the crisis, but it had its shameful epilogue in the scandal of Watergate and President Richard Nixon's forced resignation.

The credibility gap—a shorthand term for the people's loss of confidence in statements made by public officials—points to the central feature of the revolutionary situation as it affected the civic culture: constituted authority was discredited, while ideas and conduct previously disapproved of or disallowed gained legitimacy.[7] All the aforementioned factors contributed to this result, but the civil rights and black power movement played the crucial role because it was the first to develop, because it pioneered the tactics used in other protest movements, and because it established a presumption of moral superiority on the part of those who, in the name of a higher law, dissented from, disobeyed, resisted, or even employed violence against constituted authority.

Of course the leaders of the postwar civil rights movement were not the first to call constituted authority into question: it was, rather, the opponents of the Supreme Court's desegregation rulings who first defied the law of the land, resorting to violence, intimidation, and outright terrorism to preserve a system based on the repellent doctrine of white supremacy (Belknap 1987). The civil rights movement under Dr. Martin Luther King Jr. was, by contrast, committed to the most sublime of ideals—color-blind justice to be achieved through nonviolent witness, self-sacrifice, love, and forgiveness of the oppressor. Nonviolence did not translate as passivity, however. On the contrary, it was embodied in action as the movement took to the streets in direct-action tactics, which escalated from the Montgomery bus boycott of 1955 and 1956 through the sit-ins, freedom rides, and massive marches and confrontations of the early 1960s (Sitkoff 1993; Thernstrom and Thernstrom 1997, chapters 1–6; Higham 1997, chapters 1, 10). These provoked, as they were designed to provoke, ever more violent reactions by white supremacists, a scenario that dramatized and reinforced the moral superiority of the protesting African Americans and thereby simultaneously justified their action in flouting the Jim Crow laws of the South. Discriminatory laws enforced with fire hoses and police dogs were immoral and un-American, and it was quite proper to break them.

As the violence directed against them mounted, however, black leaders grew disillusioned by the inadequate response of federal authorities and moved toward the view that the entire governmental system, not just the Jim Crow South, was racist and therefore lacking in legitimacy. This conviction grew when those in control of the 1964 Democratic nominating convention refused to seat delegates elected by the (black) Mississippi Freedom Democratic Party and when Dr. King carried the civil rights movement to northern cities to address "de facto segregation," where his protest marches were met by hate-filled mobs (Carmichael and Hamilton 1967, chapter 4; Ralph 1993).

Attacking legalized segregation was, it seemed, only the beginning. The institutional racism built into the very structure of American society and government meant that the same defect that legitimated the violation of Jim Crow laws in the South might well justify violation of the law across the board. The perception that the whole system was tainted and lacking in legitimacy affected reactions to the outbursts of rioting that, though begun earlier, exploded on a wider scale and with greater intensity in the second half of the decade. The conclusion of the Kerner Report, set up to investigate the riots, was that America had failed the black people of the inner cities; that their rage and desperation were understandable; and that the violence they produced was really a cry for help, which demanded not repression but redress (National Advisory Commission on Civil Disorders 1968). Reinforcing this line of thinking was the rediscovery of poverty announced in Michael Harrington's *The Other America* (1962) and the perception that it was disproportionately located among African Americans (Patterson 1986, chapters 6–7). For Harrington, who was a socialist, and even more for adherents of the New Left, which was growing rapidly on college campuses, poverty was the inevitable result of the perverted system of liberal capitalism, and the nation's much-vaunted "democratic creed" was but hypocritical pretense designed to provide an ideological smokescreen for exploitation (Unger 1974).

Against this background, a new cadre of militant black leaders like Stokely Carmichael and H. Rap Brown frankly repudiated nonviolence and the goal of integration into an inherently evil system. Aligning themselves with a long-standing tradition of black nationalism recently revivified by Malcolm X, they demanded "black power," promoted racial pride, preached hostility toward whites ("honkies"), especially the police ("pigs") and other authority figures, and advanced strictly in-group cultural, social, and political causes (Carmichael and Hamilton 1967; Burner 1996, chapter 2). This development did not altogether displace more moderate black leaders, but it changed the dynamics of the black movement, further discredited constituted authority, and bestowed legitimacy on the kind of group-centered thinking and actions previously deplored as ethnocentric.

In the meantime, the escalation of the Vietnam War, and resistance to it, had results analogous to those wrought by the racial issue. For just as the civil rights and black power movement delegitimated the American system domestically, the Vietnam War discredited it internationally. The two issues became intermingled as the Vietnam engagement was portrayed as a racist war against an Asian people and as one in which African Americans were disproportionately represented among the young men sent into combat. Besides being tainted by racism, the war was said to reflect the nation's arrogance, militarism, imperialism, colonialism, and paranoid hostility to communism and third-world liberation movements. Above all, the war's tremendous destructiveness, especially the bombing campaign and the use of napalm and defoliants, set a precedent of unexampled violence that encouraged the idea that counterviolence by war resisters was justified.[8]

Direct-action tactics pioneered in the civil rights movement were quickly adapted to the anti–Vietnam War campaign and other protest movements, especially on college campuses, where the war became a personal issue for male "baby boomers" of military age, thousands of whom defied the draft in good conscience on the grounds that it was as "immoral" as the Jim Crow laws of the South (Bander 1970; Burner 1996, chapter 5). The relatively mild early "teach-ins" were clearly inspired by civil rights sit-ins, wade-ins, and the like, and the first great campus uprising at the University of California at Berkeley was sparked by activists just back from working in Mississippi's 1964 "Freedom Summer" voter education project. As cells of the radical Students for a Democratic Society (SDS) multiplied and campus protest escalated in scale and violence, the whole of American higher education was pronounced rotten by virtue of its being embedded in racist, fascist "Amerika" (Lichtman 1968). According to SDS doctrine, students had replaced workers as the revolutionary vanguard, and the activist historian Howard Zinn exhorted college audiences to cultivate a principled "disrespect for the law" (*South Bend Tribune*, March 20, 1970).

Thus was the self-confident Americanism of the World War II generation shattered by the combined hammer blows of racial crisis, antiwar protest, and generalized social, political, and cultural radicalism. This sea change in the civic culture had important implications for matters ethnic. Before taking them up, however, we should note again that the legislation that paved the way to a new era of mass immigration—including, for first time in the twentieth century, Asians on the same basis as everyone else—was a product of this earlier mentality. The full effect of the Hart-Celler Immigration Act did not become apparent for many years, however; during the 1960s, the most obvious immigration-related issue involved Mexican Americans.

Despite their historic roots in the Southwest and a vast increase in their numbers brought about by immigration after 1910, Mexican Americans did not gain real visibility on the national scene until the agricultural workers strike led by César Chávez associated their cause with the broader civil rights movement.[9] The subsequent emergence of a more militant Chicano movement—and a similar evolution among Puerto Rican activists—reflected the mid-1960s shift toward radical protest. Because these groups, along with Native Americans, could point to a history of discrimination; because minorities were defined as victims; because African Americans had already legitimated ethnocentrism; and because the legacy of Martin Luther King's heroic idealism served as an overshadowing aegis in all such cases, claims made by advocates of "brown power" and "red power" carried prima facie justification and further undermined the legitimacy of the existing "power structure."[10]

By the late 1960s, the mood of militancy reached the ranks of second- and third-generation immigrants of European background, giving rise to what was variously called the white ethnic movement, the ethnic revival, the new ethnicity, or the new pluralism (Weed 1973; Mann 1979, chapters 1–2; Goren 1999, chapter 10). At least four elements contributed to this phenomenon: the persistence of ethnic feeling among the descendants of European immigrants and its articulation by scholars; the discrediting of assimilation and the legitimation of ethnicity; emulation of the black example, accompanied by resentment of the "special treatment" accorded blacks; and purposeful nurturing of the ethnic revival as a strategy for defusing "white backlash."

Although no longer so visibly "hyphenated" as they had been earlier in the century, the children and grandchildren of European immigrants still retained a sense of ethnic distinctiveness and preserved elements of their cultural heritages. Most of the scholarship documenting these phenomena came later, but Andrew M. Greeley had already found ethnicity to be a significant variable in national sample surveys, and two important books gave it new scholarly visibility. *Beyond the Melting Pot,* by Nathan Glazer and Daniel P. Moynihan (1963), a study of New York City's Irish, Italians, Jews, Puerto Ricans, and African Americans, argued that ethnicity persisted but was transformed by time. The latter qualification was largely overlooked while the authors' statement that the melting pot never happened became a cliché of the ethnic revival. Milton M. Gordon's *Assimilation in American Life* (1964) included the key word in the title, but he defined it in such stringent terms that his book conveyed the message that it was pluralism, rather than assimilation, that had actually "happened."[11] Although it attracted little attention at the time, an article by Rudolph J. Vecoli (1964) denying that Italian immigrants were genuinely "uprooted" anticipated what was soon to become the conventional wisdom among historians.

As these works and many others to follow impugned the reality of assimilation as a social process, the discrediting of the American Creed made it seem hateful as an ideal, for that was just what immigrants were supposed to assimilate to; and who, to paraphrase the black militants' question, would want to be assimilated to a burning building? The denigration of the ideal is vividly illustrated by the abuse poured upon the melting pot, the principal symbol of assimilation. Michael Novak's *Rise of the Unmeltable Ethnics* (1972) provides the most convenient sampling, but the literature abounds in excoriation of the melting pot as a "gruesome metaphor" for a process "which cannibalistically devoured the immigrant's past and his ethnic heritage" (Gleason 1992, chapter 2). We have already seen that the black power movement legitimated ethnocentrism; but because that word still carried irredeemably negative connotations, "ethnicity" came into general usage as a positive way of designating the "sense of peoplehood" that proved so resistant to assimilation and that deserved respect for its intrinsic importance.

As the foregoing suggests, the white ethnic movement owed much to the example of black militancy.[12] The resentment called white backlash, however, was at least equally important. First noted in 1964, it was much more pronounced by 1968, when George Wallace made major inroads on the traditional base of the Democratic Party by appealing to white resentment of the liberal elite's condoning of black violence while portraying working-class whites as bigots. The first conferences dedicated to exploring the needs of white ethnics and doing honor to their cultural traditions took place against this background. The "proven ability of neo-reactionary forces to capitalize" on white backlash "should be seen as a deep threat to America," Irving M. Levine, of the American Jewish Committee, told one such gathering in Philadelphia in June 1968 (Levine 1968, 1). To head off the likelihood of worsening racial violence, Levine added, "some of the brilliance which articulated Negro demands will have to be similarly developed to speak to and for lower middle class America. Ethnic groups must feel the security of having someone watching out for them too" (Levine 1968, 12). For several years thereafter, the American Jewish Committee pursued this strategy of "depolarizing" the racial situation through its National Project on Ethnic America, which Levine directed (Mann 1979, 25–34; Goren 1999, chapter 10).

The new ethnicity met with skepticism from African Americans and many white liberals, who feared it simply masked racism. Without its depolarizing purpose, and absent sponsorship by the American Jewish Committee, which had a strong civil rights record, one may doubt that it would have received support from the Ford Foundation, which funded organizational work undertaken by the committee and by Geno Baroni's National Center for Urban Ethnic Affairs in Washington, as well as social scientific research carried out by Andrew Greeley's Center for the Study of American Pluralism in Chicago. Baroni and Greeley were both priests; their participation in the movement reflected the fact that Catholics—mainly of Italian and Slavic background—constituted the bulk of the white ethnic population. For them, the ethnic revival was not about having someone "speak for them" but about speaking for themselves. This was particularly evident in the case of Michael Novak (1972), a lay Catholic intellectual of Slovak background, whose *Unmeltable Ethnics* was stridently populist in its denunciation of the white Anglo-Saxon Protestant establishment that looked down upon and exploited blue-collar white ethnics (virtually interchangeable labels for Novak).[13]

Explosive growth in historical scholarship on European immigrant groups paralleled and interacted with the more activist dimension of the ethnic revival (Vecoli 1979). This was congruent with, and tended to reinforce, the most important effect of the activist revival—the universalizing of particularism that resulted from the revival's so greatly enlarging the number of Americans who were encouraged to think of themselves as belonging to descent-based identity groups. The movement's one major legislative accomplishment—which was also an early landmark in governmental support for multicultural education—illustrates this universalizing effect. The Ethnic Heritage Studies Program Act of 1972, originally introduced by a Polish American congressional representative (Roman Pucinski of Chicago), provided for the development of curricular materials relating to white ethnic heritages as well as those of blacks and others already singled out as official minorities.

The dominant civic culture was thus decidedly different in the early 1970s from what it was when John F. Kennedy spoke boldly of a new frontier. The most alienated groups were all but literally up in arms against their country, while the proverbially patriotic "hard hats" were being told they too had much to be aggrieved about. The revolutionary situation had not produced actual revolution, but it did produce lasting consequences.

THE AFTEREFFECTS OF CRISIS

The aftereffects most pertinent for us were not consciously intended; rather, they evolved naturally from the dynamic of events and the implications of the sea change described earlier. The crucial developments were the reestablishment of race as both an acceptable category of social analysis and a normative guide to social policy, and the erosion of the conviction that rights inhere in individuals and the emergence of an implicit doctrine of group rights. Affirmative action, introduced in the late 1960s and elaborated over the next two decades, acted as the catalyst that precipitated these two developments into a state of real, though largely unacknowledged, actuality. In combination with increases in the volume and composition of immigration, the new racialism and emphasis on group rights significantly affected thinking about the adjustment of immigrants to American life.

Affirmative action is a complex, technical, and controversial issue that has generated an immense literature (Moreno 1997; Graham 1990; Skrentny 1996; Nieli 1991). Not even a sketchy survey can be attempted here; the following discussion assumes a general familiarity with the policy and concentrates on how it relates to the two shifts previously identified. Its connection with both, though clear in retrospect, is implicit rather than explicit. In the case of race, affirmative action did not, of course, introduce something altogether new. On the contrary, the policy took shape against the background of black militancy and frankly avowed racial pride, on the one hand, and a heightened emphasis on the endemic quality of "white racism," on the other. Although educated opinion had long accepted the view that race is a biological fiction, the social results of that fiction could hardly be overlooked when racial violence rocked the nation. Yet the insistence by Chicanos that "la raza" means "the people," not "the race," showed that racialism was still too disreputable to be openly acknowledged. Its rehabilitation—not fully acknowledged even today—was mediated by the concepts of ethnicity and minority.

The previously noted legitimation of ethnicity created a conceptual blurriness favorable to racialism's reestablishing itself more or less unobserved. The well-known anthropologist Ashley Montagu (1942, 1945, 1972), who considered race "man's most dangerous myth," worked tirelessly in the 1940s and 1950s to get rid of the word "race" and promote the use of "ethnic group" in its place. The older term was never completely eliminated, however, and by the 1970s "ethnic and racial studies" existed in tandem—though there was disagreement as to how the two related to each other (Smith 1982). Nevertheless, ethnicity talk created a semantic field within which the word "minority" (which, we recall, entailed the idea of victimization) played the crucial role in mediating the racialism implicit in affirmative action. In due course, affirmative action effected an important practical differentiation between race and ethnicity.

All this occurred in connection with the transition whereby affirmative action came to be understood not simply as requiring special efforts of outreach in the recruitment and training of blacks but also as involving the setting of numerical goals to be achieved in these and other areas. This version of the policy was first implemented in the Philadelphia Plan, which was put in place in 1969 to ensure equitable hiring of blacks in the construction industry and later extended to cover virtually the whole spectrum of employment, education, and business activity. Although the Philadelphia Plan was really aimed at African Americans, the administrative order setting it up did not specify that; rather, it required "minorities" to be employed in proportion to their presence in the labor force.

A listing of the groups falling under the heading "minorities" was obviously required—and quickly produced. It has, with minor variations, remained canonical: African Americans, Hispanics, Native Americans, Alaskan Natives, Asians, and Pacific Islanders are the minorities eligible for preferential treatment under affirmative action. Women were included on a coequal basis with minorities, and by 1995 some 160 federal affirmative-action programs reached out into virtually all areas of American life

(Graham 1990, chapters 11, 13; Moreno 1997, chapter 9; Eastland 1996, 179).

Because the groups constituting the designated minorities are (with the partial exception of Hispanics) distinguished by phenotypical features popularly thought of as racial, and because African Americans had unquestionably suffered from racism, the practical logic of the situation suggested that something called race did indeed exist and that the wrongs suffered by racial minorities were different in kind from those experienced by merely ethnic minorities, such as Jews, Italians, and so on.

Because only they are eligible for preferential treatment, racial minorities came to be widely viewed as the only real minorities. In 1977, Justice Lewis Powell's opinion in the *Bakke* case extended the protective framework of affirmative action to include preferential treatment aimed at achieving "diversity" in educational settings and, by implication, elsewhere (Eastland 1996, chapter 4). That in turn reinforced a tendency to link race and culture, because it was assumed that increasing the representation of racial minorities would automatically enhance the cultural diversity that was the ostensible justification for preferential treatment. Even such a supporter of affirmative action as the intellectual historian David Hollinger has lamented the resulting equation of race with culture, which is taken for granted by virtually all champions of multiculturalism (Hollinger 1995, 35–37; also see Sleeper 1997, 79–85). It is sobering to recall that the linkage between race and culture was a central feature of racialism in the World War I era. The earlier linkage had harsher implications for policy, but the reappearance of a more benign analogue testifies to the pervasiveness of today's racialism and suggests its troubling potentialities.

Besides encouraging a new racialism by singling out groups thought of as racial for preferential treatment, and in connection with that development, affirmative action also shifted thinking about rights in the direction of group rather than individual rights (Killian 1981, 46–49). This came about through a redefinition of racial justice in terms of substantial equality of result rather than equality of opportunity. The shift toward group rights is largely tacit, being discussed explicitly more often by critics of affirmative action than by its proponents. Indeed, a prominent defender of affirmative action has called it a "popular misunderstanding" and a "plain mistake" to hold that the policy "assume[s] that racial or ethnic groups are entitled to proportionate shares of opportunities" (Nieli 1991, 182). Yet a book written as a guide for personnel officers and corporate lawyers, and not at all unfriendly to the policy, explains that in the view of supporters of affirmative action, "protected *groups* should be represented in the workplace in exact or approximate proportion to their availability in, or composition of, the relevant labor force. Such an approach comports with a model of group justice in which discrimination, viewed from a group-based perspective, is to be addressed for remediation purposes by approaches which extend to the group and to the group's members" (Turner 1990, 6–7, italics in original).[14]

In practical terms, the crucial shift in the direction of group rights was the application in employment, education, and other areas of statistical underrepresentation on the part of minorities and women as evidence of discrimination sufficient to require remedial efforts in the form of goals and timetables (called "quotas" by critics) designed to bring the presence or participation of the groups in question up to a specified point. Provided for in the Voting Rights Act of 1965 as a weapon against systematic exclusion of African Americans from the polls in Jim Crow states, statistical tests for discrimination were extended to other areas by administrative fiat and were subsequently approved by the courts (Glazer 1975; Belz 1991). Although the group-rights orientation is obvious in the actual workings of affirmative action, theoretical justification has lagged far behind practice.[15] At least on the level of popular commentary, the assumption that ethnic and racial groups are corporate entities that have rights seems to have established itself (to the degree that it has done so) under the conceptual umbrella of "cultural pluralism" and "multiculturalism."

Both of these concepts exist in so many versions that the terms alone signify nothing definite. The earliest version of cultural pluralism prescribed a high degree of ethnic-group autonomy, and Horace Kallen, who introduced the expression, argued at the time that individual rights find their true fulfillment in group rights. By the time the expression entered into popular usage in the 1940s, however, the hard edge was gone; cultural pluralism had dissolved, even in Kallen's usage, into a nebulous prizing of the "diverse utterance of diversities" within an overarching framework of liberal Americanism (Kallen 1924, 1956, 98; Gleason 1992, chapter 3). The term was widely used in this assimilationist sense through the middle decades of the century and into the 1980s. Only with the previously discussed ethnic revival—which augmented its usage geometrically—did cultural pluralism begin once again to signify that "cultures have rights paralleling those of people" (Stent, Hazard, and Rivlin 1973, 15).

Although seldom put so explicitly by its champions, the group-rights drift had emerged clearly enough by 1981 for Milton Gordon (1981) to draw up a systematic contrast between "liberal pluralism," as he called the assimilationist version, and a species of "corporate pluralism," which, among other things, recognized group rights and defined equality in terms of proportionately equal outcomes for groups. Semantically, cultural pluralism wobbled blurrily between those two poles for the next few years and then dropped completely out of the picture when "multiculturalism" burst suddenly upon the scene. This term inherited all of cultural pluralism's conceptual ambiguities and added a distinctive mystification of its own deriving from its frequent association with postmodernism (Sollors 1998; Glazer 1997). Despite its protean nature, however, multiculturalism has clearly moved the semantic scales in the corporate, group-rights direction. As the authors of a recent study of American nationalism observe, "Multiculturalism construes racial group identity as the *preferred* choice of self-definition and validates the ongoing affirmation of ethnic distinctiveness"; justifies claims for "a larger share of society's goods" made on the basis of group identity; and in general makes "communal representation" the guiding principle in policymaking (Citrin et al. 1994, 9–10, italics in original).

The impact of pervasive racialism and the emergence of group-rights thinking on immigration and the adjustment of immigrants to American life has received little scholarly attention.[16] All that can be done here is to note a few points deserving of systematic study, especially considering the scope and nature of recent immigration. Between 1971 and 1997 almost 19 million immigrants entered the United States legally, plus an unknown but quite substantial number who did so illegally. In terms of volume, this rivals the great flood of immigrants of the early twentieth century, although the foreign born constituted a larger percentage of the nation's total population in those days (14.7 percent in 1910, 9.7 percent in 1997).

What makes the numbers more significant is the fact the overwhelming majority of these immigrants, being of Asian and Latin American origin, qualify as protected minorities under affirmative action. Indeed, immigration has significantly altered the character of the population eligible for preferential treatment—African Americans made up two-thirds of that population in 1970; by the late 1990s, Hispanics and Asians made up more than half (Eastland 1996, 149–50). Bestowing benefits primarily intended for African Americans upon newly arrived immigrants has, as Peter Skerry observes, led to much confusion: "it distorts the common understanding of the problems immigrants face; complicates our efforts to solve them; encourages immigrants, who come with hopes of advancing themselves in a free society, to see themselves as victims of deprivation and discrimination; and results in policies that are frequently inappropriate" (Skerry 1989, 89–90).

Hispanics, who were present in large numbers through the entire era of affirmative action, have benefited most conspicuously by extension to cover their case of voting-rights laws interpreted as requiring "majority-minority" districts. This development, which is too complex for elaboration here, directly affects the political incorporation of immigrants and has come under closer judicial scrutiny as well as scholarly criticism (Thernstrom 1987; Skerry 1993). Hispanic and Asian immigrants are also eligible for preferential treatment in education, employment, and contracting. To say that recent immigrants recognize the desirability of such classification and act upon it is not to accuse them of cynicism; their doing so is, rather, perfectly understandable in view of the way public policy is presently structured. Given that public opinion has never supported preferential treatment based on race, and noting in addition that recent immigrants cannot claim as its justification a history of slavery and segregation comparable to that of African Americans, it seems reasonable to conclude that making affirmative action's special benefits available to recent immigrants is not only a divisive factor in interminority relations but also feeds anti-immigration sentiments in the general population.

Aside from these direct connections with affirmative action, the atmosphere of racialism and group-centeredness affected thinking about immigrants and their adjustment to American life in more general ways. It reinforced the overall antiassimilationist tendency that, as noted earlier, emerged in immigration scholarship around 1970, and it particularly encouraged the view that the experience of earlier immigrants was entirely different from that of recent immigrants because the former did not differ racially from the American majority. The mistaken assumption that things are utterly different today in turn underlies some of the current theorizing about the phenomenon of "transnationalism." Similarly, the emphasis on race as the crucial marker manifests itself in the growing acceptance of the category "Euro-American," which lumps into an omnium gatherum everyone except the officially designated "minorities," and in the tendency to make race the central touchstone in the interpretation of American history, a tendency most evident in recent studies of "whiteness."[17] The ultimate conclusion to which this line of thinking leads is that "American identity, encoded in the civic culture, was [from the beginning] *constituted* upon exclusions" and that racism is still "the foundation of identity in America" (Schultz 1993, 643, 646 italics in original).

The last-quoted passage can be taken as epitomizing the aftereffects of the sea change of the 1960s, since it is taken from a multiculturalist's critique of *The American Kaleidoscope*, by Lawrence H. Fuchs (1990), an encyclopedic survey of "race, ethnicity, and the civic culture" written from a perspective very much in line with the liberal universalism of the pre-1965 era. Yet the appearance of Fuchs's book testifies to the fact that the older understanding of the civic culture has not been utterly swept away. On the contrary, it has been galvanized to new life, largely in reaction to the more extreme versions of multiculturalism that circulated in the early 1990s. With respect to immigration as such, the resurgence of liberal universalism has expressed itself not merely in criticism of "strong multiculturalism" but also in reaffirmation of the fact that, as Nathan Glazer puts it, "properly understood, assimilation is still the most powerful force affecting the ethnic and racial elements of the United States" (Glazer 1993, 123).

Among historians, rehabilitation of the concept of assimilation had proceeded by 1995 to the point of meriting a review essay in the leading professional journal (Kazal 1995); since then a professor of urban affairs has written the first book-length argument in favor of assimilation to appear in decades (Salins 1997). Most daringly, perhaps, the U. S. Commission on Immigration Reform, first chaired by the late Barbara Jordan, undertook to redeem the long-discredited term "Americanization" by using it to designate "the cultivation of a shared commitment to the American values of liberty, democracy, and equal opportunity." "We view Americanization positively," the commission's 1995 report adds, "as the *inclusion* of all who wish to embrace the civic culture which holds our nation together" (U. S. Commission on Immigration Reform 1995, 177, italics in original). These developments offer encouragement to those who cherish the older "American Creed" understanding of the civic culture. Nevertheless, the sea change of the 1960s fostered patterns of racialist and group-rights thinking that are deeply entrenched. The situation thus remains contested, its outcome still in doubt.

NOTES

1. King's analysis draws on Smith's work.
2. Paul Moreno (1997, chapters 3–5) does not use these terms, but his findings confirm the same point.
3. For more on Wirth's liberal individualism, see Matthews 1987.
4. The Rodgers and Hammerstein musical, *South Pacific*, was first produced in 1949.
5. The placement of Negroes last in the listing of groups in the psychologists' manifesto indicates that the black-white issue had not yet become *the* racial problem. A few years later, two sociologists prominent in the study of intergroup relations spoke of the shift of focus from immigrant assimilation to black-white relations as a recent phenomenon (Hughes and Hughes 1952, 31).
6. For recent general treatments of the 1960s, see Cavallo 1999, Burner 1996, and the relevant chapters of Patterson 1996. Matusow 1984, somewhat older, is also excellent. O'Neill 1971, though uninterpretive, was written very close to the events described and presents them with vivid immediacy.
7. As Robert Bellah has observed of the 1960s, "Far more serious than any of the startling events of the decade was the massive erosion of the legitimacy of American institutions—business, government, education, the churches, the family—that set in particularly among young people" (Bellah 1976, 333–4).

8. Olson 1993 provides a guide to the immense literature on these topics.

9. An organizer for the farm workers, Marshall Ganz, whose experience in the Mississippi Freedom Summer of 1964 opened his eyes to injustice in his native California, reports that Chávez "seemed very interested in people who had experience in the civil rights movement" (Ferriss and Sandoval 1997, 102–3).

10. Although it is specialized and rather slight, Rhea 1997 accords with this interpretation.

11. For discussion of these works, see Gleason 1992, 71–75.

12. As Greeley notes, "*The new consciousness of ethnicity is in part based on the fact that the blacks have legitimated cultural pluralism as it has perhaps never been legitimated before.* Other Americans, observing that now it is all right to be proud of being black, wonder, quite legitimately, why it is not all right to be proud of being Italian or Polish" (1972, 273, italics in original).

13. For additional examples, see Friedman 1971; Wenk, Tomasi, and Baroni 1972; and Colburn and Pozzetta 1979.

14. Moreno, who is sympathetic to affirmative action, concludes that between 1964 and 1970, law and policy dealing with employment discrimination were "radically transformed"; that federal agencies "had advanced doctrines that made fair employment a group rather than an individual right"; that "racial proportionalism" was both the measure and the remedy for discrimination; that the remedy involved "preferential treatment and quotas"; and that the Supreme Court ratified these developments by its decision in the 1970 *Griggs* case (1997, 266).

15. Stanley Katz (1998) notes this point and indicates that a change in legal thinking is in order.

16. The work of Peter Skerry (1989, 1993, 1994) constitutes a major exception; see also Lescott-Leszczynski 1984.

17. As Nathan Glazer points out in a critique of one of the leading studies, the "whiteness thesis is designed to counter the thesis that American values of equality and inclusiveness—present . . . in the founding documents, even if they were limited and compromised by slavery and racist prejudice—have steadily expanded their reach to the point where the original promise has been fulfilled" (1998, 45).

REFERENCES

Allport, Gordon W. 1954. *The Nature of Prejudice*. Cambridge, Mass.: Addison-Wesley.

Balogh, Brian. 1996. *Integrating the Sixties.* University Park, Pa.: Pennsylvania State University Press.

Bander, Edward J., ed. 1970. *Turmoil on the Campus.* New York: H. W. Wilson.

Banton, Michael. 1988. *Racial Consciousness.* London: Longman.

Becker, Carl. 1935. *Everyman His Own Historian.* New York: Appleton-Century-Crofts.

———. 1940. "Some Generalities That Still Glitter." *Yale Review* 29(June): 649–67.

Belknap, Michal R. 1987. *Federal Law and Southern Order.* Athens, Ga.: University of Georgia Press.

Bellah, Robert N. 1976. "The New Religious Consciousness and the Crisis of Modernity." In *The New Religious Consciousness,* edited by Charles Y. Glock and Robert N. Bellah. Berkeley: University of California Press.

Belz, Herman. 1991. *Equality Transformed.* New Brunswick, N.J.: Transaction.

Britt, George. 1940. *The Fifth Column Is Here.* New York: Wilfred Funk.

Burner, David. 1996. *Making Peace with the 60s.* Princeton: Princeton University Press.

Carmichael, Stokely, and Charles V. Hamilton. 1967. *Black Power.* New York: Random House.

Cavallo, Dominick. 1999. *A Fiction of the Past.* New York: St. Martins Press.

Citrin, Jack, Ernst B. Haas, Christopher Muste, and Beth Reingold. 1994. "Is American Nationalism Changing?" *International Studies Quarterly* 38: 1–31.

Colburn, David R., and George E. Pozzetta, eds. 1979. *America and the New Ethnicity.* Port Washington, N.Y.: Kennikat.

Eastland, Terry. 1996. *Ending Affirmative Action.* New York: Basic Books.

Ferriss, Susan, and Ricardo Sandoval. 1997. *The Fight in the Fields.* New York: Harcourt.

Friedman, Murray. 1971. *Overcoming Middle-Class Rage.* Philadelphia: Westminster.

Fuchs, Lawrence H. 1990. *The American Kaleidoscope.* Middletown, Conn.: Wesleyan University Press.

Glazer, Nathan. 1975. *Affirmative Discrimination.* New York: Basic Books.

———. 1993. "Is Assimilation Dead?" *Annals of the American Academy of Political and Social Science* 530(November): 123–36.

———. 1997. *We Are All Multiculturalists Now.* Cambridge, Mass.: Harvard University Press.

———. 1998. Review of *Whiteness of a Different Color*, by Matthew Frye Jacobson. *New Republic* 219(October): 43–46.

Glazer, Nathan, and Daniel P. Moynihan. 1963. *Beyond the Melting Pot.* Cambridge, Mass.: MIT Press.

Gleason, Philip. 1980. "American Identity and Americanization." In *Harvard Encyclopedia of American Ethnic Groups*, edited by Stephan Thernstrom, Ann Orlov, and Oscar Handlin. Cambridge, Mass.: Harvard University Press.

———. 1992. *Speaking of Diversity.* Baltimore: Johns Hopkins University Press.

Gordon, Milton M. 1964. *Assimilation in American Life.* New York: Oxford University Press.

———. 1981. "Models of Pluralism." *Annals of the American Academy of Political and Social Science* 454(March): 178–88.

Goren, Arthur A. 1999. *The Politics and Public Culture of American Jews.* Bloomington: Indiana University Press.

Graham, Hugh Davis. 1990. *The Civil Rights Era.* New York: Oxford University Press.

———. 1998. "Legacies of the 1960s." *Journal of Policy History* 10(3): 267–88.

Greeley, Andrew M. 1972. "New Ethnicity and Blue Collars." *Dissent* 19(Winter): 270–77.

Harding, John, Harold Proshansky, Bernard Kutner, and Isidor Chein. 1968. "Prejudice and Ethnic Relations." Vol. 5 of *Handbook of Social Psychology*, 2d ed., edited by Gardner Lindzey and Eliot Aronson. Reading, Mass.: Addison-Wesley.

Harrington, Michael. 1962. *The Other America.* New York: Macmillan.

Higham, John. 1997. *Civil Rights and Social Wrongs.* University Park, Pa.: Pennsylvania State University Press.

Hollinger, David. 1995. *Postethnic America.* New York: Basic Books.

Hughes, Everett C., and Helen M. Hughes. 1952. *Where Peoples Meet.* Glencoe, Ill.: Free Press.

Huntington, Samuel P. 1981. *American Politics.* Cambridge, Mass.: Harvard University Press.

Jackson, Walter A. 1990. *Gunnar Myrdal and America's Conscience.* Chapel Hill: University of North Carolina Press.

Kallen, Horace M. 1924. *Culture and Democracy in the United States.* New York: Boni and Liveright.

———. 1946. "Of the American Spirit." *English Journal* 35(June): 293–94.

———. 1956. *Cultural Pluralism and the American Idea.* Philadelphia: University of Pennsylvania Press.

Katz, Stanley. 1998. "The Legal Framework of American Pluralism." In

Beyond Pluralism, edited by Wendy F. Katkin, Ned Landsman, and Andrea Tyree. Urbana, Ill.: University of Illinois Press.

Kazal, Russell. 1995. "Revisiting Assimilation." *American Historical Review* 100(April): 437–72.

Kettner, James H. 1978. *The Development of American Citizenship*. Chapel Hill: University of North Carolina Press.

Killian, Lewis M. 1981. "Black Power and White Reactions." *Annals of the American Academy of Political and Social Science* 454(March): 42–54.

King, Morton B., Jr. 1956. "The Minority Course." *American Sociological Review* 21(February): 80–83.

Lescott-Leszczynski, John. 1984. *The History of U. S. Ethnic Policy and Its Impact on European Ethnics*. Boulder, Colo.: Westview.

Levine, Irving M. 1968. "A Strategy for White Ethnic America." Paper presented at the Conference on the Problems of White Ethnic America. Philadelphia (June). Mimeo distributed by the American Jewish Committee.

Leyburn, James G. 1952 [1944]. "The Problem of Ethnic and National Impact from a Sociological Point of View." In *Foreign Influences in American Life*, edited by David F. Bowers. New York: Peter Smith.

Lichtman, Richard. 1968. "The University, Mask for Privilege." *Center Magazine* 1(January): 2–17.

Locke, Alain. 1942. "Pluralism and Intellectual Democracy." In *Science, Philosophy, and Religion: Second Symposium*. New York: Conference on Science, Philosophy, and Religion.

Mann, Arthur. 1979. *The One and the Many*. Chicago: University of Chicago Press.

Matthews, Fred. 1987. "Louis Wirth and American Ethnic Studies." In *The Jews of North America*, edited by Moses Rischin. Detroit: Wayne State University Press.

Matusow, Allen. 1984. *The Unraveling of America*. New York: Harper and Row.

Miller, David, and Michael Walzer, eds. 1995. *Pluralism, Justice, and Equality*. New York: Oxford University Press.

Montagu, M. F. Ashley. 1942. *Man's Most Dangerous Myth*. New York: Columbia University Press.

———. 1945. "On the Phrase 'Ethnic Group' in Anthropology." *Psychiatry* 8(February): 27–33.

———. 1972. *Statement on Race*. 3d ed. New York: Oxford University Press.

Montalto, Nicholas V. 1978. "The Forgotten Dream: A History of the Intercultural Education Movement, 1924–1941." Ph.D. diss., University of Minnesota.

Moreno, Paul D. 1997. *From Direct Action to Affirmative Action.* Baton Rouge: Louisiana State University Press.

Murphy, Gardner, ed. 1945. *Human Nature and Enduring Peace.* Boston: Houghton Mifflin.

Myrdal, Gunnar. 1962 [1944]. *An American Dilemma: The Negro Problem and Modern Democracy.* New York: Harper and Row.

Nagel, Paul. 1971. *This Sacred Trust.* New York: Oxford University Press.

National Advisory Commission on Civil Disorders. 1968. *Report of the National Advisory Commission on Civil Disorders* [Kerner Report]. Washington: Government Printing Office.

Nieli, Russell, ed. 1991. *Racial Preference and Racial Justice.* Washington, D.C.: Ethics and Public Policy Center.

Novak, Michael. 1972. *The Rise of the Unmeltable Ethnics.* New York: Macmillan.

Olson, James S. 1993. *The Vietnam War: Handbook of the Literature and Research.* Westport, Conn.: Greenwood.

O'Neill, William L. 1971. *Coming Apart.* Chicago: Quadrangle.

Palmer, Robert R. 1959. *The Age of Democratic Revolution.* 2 vols. Princeton: Princeton University Press.

Patterson, James T. 1986. *America's Struggle Against Poverty, 1900–1985.* 2d. ed. Cambridge, Mass.: Harvard University Press.

———. 1996. *Grand Expectations.* New York: Oxford University Press.

Pole, J. R. 1978. *The Pursuit of Equality in American History.* Berkeley: University of California Press.

Ralph, James R., Jr. 1993. *Northern Protest.* Cambridge, Mass.: Harvard University Press.

Rhea, Joseph Tilden. 1997. *Race Pride and American Identity.* Cambridge, Mass.: Harvard University Press.

Ringer, Benjamin B. 1983. *"We the People" and Others.* New York: Tavistock.

Rose, Peter I. 1968. *The Subject Is Race.* New York: Oxford University Press.

Salins, Peter D. 1997. *Assimilation, American Style.* New York: Basic Books.

Schultz, April. 1993. "Searching for a Unified America." *American Quarterly* 45(December): 639–48.

Sitkoff, Harvard. 1993. *The Struggle for Black Equality, 1954–1992.* New York: Hill and Wang.

Skerry, Peter. 1989. "Borders and Quotas." *Public Interest* 96(Summer): 86–102.

———. 1993. *Mexican-Americans.* New York: Free Press.

———. 1994. "The New Politics of Immigration." In *Unum Conversation.* Washington, D.C.: Ethics and Public Policy Center.

Skrentny, David. 1996. *The Ironies of Affirmative Action*. Chicago: University of Chicago Press.

Sleeper, Jim. 1997. *Liberal Racism*. New York: Viking.

Smith, M. G. 1982. "Ethnicity and Ethnic Groups in America." *Ethnic and Racial Studies* 5: 1–22.

Smith, Rogers M. 1988. "The 'American Creed' and American Identity." *Western Political Quarterly* 41(June): 225–51.

———. 1993. "Beyond Tocqueville, Myrdal, and Hartz." *American Political Science Review* 87(September): 549–66.

———. 1997. *Civic Ideals*. New Haven: Yale University Press.

Sollors, Werner. 1998. "The Multiculturalism Debate as Cultural Text." In *Beyond Pluralism*, edited by Wendy F. Katkin, Ned Landsman, and Andrea Tyree. Urbana, Ill.: University of Illinois Press.

Southern, David W. 1987. *Gunnar Myrdal and Black-White Relations*. Baton Rouge: Louisiana State University Press.

Stent, Madelon D., William R. Hazard, and Harry N. Rivlin. 1973. *Cultural Pluralism in Education*. New York: Appleton-Century-Crofts.

Thernstrom, Abigail. 1987. *Whose Votes Count?* Cambridge, Mass.: Harvard University Press.

Thernstrom, Stephan, and Abigail Thernstrom. 1997. *America in Black and White*. New York: Simon & Schuster.

Turner, Ronald. 1990. *The Past and Future of Affirmative Action*. New York: Quorum.

Unger, Irwin. 1974. *The Movement*. New York: Harper and Row.

U.S. Commission on Immigration Reform. 1995. *Legal Immigration: Setting Priorities*. Washington, D.C.

U.S. Office of Education. 1942. *Helping the Foreign-Born Achieve Citizenship*. Pamphlet 21. Education and National Defense Series. Washington: U.S. Federal Security Agency.

Vecoli, Rudolph J. 1964. "*Contadini* in Chicago." *Journal of American History* 51(December): 404–17.

———. 1979. "The Resurgence of American Immigration History." *American Studies International* 17(Winter): 46–66.

Vickery, William E., and Steward G. Cole. 1943. *Intercultural Education in American Schools*. New York: Harper.

Watson, Goodwin. 1947. *Action for Unity*. New York: Harper.

Weed, Perry L. 1973. *The White Ethnic Movement and Ethnic Politics*. New York: Praeger.

Wenk, Michael, Silvano M. Tomasi, and Geno Baroni, eds. 1972. *Pieces of a Dream*. New York: Center for Migration Studies.

Williams, Robin M., Jr. 1947. *The Reduction of Intergroup Tensions*. New York: Social Science Research Council.

Wirth, Louis. 1943. "The Effect of War on American Minorities: A Research Memorandum." Mimeograph in Wirth papers, Regenstein Library, University of Chicago.

———. 1945. "The Problem of Minority Groups." In *The Science of Man in the World Crisis*, edited by Ralph Linton. New York: Columbia University Press.

Wolfe, Harry C. 1939. *Human Dynamite*. New York: Foreign Policy Association.

—— Chapter 4 ——

Making Americans:
Immigration Meets Race

Desmond King

O NE DOMINANT INTERPRETATION of the experience of immigration and assimilation in the United States assumes an optimistic form. Its advocates recognize that during certain periods of U.S. history—notably, the 1880s, 1920s, and 1950s—federal policy toward immigrants was hostile and discriminatory, in that racist calibrations were introduced to distinguish between types of immigrants, but they argue that in a broader framework the historical record is one of gradual broadening and elimination of invidious distinctions in policy. In this interpretation the Hart-Celler Immigration Act of 1965 marks the culmination of efforts to liberalize immigration policy. Fundamental to this interpretation is the ideology or creed informing U.S. political culture, which, despite the historical record of inequities in the treatment of some groups and citizens, has acted consistently as a source of political values available to those seeking equality and inclusion. Philip Gleason, in chapter 3 of this volume, characterizes this creed as one of "liberal universalism" and maintains that "the universalism of the American Creed demanded tolerance of diversity. For if, as the overwhelming consensus had it, we were one people by virtue of our common commitment to the abstract ideals of democracy, it followed that differences of race, creed, color, language, or national background did not make any real difference."

In this essay I reject this interpretation of the history of immigration in the United States for several reasons. First, it glides over

143

a fundamental division between involuntary and voluntary immigration and constructs a narrative exclusively in terms of the latter category. Second, it extends an inaccurate understanding of the assimilationist Americanization programs practiced in the second and third decade of the twentieth century by ignoring their presumption of the "white" identity of the United States and the perpetuation of a historically misleading language of the melting pot. Third, the American Creed version of liberal universalism disregards and misunderstands the assumption—and, indeed, historical record—that the suppression of diversity, particularly group diversity, was a necessary condition to constructing a coherent and integrated national identity. Because the American Creed version of immigration and assimilation ignores the position of involuntary immigrants—and the racial distinctness of that category—it can never provide a plausible account of the formation of U.S. identity. Its silences are too great. That a system of segregated race relations coexisted with the development of immigration policy, the implementation of Americanization, and the construction of U.S. identity between the 1880s and the 1960s must be integrated as a primary factor in analyses of immigration and its effect on American society (Hochschild 1995; Kelley 1994; King 1995; Nobles 2000).

In support of my argument I single out the legislation enacted in the 1880s and particularly the 1920s, legislation that institutionalized consequential choices about democracy and group rights in the U.S. polity. By establishing barriers to immigrants based in part on eugenic criteria, policymakers privileged an Anglo-Saxon conception of U.S. identity, thereby rejecting the claims of other traditions in the nation, a process observable with respect to Native Americans as well as immigrants. Immigration policy helped solidify the second-class position of nonwhites, notably African Americans, already exposed to segregated race relations. Federal public policy in the 1920s presented a two-sided discrimination—externally, toward certain types of immigrants, and domestically, in the system of segregation imposed on African Americans—complemented by the Americanization process that also disregarded black citizens. Structuring this discriminatory framework was a conception of U.S. identity or nationality that was biased toward the white Anglo-Saxon element of the population over others.

By circumscribing the dominant image of American identity, the possibilities of U.S. citizenship were affected in several respects. First, the common retrospective narrative of a gradually unfolding and expanding American citizenship is rendered problematic, because efforts to systematically prevent this broadening are so readily identifiable. Second, the possibility of acknowledging a U.S. identity composed of "multiple traditions" was preempted by policymakers' efforts to impose uniformity and to devalue diversity, a course explicitly endorsed in national policy in the 1920s toward resident aliens and potential immigrants. Third, because these processes were realized, in significant part, through an active strategy of Americanization, this concept was rendered problematic, more commonly associated with division than with integration. As the historian Gary Gerstle pointedly observes, "Any analysis of Americanization, past and present, must accord coercion a role in the making of Americans" (Gerstle 1997, 558; Gerstle 1989, 1999, 2001). In particular the perception of those nonwhites already present in the United States, as articulated implicitly and explicitly in interwar Americanization programs, left a profound mark on the polity's political culture.

These characteristics of immigration and Americanization policy contributed powerfully to the development of multiculturalism in the past two decades. Multiculturalism refers to a range of public policies, including educational reform and compensatory schemes, that aim to include recognition of the historical role, traditions, and values of groups who have suffered discrimination and dismissal in the history of the United States. Because the process of expanding the content of U.S. identity has been slow and because it was historically associated with a denial of diversity, it is unremarkable that a new style of politics developed after the United States became a full democracy, extending rights of citizenship to all its members, in the late 1960s.

AMERICANIZATION AS MELTING POT

Immigration policy and the experience of immigrants in the United States have been driven by the issue of assimilability. As policymakers, politicians, experts, and populists turned their attention to immigration they bemoaned the problems of integrating new immigrants with the mainstream of American society. Until comparatively recently—the 1970s, perhaps—that mainstream has been narrowly drawn. It excluded Native Americans and African Americans from the time of the founding of the republic; the Chinese were specifically excluded from the 1880s, and the Japanese from 1905, until the 1940s; in the nineteenth century, Irish and to a lesser extent German immigrants were initially excluded (because of both penury and Catholicism) and then gradually integrated to cement the political support of the dominant groups in the United States by the 1910s; and from the 1900s until the 1950s, southern and eastern European immigrants were treated partially. Throughout this period, however, the dominant rhetorical and political construction of U.S. identity has been rooted in the image of an immigrant society and one in which J. Hector St. John de Crevecoeur's famous "melting-pot" process has integrated diverse elements into a "new man." Like many entrenched images of a society's history, it is invented and at best partial and inaccurate in important respects (Gyory 1998).

The melting-pot image is closely associated with the liberal universalism of the American Creed. Each celebrates the powers of absorption of the United States and explains historical inequities as regrettable deviations now rectified. Such an account serves to perpetuate the existing narrative of the development of diversity in the United States, however, rather than recognizing that the presence of numerous groups since the polity's foundation have fundamentally shaped it, often by presenting a model against which policymakers could define the American Creed. Thus the image of the United States as a society based on immigrants consistently displaces the position of involuntary immigrants and their descendants, historically writing them out of the invention of the U.S. polity. This practice was conveyed by Woodrow Wilson when he exhorted a group of newly naturalized citizens in 1915 that "this country is constantly drinking strength out of new sources by the voluntary association with it of great bodies of strong men and forward-looking women of other lands" (quoted in Talbot 1920, 78).

The plausibility of the melting-pot metaphor collapses during the decades from 1880 to 1929 (and arguably into the 1950s, when efforts to reform the restrictionist 1924 law foundered), when federal policy was designed to systematically select certain groups for "melting" and to exclude others. The vacuity of this melting-pot framework is powerfully exposed in the decades preceding the enactment of the eugenics-inspired Johnson-Reed Act of 1924. In these years both the main restrictionist movements and the principal policymakers in Congress and the federal government were— like political elites in most Western Hemisphere democracies in these years—deeply influenced by the arguments of eugenicists that meaningful distinctions could be drawn between people and "races" in terms of a range of physiological, mental, and qualitative criteria (King 1999a, 2000b).

Eugenic Exclusion

The practice of basing immigration standards on national origins, enacted in the Johnson-Reed Act of 1924, represented the convergence of commonplace stereotypes of and electoral hostility to immigrants and the pseudoscience propagated by eugenicists in the opening decades of the twentieth century. Attitudes and prejudices hitherto foisted on African Americans, Asians, and to a lesser extent Native Americans were now targeted on the immigrants arriving from eastern and southern Europe. Patrician and "old-stock" American descendants feared the racial imbroglio posed by the new immigrants. Advancing extravagant claims about the scientific rigor of their racial research, eugenicists presented expertise about racial hierarchies, racial degeneracy, and the sources of mental competence that were used to bolster the propositions of anti-immigration restrictionists in Congress and among the political elite. This expertise, which was consistently cited and rarely challenged (and never successfully challenged) from 1910 through the 1920s, provided an apparently scientific gloss to the hard edge of populist anti-immigrant rhetoric.

Eugenicists favored severe restriction on immigration as part of a general program to prevent dilution of the American "race" or "stock." In 1914, both the Medical Society of New York State and the Massachusetts Medical Society complained to the House of Representatives Immigration Committee about the failure to adequately screen immigrants to exclude what both termed the "mentally defective." The Massachusetts Medical Society warned of the "direful consequences of [immigrants'] being allowed to marry and to propagate and so deteriorate the mental health of the nation" (National Archives, RG 233, HR63A-H8.1). More than a decade later, the president of the Eugenics Research Association warned Representative Albert Johnson, chair of the House Immigration Committee, of the excessive fecundity of immigrants: "it is necessary to protect—as far as possible—our best stock" (National Archives, RG 233, HR69A-F20.1).

Two figures were crucial to the influence of eugenics on immigration legislation (King 1999a, 2000b): Dr. Harry Laughlin, who worked at the Eugenics Record Office at Cold Spring Harbor, Long Island, and who served from 1920 until 1932 as expert eugenics agent to the House Immigration Committee, and Representative Albert Johnson, from Washington state, who served as chairman of the House Immigration Committee. Johnson appointed Laughlin to his expert position and relied on Laughlin's scientific research in advancing the restrictionist arguments institutionalized in legislation in 1921, 1924, and 1929. Laughlin produced a series of detailed and prolix reports for the House Committee on Immigration, each of which was widely circulated among policymakers and the subject of national press attention. In 1922, Laughlin produced an analysis of America's melting pot, in 1924 he reported his extensive field research in the main emigrant-exporting countries of Europe, and in 1928 he discoursed on the "eugenical aspects of deportation" (70th Congress, 1st session, Committee on Immigration and Naturalization. 21 Feb 1928).

Laughlin's research, complemented by that of other eugenicists, hammered home three themes about the eugenic threats posed by immigrants. First, immigrants were in danger of "degenerating" the American population, because those arriving were too often mentally inferior to U.S. citizens; mental degeneracy was thought to be an inheritable condition, making its introduction into a population fundamentally dangerous. Second, immigrants created a fiscal burden significantly in excess of their share of the population because of their tendency to require institutional treatment and residence. Third, policymakers had to design an immigration regime that would permit the careful selection of immigrants most appropriate to building up the American national stock and excluding those having the obverse effect. As Laughlin explained, "In our future immigration legislation it will be necessary to include the element of family history or biological pedigree, if we are to improve the American human stock by immigration." The federal government had a central role in such selective breeding because it controlled "the hereditary quality of the immigration stream" (U.S. House 1922, 757).

Dr. Laughlin considered the national-origins scheme a mechanism to make immigration consistent with the "racial makeup of the entire people," one that would "keep America American" (Notes for the Fourth Report of the Committee on Selective Immigration of the American Eugenics Society, 2, Laughlin Papers, Truman State University). It was an agenda warmly endorsed by Representative Johnson, who concluded one committee hearing with the declaration that "the task of our committee is to prepare proposed duties which will develop the American people along the racial and institutional lines laid down by the founders of the country, so far as the control of immigration can do it" (U.S. House 1928, 717). This "racial and institutional" conception of the "American people" did not include African Americans, Native Americans, or Asians. Laughlin and Johnson, together with supporters among anti-immigration advocates, judged the 1924 national-origins system a triumph for eugenic arguments.

Americanization and Immigrants

Organized Americanization arose for political reasons as World War I and the postwar years prompted an intensification in anti-immigrant feelings and an anxiety about the absence of "Americanism" among aliens who had made no declaration to naturalize as U.S. citizens. Legislation passed in 1918 permitted the federal Bureau of Naturalization to actively propagate citizenship classes and to provide educational materials (in 1906, Congress had made competence in English a condition for naturalization). In 1920 alone, the Bureau of Naturalization distributed 98,958 textbooks on citizenship to public schools that administered classes for candidates for naturalization. The bureau maintained liaisons with a range of public and private organizations, including the Bureau of Education, the Departments of Interior and Labor, and the New York originating National Americanization Committee. The U.S.

Commissioner of Naturalization launched the American First program and the National Committee of One Hundred, aiming to make immigrants learn English and prepare for naturalization. A monthly bulletin, *Americanization*, was circulated to public and private officials involved in Americanization work. By 1918 every state had an Americanization committee, and many city governments had their own committees.

Galvanized by the aim of both preparing immigrants for citizenship and deflecting anti-American propaganda and politics (especially during and after World War I), Americanization was a national movement affecting hundreds of thousands of new immigrants. This agenda was embraced by employers and industrialists who made learning English a priority for immigrant workers. Many employers ran Americanization classes. In these aims employers were supported by the National Americanization Committee and the U.S. Chamber of Commerce, which appointed its own immigration committee in December 1918.

From 1920, Americanization was motivated by a political as well as an educational concern. Americanization was now promoted zealously by political critics of immigration and of immigrants' values. Failure to seek papers for naturalization was judged a political act, one hostile to American values and identity. During World War I, the One Hundred Percent campaign chastised the retention of ethnic identities, and the German language, previously used in many schools in the Midwest, was dropped. The principal claim of political Americanizers—from Presidents Theodore Roosevelt and Woodrow Wilson down to city officials and voluntary workers—was that becoming an American required immigrants to divest themselves of their previous ethnic and group loyalties. The humanitarian efforts of early Americanizers associated with the settlement movement leaders, such as Jane Addams, in cities like Chicago, Philadelphia, and New York were judged wanting by the proselytizers, who considered most of the new immigrants unassimilable except through a process of explicit and highly directive Americanization (Gerstle 1989, 1997, 1999; Hartmann 1948; King 2000b).

The impact of Americanization was a downgrading of group loyalties. Americanization was defined, at least implicitly, as the opposite of ethnic loyalty: it placed individual commitment to the United States above collective ethnic identity and did so in a coercive way (Gerstle 1997). Thus, the concern expressed in the Dillingham Commission report about the tendency of new immigrants to live in ethnic ghettos or foreign colonies leads directly into Americanization, as does the alleged "ignorance" and backwardness of immigrants who had therefore to be inculcated in American practices and culture. Such a message was conveyed, for instance, by Woodrow Wilson to new citizens:

> You cannot dedicate yourself to America unless you become in every respect and with every purpose of your will thorough Americans. You can not become thorough Americans if you think of yourselves in groups. America does not consist of groups. A man who thinks of himself as belonging to a particular national group in America has not yet become an American, and the man who goes among you to trade upon your nationality is no worthy son to live under the Stars and Stripes. (National Archives, RG 12, "Message to Newly Naturalized Citizens")

Wilson's passage and sentiments were widely cited in official texts about Americanization. It was the abstract, autonomous individual whom Americanizers both praised and presented as the ideal citizen. The cumulative effect of this message in civics education, Americanization programs, and official ceremonies was to delegitimate ethnic or group values.

Two long-term effects of this intense Americanization are notable. First, the emphasis upon group disavowal and its substitution with loyalty to the United States worked in the short term (and was greatly enhanced by World War II's needs) but did not succeed in ending Americans' interests in their ethnic values and traditions; it was these latter interests that constituted a basis for both the white resistance to post-1954 desegregation in northern and midwestern cities and a tendency toward a white backlash in politics (King 2000b; Sugrue 1996). Second, the conception of who constituted an American was narrowly drawn, excluding nonwhites and carrying lingering uncertainties about eastern and southern Europeans. Both consequences profoundly shaped aspects of American politics from the 1960s.

NATIVE AMERICANS AND U.S. IDENTITY

Despite intense efforts to Americanize Native Americans between the 1870s and 1920s, the dominant images of Native Americans— conveyed, for instance, in Hollywood movies—was one of unassimilability and of a backward "savagery." In John Ford's 1958 movie, *The Searchers*, one character, upon encountering captives freed from Comanche Indians, remarks, "It's hard to believe they're white," to which Ethan Edwards (played by John Wayne) snaps back, "They ain't white anymore. They're Comanches." Considered one of Ford's finest achievements, *The Searchers* nonetheless retains and disseminates a traditional view of Native Americans as outside the mainstream of U.S. identity because they are not white and are, therefore, unassimilable. In another John Ford film, *Two Rode Together* (1961), a description—issued drunkenly by Guthrie MacCambe (played by James Stewart)—of the experience of capture paints a picture of savagery and grotesqueness (Derounian-Stodola 1998). Asked by a woman to search for her brother who had been captured twelve years earlier, at the age of five, Stewart responds,

> Do you know what this little angel looks like now? Let me tell you something. That kid has braids down to here now [pointing to his chest], stinking braids full of buffalo grease; and he has a scar on his shoulders where they stuck the pins right through; and they got some rawhide ropes and hung the kid up dangling till the kid tore himself off these pins just to prove to himself that he's a man. . . . He's forgot his English; he just grunts Comanche, he just grunts; and he's killed and he's taken scalps, white man's scalps, and given the chance, sister, he'd rape you and when he finished he'd trade you off to one of the other bucks for a good knife or a bad rifle.

This movie was made as recently as 1960. From *Stagecoach* (1939) onward, Ford's directorial presence in cinematic constructions of American history was immense. His Westerns are rooted in a sentimental and mythologizing perspective about the integration of the West into American civilization through the defeat of "savage" Native Americans. *The Searchers* being a partial exception, Ford's Westerns are patriotic and serious distortions of the course of

American history. There is rarely a critical perspective brought to bear on the actions of Ford's western heroes; instead, the narratives are dogged by a sentimentality parading as seriousness and, more damagingly, as historical record. Often such Westerns appear simply to film the images portrayed in Frederic Remington's famous western paintings, like *Fight for the Waterhole* (1903) or *Defending the Stockade* (1905). It is difficult to reconcile these images of the West with the populist melting-pot story of self-development. Despite the implication that Native Americans were proud and independent peoples, the proposition that their values and traditions could in any way be integrated with those of the civilization that informed U.S. identity is never entertained in these or other images of the time.

Subsequent films—notably, Abraham Polonsky's *Tell Them Willie Boy is Here* (1969) and Delmer Daves' *Broken Arrow* (1950)—offer more nuanced treatments of Native Americans in the United States, but they are valiant attempts to buck a powerful and widely entrenched commonplace view of Native Americans as unassimilable in part because of their nonwhiteness. By 1970, however, and the release of Arthur Penn's *Little Big Man,* a more honest account of Native Americans' experience of the United States was possible; this film version of Thomas Berger's novel imposed a much needed, if disturbing, historical perspective to the treatment of Native Americans at the hands of the United States. Dee Brown's (1991) major study, *Bury My Heart At Wounded Knee,* also reignited interest in accurately grasping the historical experience of Native Americans. Michael Mann's extraordinary film, *The Last of the Mohicans* (1992) is the cinematic culmination of this more nuanced cultural engagement with Native American history.

Native Americans faced formidable barriers to membership of the U.S. polity as full citizens (McClain and Stewart 1998; Prucha 1962). Michael Rogin characteristically captures the core mythological element played by Native Americans in the invention of U.S. identity: "Not the Indians alive, then, but their destruction symbolized the American experience. The conquest of the Indians made the country uniquely American" (Rogin 1975, 7; also see Dippie 1982; Stannard 1992). This conquest underpinned the doctrine and aims of Manifest Destiny and found support in mid-nineteenth-century American racial typologies espoused by scientists such as Francis Parkman and Samuel George Morton; Parkman wrote of "an impassable gulf between [a civilized white man] and his red brethren" (quoted in Dippie 1982, 85). Throughout the nineteenth century, judicial decisions with respect to the property and tribal rights of Native Americans served the U.S. government's expansion into Indian territories. The Fourteenth Amendment, passed in 1868, judged American Indians not to be citizens and not to be eligible for citizenship. This view was upheld by the Supreme Court in 1884 (*Elk v. Wilson* [112 U.S. 94]). Citizenship was granted by Congress to the Five Tribes in 1901, but it was not until 1924 that the Indian Citizenship Act imparted full rights of citizenship to all Native Americans—the same year, ironically, that the Johnson-Reed Immigration Act implemented a discriminatory immigration regime.

Native Americans and Americanization

American Indians were subject to systematic Americanization measures beginning in the late nineteenth century, encouraged by the assimilationist philosophy of the settlement reached in the General Allotment (Dawes) Act of 1887, which allocated small allotments to Indians and broke up reservations; its logic was an assimilationist one (Dippie 1982, 177). After the passage of the Dawes Act, James Wilson writes, "the process of 'Americanization' began with the legalistic 'tribal rolls' drawn up by federal agents, which undermined the Indians' own sense of who they were— derived from the oral traditions and a common knowledge of clan and band affiliations—by registering them according to Anglo-American notions of family and individuality" (Wilson 1998, 307). Allotments—a process that also yielded considerable "surplus" land to the state—established a traditional Anglo-American familial structure in place of tribal life, thereby socially isolating Native Americans from one another.

These legal changes were complemented by a program of Americanization. The principal strategy has been to Americanize Native American children into the U.S. identity and way of life through education and, at times, removal from their families (Hoxie 1989; Prucha 1984, volume 2). Despite the framework within which relations between the U.S. government and Native Americans were supposedly conducted—in effect, two governments—federal policymakers, commonly helped by religious and voluntary bodies, aimed to Americanize Indian children. This approach began as a benevolent response among critics of government policy toward Native Americans in the mid-nineteenth century, the former fearing that existing policy would result in the extinction of Native Americans. In this context it was argued that a policy of systematic Americanization or, as it was generally known in its earlier guise, "civilizing" should be imposed upon Native Americans, focused in particular on the children; such civilization was imbued with a heavy Christianity. Reformers rejected the Indian reservation policy on grounds that it isolated Native Americans and thereby reinforced their exclusion from the civilizing effects of American society. This approach gathered momentum in the 1880s and 1890s—not coincidentally, the decades in which national politics was increasingly dominated by immigration policy and the alleged dangers of "feeble-minded" immigrants diluting the "national stock." In this context, assimilation of Native Americans was pursued to consolidate U.S. identity and progress.

As in other aspects of late-nineteenth-century progressivism, schools and education were identified as key media through which to civilize or Americanize outsiders (Adams 1995; Prucha 1984). (The Dillingham Commission, for instance, emphasized the importance of schools in Americanizing immigrant children to the United States.) Led by a former army officer, Captain Richard Pratt, the Carlisle Indian School in Pennsylvania was established in 1879, the first institution of the Americanization policy. Uninterested in, and in some ways hostile to, Native American cultures, Pratt's Americanization strategy rested on removing Indian children from their immediate environments (Prucha 1984, 2: 694–700). Pratt explained his aims in terms of building a national identity to which Native Americans would subscribe in common with other Americans: "Under our principles we have established the public school system, where people of all races may become unified in every way, and loyal to the government; but we do not gather the people of one nation into schools by themselves, and the people of another nation into schools by themselves, but we invite the youth of all peoples into all schools. We shall not succeed in Americanizing the Indian unless we take him in exactly the same way" (Pratt 1973a, 266).

Pratt was convinced of the power of assimilationist Americanization to transcend tribal ties and abhorred what he saw as the segregationist system institutionalized in reservations: "It is a great mistake to think that the Indian is born an inevitable savage. He is born a blank, like the rest of us. Left in the surroundings of savagery, he grows to possess a savage language, superstition, and life. We, left in the surroundings of civilization, grow to possess a civilized language, superstition, and habit. Transfer the savage-born infant to the surroundings of civilization, and he will grow to possess a civilized language and habit" (Pratt 1973a, 268).

Under the Carlisle School philosophy, this approach entailed giving the children American names, cutting boys' hair short, and dressing them in Euro-American clothes; as Pratt inveighed, "If we simply keep him in school *as an Indian*, he does not gain that which will make him capable of filling his place as an American citizen" (Pratt 1973b, 279; emphasis in original). Speaking Native American languages was forbidden (the so-called outing system [Pratt 1973c, 272–76]), and the children were educated in preparation for army jobs (for boys) and domestic work (for girls). The resulting transformations were captured in a series of "before" and "after" portraits of the children. The Carlisle model was followed in other off-reservation boarding schools in the next two decades.

By 1900, 10 percent of Native American children were placed in 307 schools across the United States modeled on the Carlisle (Adams 1995, 58; Prucha 1984, 2: 816). The majority were boarding schools, though many were located on reservations, and this latter became the dominant practice after 1906; from about 1915 onward, Native American children increasingly attended normal public schools. The schools shared a dedication to assimilating Native American children by eradicating use of their native languages and customs and preparing them for participation in the national labor market. Many died of illnesses such as tuberculosis and influenza (Adams 1995, 124–35; Prucha 1984, 2: 841–62); numerous children ran away; and because the curriculum taught American history as a story of progress and advancing civilization, the traditions and values of Native Americans were denigrated. There was no room for acknowledgment of multiple traditions in the single narrative of American history or for weakening the homogeneity of U.S. identity promulgated; as David Adams remarks, "Pratt liked Indians, but he had little use for Indian cultures," a view at variance with those of both Theodore Roosevelt and an influential commissioner of Indian affairs, Francis Leupp (Adams 1995, 51). The latter, who served as commissioner from 1904 to 1909, fostered the shift away from off-reservation schooling.

The educational directive to reject all aspects of their background and traditions could not but be traumatic for thousands of Native Americans. It is a indication of the high and brutal cost assimilationism can extract. The historian Frederick Hoxie concludes of this period as follows: "To be sure, Native Americans were incorporated into the nation, but their new status bore a greater resemblance to the position of the United States' other nonwhite peoples than it did to the 'full membership' envisioned by nineteenth-century reformers. By 1920 they had become an American minority group, experiencing life on the fringes of what had come to be regarded as a 'white man's land.' The assimilation campaign was complete" (Hoxie 1989, xiii). As Hoxie also observes, this assimilationist strategy was pursued very much as a vindication of the superiority of U.S. identity as conceived by the Anglo-Saxon elite as well as a means to ameliorate conditions for Native Americans: "The extension of citizenship and other symbols of membership in American society would reaffirm the power of the nation's institutions to mold all people to a common standard. Success in assimilating Indians would reaffirm the dominance of the white Protestant majority, for such an achievement would extend the reach of the majority's cultural norms" (Hoxie 1989, 15).

The Indian Reorganization Act of 1934—the brainchild of John Collier, Franklin D. Roosevelt's radically reforming and pro–Native American commissioner for Indian affairs—ended the allotment system and promulgated a set of measures intended to halt and reverse some of its more malign features, not least in respecting the values of Native Americans and introducing self-government; the new policy was also the first explicit acknowledgment in federal policy that Native Americans were not going to disappear, which had been the premise of government action since the 1830s, and that some coexistence with Americans, rather than complete assimilation with American society, was an appropriate aspiration. John Collier conceived of the 1934 act as "a new treaty and organic act, submitted in advance of its passage to all the Indian tribes of the country and subjected after its passage to referenda of all the tribes. The core of the act was the recognition that Indians, like everyone else, needed to organize, to function as individuals through groups of their own devising, and to make their own choices as to way of life" (letter to the editor, *New York Times,* March 12, 1950). Much remained to be done before Collier's vision was even approximated, but his period as commissioner set a new standard for policy with respect to Native Americans.

THE DOMINANCE OF WHITENESS

The assumption of U.S. identity as a white one was fundamental from the founding of the republic until the late 1960s. This precept significantly influenced attitudes toward immigration until the mid-twentieth century and shaped policymakers' approach to the Americanization programs of the second and third decades of the twentieth century. The dominant assumption of federal and state policymakers was that immigrants should be admitted based on their compatibility with the original English settlers, an approach that privileged Nordic Europeans over others. However, that the whiteness of this latter group was a sociologically constructed and contested one (Fields 1990) is illustrated by the initial exclusion of Irish immigrants, in the second half of the nineteenth century and opening years of the twentieth, from the dominant majority on the grounds that they were not white (Ignatiev 1995). The presumption of U.S. identity as white structured immigration debates until the middle of the twentieth century, a point underlined by the sociologist Orlando Patterson, who remarks that "no 'white' person in his right mind considered the Irish 'white' up to as late as the 1920s" (Patterson 1997, 75).

Legalizing Whiteness

As early as the mid-nineteenth century, American jurists were constructing a racialist conception of U.S. jurisprudence. In 1854, the California Supreme Court judged that the Chinese were not eligible for equal protection under the law and excluded Chinese witnesses from testifying in that state's courtrooms (*People v. Hall* [4 Cal. 399]). The same decade saw the flowering of the KnowNothing Party, whose members considered Catholics inappropriate for U.S. citizenship, let alone the Chinese or African Americans. Lacking judicial protection radically enhanced the vulnerability of the Chinese in the United States to malfeasance and to personal abuse and violence. The populist nativism articulated against Chinese immigrants—a populism often associated with labor organizations—was to prove an entrenched and significant strand in American politics until the 1930s (Higham 1995).

The failure of state immigration laws and restrictions to win judicial endorsement consistently fueled pressure for national legislation, a demand that culminated, in 1882, in the passage by the U.S. Congress of the first Chinese labor exclusion law. The language in which such demands were expressed was intemperate and racist, contributing to a view of the Chinese and the Japanese as "unfit" for assimilation with Americans; this view endured, as comments conveyed forty years later by Secretary of Labor James Davis to the Union of American Hebrew Congregations indicate: "You would throw down the bars and admit the Chinese and other Eastern races indiscriminately. . . . It is not only evident to truly American peoples but even to these Orientals themselves that they will never become assimilated into a united American Republic. They are not of us. Their economic and moral standards are those of a thousand years ago" (National Archives, RG 174). As one senator, opposing an amendment to the naturalization laws that would allow Chinese immigrants to become citizens, asked rhetorically, "Is there anybody who will say that the Chinese is a desirable population?," adding that "Mongolians, no matter how long they have lived in the United States, will never lose their identity as a peculiar and separate people. They will never amalgamate with persons of European descent" (*Congressional Globe* 1870, vol. 40, part 6: 5156).

Proscribing Black Immigrants

The racially biased system of national origins implemented between 1924 and 1929 excluded the descendants of those who arrived involuntarily in the United States or were already present before the colonizers arrived in its calculation of nationality quotas. These remarkable eligibility decisions marginalized African Americans in federal immigration policy in a way consistent with the politics of segregation: the policy meant that they were not counted as citizens for purposes of defining the nationality composition of the U.S. population (Ngai 1999). Although the self-image of the United States as an immigrant nation has been an intensely powerful one among Americans, until comparatively recently this conception ignored the position of those citizens descended from slaves.

Before the 1920s an even more extreme treatment of African Americans was pursued. In 1914, the U.S. Senate passed a bill proscribing black immigration. It was aimed in particular at West Indian immigrants, whom one U.S. senator, from Mississippi, compared unflatteringly with Chinese and Japanese aliens: "You have already a law whereby you exclude Chinese. Chinese are as much superior to Negroes as can be, almost. You have a gentleman's agreement with Japan by means of which you excluded Japanese." The same senator identified a particular threat with respect to West Indian immigrants, their potential disruption of the segregationist order: "the West Indian Negro, as a rule, is a man who is accustomed to political and social equality" (*Congressional Record* 1914, 805, 807). Indeed, many West Indians were involved in the civil rights movement in the 1920s, including both the National Association for the Advancement of Colored People (NAACP) and the Universal Negro Improvement Association (James 1997; King 2000b). This exclusionist initiative—subsequently rejected by the House of Representatives (74 in favor, 253 opposing, and 99 abstaining)—is one of the most dramatic expressions of the U.S. identity conceived of as a white one, a strategy uppermost in the congressional speeches unsuccessfully supporting the bill.

"Whites-Only" Naturalization

The naturalization laws of the United States, from its origins, were restrictive. The Naturalization Act of 1790 restricted the right to naturalize to free white men, a qualification that survived the fifteen changes to the naturalization law enacted by Congress between 1790 and 1854, and it remained operative for another hundred years. The Naturalization Act of 1870 allowed persons of African descent to naturalize but did not obviate the general restriction.

The term "free white persons" proved a powerful tool with which to exclude nonwhites, including Chinese and black immigrants, from naturalized status. A congressional initiative in the 1870s to substitute the term "free persons" for "free white persons" with respect to naturalization laws was defeated in the Senate by a vote of twenty-six to twelve (*Congressional Globe* 1870, vol. 60, part 6: 5148–77; for the breakdown of votes, see 5177). Massachusetts senator Charles Sumner, who proposed this amendment, told his colleagues that "it is 'all men' and not a race or color that are placed under protection of the Declaration; and such was the voice of our fathers on the 4th day of July, 1776" (ibidem, 5155; for the wider political context, see U.S. Senate 1877). In western states, the naturalization restriction against Asians was complemented by others regarding the rights to own property, to serve on juries, and to enter identified occupations. The length of time required before naturalization could be pursued varied in the United States, with the pressures of the Know-Nothing Party in the mid-nineteenth century leading to its extension. In the second and third decades of the twentieth century, the pressure to naturalize—from which so many others were excluded—was applied to white southern and eastern European immigrants who were to be integrated with the political majority.

The tenacity and narrowness of the "whites-only" right to naturalize was refined by the U.S. Supreme Court in two important decisions taken in the 1920s and the subject of close analysis by Ian Haney López. Dissecting the language and logic behind a series of judicial decisions, Haney López finds that the use of "common sense" and so-called scientific evidence (often eugenics influenced) in demarcating white from nonwhite has fluctuated with jurisprudential need. It was specifically with respect to determining plaintiffs' whiteness that this process operated: "the social construction of the White race is manifest in the [Supreme] Court's repudiation of science and its installation of common knowledge as the appropriate racial meter of Whiteness" (Haney López 1996, 9).

In his study, Haney López investigates the effects of the constitutional restriction, in place from 1790 to 1952 (despite efforts to
amend it, such as that by Senator Charles Sumner in 1870 [*Congressional Globe,* 1870, vol. 60, part 6: 1549–71]), that only white
persons could acquire U.S. citizenship through naturalization.
Thus, in the case of *Ozawa v. United States* (260 U.S. 178 [1922]),
the plaintiff was denied the right to naturalize because he was a
member of the "yellow" race rather than the Caucasian race and
therefore not white, whereas in *United States v. Thind* [261 U.S.
204 (1923)], the plaintiff, who was a Hindu and considered a Caucasian by ethnologists, was not white "in accordance with the understanding of the common man" (also see Haney López 1996,
chapter 4). The tortuous contortions that were marshaled to define
whiteness by the courts illustrates vividly not just how such categories are socially constructed but also the political effects of such
construction: "the legal reification of racial categories has made
race an inescapable material reality in our society, one which at
every turn seems to reinvigorate race with the appearance of reality" (Haney López, 19).

African Americans Outside Americanization

In general, Americanizers turned a blind eye to the position of
African Americans in the United States and expressed no concern
about their education or the denial of rights of citizenship they
endured. This incongruity struck the first president of the NAACP,
Moorfield Storey, who noted to the association's members that
"the poorest and more ignorant foreigner, just naturalized, has the
right to fill any office in the country save that of President, but the
most highly educated native citizen in whose veins runs a little
colored blood cannot even vote. Ignorance and worthlessness do
not unfit a man for suffrage, but the slightest shade of color will"
(Storey 1921, 4).

The palpable contradiction between the intense Americanization of foreign-born aliens and the disregard of the native-born
population occasionally burst through to the surface of politics in
the post–World War I years. One director of Americanization in
the Bureau of Education, Fred Butler, was alert to this discrepancy. "It becomes clear to me," he observed, "that there are some

American born who are not so clear upon the subject of citizenship as others; some of our citizens are not so intelligent as the rest on their duties to the republic." Butler singled out African Americans: "We have millions of negroes who have practically no education and who have not had an opportunity to participate in our political life. They lack schooling and they lack experience. They are children in their mental and social development" (National Archives, RG 12, "Americanization: Its Purpose and Process," 2). For Butler, the gap between foreign-born aliens' lack of Americanism and the inherent limits of some native-born African Americans was a cause for alarm; that this state of affairs reflected the segregationist order in the United States was entirely overlooked.

Butler's analysis underlines two key aspects of the Americanization process. First, it illustrates that immigrants were its principal focus; Butler's remarks are a rare instance of an Americanizer considering other members of the U.S. population. Second, his analysis demonstrates the narrowness of assimilationist Americanization in practice (what he calls the "assimilation of the foreign-born and making Americans of them" [National Archives RG-12, "Americanization: Its Purpose and Process."]). His comments about the mental limits of certain groups in the United States reproduces the assumptions of eugenic arguments, at this time a major influence on debates about immigrants and Americanization.

What is perhaps most extraordinary about Butler's analysis, however, is his failure—one shared with most Americanizers—to recognize the degree to which his understanding of Americanism was so partially established in existing U.S. institutions. He defined the social philosophy of Americanism as resting in identifiable core ideas, "such as freedom of speech, of religion, and of the press, the right of the majority to rule, full participation of the individual in government, and personal freedom" (National Archives RG-12, "Americanization: Its Purpose and Process," 1). That African Americans, as revealed in the speeches and debates of NAACP officers, were powerfully aware of this contradictory and limited character of Americanization there can be no doubt. There was, of course, an important contemporary debate about education policy for African Americans, conducted between Booker T. Washington, head of the Tuskegee Institute and an advocate of limited education, and the intellectual W. E. B. Du Bois, editor of the *Crisis,* who, having himself benefited from university education (including his doctorate from Harvard) saw no reason to prescribe a limited nonacademic curriculum for African Americans. These debates were far removed from the world of federal policymakers, however, whose task it was to expand educational resources for immigrants. What is surprising is that the efforts mobilized with respect to Native American education for Americanization found no counterpart for black Americans.

DENYING DIVERSITY AND MULTIPLE TRADITIONS

The enactment of the Chinese Exclusion Act in 1882 marked a fundamental break with existing immigration policy. From being a country open to all potential immigrants—an openness that produced a massive inflow of immigrants during the mid-nineteenth century—the United States changed policy. Furthermore, the 1882 exclusion was tinged with the assumptions of eugenic arguments that achieved enormous intellectual and political influence in the ensuing four decades and fundamentally shaped the content— chiefly, the system of national-origins quotas—of the restrictionist Johnson-Reed Immigration Act passed in 1924.

Debate about immigration policy in the United States from 1900 to 1929 was saturated with a fear of inferior "stock," "races," or "nationalities" "invading" and commingling with the "real American stock"—that is, white descendants of the northwestern Europeans who first settled the New World colonies. African American descendants are considered as involuntary members of the U.S. population and as basically unassimilable, an assumption that served as the foundation of the federal government's pernicious system of segregated race relations (Kelley 1994; King 1995). The ethos that immigrants should be assimilable with the dominant "American race" underpinned the debates about immigration; assimilation occurred through a melting pot, but the ingredients were predetermined. This debate is significant for what it reveals about the notion of equality within a liberal democratic polity. In essence, immigration policymakers were determining who would be entitled to become members of the polity and thereby have the opportunity to exercise such equal rights. In 1952, President Harry Truman characterized the law enacted in 1924 as "a slur on the patriotism, the capacity and the decency of a large part of our citizenry" (quoted in U.S. Senate 1979, I).

In a series of articles and a major book, the Yale University political scientist Rogers Smith has articulated the idea of multiple traditions as a means to gain purchase on the complexity of the historical formation of U.S. national identity. Instead of perpetuating the commonplace sanguine narrative about the gradual triumph of the American Creed of liberal universalism, Smith explains how multiple traditions—many ascriptive, illiberal, discriminatory, and racist—have coexisted and recurred in American history (Smith 1993, 1997; also see King 1999a, 2000a).

Analytically, the multiple traditions approach does not mean just that the United States is composed of groups other than a dominant white-based elite but that those groups' distinctions and diverse traditions were fostered and formed in the very development of the polity and contributed to that development. The two cannot be separated. To take an influential model, Seymour Martin Lipset's (1996) recent book on American exceptionalism continues to advance a partial and limited account of the development of the U.S. polity and its values. Lipset addresses the place of African Americans in the history of the United States, acknowledging their involuntary arrival and the effects of that circumstance. (It is notable that these details were overlooked in his earlier volume [Lipset 1967].) Assuming that other immigrants broadly conform to the assimilationist model, Lipset writes of African Americans that "they are the great exception to the American Creed, to American ideological exceptionalism" (Lipset 1996, 113); this view not only reduces racial inequality to a problem of hypocrisy rather than a problem arising from identifiable historical processes of inclusion and exclusion in the construction of U.S. national identity but also neglects the centrality of African Americans in American political development. Lipset dismisses issues of multiculturalism as concerns exclusive to the intellectual class, with "little impact on mass behavior"; consequently, "the 'melting pot' remains as appropriate an image as ever" (Lipset 1996, 250). This conclusion undercuts the implications of Lipset's own admission about the marginality constructed for African Americans within the assimilationist framework: that an exception has to be made exposes the analytical weaknesses of the assumptions of a general American Creed framework.

CONCLUSION

Is there a distinct American "race" or people? Despite Horace Kallen's unequivocal warning in 1915 that "the 'American race' is a totally unknown thing," this question nonetheless has taxed policymakers and intellectuals since 1900, when immigration began to gain in political salience (Kallen 1915, 219). The question of identity was of profound importance, because restrictionists increasingly presented their arguments in terms of the unassimilability of certain immigrants with existing Americans. The ardent restrictionist senator Henry Cabot Lodge warned against the southern and eastern European immigrants who were, he argued, "from races most alien to the body of the American people and from the lowest and most illiterate classes among those races" (Lodge 1891, 32). Throughout this discussion, the place of African Americans—weighed down in segregation—was ignored, and because almost all the key policymakers presumed a "whites-only" immigration policy, African Americans were assumed to be unassimilable with the U.S. "people."

Scholars of immigration have traditionally occupied a separate intellectual and historical terrain from those writing about race in the United States. This fragmentation has resulted in a partial and inadequate account—indeed, often no account—of the interaction between immigration and race in the construction of a national identity in the United States. The analytic cost has been the maintenance of a historically limited and intellectually incomplete understanding of U.S. identity. It is one that continues to inform scholarship but is no longer defensible. Its retention constitutes a major barrier to understanding the sources of multiculturalism and the likely persistence of such a politics. A new generation of historians of immigration and immigrant history take a more nuanced view as the stories of particular communities or particular ethnic groups are told (Butler 1983; Olson 1979; Morawska 1985).

This conclusion plainly conflicts with the view of U.S. immigration and politics presented by the distinguished historian Philip Gleason, in chapter 3 of this volume. The coincidence of a political challenge to the liberal universalist consensus—that is, the legislation on civil rights, voting rights, and immigration in the mid-1960s—and the articulation of a multiculturalist agenda by groups previously marginalized or the subject of historical inequalities has certainly compelled a reconsideration of the established understanding of American history. In the view of some commentators this disruption to the liberal universalist consensus is politically damaging because it injects a group-based set of demands into the policy process (for instance, with respect to multiculturalism in education or affirmative-action programs) and exacerbates fragmentation and dissent in political debate.

However, these conclusions rest upon ahistorical propositions. First, as the text of this essay has attempted to demonstrate, the liberal universalist narrative of the development of the United States can only be sustained if the exclusion of certain groups is either ignored or treated as trivial. In practice, liberal universalism had no place for African Americans until the 1960s and denied substantial numbers of residents the right to naturalize until the 1940s. Second, the proposition that a group-based politics is a new phenomenon in American politics is historically inaccurate. For instance, veterans are a group of Americans who have received special treatment based on their membership of a particular category since the middle of the nineteenth century. The exclusion of African Americans, under segregated race relations, from senior administrative positions in the federal government between the 1890s and 1960s effected a system of partiality for white employees (King 1999b). It would be difficult to find a more pellucid instance of group preference than the "whites-only" naturalization eligibility rule outlined above.

Judging whether the changes since the 1960s are positive or negative for politics and political culture in the United States depends in part upon the significance attributed to the previous exclusions. If these latter are considered significant—as I believe they should be—then political reform to ensure inclusion of those previously overlooked and dissipation of the artificial liberal universalist consensus was an unavoidable and desirable corrective. Plainly, those commentators retaining a traditional understanding of the American narrative—one that gives no attention at all to the idea and implications of a multiple traditions perspective—will greet the changes with alarm.

Furthermore, recognizing the inadequacy of the conventional narrative with respect to excluded groups such as African Americans or Native Americans provides a more promising basis for the political incorporation of those immigrants entering the United States since the 1980s. Although the political battles of the 1960s may have weakened the sense of a strong nationhood in the United States (though this outcome is a contested one), they have not altered a defining feature of immigrants: they come to the United States voluntarily and, for the most part, are eager to embrace U.S. identity and the values of Americanism. That they can do so without having to belittle their own cultures and traditions—as used to be required—constitutes the basis for an even stronger attachment to the United States than that expressed by earlier generations of immigrants. The current conception of Americanism or Americanization is unquestionably broader and culturally richer than the one prevalent a century ago. It is in many respects a multicultural Americanism. It is not inherently centrifugal in its political effects but is likely to facilitate a broader and richer definition of nationhood. The historical record of U.S. development would seem to confirm this sort of resilience in the polity's political institutions and policies.

REFERENCES

Adams, David Wallace. 1995. *Education for Extinction: American Indians and the Boarding School Experience, 1875–1928*. Lawrence, Kans.: University Press of Kansas.

Brown, Dee. 1991. *Bury My Heart at Wounded Knee*. London: Vintage.

Butler, Jon. 1983. *The Huguenots in America*. Cambridge, Mass.: Harvard University Press.

Congressional Globe. 1833–73. 46 vols. Washington, D.C., 1834–73.

Congressional Record. 1914. 58th Cong., 2d sess. Vol. 52, pt. 1.

Debo, Angie. 1995. *A History of the Indians of the United States*. London: Pimlico.

Derounian-Stodola, Kathryn Zabelle, ed. 1998 *Women's Indian Captivity Narratives*. Harmondsworth, England: Penguin Books.

Dippie, Brian W. 1982. *The Vanishing American: White Attitudes and U.S. Indian Policy.* Middletown, Conn.: Wesleyan University Press.

Fetzer, Joel S. 2000. *Public Attitudes Toward Immigration in the United States, France, and Germany.* New York: Cambridge University Press.

Fields, Barbara J. 1990. "Slavery, Race, and Ideology in the United States of America." *New Left Review* 181:95–118.

Fitzgerald, Keith. 1996. *The Face of the Nation.* Stanford: Stanford University Press.

Gerstle, Gary. 1989. *Working-Class Americanism: The Politics of Labor in a Textile City, 1914–1960.* New York: Cambridge University Press.

———. 1994. "The Protean Character of American Liberalism." *American Historical Review* 99(5): 1043–73.

———. 1997. "Liberty, Coercion, and the Making of Americans." *Journal of American History* 84: 524–58.

———. 1999. "Theodore Roosevelt and the Divided Character of American Nationalism." *Journal of American History* 86: 1280–1307.

———. 2001. *American Crucible.* Princeton, N.J.: Princeton University Press.

Glazer, Nathan. 1997. *We Are All Multiculturalists Now.* Cambridge, Mass.: Harvard University Press.

Gyory, Andrew. 1998. *Closing the Gate.* Chapel Hill: University of North Carolina Press.

Haney López, Ian F. 1996. *White by Law.* New York: New York University Press.

Hartmann, Edward G. 1948. *The Movement to Americanize the Immigrant.* New York: Columbia University Press.

Higham, John. 1995. 2d ed. *Strangers in the Land.* New Brunswick, N.J.: Rutgers University Press.

Hochschild, Jennifer. 1995. *Facing Up to the American Dream.* Princeton, N.J.: Princeton University Press.

Hollifield, James. 1992. *Immigrants, Markets, and States.* Cambridge, Mass.: Harvard University Press.

Hoxie, Frederick E. 1989. *A Final Promise: The Campaign to Assimilate the Indians, 1880–1920.* New York: Cambridge University Press.

Ignatiev, Noel. 1995. *How the Irish Became White.* New York: Routledge.

Jacobson, Matthew F. 1998. *Whiteness of a Different Color.* Cambridge, Mass.: Harvard University Press.

James, Winston. 1997. *Holding Aloft the Banner of Ethiopia.* London: Verso.

Kallen, Horace. 1915. "Democracy Versus the Melting-Pot." Part 2. *Nation,* February 25.

Kelley, Robin R. D. 1994. *Race Rebels.* New York: Free Press.

King, Desmond. 1995. *Separate and Unequal: Black Americans and the U.S. Federal Government.* New York: Oxford University Press.

———. 1999a. *In the Name of Liberalism: Illiberal Social Policy in the U.S.A. and Britain.* New York: Oxford University Press.

———. 1999b. "The Racial Bureaucracy: African Americans and the Federal Government in the Era of Segregated Race Relations." *Governance* 12: 345–77.

———. 2000a. "Liberal and Illiberal Immigration Policy: A Comparison of Early British (1905) and U.S. (1924) Legislation." *Totalitarian Movements and Political Religions* 1: 78–96.

———. 2000b. *Making Americans: Immigration, Race, and the Origins of the Diverse Democracy.* Cambridge, Mass.: Harvard University Press.

Lieberman, Robert. 1998. *Shifting the Color Line.* Cambridge, Mass.: Harvard University Press.

Lipset, Seymour Martin. 1967. *The First New Nation.* New York: Anchor.

———. 1996. *American Exceptionalism.* New York: Norton.

Lodge, H. C. 1891. "The Restriction of Immigration." *North American Review* 152: 28–36.

McClain, Paula, and Joseph Stewart. 1998. *Can We All Get Along? Racial and Ethnic Minorities in America.* Boulder: Westview.

Morawska, Ewa T. 1985. *For Bread with Butter.* New York: Cambridge University Press.

National Archives. RG 12. "Americanization: Its Purpose and Process," by Fred C. Butler. Records of the Office of the Commissioner. Historical Files, 1870–1950. Folder, Americanization. Box 11. Entry 6.

———. RG 12. "Message to Newly Naturalized Citizens," by Woodrow Wilson. Records of the Office of the Commissioner. Historical Files, 1870–1950. Folder, Americanization. Box 11. Entry 6.

———. RG 174. Letter from James Davis to Simon Wolf, Union of American Hebrew Congregations. March 5, 1923. General Records, 1907–42. Box 165. Folder 163/127C.

———. RG 233. Files of the House Committee on Immigration. Box 458. File HR63A-H8.1.

———. RG 233. Letter from Frank Babbott to Albert Johnson. March 31, 1927. Files of the House Committee on Immigration. Box 341. Folder HR69A-F20.1.

Ngai, M. M. 1999. "The Architecture of Race in American Immigration Law: A Reexamination of the Immigration Act of 1924." *Journal of American History* 86: 67–92.

Nobles, Melissa. 2000. *Shades of Citizenship.* Stanford: Stanford University Press.

Olson, James S. 1979. *The Ethnic Dimension in American History.* New York: St. Martin's Press.

Patterson, Orlando. 1997. *The Ordeal of Integration.* Washington, D.C.: Civitas.

Pratt, Richard. 1973a. "The Advantages of Mingling Indians with Whites." In *Americanizing the American Indians,* edited by Francis Paul Prucha. Cambridge, Mass.: Harvard University Press.

———. 1973b. "Remarks on Indian Education." In *Americanizing the American Indians,* edited by Francis Paul Prucha. Cambridge, Mass.: Harvard University Press.

———. 1973c. "A Way Out." In *Americanizing the American Indians,* edited by Francis Paul Prucha. Cambridge, Mass.: Harvard University Press.

Prucha, Francis Paul. 1962. *American Indian Policy in the Formative Years.* Cambridge, Mass.: Harvard University Press.

———. 1979. *The Churches and the Indian Schools, 1888–1912.* Lincoln, Nebr.: University of Nebraska Press.

———. 1984. *The Great Father: The United States Government and the American Indians.* Vols. 1 and 2. Lincoln, Nebr.: University of Nebraska Press.

Rogin, Michael Paul. 1975. *Fathers and Children: Andrew Jackson and the Subjugation of the American Indian.* New York: Knopf.

Schlesinger, Arthur, Jr. 2000. "The Two Jones—and Korea." *Times Literary Supplement.* September 22: 14–15.

Smith, Rogers M. 1993. "Beyond Tocqueville, Myrdal, and Hartz: The Multiple Traditions in America." *American Political Science Review* 87: 549–66.

———. 1997. *Civic Ideals: Conflicting Visions of Citizenship in U.S. History.* New Haven: Yale University Press.

Stannard, David E. 1992. *American Holocaust.* New York: Oxford University Press.

Storey, Moorfield. 1921. Address to the annual conference of the National Association for the Advancement of Colored People. Detroit. NAACP I Papers. Box B-5. Folder, Annual Conference, Speeches, 1921. Washington, D.C.: Library of Congress.

Sugrue, Thomas J. 1996. *The Origins of the Urban Crisis.* Princeton, N.J.: Princeton University Press.

Talbot, William, ed. 1920. *Americanization.* New York: H. W. Wilson.

Tichenor, Daniel J. 1994. "The Politics of Immigration Reform in the United States." *Polity* 26: 333–62.

———. Forthcoming. *Regulating Community: Immigration Control, Nationhood, and American Political Development.*

U.S. House. 1922. Committee on Immigration and Naturalization. *Analysis of America's Modern Melting Pot: Hearings on H.R. 66.* 67th Cong., 3d sess. November 21.

———. 1928. Committee on Immigration and Naturalization. *Immigration from Countries of the Western Hemisphere: Hearings on H.R. 63.* 70th Cong., 1st sess. February 21.

U.S. Senate. 1877. *Report of the Joint Special Committee to Investigate Chinese Immigration.* 44th Cong., 2d sess. S. Rept. 689.

———. 1979. Committee on the Judiciary. *U.S. Immigration Law and Policy, 1952–1979.* 96th Cong., 1st sess.

Wilson, James. 1998. *The Earth Shall Weep: A History of Native America.* London: Picador.

— Part III —

Transnationalism and the Political Behavior of Immigrants

—— Chapter 5 ——

Immigrants, Transnationalism, and Ethnicization: A Comparison of This Great Wave and the Last

Ewa Morawska

A VIGOROUS ACADEMIC industry has developed in the past few years around the idea of a new transnationalism. It has attracted adherents from both sides of the Atlantic among political scientists, international-relations and legal scholars, sociologists, and anthropologists and has already produced a crop of specialists in "transnational cultural studies," gathered around journals like *Public Culture, Social Text,* and *Diaspora.* All agree that the mass migrations now crisscrossing the globe are an important, even central, agent in diffusing this new transnationalism.

Representatives of the different scholarly orientations have unavoidably assigned different meanings to the concept of transnationalism and apply it to diverse phenomena as they pursue their different academic agendas (Faist 2000; Joppke 1998b; Aleinikoff 1998; Kivisto 2001). In particular, North American and western European scholars have used somewhat different interpretations of the prefix "trans" that reflect the prevailing ideas and practices regarding civic and national membership (Brubaker 1989; Hammar 1990; Glazer 1996; Bade and Weiner 1997; Joppke 1998a).

The first interpretation treats transnationalism as a combination of civic-political memberships, economic involvements, social networks, and cultural identities that links people and institutions in two or more nation-states in diverse, multilayered patterns. These cross-border connections are mainly constructed by international migrants, who create "new transnational spaces" that deterritorialize or extend (rather than undermine) the nation-states they link. This interpretation has been most common among anthropologists, "transnational culturologists," and sociologists. The immigrant actors and transnational spaces they describe are most often anchored in North America (see, for example, Basch, Glick Schiller, and Blanc 1994; Glick Schiller 1996; Portes 1997; Jacobson 1996; Smith and Guarnizo 1998; Pattie 1994; Levitt 2001; Jacobson 1995).[1]

The second interpretation understands transnationalism as a shift beyond or, as it were, vertically over (rather than horizontally across) the accustomed territorial state-level memberships, state-bound national identities, and civic-political claims. This new realm inscribes more-encompassing involvements and identities resting on highest-order, universal humanity or human rights, suprastatal memberships and entitlements (those, for example, evident in the European Union), and panethnic or religious solidarities (for example, Hispanic in the United States or Muslim in western Europe). This interpretation focuses on the "decline of the nation-state" and how the supranational civic-political claims and entitlements of immigrants may undermine nation-states' abilities to control and regulate activities within their borders. This approach has been most common among political scientists, political sociologists, lawyers, and international relations specialists and primarily in western Europe, especially in relation to the emerging European Union (see, for example, Feldblum 1998; Soysal 1994; Kastoryano 1994; Miyoshi 1993; Sassen 1998; for critical discussions of this concept, see Mann 1993; Brubaker 1996; Joppke 1998b). Specialists in transnational culture have also focused on the postnational or "third-space" identities of contemporary globetrotters (for example, Kearney 1991, 1995; Rouse 1992; Holston and Appadurai 1996).[2]

In this essay I use the first interpretation because it informs most of the recent studies of present-day immigrants in the United States. These studies have focused primarily on the cross-border life spaces of immigrants themselves—their economic pursuits, social relations, support networks, and civic-national identities and involvements—and on ways these new "transnational spaces" allow immigrants both to leverage their political demands at two or more ends of the migration circuit and to use their cross-border bonds and activities for their own competitive advantage.

The claim in this literature that transnationalism is "new" rests on several incorrect assumptions about the last great wave of immigration to the United States, from the 1880s to 1914, and the historiography it generated, particularly regarding the supposed absence of transnational involvements among these turn-of-the-century immigrants. I take issue with four such claims of the new transnationalists regarding broader-context mechanisms of present-day international migrations, the character of the migration process, and immigrants' concerns and activities (see also the somewhat differently argued discussion of the old as against the new immigrant transnationalism in Foner 1997, 20).

First, the new transnationalists are mistaken in the view that the "multiple, circular, and return migrations" of present-day movements differ substantially from the "singular great journeys from one sedentary space to another" that characterized turn-of-the-century journeys to America (Lie 1995, 304; see also Jones 1992, 219, for a similar statement). They are also wrong in claiming that earlier immigrants, as one-way transplants, experienced "permanent ruptures" with home-country affairs, irrevocably dividing their past and present lives, whereas present-day shuttlers' "networks, activities, patterns of living, and ideologies . . . span their home and the host society" in new transnational spaces (Basch, Glick Schiller, and Blanc 1994, 3–4; see also Portes 1997, 812–13, for a similar proposition). Third, the view that the last wave of immigration lacked a transnational sphere in which immigrants engaged political leaders in the home countries and the host-country establishment in a "new form of nation-building" on a "deterritorialized" plane (Basch, Glick Schiller, and Blanc 1994, 46; see also Gutierrez 1997) is also unfounded.

Finally, the discussion has been informed by the perception that this new transnationalism has been generated by the globalization of the late twentieth century and, in particular, by the "dependent" incorporation of less-developed southeastern regions of the world into the capitalist world system dominated by its north-

western "core." This historically inaccurate perception is com-
pounded by the belief that the new transnational quality of immigrants' lives has been sustained by racist attitudes and discrimination against new nonwhite immigrants in receiver societies that
the earlier, white European arrivals were spared (Basch, Glick
Schiller, and Blanc 1994; Glick Schiller 1996; Portes and Zhou
1993; see also Lie 1995; Jones 1992).

In point of fact, though they differ in important respects, the
lifeworlds and diaspora politics of turn-of-the-century immigrants
share many of the supposedly novel features of present-day transnationalism. Some of these similarities have been generated by the
same macroscopic historical forces, others by similar microscopic
social mechanisms that, though embedded in different contexts,
have yielded similar results. Mass transatlantic migrations from
southern and eastern Europe were an integral part of the dependent incorporation of these regions into the Atlantic capitalist
world system "superpowered" by the most highly developed
countries in western Europe and the United States. Native-born
white residents of these countries viewed "Sclavish" (Slavic),
"wop" (Italian), "Hunkie" (Hungarian), and "Hebrew" immigrants
as racially distinct from and inferior to Nordic groups and openly
discriminated against them on these grounds. Late-nineteenth-
century advancements in transportation and communication tech-
nologies facilitated considerable return and circular movement between the sending and receiving countries, and intense economic
and social contacts between immigrants and their home villages
created complex transatlantic networks of communication and
assistance. Immigrants had significant involvement in their home-
country politics. Their U.S.-born offspring also had strong concerns, if transformed and recomposed in relation to American
politics, about the involvement of diasporic communities in home-
country politics.

The new transnationalists' assessment of the approach of immigration historians as focused on "questions of socioeconomic
and cultural assimilation"—understood as the progressive abandonment by earlier-wave immigrants of their home societies' ways
of life and their replacement with the host, American ones—is
also mistaken (Lie 1995, 303). Historians of immigration have long
since abandoned the straight-line assimilation model and have de-

veloped instead the much more sophisticated concept of ethnicization. They have shown how immigrants' lifestyles, identities, and commitments have evolved through the interplay between knowledgeable, purposeful, and creative social actors and their multilayered environments at both macro and micro levels, past and present, including translocal attachments such as home-country loyalties and connections, reference frameworks, and traditions (see, for example, Greene 1975; Sarna 1978; Vecoli 1973; Archdeacon 1983; Conzen et al. 1992; Hoerder 1996; Gabaccia 1994; see also Yinger 1994; Kazal 1995).[3] This approach views the specific forms, "contents," and pace of ethnicization as resulting from the mixing and recombining of home and host elements at work, in church, through politics, and in social practices. It views group boundaries and identities as inherently contingent on specific spatial and temporal circumstances and, therefore, as never fully determined.

The ways that students of contemporary migration use the concept of transnationalism and historians the concept of ethnicization to make sense of the prior wave of migration are theoretically related and can be partially "translated" into one another. The advocates of these two approaches can both gain from initiating a conversation, especially because, unlike immigration sociologists whose work the new transnationalists recognize and often treat as the adversary, immigration historians' studies have been amazingly absent from their field of perception.[4]

COMPARING TRANSNATIONALISM IN THE LAST TWO GREAT WAVES OF MIGRATION

This essay considers, first, the enduring features in the broader contexts of past and present international population movements and in the migrants' transnational connections and, next, the new, contemporary macro- and micro-level developments that make the pressures and opportunities of present-day immigrants' transnational lives distinct from those confronted by their turn-of-the-century predecessors. Because they constituted the majority—more than 70 percent—of the turn-of-the-past-century immigrants to America, southern and eastern Europeans are the focus of this historical comparison.[5]

During the long turn of the century (from 1870 to 1914), which witnessed the spread of modern rail and ship transportation, the rise of electronic communication, and Western capital investment in the belated industrialization of southern and eastern Europe, those regions were incorporated into the Atlantic world system, uprooting millions of local inhabitants from their rural lives and setting them in search of livelihoods in more highly developed western parts of the Continent and North America. The total volume of cross-border comings and goings of southern and eastern Europeans during that period is estimated at a staggering 35 million to 45 million (Ferenczi and Willcox 1929; Gould 1979, 1980; Berend and Ranki 1982; Bade 1992; Olsson 1996.)[6]

The 1910 census of the United States reports that more than 7 million immigrants from southern and eastern Europe had settled into tightly knit "foreign colonies" in the rapidly growing industrial cities of the United States. Almost all of them went to work as unskilled laborers in factories, steel mills, coal mines, and railroad and building construction (except for eastern European Jews, two-thirds of whom were employed as skilled manual workers) (Sheridan 1907; Balch 1969 [1910]; U.S. Immigration Commission 1911a, 1911b; Hutchinson 1956; Lieberson 1963; Lestschinsky 1955).

Contrary to the view of the new transnationalists, these immigrants' racial identification did not facilitate their adaptation to America. The meaning of "race" at that time differed from our present-day understanding in that it was more inclusive and ambiguous. During the early decades of the twentieth century, widely recognized "scholarly" racist theories provided dominant, native-born American public opinion with authority for the view that groups we define today as white were racially differentiated by physical features, skin "hues," and genetically determined mental capacities, with the "Nordic race" being superior to all others.

In this scheme, southern and eastern Europeans—both immigrants and their U.S.-born children—were perceived as racially, not just nationally or ethnically, distinct from and inferior to the dominant Anglo-Saxon and other northwestern European groups. Made of "germ plasm," "the Slavs are immune to certain kinds of dirt. They can stand what would kill a white man." Italians' "dark

complexion . . . resembles African more than Caucasian hues."
Jews or "furtive Yacoobs . . . snarl in weird yiddish" (Nugent 1992,
158; Lieberson 1980, 25; DeWind and Kasinitz 1997, 1100; Rieder
1985, 32). Such racist pronouncements about those "suspicious
aliens of inferior species" were commonly heard from respectable
public persons in respectable American institutions such as the
Congress, Harvard University, the American Census Bureau, and
the American Federation of Labor (Wyman 1993, 101; see also
Higham 1967, 1975; Gerber 1987; Jacobson 1995; Perlmann and
Waldinger 1997; on the historical changes in the understandings
of "race," see Rex 1998).

Because of these accepted perceptions, as immigration and
ethnic historians have amply documented, southern and eastern
European immigrants and their offspring had remained excluded
from closer social relations with the natives and had been openly
discriminated against at work. (By 1929, 75 to 80 percent of Slavic
and Italian Americans were still employed in lower-echelon manual jobs in the industrial labor market, while eastern European
Jews, who, by the interwar period, had moved into colleges and
white-collar jobs, were met with restrictive entry quotas and out-
spoken anti-Semitism on campuses and in offices.)

As late as the 1940s, referring to Americans of southern and
eastern European backgrounds, W. Lloyd Warner and Leo Srole,
the leading American sociologists, discussed the dim prospects for
assimilation among those darker-skin "mixtures of Caucasoid and
Mongoloid" blood (Warner and Srole 1945, 286). As Joel Perlmann
and Roger Waldinger have pointed out, only in subsequent decades did those "dark Caucasoids" became "white ethnics" (Perlmann and Waldinger 1997, 903; see also Novak 1972; on the earlier mainstream integration of the Irish, the Germans, and
southern and eastern Europeans' predecessors in America through
"becoming white," see Roediger 1991; Ignatiev 1995; Kazal 1998).

Prejudice and social exclusion by members of dominant groups
against southern and eastern Europeans at the beginning of the
twentieth century naturally sustained the latter's focus on themselves and their personal connections with the home country and
its public affairs. Several other factors also contributed to the forging and maintenance of these transnational liaisons. Most Slavic
and Italian migrants intended their transatlantic sojourns to be

temporary. Between 30 and 40 percent actually went back to their home countries, and between 15 and 30 percent, according to contemporary studies, made repeated visits.[7] (Eastern European Jews again took a contrasting path, with fewer than 10 percent going back.)[8]

Immigrants' letters home, their diaries, and the contemporaneous immigrant press confirm that they continued to think about returning home throughout the interwar period. Because many perceived their sojourns as temporary, most sustained close economic and social contacts with their families and friends in Europe (see Wyman 1993; Morawska 1989; Cerase 1971; Daniels 1990; Taylor 1971; Saloutos 1956; Baily and Ramella 1988; *Listy Emigrantów* 1973; *Pamiętniki Emigrantów* 1977; Cinel 1979; Puskaś 1982; Kantor 1990). Indeed, migrants remained part of their home communities across the ocean even after their sojourns significantly exceeded their expected duration (Merton 1982). William Thomas and Florian Znaniecki observed in 1918 that "the [village] community [does not] reconcile itself to the idea that the emigrant may never return, may ever cease to be a real member of his original group" (Thomas and Znaniecki 1918–20, 5: 11). Between 1900 and 1906 alone, American sojourners sent 5 million letters to Russia and Austria-Hungary. The back-and-forth flow of migrants and the density of this correspondence created an effective transnational system of communication, social control, household management, and travel and employment assistance that extended forward from the immigrants' native places in Europe into the United States and backward from America to their original homelands.

Letters and migrants returning from America to the European villages spread information about living and working conditions, wages (four to six times higher than at home), and possibilities for savings (up to 75 percent of the average laborer's pay). They helped to make travel arrangements for those willing to leave (Taylor 1971; Puskaś 1993; *Listy Emigrantów* 1973; *Pamiętniki Emigrantów* 1977; Baily and Ramella 1988; Rosoli 1993; Klemenćic 1993; Morawska 1989; Wyman 1993; Benkart 1975; Stolarik 1980). Kin or acquaintances who had already made the journey paid for the transatlantic travel of almost two-thirds of the southern and eastern European arrivals in America. The same people helped them to find lodging in densely populated "foreign colonies" in American cities and work among their own kind in American mills and factories.

From across the ocean, immigrants supervised their family affairs and managed their farms back home. "You went with piglets to Rzeszow and Niebylec," a Detroit immigrant wrote to his wife in Babica, in southeastern Poland, "but you did not sell them, did you? Because I know every movement in the village." In a follow-up letter, he commented on some unpleasant gossip he had heard about his wife: "Every movement in Babica I know, because I live here among the Babicans, and I hope it is not all true [what] I have been told about you" (quoted in Duda-Dziewierz 1938, 27). Jozefa Pawiak, from Budziwoj, wrote to her husband in America, "Now dear husband, I wrote you for advice, what to do with this house which is for sale. . . . Now people give for it 530 renski. It seems to me too expensive, but if you order, dear husband, I shall buy it for this money, because it would be good for us. But if you don't order, I won't buy" (quoted in Thomas and Znaniecki 1918–20, 2:300). A Polish emigrant in Webster, Massachusetts, wrote his mother in Golub, "Tell me how was the weather, the crops, and how big the harvest. . . . Buy potatoes and you may buy a pig. . . . But the thing [that] does not please me too much is that you bought yourself a cow and paid for her 29.5 rubles, which is a lot of money" (quoted in *Listy Emigrantów* 1973, 57).

Such long-distance management required American "emissaries" to pay continuous attention and, above all, provide the financial means of support expected—and demanded—by the migrants' families at home. "Homefolk passed judgement on their own in America . . . by the standard of the remittances: this one sends much and frequently, so he is diligent and thrifty; that one sends but little and irregularly so he is negligent and wasteful" (Molek 1979, 45). The enormous sums of money that flowed into southern and eastern Europe during the peak years of overseas migration provide empirical evidence that those emissaries fulfilled their social obligations as managers of the family farms and members of their village communities. Between 1900 and 1906, the immigrant colonies in America sent a staggering $69 million in money orders to Russia and Austria-Hungary. Local figures are perhaps even more impressive. In 1903, Hungarian emigrants from Veszprem County sent $290,000 to their villages. In 1910, the Slovak villages of Butka and Zdiara in the Zemplin region each received about $15,000, an average of about $200 for each emigrant household. Existing estimates indicate that these immigrant remittances made up between a quarter and more than a third of the sender regions' balances of payment (Balch 1969 [1910], 140, 183; Wyman 1993; Puskaś 1982, 77; Tajtak 1961, 242; see also Benkart 1975; Hanzlik 1975; Murdzek 1977; Morawska 1987, 1989).

The last persistent feature of transnationalism involves the civic-political sphere. The new transnationalists posit the novel rise of a transnational sphere of politics and nation-building that bridges the gap between sending and receiving societies through home-country involvements of immigrants in the United States and diaspora-centered initiatives of home nation-states. In fact, such bonds already existed, even thrived, at the turn of the twentieth century and endured through the interwar period.

By the late nineteenth century most of the home countries of southern and eastern European immigrants were still deeply immersed in building the encompassing national allegiance of their larger populations. Several of them, especially in eastern parts of the Continent, struggled to gain (or regain) state-national sovereignty. The overwhelming majority of turn-of-the-twentieth-century Slavic and Italian arrivals in the United States, more than 90 percent of whom were of rural backgrounds, came to this country with a group identity and a sense of belonging that extended no further than the "okolica" (local countryside). Paradoxically, only after they came to America, and began to create organized immigrant networks for assistance and self-expression and to establish group boundaries as they encountered an ethnically pluralistic and often hostile environment, did these immigrants develop translocal national identities with—to use a distinction of the Polish sociologist, Stanisław Ossowski—their old-country ideological "Vaterlands" or the imagined communities of the encompassing "patrias," as distinct from the "heimats," or the local homelands, as Italians, Poles, Ukrainians, Slovaks, Lithuanians, and so on (Ossowski 1967; see also Anderson 1983). (Jews, who brought with them their "mobile" spiritual community of "klal-Yisroel" that stretched back sixty centuries, were again the exception.) Lithuanians have referred to the United States as "the second birthplace of the[ir] nationality," and the same may be said of the others (quoted in Park 1922, 51; see also Conzen et al. 1992; Wyman 1993; Hoerder and Moch 1996; Harzig and Hoerder 1985; Jacobson 1995).

Among the variety of agencies that immigrants created between 1880 and 1920 to help them confront the new environment, the foreign-language press played an important role in defining ethnic-group boundaries and fostering solidarity by propagating identification with and commitment to the old-country fatherland. "[These newspapers] . . . devote more space to European affairs than to America," noted one contemporary observer. Between 1907 and 1912, editorials in the Chicago-based Polish daily *Zgoda* dealing with American issues made up about 20 percent of the total; the remainder mostly focused on the homeland.[9]

In addition to current news from the homeland, all these newspapers regularly carried sections devoted to their group national history and reprinted (and advertised) novels and poetry by heralds of nationalism and patriotism in their respective countries. So intense was this preoccupation with the home-country fatherland that the American (read German and Irish) church hierarchy and educational institutions, with whom Slavic and Italian immigrant leaders battled over language rights in parish and classroom, were commonly depicted as "extensions" of home-country enemies, such as, in the case of Poles referring to the situation in their then partitioned fatherland, "Prussian policemen," "Muscovite spies," and so on (quoted in Park 1922, 51–55; see also Wyman 1993; Jacobson 1995; Kantowicz 1975; Nelli 1979; Morawska 1993a).

The cultural and political elites of southern and eastern European sender societies were not indifferent to this nation-building process that occurred in immigrant communities across the ocean, either; in fact, they repeatedly intervened in it by trying to mobilize "their" emigrants' national loyalty and to engage them for home-country political purposes or to squash their political activities that were deemed subversive. Thus, for example, several organized groups in Italy, such as the Instituto di San Raffaele or the Instituto Coloniale, concerned with "keep[ing] alive in the hearts of Italians [in the United States] . . . the sentiment of nationality and affection for the mother country," sought (and obtained) government aid for Italian schools in America and supervised their programs by participating in "bilateral" committees composed of representatives from both sides of the ocean (quoted in Wyman 1993, 94). Poles organized home-based agencies to recruit qualified Polish language and history teachers, and contributed educational material toward the same purpose, in Polish American colonies. Lithuanian nationalists came to the United States to help "awaken a Lithuanian spirit among those who had emigrated" (quoted in Rubchak 1992, 120; see also Brożek 1977; Caro 1914; Saloutos 1956; Nelli 1979; Cinel 1991; Gilkey 1950; Kantowicz 1975).

The Hungarian political elite, concerned with the growing national consciousness and separatist aspirations among émigrés from non-Hungarian groups, especially Slovak and Rusyn, under the multiethnic Hungarian Monarchy, launched a systematic propaganda action in these immigrant communities to ensure that their members in America remained "good Hungarian citizens" and did not fall under the influence of "bad-intentioned leaders" who might "corrupt [them] from the national point of view" (quoted in Wyman 1993, 95). From the Russian consulates in American cities with large concentrations of Poles and Lithuanians—members of subordinate national minorities in the Russian empire—regular reports were sent to St. Petersburg about the national activities of those immigrants, with warnings about the importation of these and other (democratic) subversive ideas and practices into their hometowns by immigrant press sent from America and by returning "Amerikanci" migrants (Stolarik 1980; Puskaś 1982; Glettler 1980; Conzen et al. 1992).

Encouraged by or in opposition to the "transnational politics" of the home-country elites carried out in America, immigrants developed national identities as Slovaks, Hungarians, Lithuanians, and Poles and became organizational leaders or "silent" participants (Iwanska 1981) in mobilizations around important events or issues in the political affairs of their European fatherlands. The beginning of the twentieth century provided many such mobilizing issues, especially with regard to political discrimination against nationally "awakening" groups in eastern Europe, millions of whose members resided in the United States.

With help from their longer-established and better-connected

German coreligionists, eastern European Jews conducted massive protest demonstrations against the bloody pogrom of the Kishinev Jews in Russia in 1903 and successfully lobbied the American government to issue an official protest (Soltes 1969 [1924]; Morawska 1993a). The imprisonment in Hungary in 1907 of the Reverend Andrej Hlinka, leader of the nationalist Slovak People's Party, resulted in a series of "indignation meetings" in the Slovak immigrant communities across America to protest the enforced Magyarization policy of the Hungarian government. Members of these communities undertook a concerted action to buy and mail to Slovakia all American Slovak-language newspapers protesting this violence (Zecker 1998). World War I and the subsequent remaking of central Europe's political order, particularly the regaining of national sovereignty by Poland, Czechoslovakia, Latvia, and Lithuania, aided a remarkable "transnational mobilization" on their behalf in the eastern European communities in the United States (see Park 1922; Stolarik 1968; Wyman 1993; Vardy 1985; Kantowicz 1975; Reichman 1937).

By the end of World War I, an upsurge of American nativist hostility to immigrants' "foreignness" and "alien loyalties," combined with a vigorous Americanization campaign launched by the U.S. government and the media, effectively "demobilized" these home-country enthusiasms and redirected immigrants' attention to domestic, American issues and engagements (Higham 1967; Ueda 1997). The immigration restrictions of the 1920s also undercut the previously intense circulation of people and news across the Atlantic. These factors, as well as the lengthening sojourn of transatlantic migrants, growing intermarriage, the purchase of homes, the learning of (some) English, and the bearing of children in the new country, caused immigrants to develop local, American attachments and interests and to assume (not unproblematic) ethnicized identities as Hungarian Americans, Italian Americans, Lithuanian Americans, and Polish Americans (Vecoli 1973; Nelli 1979, 1984; Conzen et al. 1992; Bukowczyk 1984; Jones and Holli 1977; Morawska 1993a).

In the 1930s, the pluralist spirit of New Deal politics and the founding of the immigrant-friendly national labor organization, the Congress of Industrial Organizations, also encouraged foreign-born and, especially, second-generation Slavs and Italians to participate in American urban politics and industrial workers' unions (Bayor 1988; Bodnar 1985; Brody 1980; Fink 1977; Galenson 1960; Montgomery 1979; Kolko 1976; Slayton 1986; Glazer and Moynihan 1970). The "transnational" attachments of Hungarian, Italian, Polish, and Lithuanian Americans did not wane, however, but were reconfigured into new ethnic identities that became an increasingly important reference point for their activities within the American context. Letters and financial assistance continued to cross from the Amerikanci to their "dependents" in Europe. Material objects were regularly exchanged: old-country family members and friends solicited "modern" gadgets from the Amerikanci, who in turn sought articles of sentimental value, tokens of the heimat, to assuage their nostalgia. The observation of a mid-1930s study on relations between residents of the Polish village Babica and their American compatriots applies to other parts of eastern and southern Europe: "To the American relatives people wrote asking for money, better fabrics for clothing, ready-made clothing, watches, various small innovations for household use, etc. . . . *Z kraju* (from the home country), the immigrants asked for local honey, mushrooms from nearby woods, kasha, goose feathers for the pillows, pinewood pipes, embroidered shawls, religious medallions, pictures of patron saints, etc." (Duda-Dziewierz 1938, 50; for similar accounts see Gliwicówna 1937; *Pamiętniki Emigrantów* 1977; Puskaś 1991; Chałasiński 1934; Molek 1979; Wyman 1993; on the spread of techno-consumer culture in interwar America and on the eager participation therein of immigrant ethnics, see Fox and Lears 1983; Rosenzweig 1984; Heinze 1992).

Associations such as the Polish Mechanics' Association (headquartered in Toledo, Ohio), the local lodges of ethnic American labor organizations, mutual help cooperatives, the Latvian Mazpulks (a youth group based on the American 4-H movement), Slovak Sokols, the Polish National Catholic Church affiliates, and the dissident religious movement of Polish immigrants maintained transnational contacts with parallel branches in Europe throughout the interwar period. (On transnational connections between Italian and Slavic organizations in America and Europe during the interwar period, see Koht 1946; Wyman 1993; Cerase 1971; Nelli 1979; Saloutos 1956; Cinel 1991; Gołda 1976; Morawska 1993a).

By the 1930s, fewer than one-half of all southern and eastern

European immigrants had become naturalized (again except for Jews, the majority of whom took out citizenship papers). Reports of clashes between different immigrant groups over home-centered nationalist issues and resentments were common in American and foreign-language newspapers (see Wyman 1993; Bayor 1988; Glazer and Moynihan 1970; Diggins 1972; Nelli 1979; Kantowicz 1975). When compared with the earlier period, the immigrant press devoted considerably more attention to the American homeland and less to the immigrants' native countries in eastern and southern Europe. Nevertheless, topics related to native countries accounted for 35 to 40 percent of the editorials (but barely half that in the Jewish newspapers).[10] "English pages" became a regular feature in the Slavic and Italian press, but they printed old-country national histories beside stories from the American past. In 1929, for example, the Hungarian *Szabadsag* published a serial "History of the Magyar Nation" and a detailed account of the Battle of Gettysburg on the same page. In 1935, the Slovak *Jednota* ran the legend of Janosik, a national hero of the Tatra Mountains, next to a history of the American Civil War.

After World War II, American ethnic groups of eastern European origin remobilized a "transnational politics" on behalf of fatherlands that had fallen under Soviet rule. Although this phenomenon extends beyond the scope of this discussion, it provides an excellent illustration of the advantages of the ethnicization model and, especially, its emphasis on how immigrant ethnic identities are reconfigured as the context changes. In this case, an external player-sponsor, the host state, had the greatest impact, in contrast with the earlier period, when home-country political elites played the central role.

The U.S. government's Cold War with the Soviet Union led it to encourage eastern European ethnic leaders and organizations to pressure Communist governments about human rights issues and persecuted groups or individuals, to broadcast uncensored information and anti-Soviet propaganda into eastern Europe, and to solicit material help for dissident groups. When political unrest occurred in these countries—in Hungary in 1956, in Czechoslovakia in 1968, and in Poland in 1980 and 1981—the "silent" members of American ethnic communities joined in transnational politics on behalf of their old homelands (Shain 1991, 1994–95;

Nash 1989; Rubchak 1992; Safran 1991; Jacobson 1995; Misiunas 1991).

This recitation amply documents the multiple transatlantic networks that earlier-wave European immigrants and their U.S.-born children sustained with their old fatherlands and their simultaneous involvement in host- and home-country political domains. This is not to say, of course, that the present is an exact replica of the past. The contemporary situation has clearly been shaped by new developments in addition to enduring circumstances. At the macro level, these developments include the expansion and increasingly dense interconnectedness of the world economy dominated by the most highly developed northwestern core countries and regions and the penetration through the global media of cultural values and orientations of the world's northwestern core into semiperipheral southeastern societies, both greatly facilitated by the "compression of time and space" resulting from the transportation and communication revolutions. In the receiving American society, the restructuring of the economy has created an "underclass" of permanently unemployed or underemployed labor and a rapidly growing informal sector offering variable wages (usually substandard) and no employment security and unattached to the legal-institutional structures of the fiscal and welfare systems, on the one hand, and the highly skilled professional sector, on the other. In the sending societies, the educational and occupational differentiation of the population has increased the potential supply of international migrants into both the lower- and upper-level sectors of the American economy.

The politicization of international migration by the receiver states (through controls of the entry, duration of sojourn, and permissible pursuits of migrants) has created there a growing army of marginalized "illegal" migrants.[11] Simultaneously, however, and as a counterinfluence on these measures, in the American public discourse a renaissance of the ideology of cultural pluralism has occurred since the 1960s, this time combined with practical implementation in the legal system and public institutions. At the same time, civic-political movements and organizations of laws and declarations upholding universal human rights, civic entitlements of groups and individuals, social justice, and democratic representation and pluralism have proliferated across the globe and trickled down to the national level.

Finally, most of the present-day societies that send out the largest numbers of international migrants have already completed, or find themselves in an advanced stage of, the nation-building process. As a result, their laws regarding national membership and loyalty, their political discourse, and their cultural representations are considerably less exclusive and more accommodating of immigrants' plural national commitments and participation than were those during the turn-of-the-twentieth-century nation-building processes in southern and eastern Europe (Castells 1996; Freeman 1998; Koslovsky 1998; Cornelius, Martin, and Hollifield 1994; Teitelbaum and Weiner 1995; Rumbaut 1994; see also chapter 6 in this volume).

At the micro level, the new elements include the already noted socioeconomic diversification of contemporary travelers. Because a large share of present-day migrants originate from regions geographically close to the United States, return and circular movements are made easier and take place with greater intensity. (Noteworthy as it is, however, this difference is one of degree, not kind.) A new, increasingly common phenomenon among contemporary legal migrants, tacitly tolerated and often encouraged by sending and receiving nation-states alike, has been the rise of dual citizenship. American public opinion has become much more tolerant and cosmopolitan regarding foreign or "other" things and people, including immigrants and their lifestyles. Another new development related to intensified transnationalism of contemporary immigrants has been premigration Westernization—or, more precisely, Americanization—of potential travelers in their home countries under the impact of the global media and frequent contacts with émigré and returnee family and friends (Rumbaut 1997a, 1997b; Levitt 2001; Grasmuck and Pessar 1991; Gabaccia 1994; Lieberson and Waters 1988; also Alba and Nee 1997).

Shaped by both enduring and new elements, the transnationalism of present-day immigrants differs from that of their turn-of-the-twentieth-century predecessors in two major ways. First, it is much more variegated or plural in form and content, because contemporary immigrants themselves are much more diverse in their regional origins, racial identifications, gender, socioeconomic backgrounds, and cultural orientations. Within the host society, they also take on more-varied legal statuses, work in more-varied economic sectors, and adopt newer modes of acculturation into the dominant society. Both sending and receiving nation-states are more tolerant of such differences than they have been in the past.

Reflecting this diversity, contemporary transnationalism runs the gamut from intense rotation of nonwhite "indocumentados" in the informal economic sector—whereby immigrants' homes, work, incomes, friends, and entertainment actually (and symbolically) "happen" between two or more sides of states' borders—through ethnic configurations based on a variety of home-host compositions, including the postnational globetrotting of highly skilled professional employees of transnational corporations, nongovernmental organizations, and the like. Unfortunately, few scholars have investigated the gender effects on these transnational identities and involvements. Existing studies report both that women's national and ethnic identities tend to be more "trans," more "fluid and permeable," than those of men (Waters 1996) and that they are more sharply focused or delineated (Gabaccia 1994; see also Pessar and Graham forthcoming; Das Gupta 1997; Waters 1996 on gendered processes of assimilation and transnationalism). More research obviously needs to be done on this question, but it seems likely that transnationalisms are gendered in different ways depending on the specific features of the actors, environments, and interactions involved.

Second, whereas both home and host nation-states exerted exclusionary demands on earlier-wave immigrants regarding their national commitments and showed little tolerance or protection for diversity, contemporary successors have many more legitimate options in terms of identities and participation, ranging from global to transnational, national, local, and different combinations thereof. Although a "just pluralism" does not equally embrace all communities, especially those of the nonwhites who make up the bulk of contemporary immigrants, law and public discourse create institutional channels and a juridicopolitical climate in which groups and individuals can pursue their grievances or remain "other" without fear of opprobrium and accusations of disloyalty.

At the beginning of the twentieth century, the interest and involvement of eastern and southern Europeans in their home countries encountered pervasive nativist suspicion about foreigners' anti-Americanism and wide support for President Woodrow Wilson's renowned "infallible test" for proper hyphenated Americans (who might retain "ancient affections" but must center their "hearts and thoughts . . . nowhere but in the emotions and the purposes and the policies of the U.S.A.") (quoted in Arthur 1991, 144). At the same time, cultural elites of the stateless or recently politically unified nations of southern and eastern Europe and immigrant secular and religious leaders, newspapers, and parochial school texts promulgated the idea of a home-country patria as a primordial, morally imperative, and exclusive symbolic community.

In this situation, pre–World War II immigrants and especially their U.S.-born children, who were still viewed by the dominant groups as "suspicious aliens of inferior species," experienced their transnational identities and attachments as contradictory in a painful, "raw-on-the-inside" way—a predicament to cope with and resolve with minimum exposure to the accusation of national betrayal in their own minds and hearts and in the eyes of representatives of the two nation-states of which they felt themselves to be members. When asked why he did not become an American citizen, one Slovak in prewar Pittsburgh explained that he did not want to "forswear himself" (Morawska 1993b, 75). Members of the Slavic and Hungarian communities of a Pennsylvania steel town who did obtain American citizenship felt a pervasive sense of discomfort. Although differently "textured," this feeling also existed among their U.S.-born children, for whom their parents' old homelands were, to use Hans Kohut's apt distinction, experience-distant, whereas America was experience-near. In comparison with those "closet transnationalists," today immigrants can espouse their transnationalism publicly, including simultaneous involvement in the civic and political affairs of their home and host countries. This has become a matter-of-fact condition or choice for them, though one that is not without tensions. Contemporary immigrants do not experience their transnational identities as intensely problematic and uncomfortable, as did their predecessors, because of the legitimation of "le droit à la différence" in contemporary American society and the sense of civic-political entitlement resulting therefrom.

ON THE BENEFITS OF HISTORICAL COMPARISONS
(IN LIEU OF A CONCLUSION)

What lessons, then, can be drawn from this historical comparison? What historical considerations should inform the contemporary debate about transnationalism? What should historians draw from the latter work?

The "new transnationalists" could derive four epistemic gains from a more historical and comparative perspective on their subject. First and most general would be the recognition that history matters or, put differently, the acknowledgment that long-term historical processes have an impact on both sustaining and transforming immigrants' attitudes and behavioral patterns. The lasting presence of immigrant transnationalism and its sources are obvious, as is the need for a historical perspective on immigrants' acculturation to the host society. One of the premises of the "new transnationalism" is the weakness of assimilation among recent immigrants in the United States, who, it is argued, are reluctant to learn English and are uninterested in obtaining American citizenship and participating in American politics as concerned American citizens (rather than merely for ethnic or home-national purposes). The historical process of ethnicizing turn-of-the-twentieth-century immigrants took many decades. Although some present-day immigrants maintain more dense and intense home-country involvements and identities than those of some earlier-wave groups, the duration of their stay in the United States has not yet been long enough to determine conclusively whether transnationalism and dissimilation will persist. Existing data show steady increases in English proficiency (differently paced for different groups), gradual residential dispersion, and increasing naturalization among new immigrants from Latin America, the Caribbean, and Asia (see, for example, Rumbaut 1994; Rumbaut and Cornelius 1995; Rumbaut and Hohm 1997; also Alba and Nee 1997). This suggests progress toward, rather than a retreat from or stalling of, ethnicization.

Second, a historical-comparative treatment of immigrant transnationalism would contribute to a better understanding of how nation-states on both sides of the migration process enhance or suppress transnational identities and involvements for their own political, economic, or military goals, which may or may not coincide with purposes of the immigrant ethnic groups. In spite of the advancement of globalization and the rise of cross-national networks of people, ideas, and institutions, nation-states continue to have a strong "formatting" influence on group identities. As the foregoing discussion has shown, however, the strength, direction, and effectiveness of this influence has varied historically and should therefore be assessed in specific contexts rather than generalized in dichotomizing statements about declining or "fortress" nation-states.

Reciprocally, over shorter or, usually, more extended periods of time, identificational, civic-political, and economic transnational engagement of immigrant ethnic actors in their home and host countries affects the popular cultures and national self-perceptions, occupational distributions, and domestic and international politics of both sender and receiver societies. These reverse impacts must also be considered as historically contingent on the changing characteristics of the actors and their environments.

A historical-comparative approach would also strengthen the methodological base of the study of contemporary transnationalism. This is predicated on the theoretical kinship between the concept of ethnicization that informs historical research on immigrant lifestyles and activities and the concept of transnationalism that informs contemporary studies. The ethnicization model posits an "imperfect" reciprocity between structures and agency resulting both from the multiplicity and "polysemy" of actors' everyday practices and their ability to transpose sociocultural resources from old environments to new ones. This refocuses the discussion about the origins and persistence of ethnicity from the primordialist "being" or the instrumentalist-constructivist "doing" to the continuous becoming and "blending" of different components.

Michael Kearney describes the multifaceted, malleable identities of contemporary immigrants as "coalesc[ing] as *ethnicity*, as an ethnic consciousness, which is the supremely appropriate form for identity to take in the age of transnationalism" (Kearney 1991, 62, emphasis added). In their essay, "Transnationalism: A New Analytic Framework for Understanding Migration," Nina Glick Schiller, Linda Basch, and Cristina Blanc-Szanton invoke Ulf

Hannerz's concept of "creolization" or mixing as a useful analytic tool for the understanding of "the dynamic of migration and differentiation . . . as transmigrants live in several societies simultaneously [and] within their complex web of social relations draw upon and create fluid and multiple identities" (Glick Schiller, Basch, and Blanc-Szanton 1992, 11). To the extent that the concept of transnationalism embraces a multiplicity and flexibility of impacts and a dynamic processual treatment of social practices and cultural identities, it is cognate with the idea of ethnicization.

Historically minded students of immigration and ethnicity prefer to look for the "flexible and fluxible," yet time- and place-bounded circumstances, not completely fluid social processes and phenomena. This allows them to search for historical patterns of attitudes and behaviors. In explaining why things happened, social historians and historical sociologists of immigration and ethnicity use the configural method to reconstruct how they happened (Abrams 1982) by identifying and explaining particular combinations of the macro- and micro-level events, actions, and circumstances that contribute to the explication. For two decades, they have been perfecting the strategies of configurational analysis so that they can test general models, analyze causal regularities, and contextualize specific cases (see Skocpol 1984; Abbott 1992; Griffin 1992; Isaac 1997; Quadagno and Knapp 1992; Aminzade 1992; Ragin 1987). Advocates of transnationalism may find this work a useful corrective.

For those who might be interested in pursuing the configurational method of analysis, from the literature on transnational involvement of contemporary migrants and from similarly focused studies (or parts thereof) of immigration and ethnic historians I have compiled a list of conditions—global, in immigrants' home and host societies, in immigrants' communities, and regarding characteristics of the immigrant group itself—that seem to affect immigrants' transnationalism. If one considers multiple interactions among the contributing factors and reciprocal effects between those conditions and their outcomes complexified even further by the effects of class, racial and ethnic origin, gender, the duration of American sojourn, and so on and "sets in motion" this gyroscopic construction, "polyfractal" would probably be the best term to describe these relationships.

Such a "moving picture" configurational analysis cannot generate general conclusions about all transmigrants, past and present. It does, however, allow a researcher to rearrange, in kaleidoscope fashion, component elements to explain comparatively, for example, civic-political practices of the majority of recently surveyed Mexicans who reportedly take part in neither mainstream American political activities nor their own ethnic organizations or home-country public affairs and the minority actively involved in home-country and American ethnic politics (after Jusdanis 1996, 154). Then, should anybody be interested in a more encompassing project, he or she could compare the more American-bound political involvement of Brazilian immigrants from Governador Valaderes, for example, with the "equally distributed" commitments to home and host countries of Gujarati Indians.

The benefits of the transnationalism-ethnicization encounter are, of course, not one-sided. Practitioners of the ethnicization approach could readily benefit from integrating elements of the transnationalism paradigm. Given historians' recognition of immigrants' cross-statal connections and of the "glocal" quality of their life worlds, it would make sense to expand the analysis of ethnicization, which has traditionally focused exclusively on immigrant ethnic communities in their host-country environment, to consider as well similar effects in micro- and macro-level economies and social institutions, state- and local-level politics, and cultures of immigrants' home countries and to problematize the relationships of these processes. (The differentiating impact of class and gender considered over time would be, of course, of interest.) The transnational perspective directs the attention of students of ethnicization—which has been focused on migrants' binational networks, involvements, and identities stretched between home countries and immigrant communities—to the possibility of plural pan-ethnic and pan-national connections and commitments as immigrants and their offspring in the United States lived next to, worked with, struggled for in "panethnic" labor unions, befriended, or even married members of other immigrant groups. (Again, the effects of gender, generation, and the emerging class differences would be of great interest.) It also refocuses the customary interpretation of the involvement of immigrant-ethnics in

TABLE 5.1 **Factors Influencing Immigrant Transnationalism**

Sending Country	Receiving Country
Geographic proximity to receiving country	Transportation and communication technology
Transportation and communication technology	State-national model of civic-political integration*
Dynamics of economic development	Civic culture-practice of inclusion or exclusion of immigrants
Civic-political culture, especially exclusive vs. inclusive (civic) national membership and loyalty	State policy toward immigrants (undocumented status double citizenship and other transnational activities)
Government interest in cooperation (economic, political) with receiving country	State policy toward–relations with sending country
Government attitudes-behavior toward émigrés in receiving country	Structure and dynamics of the economy
Political system-political causes of emigration	Significance of race in culture and social stratification

Local Conditions in Immigrants' Place of Settlement in Receiving Country

External	Intragroup
Structure and dynamics of the economy	Group size and residential segregation from Native-born Americans
Degree and institutional embeddedness of ethnic-racial segregation-concentration	Proportions of foreign- and American-borns
Civic-political culture and practice regarding immigrants, particularly of different race	Group socioeconomic characteristics
	Sojourn-diasporic collective mentality
Openness-closure of local political system	Internal organization and leadership (transnational orientations and activities)
Native perceptions of–behavior toward immigrants, especially of different race	Group sense of disenfranchisement-rejection in host society
Degree of inter-group social exclusion-inclusion	

Characteristics of (Individual) Immigrants

Economic and cultural capital (education, occupational skills, access to technological resources, life goals and values)
Density of transnational social networks
Race
Gender
Socioeconomic position and prospects of mobility

TABLE 5.1 *Continued*

Characteristics of (Individual) Immigrants

Residential-work isolation from or contact with native-born Americans
Number of years spent in receiving country
Sojourn or permanent (im)migration
Presence-number of economically dependent family members in home country
  or real estate–other possessions
Intensity of ideological or emotional attachment to home country

Source: Author's compilation.

American politics as reflecting the increment in "host" components in the ethnicization melange by suggesting the consideration of such engagement as, precisely, ethnic-as-*trans*national.

Finally, by positing the possibility of new, *post*national involvements and identities—the variety of transnationalism identified but not discussed here has not (yet?) formed into discernible social patterns among ordinary immigrants, especially in North America, which lacks suprastatal structures comparable to those of the emergent European Union—the ethnicization-as-transnationalization approach would permit its practitioners to formulate and test research questions that, if supported by data, might require reworking of the concept of ethnicization as creolized combinations of existing, national options including the specification of circumstances in which it does not occur.

NOTES

1. Apparently under the influence of the American immigration specialists who advocate the new transnationalism, studies of polynational involvements of immigrant residents of western Europe have begun to appear in the last decade. See, for example, Haug 1998; Amiraux 1998; Cesari 1998; Pries 1997.
2. Although not explicitly identified with the new transnationalism paradigm, a third approach stresses how members of national-ethnic diasporas living outside of their native countries can be linked into a single, symbolic, deterritorialized national-ethnic community based on nearly exclusive identities and commitments. These are unlike the inclusive and plural connections identified in the first approach.

Studies of this sort have been authored by political scientists and international relations specialists as well as political and cultural sociologists; see, for example, Van der Laan 1975; Singh 1977; Iwanska 1981; Chaliand and Ternon 1983; Sheffer 1993; Shain 1991; Hourani and Shehadi 1992; Hovanissian 1992; see also Cohen 1997; Clifford 1998.

3. Other commonly used conceptualizations of ethnicity as instrumental-situational, negotiated, or for that matter, also the assimilation model, if properly "historicized"—can also be encompassed within the ethnicization framework. For a review of different conceptualizations of ethnicity and immigrants' adaptation to the host society, see Sollors 1996; Hutchinson and Smith 1996.

4. However, see Sollors 1996, Hutchinson and Smith 1996, and Gans 1997 for overviews of postassimilationist models developed by sociologists that the new transnationalists have neglected. These studies either emphasize or allow for sociocultural continuities between immigrants' home and host environments.

5. Although two among (non-Jewish) eastern European immigrant groups considered here—Hungarians and Lithuanians—are not Slavs, admittedly in a violation of cultural realities but in order to avoid repeated lengthy references to "Slavs, Lithuanians, and Hungarians," I subsume here these two groups under the general term "Slavic."

6. Because Russia was less subject to the forces incorporating eastern Europe into the Atlantic world system, we should separately record the emigration to Siberia and Central Asia of 5 million to 8 million persons of Russian peasantry during the same era (see Obolensky-Ossinsky 1929).

7. European sources report higher numbers, and American lower numbers, of such repeated journeys; my examination of early-twentieth-century ethnographic studies in eastern Europe indicates the proportion of repeaters among returned Amerikanci in the villages as ranging between 25 and 40 percent, whereas the 1908 U.S. Immigration Commission and port records for 1899 to 1906 report 12 to 17 percent (see Wyman 1993, 82–83).

8. A surprisingly high proportion of Jews, 20 percent or more, returned to eastern Europe between 1880 and 1900, according to Jonathan Sarna (1981).

9. On the domination of European affairs in the Slavic and Italian immigrant press, see Soltes 1969 [1924], 175–76. I estimated the *Zgoda* editorials from a content analysis of this newspaper at the Immigration History Research Center at the University of Minnesota.

10. Estimate derived from my content analysis of foreign-language

newspapers held at the Immigration History Research Center at the University of Minnesota.

11. Although to a much lesser degree and without the legal-institutional apparatus designed for this very purpose, the entry of immigrants into the United States has been actually controlled by the state even before the immigration restriction laws of the 1920s—through the federal supervision of the number of foreign ships entering U.S. ports and the authority to set the standards of "health" and refuse entry to disembarking immigrants who failed the prescribed tests (Higham 1967, 1975; Ueda 1997; Weil 1997; Kraut 1994).

REFERENCES

Abbott, Andrew. 1992. "From Causes to Events: Notes on Narrative Positivism." *Sociological Methods and Research* 20(4): 428–55.

Abrams, Philip. 1982. *Historical Sociology*. Ithaca, N.Y.: Cornell University Press.

Alba, Richard, and Victor Nee. 1997. "Rethinking Assimilation Theory for New Era of Immigration." *International Migration Review* 31(4): 826–74.

Aleinikoff, Alexander. 1998. "National and Postnational Membership in the United States." Paper presented to the European University Institute, Conference on Integrating Immigrants in Liberal States. Florence, Italy, May 8–9.

Aminzade, Ronald. 1992. "Historical Sociology and Time." *Sociological Methods and Research* 20(4): 456–80.

Amiraux, Valerie. 1998. "New Perspectives on Turkish Islam in Germany: The Transnationalism of Social Space." Paper presented to the European University Institute, Conference on Integrating Immigrants in Liberal States. Florence, Italy (May 8 and 9).

Anderson, Benedict. 1983. *Imagined Communities*. London: Verso.

Archdeacon, Thomas. 1983. *Becoming American: An Ethnic History*. New York: Free Press.

Arthur, Paul. 1991. "Diasporan Intervention in International Affairs: Irish America as a Case Study." *Diaspora* 1(2): 143–59.

Bade, Klaus. 1992. *Deutsche im Ausland, Fremde in Deutschland: Migration in Geschichte und Gegenwart*. Munchen: Verlag C. H. Beck.

Bade, Klaus, and Myron Weiner, eds. 1997. *Migration Past, Migration Future: Germany and the United States*. Providence, R.I.: Berghahn Books.

Baily, Samuel, and Franco Ramella, eds. 1988. *One Family, Two Worlds: An Italian Family's Correspondence Across the Atlantic, 1901–1922*. New Brunswick, N.J.: Transaction Books.

Balch, Emily. 1969. *Our Slavic Fellow Citizens*. 1910. Reprint, New York: Arno Press.

Basch, Linda, Nina Glick Schiller, and Cristina Szanton Blanc. 1994. *Nations Unbound: Transnational Projects, Postcolonial Predicaments, and Deterritorialized Nation-States*. Amsterdam: Gordon and Breach.

Bayor, Ronald. 1988. *Neighbors in Conflict: The Irish, Germans, Jews, and Italians in New York City, 1921–1941*. Urbana, Ill.: University of Illinois Press.

Benkart, Paula. 1975. "Religion, Family, and Continuity Among Hungarians Emigrating to American Cities." Ph.D. diss., Johns Hopkins University.

Berend, Ivan, and Gyorgi Ranki. 1982. *The European Periphery and Industrialization, 1780–1914*. New York: Columbia University Press.

Bodnar, John. 1985. *The Transplanted: A History of Immigrants in Urban America*. Bloomington, Ind.: Indiana University Press.

Brody, David. 1980. *Workers in Industrial America: Essays on the Twentieth-Century Struggle*. New York: Oxford University Press.

Brożek, Andrzej. 1977. *Polonia Amerykańska, 1854–1939*. Warsaw: PWN.

Brubaker, Rogers. 1989. *Immigration and the Politics of Citizenship in Europe and North America*. Washington, D.C.: German Marshall Fund and University Press of America.

———. 1996. *Nationalism Reframed*. New York: Cambridge University Press.

Bukowczyk, John. 1984. "The Transformation of Working-Class Ethnicity: Corporate Control, Americanization, and the Polish Immigrant Middle Class in Bayonne, New Jersey, 1915–1925." *Labor History* 25(1): 53–82.

Caro, Leopold. 1914. *Emigracja i polityka emigracyjna ze szczegolnym uwzglednieniem ziem polskich*. Poznan: Gebethner.

Castells, Manuel. 1996. *The Rise of the Network Society*. New York: Blackwell.

Cerase, Francesco. 1971. "From Italy to the United States and Back: Return Migrants, Conservative or Innovative?" Ph.D. diss., Columbia University.

Cesari, Jocelyne. 1998. "Transnational Networks Between Europe and Maghreb: A Risk for Nation-States?" Paper presented to the European University Institute, Conference on Integrating Immigrants in Liberal States. Florence, Italy (May 8 and 9).

Chałasiński, Jozef. 1934. "Wśród Robotników polskich w Ameryce." *Wiedza i Życie* 8–9: 651–70.

Chaliand, Gerard, and Yves Ternon. 1983. *The Armenians: From Genocide to Resistance*. London: Zed Books.

Cinel, Dino. 1979. "Conservative Adventurers: Italian Migrants in Italy and San Francisco." Ph.D. diss., Stanford University.

———. 1991. *The National Integration of Italian Return Migration, 1870–1929.* Cambridge, Mass.: Harvard University Press.

Clifford, James. 1998. "Diasporas." In *The Ethnicity Reader*, edited by Maria Montserrat Guibernau and John Rex. Oxford: Polity Press.

Cohen, Lizabeth. 1990. *Making a New Deal: Industrial Workers in Chicago, 1919–1930.* New York: Cambridge University Press.

Cohen, Robin. 1997. "Diasporas, the Nation-State, and Globalization." In *Global History and Migrations*, edited by Wang Gungwu. Boulder, Colo.: Westview Press.

Conzen, Kathleen, David Gerber Neils, Ewa Morawska, George Prozzetta, and Rudolph Vecoli. 1992. "The Invention of Ethnicity: A Perspective from the U.S.A." *Journal of American Ethnic History* 12(1): 3–41.

Cornelius, Wayne, Philip Martin, and James Hollifield, eds. 1994. *Controlling Immigration: A Global Perspective.* Stanford: Stanford University Press.

Daniels, Roger. 1990. *Coming to America: A History of Immigration and Ethnicity in American Life.* New York: HarperCollins.

Das Gupta, Kasturi. 1997. "Raising Bicultural Children." In *Asian Indian Immigrants,* edited by Brih Khare. Dubugue, Iowa: Kendall/Hunt.

DeWind, Josh, and Philip Kasinitz. 1997. "Everything Old Is New Again? Processes and Theories of Immigrant Incorporation." *International Migration Review* 31(4): 1096–1111.

Diggins, John. 1972. *Mussolini and Fascism: A View from America.* Princeton, N.J.: Princeton University Press.

Duda-Dziewierz, Krystyna. 1938. *Wieś malopolska a emigracja Amerykanśka.* Warsaw: Instytut Socjologii U.W.

Faist, Thomas. 2000. "Transnationalization in International Migration: Implications for the Study of Citizenship and Culture." *Ethnic and Racial Studies* 23(2): 189–222.

Feldblum, Miriam. 1998. "Reconfiguring Citizenship in Western Europe." In *Challenge to the Nation-State: Immigration in Western Europe and the United States,* edited by Christian Joppke. Oxford: Oxford University Press.

Ferenczi, Imre, and Walter Willcox. 1929. *International Migrations.* 2 vols. Geneva: International Labor Office.

Foner, Nancy. 2000. *From Ellis Island to JFK: New York's Two Great Waves of Immigration.* New York: Russell Sage Foundation.

———. 1997. What's New About Transnationalism? New York Immigrants Today and at the Turn of the Century. *Diaspora* 6(3): 355–75.

Fink, Gary, ed. 1977. *Labor Unions.* Westport, Conn.: Greenwood Press.

Fox, Richard Wightman, and Y. J. Jackson Lears, eds. 1983. *The Culture of Consumption*. New York: Pantheon Books.

Freeman, Gary. 1998. "The Decline of Sovereignty? Politics and Immigration Restriction in Liberal States." In *Challenge to the Nation-State: Immigration in Western Europe and the United States*, edited by Christian Joppke. Oxford: Oxford University Press.

Gabaccia, Donna. 1994. *From the Other Side: Women, Gender, and Immigrant Life in the United States, 1820–1990*. Bloomington, Ind.: Indiana University Press.

Galenson, Walter. 1960. *The CIO Challenge to the AFL*. New York: Russell and Russell.

Gans, Herbert. 1997. "Toward a Reconciliation of 'Assimilation' and 'Pluralism': The Interplay of Acculturation and Ethnic Retention." *International Migration Review* 31(4): 875–93.

Gerber, David, ed. 1987. *Anti-Semitism in American History*. Urbana, Ill.: University of Illinois Press.

Gilkey, George. 1950. "The Effects of Emigration on Italy, 1900 to 1923." Ph.D. diss., Northwestern University.

Glazer, Nathan. 1996. "Multiculturalism and American Exceptionalism." Paper presented to European University Institute, Conference on Multiculturalism, Minorities, and Citizenship. Florence, Italy (April 18 to 23).

Glazer, Nathan, and Patrick Moynihan. 1970. *Beyond the Melting Pot*. Cambridge, Mass.: MIT Press.

Glettler, Monika. 1980. *Pittsburgh, Wien, Budapest: Programm und Praxis der Nationalitatenpolitik bei Auswanderung der ungarischen Slowaken nach Amerika um 1900*. Wien: Böhlau.

Glick Schiller, Nina, Linda Basch, and Cristina Blanc-Szanton. 1992. "Transnationalism: A New Analytic Framework for Understanding Migration." *Annals of the New York Academy of Sciences* 645(July 6): 1–24.

———. 1996. "From Immigrant to Transmigrants: Theorizing Transnational Migration." *Anthropological Quarterly* 68(1): 48–63.

Gliwicówna, Maria. 1937. "Drogi Emigracji." *Przeglad Socjologiczny*, 4.

Golda, Barbara. 1974. "Konsekwencje emgracji w życiu Wiejskiej społecznosci plskiej." *Przeglad Polonijny* 2(1): 94–119.

Gould, J. D. 1979. "European Intercontinental Emigration, 1815–1914: Patterns and Causes." *Journal of European Economic History* 8: 593–681.

———. 1980. "European Intercontinental Emigration: The Role of 'Diffusion' and Feedback." *Journal of European Economic History* 9: 41–112.

Grasmuck, Sherri, and Patricia Pessar. 1991. *Between Two Islands: Dominican International Migration.* Berkeley: University of California Press.

Greene, Victor. 1975. *For God and Country: The Rise of Polish and Lithuanian Consciousness in America.* Madison, Wis.: State Historical Society of Wisconsin.

Griffin, Larry. 1992. "Temporality, Events, and Explanation in Historical Sociology." *Sociological Methods and Research* 20(4): 403–27.

Gutierez, David. 1997. "Transnationalism and Ethnic Politics in the United States: Reflections on Recent History." Paper presented to the Social Science Research Council, Conference on Immigrants, Civic Culture, and Modes of Political Incorporation. Santa Fe (May 2 to 4).

Hammar, Thomas. 1990. *Democracy and the Nation-State: Aliens, Denizens, and Citizens in a World of International Migration.* Aldershot, England: Avebury.

Hanzlik, Jan. 1975. "Zaciatky vystahovaleśtva ze Slovenska do USA a jeho priebeh az do roku 1918, jeho priśiny a nasledky." In *Zaciatky ceskej a slovensky emigracji do USA,* edited by Josef Polisensky. Bratislava, Czechoslovakia: Matica Slovenska.

Harzig, Christiane, and Dirk Hoerder, eds. 1985. *The Press of Labor Migrants in Europe and North America, 1880s–1930s.* Bremen, Germany: Bremen University Press.

Haug, Sonja. 1998. "Transnational Migrant Communities: The Case of the Italian Migrants in Germany." Paper presented to the European University Institute, Conference on Integrating Immigrants in Liberal States. Florence, Italy, May 8–9.

Heinze, Andrew. 1992. *Adapting to Abundance: Jewish Immigrants, Mass Consumption, and the Search for American Identity.* New York: Columbia University Press.

Higham, John. 1967. *Strangers in the Land: Patterns of American Nativism, 1860–1925.* New York: Atheneum.

———. 1975. *Send These to Me: Jews and Other Immigrants in Urban America.* New York: Atheneum.

Hoerder, Dirk. 1996. "From Migrants to Ethnics: Acculturation in a Societal Framework." In *European Migrants: Global and Local Perspectives,* edited by Dirk Hoerder and Leslie Moch. Boston: Northeastern University Press.

Hoerder, Dirk, and Leslie Moch, eds. 1996. *European Migrants: Global and Local Perspectives.* Boston: Northeastern University Press.

Holston, James, and Arjun Appadurai. 1996. "Cities and Citizenship." *Public Culture* 8(2): 187–204.

Hourani, Albert Habib, and Nadim Shehadi, eds. 1992. *The Lebanese in the World: A Century of Emigration.* London: I. B. Tauris for the Centre for Lebanese Studies.

Hovanissian, Mihran. 1992. *Le lien communautaire: Trois generations d'Armeniens.* Paris: Arman Colin.

Hutchinson, E. P. 1956. *Immigrants and Their Children, 1850–1950.* New York: John Wiley.

Hutchinson, John, and Anthony Smith, eds. 1996. *Ethnicity.* New York: Oxford University Press.

Ignatiev, Noel. 1995. *How the Irish Became White.* New York: Routledge.

Isaac, Larry. 1997. "Transforming Localities: Reflections on Time, Causality, and Narrative in Contemporary Historical Sociology." *Historical Methods* 30(1): 4–13.

Iwanska, Alicja. 1981. *Exiled Governments: Spanish and Polish.* Cambridge, Mass.: Schenkman Publishing.

Jacobson, David. 1996. *Rights Across Borders: Immigration and the Decline of Citizenship.* Baltimore: Johns Hopkins University Press.

Jacobson, Matthew Frye. 1995. *Special Sorrows: The Diasporic Imagination of Irish, Polish, and Jewish Immigrants in the United States.* Cambridge, Mass.: Harvard University Press.

Jones, Delmos. 1992. "Which Migrants? Temporary or Permanent?" *Annals of the New York Academy of Sciences* 645(July): 217–30.

Jones, Peter d'A., and Melvin Holli, eds. 1997. *Ethnic Frontier.* Grand Rapids, Mich.: William B. Eerdmans.

Joppke, Christian, ed. 1998a. *Challenge to the Nation-State: Immigration in Western Europe and the United States.* Oxford: Oxford University Press.

———. 1998b. "Immigration Challenges the Nation-State." In *Challenge to the Nation-State: Immigration in Western Europe and the United States,* edited by Christian Joppke. Oxford: Oxford University Press.

Jusdanis, Gregory. 1996. "Culture, Culture Everywhere: The Swell of Globalization Theory." *Diaspora* 5(1): 141–61.

Kantor, Ryszard. 1990. *Między Zaborowem a Chicago: kulturowe konsekwencje istnienia zbiorowości imigrantow z parafii zaborowskiej w Chicago i jej Kontaktów z Rodzinnymi wsiami.* Wrocław-Warsaw: Ossolineum.

Kantowicz, Edward. 1975. *Polish-American Politics in Chicago, 1888–1940.* Chicago: University of Chicago Press.

Kastoryano, Riva. 1994. "Mobilisations des migrants en Europe: Du national au transnational." *Revue Europeenne des Migrations Internationales* 10(1): 169–80.

Kazal, Russell. 1995. "Revisiting Assimilation: The Rise, Fall, and Reappraisal of a Concept in American Ethnic History." *American Historical Review* 100: 437–72.

———. 1998. "Becoming 'Old Stock': The Waning of German-American Identity in Philadelphia, 1900–1930." Ph.D. diss., University of Pennsylvania.

Kearney, Michael. 1991. "Borders and Boundaries of State and Self at the End of Empire." *Journal of Historical Sociology* 4(1): 52–73.

———. 1995. "The Local and the Global: The Anthropology of Globalization and Transnationalism." *Annual Review of Anthropology* 24(2): 547–65.

Kivisto, Peter. 2001. "Theorizing Transnational Immigration: A Critical Review of Current Efforts." *Ethnic and Racial Studies* 24(4): 549–77.

Klemenčic, Matjaz. 1993. "Images of America Among Slovene and Other Yugoslav Migrants." In *Distant Magnets: Expectations and Realities in the Immigrant Experience, 1840–1930,* edited by Dirk Hoerder and Horts Rossler. New York: Holmes and Meier.

Koht, Halvdan. 1946. *The American Spirit in Europe: A Survey of Transatlantic Influences.* Philadelphia: Temple University Press.

Kolko, Gabriel. 1976. "The American Working Class: The Immigrant Foundations." In *Main Currents in Modern American History,* edited by Gabriel Kolko. New York: Harper and Row.

Koslovsky, Rey. 1998. "European Migration Regimes: Established and Emergent." In *Challenge to the Nation-State: Immigration in Western Europe and the United States,* edited by Christian Joppke. Oxford: Oxford University Press.

Kraut, Alan. 1994. *Silent Travelers: Germs, Genes, and the "Immigrant Menace."* New York: Basic Books.

Lestschinsky, Jacob. 1955. "Economic and Social Development of American Jewry, Past and Present." *Jewish Encyclopaedic Handbook* 4: 82–93.

Levitt, Peggy. 2001. *The Transnational Villagers.* Berkeley: University of California Press.

Lie, John. 1995. "From International Migration to Transnational Diaspora." *Contemporary Sociology* 24(4): 303–6.

Lieberson, Stanley. 1963. *Ethnic Patterns in American Cities.* New York: Free Press.

———. 1980. *A Piece of the Pie: Blacks and White Immigrants Since 1880.* Berkeley: University of California Press.

Lieberson, Stanley, and Mary Waters. 1988. *From Many Strands: Ethnic and Racial Groups in Contemporary America.* New York: Russell Sage Foundation.

Listy Emigrantów, ed. 1973. *Witold Kula, Nina Assorodobraj-Kula, and Marcin Kula.* Warsaw: Spoldzielnia Ludowa.

Mann, Michael. 1993. "Nation-States in Europe and Other Continents: Diversifying, Developing, Not Dying." *Daedalus* 122(3): 115–40.

Merton, Robert. 1982. "Socially Expected Durations: A Temporal Component of Social Structure." Paper presented at the seventy-seventh annual meeting of the American Sociological Association. Boston (August 19 to 26).

Misiunas, Romuald. 1991. "Sovereignty Without Government: Baltic Diplomatic and Consular Representation, 1940–1990." In *Governments-in-Exile in Contemporary World Politics*, edited by Yossi Shain. New York: Routledge.

Miyoshi, Masao. 1993. "A Borderless World? From Colonialism to Transnationalism and the Decline of the Nation-State." *Critical Inquiry* 19(4): 726–51.

Molek, Ivan. 1979. *Slovene Immigrant History, 1900–1950: Autobiographical Sketches by Ivan Molek*, edited by Mary Molek. Dover, Del.: Lithocrafters.

Montgomery, David. 1979. *Workers' Control in America*. Cambridge, Mass.: Harvard University Press.

Morawska, Ewa. 1987. "Sociological Ambivalence: The Case of East European Peasant-Immigrant Workers in America, 1880s–1930s." *Qualitative Sociology* 10(3): 225–50.

———. 1989. "Labor Migrations of Poles in the Atlantic World-Economy, 1880–1914." *Comparative Studies in Society and History* 31(2): 237–72.

———. 1993a. "Changing Images of the Home Country in the Development of Ethnic Identity Among East European Immigrants, 1880s–1930s." *Yivo Annual of Jewish Social Science* 21: 273–341.

———. 1993b. "Une vision 'revisitée': les immigrés slaves vus par le *Pittsburgh Survey*." *Actes de la Recherche en Sciences Sociales* 99(September): 65–79.

———. 1996. "The Immigrants Pictured and Unpictured in the Pittsburgh Survey." In *Pittsburgh Surveyed: Social Science and Social Reform in the Early Twentieth Century*, edited by Maureen Greenwald and Margo Anderson. Pittsburgh: University of Pittsburgh Press.

Murdzek, Benjamin. 1977. *Emigration in Polish Social-Political Thought, 1870–1914*. New York: Columbia University Press.

Nash, Madeleine. 1989. "From Polonia with Love." *Time*, November 27, 22–23.

Nelli, Humbert. 1979. *Italians in Chicago*. New York: Oxford University Press.

———. 1984. *From Immigrants to Ethnics: The Italian Americans*. New York: Oxford University Press.

Novak, Michael. 1972. *The Rise of the Unmeltable Ethnics*. New York: Free Press.

Nugent, Walter. 1992. *Crossings: The Great Transatlantic Migrations, 1870–1914.* Bloomington, Ind.: Indiana University Press.

Obolensky-Ossinsky, Victor. 1929. "Migration from and Immigration to Russia." In *International Migrations,* edited by Imre Ferenczi and Walter Willcox. Geneva: International Labor Office.

Olsson, Lars. 1996. "Labor Migration as a Prelude to World War I." *International Migration Review* 30(4): 875–900.

Ossowski, Stanisław. 1967. "Analiza socjologiczna pojęcia ojczyzny." In *Z Zagadnień Psychologii Społecznej,* edited by Stanisław Ossowski. Warsaw: PWN.

Pamiętniki Emigrantów. 1977. Edited by Marek Drozdowski. 2 vols. Warsaw: Książka i Wiedza.

Park, Robert. 1922. *The Immigrant Press and Its Control.* New York: Harper and Brothers.

Pattie, Susan. 1994. "At Home in Diaspora: Armenians in America." *Diaspora* 3(2): 185–98.

Perlmann, Joel, and Roger Waldinger. 1997. "Second-Generation Decline? Children of Immigrants, Past and Present: A Reconsideration." *International Migration Review* 31(4): 893–923.

Pessar, Patricia and Pamela Graham. Forthcoming. "Dominican New Yorkers: Transnational Identities and Local Politics." In *New Immigrants in New York,* edited by Nancy Foner. New York: Columbia University Press.

Portes, Alejandro. 1997. "Immigration Theory for a New Century: Some Problems and Opportunities." *International Migration Review* 31(4): 799–825.

Portes, Alejandro, and Min Zhou. 1993. "The New Second Generation: Segmented Assimilation and Its Variants." *Annals of the American Academy of Political and Social Sciences* 530: 74–96.

Pries, Ludger, ed. 1997. *Transnationale Migration.* Baden-Baden, Germany: NOMOS Verlagsgesellschaft.

Puskaś, Julianna. 1982. *From Hungary to the United States, 1880–1914.* Budapest: Hungarian Academy of Science.

———. 1991. "Hungarian Overseas Migration: A Microanalysis." In *A Century of European Migrations, 1830 to 1930: Comparative Perspectives,* edited by Rudolph Vecoli. Urbana, Ill.: University of Illinois Press.

———. 1993. "Hungarian Images of America: The Siren's Song of Tinkling Dollars." In *Distant Magnets: Expectations and Realities in the Immigrant Experience, 1840–1930,* edited by Dirk Hoerder and Horst Rossler. New York: Holmes and Meier.

Quadagno, Jill, and Stanley Knapp. 1992. "Have Historical Sociologists

Forsaken Theory? Thoughts on the History/Theory Relationship." *Sociological Methods and Research* 20(4): 481–507.

Ragin, Charles. 1987. *The Comparative Method: Moving Beyond Qualitative and Quantitative Strategies.* Berkeley: University of California Press.

Reichman, John. 1937. "Czechoslovaks of Chicago: Contributions to a History of National Groups, with an Introduction on the Part of Czechoslovaks in the Development of Chicago." Chicago: Czechoslovak Historical Society of Illinois.

Rex, John. 1998. "Race and Ethnicity in Migration Research." Paper presented to the European University Institute, Forum on International Migrations. Florence, Italy (May 15).

Rieder, Jonathan. 1985. *Canarsie: The Jews and Italians of Brooklyn Against Liberalism.* Cambridge, Mass.: Harvard University Press.

Roediger, David. 1991. *The Wages of Whiteness: Race and the Making of the American Working Class.* New York: Verso.

Rosenzweig, Roy. 1984. *"Eight Hours for What We Will": Workers and Leisure in Worcester, Massachusetts, 1870–1930.* New York: Cambridge University Press.

Rosoli, Gianfausto. 1993. "From 'Promised Land' to 'Bitter Land': Italian Migrants and the Transformation of a Myth." In *Distant Magnets: Expectations and Realities in the Immigrant Experience, 1840–1930*, edited by Dirk Hoerder and Horst Rossler. New York: Holmes and Meier.

Rouse, Roger. 1992. "Making Sense of Settlement: Class Transformation, Cultural Struggle, and Transnationalism Among Mexican Migrants in the United States." *Annals of the New York Academy of Sciences* 645(July 6): 25–52.

Rubchak, Marian. 1992. "God Made Me a Lithuanian: Nationalist Ideology and the Constructions of a North American Diaspora." *Diaspora* 2(1): 117–29.

Rumbaut, Ruben. 1994. "Origins and Destinies: Immigration to the United States Since World War II." *Sociological Forum* 9(4): 583–621.

———. 1997a. "Assimilation and Its Discontents: Between Rhetoric and Reality." Working Paper 117. New York: Russell Sage Foundation.

———. 1997b. "Ties That Bind: Immigration and Immigrant Families in the United States." In *Immigration and the Family: Research and Policy on U.S. Immigrants*, edited by Alan Booth, Ann Crouter, and Nancy Landale. Mahwah, N.J.: Lawrence Erlbaum Associates.

Rumbaut, Ruben, and Wayne Cornelius, eds. 1995. *California's Immigrant Children.* San Diego: Center for U.S.-Mexican Studies.

Rumbaut, Ruben, and Steven Hohm, eds. 1997. "Immigration and Incorporation." *Sociological Perspectives* 40(3) (special issue).

Safran, William. 1991. "Diasporas in Modern Societies: Myths of Homeland and Return." *Diaspora* 1(1): 83–99.

Saloutos, Theodore. 1956. *They Remember America: The Story of the Repatriated Greek Americans.* Berkeley: University of California Press.

Sarna, Jonathan. 1978. "From Immigrants to Ethnics: Toward a New Theory of Ethnicization." *Ethnicity* 5(December): 73–78.

———. 1981. "The Myth of No Return: Jewish Return Migrations to Eastern Europe, 1891–1914." *American Jewish History* 71:256–69.

Sassen, Saskia. 1991. *The Global City: New York, London, Tokyo.* Princeton, N.J.: Princeton University Press.

———. 1998. "The De Facto Transnationalizing of Immigration Policy." In *Challenge to the Nation-State: Immigration in Western Europe and the United States,* edited by Christian Joppke. Oxford: Oxford University Press.

Shain, Yossi. 1994–95. "Ethnic Diasporas and U.S. Foreign Policy." *Political Science Quarterly* 5: 811–41.

———, ed. 1991. *Governments-in-Exile in Contemporary World Politics.* New York: Routledge.

Sheffer, Gabriel. 1993. "Ethnic Diasporas: A Threat to Their Hosts?" In *International Migration and Security,* edited by Myron Weiner. Boulder, Colo.: Westview Press.

Sheridan, Frank. 1907. "Italian, Slavic, and Hungarian Immigrant Laborers in the United States." *Bulletin of the Bureau of Labor* 72(September): 403–86.

Singh, Kumar. 1977. *A History of the Sikhs.* Vol. 1, *1839–1974.* Delhi: Oxford University Press.

Skocpol, Theda. 1984. "Emergent Agendas and Recurrent Strategies in Historical Sociology." In *Vision and Method in Historical Sociology,* edited by Theda Skocpol. New York: Cambridge University Press.

Slayton, Robert. 1986. *Back of the Yards: The Making of a Local Democracy.* Chicago: University of Chicago Press.

Smith, Michael, and Luis Guarnizo, eds. 1998. *Transnationalism from Below.* New Brunswick, N.J.: Transaction Books.

Sollors, Werner, ed. 1996. *Theories of Ethnicity.* New York: New York University Press.

Soltes, Mordechai. 1969 [1924]. *The Yiddish Press: An Americanizing Agency.* Reprint. New York: Columbia University Press [Arno Press].

Soysal, Yasemin Nuhoglu. 1994. *Limits of Citizenship: Migrants and Post-national Membership in Europe.* Chicago: University of Chicago Press.

Stolarik, Mark. 1968. "The Role of American Slovaks in the Creation of Czecho-Slovakia." *Slovak Studies* 8: 7–84.

———. 1980. *Slovak Migration from Europe to North America, 1870–1917.* Cleveland, Ohio: Cleveland Historical Society.

Tajtak, Ladislas. 1961. "Vychodoslovenske vystahovalectvo do prvej svetovej vojny." *Nove Obzory* 3: 221–47.

Taylor, Charles. 1971. *The Distant Magnet: European Emigration to the U.S.A.* New York: Harper Torchbooks.

Teitelbaum, Michael, and Myron Weiner. 1995. *Threatened Peoples, Threatened Borders: World Migration and U.S. Policy.* New York: Columbia University Press.

Thomas, William, and Florian Znaniecki. 1918–1920. *The Polish Peasant in Europe and America.* 5 vols. Boston: Richard Badger.

Ueda, Reed. 1997. "An Immigration Country of Assimilative Pluralism: Immigrant Reception and Absorption in American History." In *Migration Past, Migration Future: Germany and the United States,* edited by Klaus Bade and Myron Weiner. Providence, R.I.: Berghahn Books.

U.S. Immigration Commission. 1911a. *Reports of the Immigration Commission.* Part 2, *Immigrants in Industries.* 61st Cong., 2d sess. S. Doc. 633. Washington: Government Printing Office.

———. 1911b. *Reports of the Immigration Commission.* Part 4, *Immigrants in Cities.* 61st Cong., 2d sess. S. Doc. 338. Washington: Government Printing Office.

Van der Laan, Henry L. 1975. *The Lebanese Traders in Sierra Leone.* The Hague: Mouton for the Afrika-Studiecentrum.

Vardy, Steven Bela. 1985. *The Hungarian-Americans.* Boston: Twayne.

Vecoli, Rudolph. 1973. "European Americans: From Immigrants to Ethnics." In *The Reinterpretation of American History and Culture,* edited by William Cartwright and Richard Watson. Washington, D.C.: National Council for the Social Studies.

Warner, W. Lloyd, and Leo Srole. 1945. *The Social Systems of American Ethnic Groups.* Westport, Conn.: Greenwood Press.

Waters, Mary. 1996. "The Intersection of Gender, Race, and Ethnicity in Identity Development of Caribbean American Teens." In *Urban Girls: Resisting Stereotypes, Creating Identities,* edited by Bonnie J. Ross Leadbeater and Niobe Way. New York: New York University Press.

Weil, Patrick. 1997. "Races at the Gate: The Rise and Fall of Racial Distinctions in American Immigration Policy, 1898–1952." Paper presented to the European University Institute conference, Les Migrations dans une Perspective Historique (Migrations in Historical Perspective). Florence, Italy (October 24 and 25).

Wyman, Mark. 1993. *Round-Trip to America: The Immigrants Return to Europe, 1880–1930.* Ithaca: Cornell University Press.

Yinger, Milton. 1994. *Ethnicity.* Albany: State University of New York Press.

Zecker, Robert. 1998. "'All Our Own Kind': The Creation of a Slovak-American Community in Philadelphia, 1890–1945." Ph.D. diss., University of Pennsylvania.

—— Chapter 6 ——

On the Political Participation of Transnational Migrants: Old Practices and New Trends

Luis Eduardo Guarnizo

A LARGE NUMBER of immigrants in the United States can now legally hold citizenship in more than one country simultaneously. How has this dual membership affected their political incorporation in the United States? A comprehensive answer to such a broad question cannot be provided here, but some preliminary conclusions can be drawn by comparing contemporary transnational political practices—those evident from the 1960s through the end of the twentieth century—with the experiences of European migrants around the turn of the twentieth century—the period from 1880 until the 1920s. This chapter presents a theoretical framework for analyzing contemporary migrants' transnational practices and contextualizes the debate about its alleged novelty, using the cases of contemporary Dominican and Colombian migrants in New York City and Salvadoran migrants in Los Angeles (see Glick Schiller 1999).[1]

Many political activities undertaken by these groups indeed resemble those of past groups. The scale, meanings, and effects of these activities are significantly different from those of earlier groups, however, because both global and local contexts have changed substantially and because the social and national composition of the immigrant population has shifted. Both periods witnessed high levels of immigration and strong anti-immigrant hostility, but that hostility is today expressed against people coming from Latin America, the Caribbean, and Asia who include not only poor, illiterate peasants (the bulk of turn-of-the-century European immigrants) but also highly skilled urbanites, professionals, entrepreneurs, and laborers. Recent immigrants face political and labor market conditions markedly different from those encountered by their forerunners. Increasing economic and political global interdependence, the growing value of immigrants' remittances to their home countries, and pressure from emergent migrant elites are also forcing states of origin to formally facilitate and encourage migrants' transnational engagement.

Participation in more than one nation-state is a chief characteristic of contemporary transnational practices. Unlike the early-twentieth-century immigrants, contemporary immigrants do not forsake political incorporation into U.S. society when they engage in transnational political practices. Indeed, migrants can now be formally incorporated both "here" and "there" through privileges opened up by dual citizenship and the reach into the United States of government programs, political parties, and candidates for political office from their countries of origin. In fact, countries that send large numbers of migrants to the United States, such as Colombia, the Dominican Republic, El Salvador, Ecuador, and Mexico, are encouraging migrants to naturalize and become politically active in the United States in order to defend themselves against the anti-immigration storm. Simultaneously, these countries see their nationals living abroad as loyal supporters of their original homelands. Dual citizens can be naturalized in the United States without losing their rights "back home," undermining the jingoist ideology, dominant in home countries until recently, that saw naturalization as a betrayal of the homeland of origin. Transnational grassroots connections, traditionally built from below, are now being systematically formalized from above by nation-states of origin. This "transnationalization from above" is much more extensive than it was a century ago, and it has more far-reaching implications.

Undoubtedly, this trend has been facilitated by increasing acceptance of cultural differentiation in the United States, which, though still strongly criticized in some circles, mainstream American society considers less objectionable than in the past. Indeed, cultural differentiation even enjoys some legal protection in the United States and internationally. This more or less inclusive environment contrasts with the turn of the past century, when "Americanization" (that is, imposed Anglo conformity) was the rule and officials often approved of discrimination against cultural and ethnic minorities.

PERSPECTIVES ON TRANSNATIONALISM

In the past decade, both social scientists and cultural studies scholars have rapidly embraced the concept of transnationalism. Its swift rise to prominence, however, has been accompanied by a mounting ambiguity. We therefore need to explore and refine transnationalism as a tool for analyzing phenomena that, though not entirely new, reached particular intensity and produced distinctive effects at the end of the twentieth century.

Until recently, cultural studies scholars occupied a preeminent position in the analysis of transnational practices and processes, giving the field a particular cultural bent (Appadurai 1990, 1996; Buell 1994; Clifford 1994; Bhabha 1990; Hannerz 1996). Lately, social scientists have presented alternative visions, often linked to the idea of transmigration (Portes, Guarnizo, and Landolt 1999; Guarnizo and Smith 1998; Goldring 1996; Portes 1996; Glick Schiller, Basch, and Blanc-Szanton 1992; Basch, Glick Schiller, and Szanton Blanc 1994; Glick Schiller, Basch, and Szanton Blanc 1995; M. P. Smith 1994; R. Smith 1994; Rouse 1992; Kearney 1991). Many social scientists have joined cultural studies not only in giving transnational practices a central theoretical importance but also in seeing them as expressions of a subversive popular resistance "from below." They depict cultural hybridity, multipositional identities, and border crossing by marginal "others" as successful efforts by ordinary people to resist and even escape domination "from above" by capital and state.[2]

Other social scientists present a contrasting interpretation of transnational activities linked to migration. According to the anthropologist Nina Glick Schiller (1999), rather than liberating people, transnational practices enable sending-country states to exert power beyond their traditional territorial jurisdiction. States of origin form such "deterritorialized states" to incorporate migrants into their national projects. Rather than escaping state control, these scholars believe, transnational political participation brings migrants under sending-state purview even when they are outside the national territory (see Glick Schiller and Fouron 1999; Glick Schiller, Basch, and Szanton Blanc 1995; Basch, Glick Schiller, and Szanton Blanc 1994). Other scholars have argued that the effects of transnational ties are contingent on historical conditions in the countries of origin and destination, as well as on the social composition and mode of incorporation of migrants abroad (Portes, Guarnizo, and Landolt 1999; Kyle 1999; Guarnizo and Smith 1998).

Critics of the first generation of transnational studies point out that there is nothing novel about migrants' transnational practices (see chapter 5, this volume; Waldinger 1998). To paraphrase Stuart Hall, we have been witnessing "another version of the historical amnesia characteristic of American culture—the tyranny of the New" (Grossberg 1996, 133). The second wave of studies of transnational political practices has steered away from a concern with their novelty, however, to a focus on how they have evolved over time. Some of these studies demonstrate that although transnational practices are not new, aspects of their current uses, reach, and impact *are* new, calling for new kinds of conceptualization and analysis (Portes, Guarnizo, and Landolt 1999; Guarnizo and Smith 1998; see also Glick Schiller 1999, for a historical analysis of the relationship between transmigration and the state). As I suggest in this essay, transnational practices have a new and different scale, scope, and thrust compared with those of the past, the global and local contexts in which they are embedded is quite different, and sending countries now seek to institutionalizing them in ways that did not happen before.

TRANSNATIONAL POLITICAL PARTICIPATION AMONG EARLIER IMMIGRANTS

The historical record shows that first-generation immigrants have long participated in the political, economic, and social life of more than one country. As one especially perceptive scholar has recently noted, "A careful reading of U.S. immigrant history reveals a wealth of home ties among numerous immigrant populations"

(Glick Schiller 1996, 4). Evidence can be found in recent historical works on pre-1920s European immigration, older conventional historical works, and a wide range of ethnographies on Mexican and Asian immigrants in the United States; but as Glick Schiller points out, only recently have scholars developed a transnational perspective on the migratory process. This oversight led contemporary scholars "to emphasize the novelty of what they were observing" (Glick Schiller 1996, 4–5; see also 1999).

As Glick Schiller (1996) reminds us, the political participation of earlier immigrants was not limited to their old country but also included the new locality where they resided. Commonly dubbed "ethnic politics," the local political practices of immigrants have been intimately linked to global processes. Migrants historically sought to influence many more aspects of U.S. domestic and foreign policymaking that just the realm of immigration legislation. They exerted this influence directly, through mobilization, as new voters and indirectly, through the wide range of inclusive, neutral, exclusive, or mixed reactions their presence elicited from mainstream society. The types of local and national political participation undertaken by these migrants has been as varied as their social and cultural origins. Although most nineteenth-century migrants supported the Democratic Party, a good proportion of them were strongly Republican. Their shared status as migrants, however, often led to coalitions that cut across ideological cleavages. Italians, Jews, Poles, Slavs, Germans, and the Irish, for example, cooperated in opposing Prohibition and the restriction of immigration (Duff 1967, 111).[3]

The voting behavior of immigrants and their offspring has had an enduring influence on partisan political development in the United States as well as on U.S. foreign policy.[4] As Thomas Bailey notes, "When wars, revolutions, and persecutions have convulsed the homeland, Irish-hyphen-Americans, German-hyphen-Americans, Polish-hyphen-Americans, Jewish-hyphen-Americans, and others have brought pressure on the Washington government to shape foreign policy interests" (Bailey 1958, 5).[5] Their efforts to influence foreign policy during World War I showed their commitment to their own "imagined communities" in Europe (see O'Grady 1967, introduction). Americans of German, Italian, and Irish descent registered a vigorous protest against President Woodrow Wilson's postwar foreign policy by voting Republican in the 1920 presidential election. As Wilson later acknowledged, his defeat owed in good part to the fact that "the three large racial [*sic*] groups, German, Irish, and Italian, had gone over to the Republican side" (cited in Duff 1967, 138). "Ethnic politics" had an essentially transnational character and was not simply an attempt to become "Americanized" at the expense of immigrants' ties and allegiance to their societies of origin.[6]

So what is different about current transnational practices? What are the theoretical and practical implications of such differences for national identity and citizenship? These questions can be tackled by looking at transnational political practices among Colombian, Dominican, and Salvadoran immigrants to the United States. My analysis in this essay is based on first-hand data, official statistics, and primary and secondary sources. Materials on Dominicans were gathered between 1989 and 1994 during three research projects carried out in New York and the three largest Dominican cities, Santo Domingo, Santiago, and San Francisco de Macorís.[7] Information about Colombian and Salvadoran migrants comes from two projects I recently concluded. One was a multiyear study conducted with Alejandro Portes comparing the economic, political, and sociocultural transnational ties connecting Colombian, Salvadoran, and Dominican migrants in the United States with their countries of origin. The second project focused on the political participation of Colombians in the New York metropolitan area. Some 120 informants were interviewed in the New York metropolitan area (Manhattan, Queens, and northern New Jersey), Los Angeles, and the Colombian cities of Bogotá, Cali, and Pereira between August 1996 and June 1997. A similar number of Salvadoran people were interviewed in Los Angeles and in San Salvador and San Miguel, El Salvador. Respondents included migrant leaders, local and national officials, politicians, nonmigrant civic leaders, and scholars.

THE ROOTS OF MIGRATION AND TRANSNATIONAL PRACTICES

Salvadoran, Dominican, and Colombian immigrants constitute the third-, fourth-, and fifth-largest Latin American groups in the current wave of migration, respectively (see table 6.1). They repre-

TABLE 6.1 **Characteristics of Immigrant Groups, by Country of Origin**

Characteristic	Dominican Republic	El Salvador	Colombia	All Latin Americans
Main group				
Rank as source of U.S. documented immigration	6	9	18	2
Rank as source of U.S. immigration, regardless of status	4	3	5	—
Size in 1990 (× 1,000)	367	459	281	7,842
Migrants as share of population of country of origin (percentage)	5.2	8.8	.9	—
Median age (years)	33.6	29.1	35.3	32.1
U.S. labor force participation (percentage)	63.6	76.2	73.7	69.7
Professional occupations (percentage of group)	10.5	5.8	16.4	10.2
High school graduates, 25 years and older (percentage of group)	33.8	28.1	51.0	26.9
College graduates, 25 years and older (percentage of group)	7.3	4.5	15.1	8.2
Per capita income (dollars)	9,326	8,397	13,538	10,173
Poverty rate (percentage)	30.5	25.1	15.4	25.7
Business participation (per 1,000)	26.7	29.6	43.5	31.0
Naturalization rate (percentage)	27.6	15.4	29.0	26.2

(Table continues on p. 220.)

TABLE 6.1 *Continued*

Characteristic	Dominican Republic	El Salvador	Colombia	All Latin Americans
Undocumented population in the United States (estimated)[a]	10.9	71.3	21.0	—
Arrivals since 1980 (percentage)	53.5	75.42	51.8	50.7
Sending country 1990 population ($\times$ 1,000,000)	7.1	5.2	32.3	—
Per capita gross national product in 1990 (dollars)	830	1,110	1,260	—
Manufacturing (as percentage of gross national product)	13	19	21	—
Foreign debt per capita (dollars)	620	410	534	—
Receiving society Most common destination	New York	Los Angeles	New York	—
Immigrants to most common destination (percentage)[b]	55.3	42.3	20.7	—
Immigrants to top three destinations (percentage)	71.0	66.2	62.7	—
Top destinations immigrant population (percentage)	19.6	7.9	2.0	—

Source: U.S. Bureau of the Census 1993a; U.S. Immigration and Naturalization Service 1994a; World Bank 1992; Instituto Nacional de Estadística, Geografía, e Informática 1992.
[a]Figures calculated based on group's total population as reported by the 1990 U.S. Census and on the INS's "Estimated Illegal Immigrant Population," as of October 1992, in U.S. Immigration and Naturalization Service 1994a, 183.
[b]Figures are annual averages for 1990 through 1994 for Dominicans and Colombians and 1993 for Salvadorans.

sent different migratory processes triggered by common global factors (such as U.S. geopolitical interests and global economic restructuring), peculiar national conditions (such as social crisis in Colombia, U.S.-backed civil strife in El Salvador, and protracted economic crisis in the Dominican Republic), and the distinctive "life history" of each group's migration chain (the consolidation of kinship and other social networks connecting would-be migrants to actual migrants). Nationals from these countries have lived in the United States since the early twentieth century, though until recently their numbers were small. Although they share certain cultural traits (the Spanish language, the predominance of Catholicism) and are classified under the common rubric "Latino" or "Hispanic," their countries of origin differ greatly along cultural, political, and economic dimensions, and their emigrants in the United States thus differ, as the data in table 6.1 show. Their average human capital appears to be quite low; but these groups are not as ill prepared to deal with U.S. society as were their turn-of-the-century counterparts, more than 90 percent of whom were poor, uneducated, rural people (Conzen et al. 1992). All three groups, even the predominantly rural Salvadorans, have much more knowledge about the United States before migration than did their predecessors. They get this knowledge not only from friends and relatives in the United States but also as a result of U.S. economic, political, and military intervention in their countries of origin as well as through U.S. media and entertainment industries (television, movies, fashion, and so forth). With a few exceptions, most of them come from urban settings, where U.S. influence is strong.

In terms of sociodemographic endowments, Colombian immigrants are, on average, closer to mainstream Americans than either Dominicans or Salvadorans. They are older (median 35.3 years of age), and they have higher levels of schooling and income and lower rates of poverty. The profile of Salvadorans, on the other hand, puts them closer to turn-of-the-century European immigrants: most come from rural areas; they have the lowest educational attainment and the lowest per capita income; they are the newest arrivals; and they have the highest proportion of undocumented people across the three groups. Although the Dominicans in the sample have a slightly higher per capita income than Salvadorans and the lowest rate of undocumented people, they have the highest level of poverty (30.5 percent). The naturalization rate, an indicator of "assimilation," is low among all three groups (15 to 29 percent) compared with non–Latin American immigrants (49 percent) (U.S. Bureau of the Census 1993a). Given their low naturalization rates, received wisdom would thus suggest that the rate of active local political incorporation on the part of these immigrants is low. However, empirical evidence does not fully support that conclusion.

The Dominican Republic is a small (7.1 million people), peripheral Caribbean country with a small, undiversified economy highly dependent on the United States. Dominican migrants to the United States are highly concentrated in New York City. The majority are unskilled wageworkers with little formal education, and they are more likely to be poor than other Latin American immigrants (see table 6.1), though most are originally from urban areas (Grasmuck and Pessar 1991, 1996). Dominicans do boast one of the highest rates of self-employment among recent immigrants; thousands of Dominican entrepreneurs have formed a dynamic ethnic economy (Guarnizo 1993; Portes and Guarnizo 1991). Their economic efforts yield an enormous amount of family remittances back to the Dominican Republic and are vital to the home-country economy. Family remittances (excluding migrants' business investments), which are the Dominican Republic's primary source of foreign exchange, are estimated to be $1.1 billion annually, or 10 percent of the country's gross domestic product (Dore et al. 1997). Social, cultural, economic, and political exchanges create a complex transnational social field that binds both sets of Dominicans together (Guarnizo 1994, 1997). Without ever leaving the United States, a Dominican can conduct a real estate or other economic transaction in the Dominican Republic, read a Dominican daily newspaper, watch Dominican television programs, or contribute to a favored political candidate. The Dominican diaspora has become a vital feature of Dominican society, and the Dominican state is seeking to embed this complex of relations in transnationalized state institutions.

Colombians started to arrive in significant numbers in New York and Los Angeles in the wake of World War II. They tended to be Colombian- and U.S.-trained professionals, especially medical doctors, dentists, and engineers; international bureaucrats who decided to stay at the end of their official missions; and some veterans of the Korean War. After the 1965 immigration reform, the number of working-class immigrants grew (Cardona et al. 1980). The proportion of semiskilled workers increased rapidly in the 1970s, while that of professionals dropped (Urrea-Giraldo 1982). Since the mid-1980s, as a result of the consolidation of social networks, the country's deepening political and economic crisis, and the expansion of the illicit drug trade, a wide variety of Colombians have sought to migrate to the United States. As have Dominicans, they have tended to settle in the New York metropolitan area. By 1990, two-fifths of the 379,000 people in the United States who were Colombian by birth or ancestry resided in New York (Urrea-Giraldo 1982). As with Dominicans, migration became a structural dimension of Colombian society, although the importance of this connection has not been as widely understood as in the Dominican Republic or El Salvador.

El Salvador is a small (5.2 million) and densely populated Central American country that has been highly dependent on U.S. economic and geopolitical interests. Migration from the country to the cities and from there to the United States has been a central aspect of the country's development. Migration generated by U.S. economic and geopolitical involvement in El Salvador was already noticeable early in the twentieth century (Mahler 1995; Hamilton and Chinchilla Stoltz 1991). At that time, some Salvadorans associated with the country's coffee oligarchy migrated to San Francisco, where U.S. coffee corporations with investments in El Salvador were based (Córdoba 1995). During the early 1960s, more Salvadorans migrated to the United States, this time including professionals, technocrats, diplomats, and wealthy investors. Well-to-do immigrants opened up new channels for migration of low-wage workers by importing Salvadoran domestic help (Repak 1995).

Above all, the twelve-year civil strife that razed the country between 1980 and 1992 set off a massive emigration to the United States, mostly from rural areas (Mahler 1995; Zolberg, Suhrke, and Aguayo 1989; Aguayo and Fagen 1988; Montes Mozo and Garcia Vasquez 1988). Eight of ten Salvadorans now in the United States arrived after 1980. By 1990, half of the Salvadoran immigrant population resided in the Los Angeles metropolitan area, where they were concentrated in low-wage jobs (Waldinger and Bozorgmehr

1996; Mahler 1995; Chinchilla, Hamilton, and Loucky 1993). Although the majority had left their country because of political violence, the U.S. government for the most part refused to recognize their claims to refugee status (Lopez, Popkin, and Tellez 1996).[8]

As with Colombia and the Dominican Republic, transnational migration has been a pivotal element of the Salvadoran social structure since the 1980s. Despite their precarious legal status and low income in the United States, Salvadoran migrants now contribute more than $1 billion each year to their native country, which constitutes its single most important source of foreign exchange (between 20 and 28 percent of the total; "Remesas fortalecen estabilidad cambiaria," *La Prensa Gráfica,* August 7, 1997, 19). These remittances have served as the basis for the country's postwar economic stability (personal interviews with officials of Banco Central de El Salvador, October 17, 1996).

THE CONTEXTS OF RECEPTION IN NEW YORK CITY AND LOS ANGELES

The states of New York and California currently have the largest number of immigrants, and the New York and Los Angeles metropolitan areas are the two largest destinations for new arrivals (U.S. Immigration and Naturalization Service 1994a; U.S. Bureau of the Census 1993b, 1993c). New York City has been the premier entry point for immigration for more than a century, though Los Angeles now seems to have pulled even, and indeed ahead (Waldinger 1996; Waldinger and Bozorgmehr 1996, 12–13). During the 1980s, the two metropolises underwent a huge change in the composition and distribution of their populations as a result of immigrant flows, along with the interrelated transformations in their local economies and labor markets (Waldinger 1996; Waldinger and Bozorgmehr 1996; Sassen 1991). Minority groups now form the majority in both New York and Los Angeles populations. Although the newest immigrants reside in central-city areas, Americans of European descent and better-off, older, non-European immigrant groups have increasingly forsaken the central cities for the suburbs. Greater Los Angeles and New York City, respectively, contain the largest and the second-largest concentrations of Latin

American immigrants in the country (U.S. Bureau of the Census 1991).[9] Recent studies suggest they are living in increasingly multiethnic but not racially segregated neighborhoods in both cities (Clark 1996; Alba et al. 1995; Horton 1995).[10]

Los Angeles and New York City have quite distinct political histories, which present different opportunities to their immigrant populations. Los Angeles's political culture developed in the late nineteenth century and was shaped by midwestern Protestant migrants "who hoped to devise an urban alternative to the 'old, corrupt' cities of the East and Midwest." Strong party organizations are virtually absent (Sonenshein 1993, 230). The far older New York has a strong tradition of white ethnic political "machines" (Mollenkopf 1991). Historically, minorities in both cities have favored Democrats. In Los Angeles, the Latino population and political leadership are overwhelmingly Mexican and Mexican American, whereas in New York they are predominantly Puerto Rican. Until the early 1960s, the minority residents of Los Angeles were for the most part excluded from local political power. Since then, African Americans have gained greater representation on the city council than their share of the population, which was only 13 percent in 1990. Latinos, by contrast, made up 37.8 percent of the population in 1990 and continued to be underrepresented in the city's government and power structure.[11] Latino political participation grew in the late 1980s, affecting African Americans' political position (Sonenshein 1993). Despite Mexican American political progress, Central Americans remain excluded. Their political marginality can be explained in part by their recent arrival, low levels of naturalization, and rampant anti-immigrant sentiments in Los Angeles, but the numeric dominance and emerging political salience of Mexicans and Mexican Americans has not helped Salvadorans in any way.

Despite New York City's liberal tradition, its political establishment has been "characterized by a conservative, primarily white, dominant electoral coalition [and] by a systematic underrepresentation of blacks and Latinos" (Mollenkopf 1991, 333; Mollenkopf 1990). Even after the first black mayor, David Dinkins, narrowly won office in 1989, he failed to institutionalize the interracial electoral coalition that had elected him. Paralleling political changes in Los Angeles, Republican Rudolph W. Giuliani broke the Democrats' long hold on City Hall in 1993. For more than 150 years, the city's political establishment has absorbed new European groups through political co-optation and succession. This process, however, "has stalled or failed for blacks and Hispanics" (Mollenkopf 1991, 336).

This situation may be changing. The electoral redistricting of the city, implemented under a mandate to increase representation among native and immigrant minorities, along with increasing naturalization among immigrants, may foster greater inclusion. The redistricting of 1991 created new seats in minority and immigrant neighborhoods that facilitated the election of minority and immigrant candidates. The pool of Latino voters has increased as their naturalization rates have skyrocketed, triggered by the anti-immigrant storm and the recent approval of dual citizenship rights in the Dominican Republic, Colombia, and Ecuador.

These changes evoke the turn-of-the-century experience that brought new immigrants to the forefront of New York politics, altering the city's exclusionary political context. Cognizant of this new electoral potential, Mayor Giuliani formally opposed and denounced anti-immigrant initiatives (many sponsored by members of his own party, especially in California), sponsoring naturalization and voter registration campaigns. These efforts may have helped Giuliani to become only the second Republican in sixty years to win a second term as the city's mayor (Isabel Butten, "Así votaron nuestros barrios: Realidad y fantasía del voto," *El Diario/La Prensa,* November 7, 1997, 4; Levitt 1997). Indeed, a preliminary analysis of the 1997 mayoral election indicates that Latino voters were the only ethnoracial group whose turnout increased that year, moving from 13 to 20 percent of the electorate and accounting for about a third of Giuliani's margin over the Democratic candidate (David Firestone, "Big Victory, but Gains for Mayor Are Modest," *New York Times,* November 6, 1997, B2).[12]

THE DOMINICAN CASE

Since the early 1980s, the Dominican Republic has been experiencing one of its worst and longest economic crises ever, from which it has only recently recovered. Once an exporter of basic commodities (sugar, tobacco, coffee, and cacao), the republic has become an exporter of services, labor, and products assembled in a growing export-processing-zone sector. Since the mid-nineteenth century, the country has been in a subaltern economic and political relation with the United States. This relation has produced lasting structural transformations and imbalances, which in part account for U.S.-bound Dominican migration (see Betances 1995; Grasmuck and Pessar 1991; Georges 1990).

Dominican Transnational Political Participation

From the turn of the century until the late 1970s, New York was a refuge for Dominican political leaders from every persuasion fleeing persecution at home. During Rafael Leonidas Trujillo's dictatorship (from 1930 to 1961), the city developed as a transnational theater for often violent Dominican political struggles (see Galíndez 1958, 140–42; Lozano 1985). Dominican migration dramatically increased after the dictator's assassination in 1961. Among the new emigrants were middle-class people fleeing the anti-oligarchical riots that followed 1961 and a significant number of political dissidents whom the new Dominican government deported to the United States with full support from the U.S. government (Grasmuck and Pessar 1991; Martin 1966, 99). Whereas these political exiles exerted a significant influence during the 1960s, today the bulk of the migrant population consists of people moving because of economic, social, and familial reasons rather than political ones.

By the late 1980s the politics of the Dominican community in New York were dominated by Dominican party competition, not informal political opposition to the regime. On the island, Dominican officials were more concerned to control migrants' growing monetary transfers to the republic than to perpetuate the repressive measures of earlier days. New York thus became a contested political territory that all Dominican political parties now seek to dominate. Mass demonstrations (both in support of and against the Dominican government) and popular celebrations of Dominican culture have become part of public life in multiethnic New York. Every Dominican political party has at least one office in the city, and candidates for high office in the Dominican Republic must campaign in New York's Dominican neighborhoods. An estimated 15 percent of the Dominican parties' fund-raising comes from New York (Graham 1997, 101). Dominican migrants also participate in the Dominican Republic's elections by influencing their relatives' voting preferences and, if they have the money and papers to travel at will, by returning to the island to vote in national and local elections themselves.

Dominican New Yorkers are participating more vigorously in transnational politics not only because of these factors but also because its emerging entrepreneurial elite is vying for power and recognition on the island. Throughout the 1980s, they pushed the Dominican Congress to approve dual citizenship so they could defend their transnational interests and gain formal power in both places. Their efforts found support among opposition parties that immigrants have historically favored, such as the Partido Revolucionario Dominicano (PRD), the Partido de la Liberación Dominicana (PLD), and more recently, the Partido de los Trabajadores Dominicanos (PTD) (Graham 1997). In August 1994, the Dominican Congress finally passed a constitutional reform bill giving full citizenship rights to Dominicans who opt for another citizenship. (For the process leading to this result, see Guarnizo 1998; Cambeira 1997; Espinal 1995; Ríos 1995.)[13]

The approval of dual citizenship revealed the complex power relationships between national and the transnational actors. The migrant population has a conflictual and multifaceted relationship to the ruling Dominican elites that oscillates between exclusion and inclusion. On the one hand, the traditional Dominican dominant elites and middle classes increasingly discriminate against, and seek to exclude, the migrant population, but they also actively attempt to incorporate them as economic actors.[14] Some Dominican writers openly attack transnational migrant practices, and migration more generally, as antinational and socially deleterious (Cury 1995a, 1995b), while the banking industry and private investors court the migrants in order to control their economic resources. Reflecting in part this tension, dual citizenship grants limited political rights; a dual citizen cannot be elected president or vice president of the country. The measure did formally change the meaning of Dominican citizenship, however, and extended both Dominican national identity and the reach of the Dominican state beyond the island's borders. The new constitution adds an essentializing jus sanguinis definition of national belonging to jus soli, which until now was the sole principle for determining membership in the nation (see article 11 of the Dominican Constitution, *Gaceta Oficial* 1994). This de jure principle of transterritorial lineage not only formally includes the expanding Dominican diaspora into the Dominican nation-state but also transterritorializes that state.[15] No matter where they are born, or what other citizenship they adopt, Dominicans remain citizens of the Dominican state.

The Dominican state and its dominant classes have dealt with migrants in a way that reflects their society's subordinate position relative to the United States and the uncertain consequences of transnationalism for interstate relations. Until recently, Santo Domingo had limited its relations with Washington on migration issues to controlling and regulating monetary transfers, informal trade, surreptitious emigration, and crime.[16] These agreements went unchallenged. Lately, however, a vocal immigrant leadership has successfully resisted similar proposals. News about negotiations to open an office of the New York Police Department in Santo Domingo to help fight drug-related crimes created an uproar among Dominican migrants and nonmigrant nationalists, who denounced the idea as an assault on the country's sovereignty. The president rushed to deny the existence of the initiative and shelved it. In the late 1990s, similar nationalist reactions from transnational migrants prevented Santo Domingo from signing an extradition agreement with the United States.

Dominican transnational political activism reached a peak in July 1996 when the PLD's candidate for the Dominican presidency, Leonel Fernández, who had lived in Washington Heights for a decade, won office with strong support from the migrant population in the United States. Fernández continued to hold his "green card" and planned to return to the Big Apple at the end of his administration (James Bennet, "Clinton, at Costa Rica Talks, Gives Pledge on Immigrants," *New York Times,* May 9, 1997, A6). Fernández's election marked a shift in the relationship between the Dominican state and Dominican nationals living abroad. His administration introduced significant reforms designed to incorporate the migrant population into the national project, and he actively promoted migrants' transnational political activism. In the 1998 Dominican elections, for example, he brokered a deal in which New York–based José Fernández (no relation to the president) was the PLD's congressional candidate from Santiago, a province in the Cibao region that is home to many Dominican migrants in New York. José Fernández became the first New York resident elected to the Dominican Congress.

After the U.S. Congress passed legislation aimed at depriving legal immigrants of public benefits, Leonel Fernández urged Dominicans who were eligible for U.S. citizenship to naturalize, reminding them that they would not lose their Dominican citizenship in the process. Becoming U.S. citizens, he emphasized, would give them "an opportunity to actively participate in politics." He asserted that this involvement would not impede but rather would increase migrants' concerns for Dominican interests (Ian Fisher, "Dominican President Takes Tour of Triumph," *New York Times,* October 5, 1996, 20). Thanks to strong migrant lobbying, in December 1997 the Dominican Congress adopted one of the most important reforms of the Fernández government, a national electoral law that allowed Dominicans residing abroad to vote in national elections starting in 2002 (Wilfredo Polanco, "Dominicana: Residentes en el extranjero podrán votar en elecciones," *El Diario/La Prensa,* December 18, 1997, 14). This constitutes another step in the institutionalization of the Dominican Republic as a transnational polity. This process gained momentum when the recently elected president, Hipólito Mejía, whose party has an impressive following among Dominican New Yorkers, promised to continue to promote it. Full political membership in the Dominican polity, in effect, neither diminishes nor precludes full political incorporation in New York City.

Dominican Political Participation in New York City

Dominicans started participating in New York City politics in the early 1980s. Like many immigrant groups before them, they began by taking part in elections to the school board in Washington Heights.[17] Several converging factors opened the door for them. First, the protracted economic crisis in the Dominican Republic made the dream of return less viable. This forced many Dominicans, especially business owners, to think of their presence in the city as more permanent and thus to deal with the precarious conditions in which most of the Dominican community lived. To gain a political voice in the city, Dominicans could build on their long grassroots organizing experience. They had formed a wide range of organizations, which became the seedbed for political action (Georges 1987, 1990; Sassen-Koob 1979). Young leaders who had arrived in the United States as small children and had been educated in New York had come to lead these organizations, and they now became involved in politics.

In 1986 and again in 1989, two of these young leaders, Angel Nuñez and Adriano Espaillat, ran unsuccessfully for the Democratic nomination to the city council against official candidates supported by the party organization. Finally in 1991, Guillermo Linares won the Democratic primary and was subsequently elected to the council from the newly drawn District 10 (Washington Heights), with full support from the county party organization. In November 1996, Adriano Espaillat won the Democratic nomination and was elected as a representative to the New York State Assembly (District 72, Washington Heights).

What explains such rapid political success? First, a reform of the city charter expanded the city council from thirty-five seats to fifty-one, and the new district lines were drawn to make possible a higher representation of minorities, as called for by local and federal court decisions and promoted by the Democratic leadership (see Mollenkopf 1991). A new district was created for the Dominican community in Washington Heights. The resulting primary campaign ended up being more a Dominican than an American event, one in which issues of Dominican identity and authenticity were central. Five candidates, four of whom had been born in the Dominican Republic, entered the primary in 1991 (Graham 1997, 108–15). Although Councilman Linares faced Dominican opponents in both the 1993 and 1997 primaries, he was reelected both times.

It would be misleading to conclude from this story that Dominicans have a high degree of political cohesion, however. An ideological cleavage between Guillermo Linares and Adriano Espaillat and their allies splits the top Dominican political leadership. Linares gained public office with the support of the Democratic Party establishment, which he won by working with them and "waiting for his turn." Espaillat, on the other hand, succeeded despite the initial opposition of the Democratic district leadership. Unlike Linares, he credits grassroots mobilization over personal arrangements with the political establishment. Espaillat is highly critical of the white ethnics who dominate the regular party clubs and professes a "stronger allegiance to my community than to the party" (personal interview with Adriano Espaillat, December 31, 1997, New York).[18] The Dominican business class in the city, the major Dominican political parties, and lately the Dominican government proper have strongly supported candidates from both camps, however. Despite these close political connections, the Dominican American politicians have all avoided any formal affiliation with Dominican parties.

Dominican political triumphs are celebrated throughout the transnational space. Just as the Dominican community in New York welcomed former president Fernández and recently elected Hipólito Mejía with all the honors as "our president," U.S. Dominican elected officials have been welcomed in the Dominican Republic like national heroes. Their political triumphs have helped promote the political empowerment of migrants back home, as the recent election of José Fernández illustrates. Simultaneously, the growing number of Dominican naturalized citizens (potential voters) and elected officials (potential political allies) in New York leads candidates for the city's mayoralty to do what Dominican politicians have done for decades: campaign overseas. In the 1997 mayoral campaign, both New York City's current mayor, Rudolph W. Giuliani, and his Democratic challenger visited the island to show their support for the community.[19] In short, a transnational political field of action has been constructed between New York and Dominican politics.

THE COLOMBIAN CASE

Colombia is a midsize country with an economy based on basic commodity production and the export of coffee, bananas, cut flowers, and light manufactured goods. The country has been highly dependent on the United States economically, militarily, and politically. Colombian migration worldwide reached significant levels in the past decade. According to the Ministry of Foreign Relations, some 3 million Colombians currently reside outside the country, mostly in the United States (see Guarnizo, Sánchez, and Roach 1999). Since the early 1980s, the export of illegal drugs has become an important source of foreign exchange and social disarray for the country. International drug trafficking has become virtually synonymous with Colombian identity and a major leitmotiv in the relations between Bogotá and Washington, D.C. In recent years, Washington has failed to certify the country as supporting the U.S.-sponsored war on drugs—a decision that could eventually carry economic sanctions. In early 2000, Washington passed a $1.3 billion military aid package to help the government eradicate coca cultivation in southern Colombia, the major source of financial support for the largest leftist guerrilla group in the country. Colombians living in New York have experienced acute stigmatization, which has hampered the group's struggle to improve its social standing. Colombian involvement in drug dealing, together with police pressure against it, have increased the levels of social fragmentation and generalized mistrust. Paradoxically, although this has weakened their social cohesion in the United States, it has strengthened Colombians' ties to their country of origin.

Colombian Transnational Political Participation

Historically, Colombian migrants have focused their political activities mainly on Colombia. The dominant Liberal and Conservative Parties, as well as opposition parties including guerrilla groups, all have representatives in the largest Colombian "colonias" in the United States—the greater New York metropolitan area, Miami, and Chicago. During the past thirty years, Jackson Heights, Queens, has emerged as a cardinal locale for Colombian transnational politics. Colombian presidential candidates from the both the Liberal and Conservative Parties make campaign visits and fund-raising efforts in the neighborhood. The local chapters of political parties mobilize their rank and file, organize political events, and honor visiting politicians.

Such activities do not necessarily encourage consensus or conformity. Like their compatriots back home, Colombians in New York City are divided by strong class, racial, and regional divisions and by their opinions about the current political situation in their country of origin.[20] Many unswervingly support the government, either out of political loyalty or in response to U.S. intervention in the country. Others, however, are steadfast critics and opponents of the regime. This political polarization has become more acute since the mid-1990s in the wake of accusations against former president Ernesto Samper, who held the office from 1994 to 1998, for receiving financial support for his campaign from the Cali drug cartel. By 2000, the major issue dividing Colombians has become the United States-sponsored Plan Colombia.

Since 1961, Colombians living abroad have been allowed to vote in Colombian presidential elections. Although the law was originally designed as a political weapon for elite refugees, middle- and working-class Colombian immigrants across the world now exercise this right.[21] Colombian national elections now fill the Colombian neighborhoods of New York City with nationalist symbols that connect them with "la patria." Ethnic and Colombia-based media intensely cover transnational political events and convey symbolic capital, social status, and, eventually, material resources on local political leaders. Nevertheless, Colombians' transnational political activism tends to be episodic and intermittent. Relatively few migrants vote in these elections, and the migrant vote has little impact on the outcome. Partisan apathy persists despite the fact that the migrant vote could, if mobilized, have a substantial electoral impact. A high official recently summed up the situation by noting that "the migrant vote, if fully exercised, can define any national election in Colombia" (personal interview, Bogotá, October 8, 1996). This is particularly true in light of the strikingly low rate of voter turnout prevalent in Colombia. It will be interesting to see if the Colombia para Todos (Colombia for everyone) program established by former president Ernesto Samper's government will change this situation (Samper Pizano 1996).

Other than voting in Colombian elections, the most important moment of transnational political action on the part of New York Colombians was the campaign to introduce dual citizenship. Migrant leaders created a task force to draft and submit a constitutional amendment to the National Constituent Assembly. This multiparty task force, which was formed by Liberal Party leaders in New York, even included representatives from some guerrilla groups (Sánchez 1996). Dual citizenship was approved in 1991. The Constituent Assembly also created a global extraterritorial electoral district to provide political representation in the national Congress for Colombians living abroad. In December 1997, the Colombian Congress granted Colombians residing abroad the right to vote for congressional candidates representing their native electoral districts in Colombia, giving migrants enhanced influence in their regions of origin.

Besides these constitutional reforms, the Colombian state is implementing new policies to address the needs of nationals living abroad. In 1996, as part of the president's Colombia para Todos program, the Ministry of Foreign Relations established the Programa para la Promoción de las Comunidades Colombianas en el Exterior (PPCCE, Program for the Promotion of Colombian Communities Abroad). The PPCCE's activities include upgrading the consular service, creating an outreach program to Colombian nationals living abroad, providing legal assistance for those incarcerated in foreign jails, promoting a renewed national pride, and surveying the needs of geographically dispersed immigrant populations. Recently, the Colombian Department of Planning launched a series of studies about the implications of recent changes in U.S. immigration laws for Colombians in the United States.[22] Andrés Pastrana's administration (from 1998 to 2002) has, for the most part, maintained these initiatives in order to gain immigrants' support for the passage of Plan Colombia, a United States-financed effort to combat the illegal drug trade in Colombia.

Together, these reforms and policies represent the institutionalization of a transnational political field in which Colombian single and dual citizens both participate in the national political process. This dynamic is fundamentally reconfiguring the state's relationship to the population both inside and outside the country, and it represents a major shift in the way mainstream Colombian society relates to the migrant population. Evidently, at least from the state's point of view, migrants are no longer merely living in "el exterior," they are also remaining integral members of the nation-state.

As might be expected in a highly fragmented population, there is considerable variation in the extent to which Colombians engage in transnational political practices. A select group of migrants who have "made it" in New York City dominate the community's politics.[23] This situation is reminiscent of the class, gender, and race relations prevalent in Colombia. The leaders of the Liberal and Conservative Parties in New York are mature, successful business owners, most of whom have been in the United States for a considerable length of time. They are light-skin mestizo men from the better-off regions of the country, such as Bogotá, the coffee region, and the departments of Antioquia and Valle del Cauca. Although women do participate, the leaders see them as valued supporters who should not occupy formal positions of leadership (see Guarnizo and Portes 2001).[24]

Colombian Participation in Local Politics in New York

Colombians have thus far had only a marginal involvement in local politics in New York, owing to their general wariness of politics, the social fragmentation of the group and its leadership, and the lack of strong organizations. There appears to be more variation in the political affiliations of those who do participate than among larger Latino groups in the city (see note 12; Falcón and Hanson-Sánchez 1996). This reflects the entrenched political, ideological, and class divisions among Latino groups, which seem to preclude political mobilization based on national identity— undoubtedly a significant drawback in a highly competitive political arena such as New York City, where coalitions are a sine qua non for political empowerment. The stigmatization of Colombians over the illicit drug trade has added to this marginalization. Indeed, the community seems to be characterized by generalized mistrust and lack of group solidarity. With the exception of major (often tragic) events that affect either the group in New York City or their country of origin, Colombian organizations avoid, rather than seek out, integration and mutual support (see Guarnizo, Sánchez, and Roach 1999; Peña Salas 1997; Sassen-Koob 1979).

Since the election of Ernesto Samper Pizano as president of Colombia in 1994, the Colombian consulate in New York has actively promoted naturalization and transnational political participation, a policy maintained by the current president, Andrés Pastrana. The consulate regularly calls on Colombian activists to participate in local and Colombian politics. It invites activists and aspiring political leaders to events on such issues as participation in the Colombian electoral process, lobbying for U.S. approval of the $1.3 billion Plan Colombia, and improvement of the condition of Colombians in New York City. Activities such as lobbying for or against Plan Colombia are highly significant for most Colombian New Yorkers and have affected the way Colombian political activists go about their business. Several activists who until recently proclaimed a pan-Latino political identity and avoided being identified as Colombian American have reversed this stance in order to maintain the support of their conationals.

Some political activists combine the promotion of local political participation with calls for participation in Colombian politics. That is, they have shifted from an almost exclusive focus on Colombia to a more inclusive, translocal orientation and from traditional rigid Colombian bipartisanship to a more fluid multiparty affiliation in the United States. The Colombian state has encouraged migrants to seek political empowerment in order to defend their own interests and those of their country of origin. The rapid increase in naturalization among Colombians since the approval of dual citizenship in Colombia in 1991 also facilitates their participation in local affairs (see Guarnizo and Sánchez 1998). Employment discrimination and anti-immigrant legislation in the United States have also prompted segments of the Colombian population in the United States to naturalize. In addition, worsening conditions in Colombia have made the prospect of definitive return less likely while also motivating many migrants to engage in the (peaceful or military) resolution of the conflict. The emergence of young politicians who were born in Colombia but completed their university education in the United States, and are thus comfortable with a bicultural politics, also contributes to this trend.

These emerging Colombian American politicians depart from the predictable Democratic affiliation of other Latinos in the city. Although active in non-Colombian communities, they retain links with Colombian organizations and are well known to the traditional Colombian leaders in the city. The small size and increasing dispersion of the Colombian population in the metropolitan area

have forced these activists to support Colombian political empowerment while simultaneously advocating a pan-Latino political
agenda. Although they have gained a political space through interethnic coalitions, few of them, ironically, have penetrated the
traditional Colombian organizations. Often, traditional leaders
have opposed emerging leaders' access by openly questioning
their Colombian "authenticity." If the new leaders succeed in
gaining control of the traditional organizations, it will enhance
their political legitimacy as leaders of the Colombian "community" and improve their ability to deliver votes. There is considerable speculation about potential Colombian candidates for city
council seats—speculation that goes hand in hand with negotiations among traditional leaders about whom to nominate for the
seat in the Colombian Congress to represent Colombians residing outside the country.

THE SALVADORAN CASE

The Salvadoran population in the United States is going through a
major transition resulting from the end of the civil war in that
country. During the 1980s, when the civil war in El Salvador was
under way, followers of the two sides residing in the United States
had high levels of cohesion and solidarity and clearly defined missions and agendas. With peace, this congruence has given way to
new forms of social and political fragmentation, which in turn are
reflected in weaker and often redundant community organizations. During the civil war, Salvadoran organizations in the United
States focused primarily on denouncing human rights abuses in El
Salvador and U.S. government support for the brutal Salvadoran
regime and on defending the rights of Salvadoran refugees. Sympathetic public opinion and solidarity movements in many parts
of the United States supported their activities. War was the driving
force behind a well-articulated network of highly effective advocacy and grassroots organizing. Ironically, peace spelled demise
for this network.

After the signing of the peace agreement between the Frente
Farabundo Martí para la Liberación Nacional (FMLN) and the Salvadoran government in 1992, long-buried political contradictions

resurfaced within and between Salvadoran organizations. New, independent, apolitical hometown associations also proliferated. This undermined the left's uncontested leadership role, enabling the maligned Salvadoran state and the political right to move slowly to center stage. Salvadorans from across the spectrum were being forced to reinvent institutions, redefine personal and political goals, and explore new alliances. Peace also brought a dramatic change in the density, scale, and scope of the transnational ties between Salvadorans in the United States and those at home, and the unsettled refugee population has been transformed into a settled immigrant population. New transnational relations tightly connect Salvadoran Angelenos with their home country, even as they seek to define their place in U.S. society.

Salvadoran Transnational Political Participation

The civil war in El Salvador taught Salvadorans many lessons. Although few Salvadoran organizations in the United States were openly partisan, all had latent political interests and affiliations. Salvadoran leaders wore many hats as they moved among different types of activities and organizations, from apolitical cultural activism to open political partisanship. The connection between politics and violence in El Salvador and the polarization of Salvadoran society, however, still makes most Salvadoran migrants wary of being associated with partisan politics. Just as drug trafficking has divided Colombians, political divisions over the war splintered Salvadorans. Most Salvadoran Angelenos react by saying "Yo no me meto en política" (I don't get involved in politics).

The official end of the war dramatically changed the political landscape of the Salvadoran community in Los Angeles. The peace accord ended a primary cause of polarization, making room for political ambiguity and causing disorientation within the left. The organizations that Salvadoran leaders had created, with the support of many U.S. citizens, to defend Salvadoran refugees—including CARECEN (formerly the Central American Refugee Center, renamed the Central American Resource Center in 1992) and El Rescate (the largest social service organization for Salvadorans in Los Angeles)—faced serious crises in leadership and were forced to redefine their missions and to restructure themselves.

The struggle by thousands of Salvadorans to regularize their status in the United States became the predominant challenge facing these organizations. A plethora of newly formed hometown associations (most of which belong to the umbrella organization COMUNIDADES [Comunidades Unificadas de Ayuda Directa a El Salvador]) has also changed the local political dynamics in Los Angeles and El Salvador. In fact, these nonpartisan organizations have become the main political vehicle for Salvadoran migrants.

The Salvadoran right has become increasingly predominant as a transnational political actor in Los Angeles. As the Salvadoran migrant community has become more important, so has the interest of the government of El Salvador (controlled by the right-wing Arena Party) in securing this population's economic and political loyalty and support. The government now actively reaches out to people it recently regarded as the enemy, displacing the organizations of the left in the process. During the 1980s, one informant explained, the consulate had little contact with the Salvadoran population in Los Angeles, and organizations like CARECEN and El Rescate acted as de facto "consulates" to represent the community and resolve day-to-day problems. Now, the official consulate, which has far more resources, has reclaimed these roles.

After 1992, CARECEN and El Rescate turned their attention to supporting the reconstruction of El Salvador and influencing the country's longer-term political and economic development. At the same time, they had to adjust to the changing circumstances of the Salvadoran population in Los Angeles, particularly its desire to stay in Los Angeles regardless, for many, of their precarious legal status. This situation prompted one long-time activist from one of the organizations to comment, "We're trying to develop two countries at once. People must think we're crazy."[25]

Before 1992, the FMLN maintained an active but clandestine presence in Los Angeles. Only in 1996, four years after the FMLN became an open political party in El Salvador, did former militants in Los Angeles organize the Comité del FMLN as an open political organization. In July 1996, the Comité was admitted as part of the FMLN proper. In the last local elections, several FMLN committees organized fund-raising drives to support their candidates, some of whom were "returned" migrants, for mayoral and city council seats in El Salvador.

The most notable grassroots transnational actors in Los Angeles are the seventy hometown associations that had been formed by migrants from across El Salvador by early 1997. In addition to representing almost every geographic region, the leaders and members of these associations come from diverse class and political backgrounds, though few upper-class people seem to belong to them. Although some cooperate closely with Arena mayors in El Salvador and with the consulate in Los Angeles, the majority deliberately avoid such relationships. Most associations are not openly partisan and protect their political autonomy, but they nonetheless have altered the power structure in their hometowns and can influence local politics through the choice of projects they support. Over the long haul, the degree to which they choose to cooperate with the Salvadoran government may determine their access to resources and power.

Salvadoran migrants care about the future of their communities in El Salvador and recognize the influence they can have from Los Angeles. In the Salvadoran elections of March 1997, members of hometown associations in Los Angeles went to El Salvador to contribute their time to campaigns, and some candidates came to Los Angeles to promote their causes. As a leader from Santa Elena said in addressing those who attended a fund-raising event, "The FMLN will only become stronger with the support of migrant committees like this one. I'd like to take you all down to Santa Elena to vote in the elections, but I can't, so it is our responsibility to organize ourselves up here."

The Salvadoran state is initiating high-level efforts to secure the loyalty of the Salvadoran population in the United States. Arena government officials have made unprecedented diplomatic gestures to establish relations with grassroots and community leaders; they have adopted a comprehensive plan for working with Salvadoran communities abroad; they are creating affiliated institutions like Casas de la Cultura and the Cámaras de Comercio; and the consulate has cultivated relations with Salvadorans in Los Angeles by providing immigration services, including helping them to register in the American Baptist Church's political asylum program in the United States. Many elected and appointed Arena officials, including the president, now regularly visit Salvadoran neighborhoods in Los Angeles.

The consulate is the crucial link in the state's strategy to strengthen its ties with the Salvadoran community in Los Angeles. As the consul put it in late 1996, "As officials of the government, our role is not to allow, under any circumstance, the rupture of the umbilical cord connecting the Salvadoran population and its country of origin." Currently, the FMLN is the only Salvadoran political party with an office and an open presence in Los Angeles. The front's representatives from El Salvador occasionally visit Los Angeles both formally and informally, but this type of contact is far less common than it was before the 1994 election. Nevertheless, both Arena and the FMLN are now seriously considering the pros and cons of granting home-country voting rights to Salvadorans living abroad.

Salvadoran Political Participation in Los Angeles

As their relationship with El Salvador has changed, Salvadoran immigrants have been learning the ropes of local politics in Los Angeles. Because of the recency of their arrival and the high proportion of undocumented people among their ranks, their formal political participation has, until recently, been almost nil. Evidently, they are single-mindedly focused on regularizing their immigration status in the United States. As is true with Colombians and Dominicans, however, the anti-immigrant storm has forced many Salvadorans in Los Angeles to become U.S. citizens. Their worsening living conditions and the Mexican American monopoly on Latino power politics have also prompted a new focus on U.S. and local politics. The most visible result has been the Organizacion Salvadorena Americana (OSA), whose premier objective is to promote the political participation of Salvadorans, first as informed voters and eventually as candidates. Building on a sense of national pride, the OSA also seeks to defend the interests of Salvadoran immigrants in general. Its leaders have already approached local and national U.S. politicians to let them know about the emerging Salvadoran electoral potential.

With the enactment of the 1996 Illegal Immigration Reform and Immigrant Responsibility Act, which called for the deportation of thousands of undocumented immigrants, left-leaning activists brokered a wide-ranging coalition within the Salvadoran population and reached out to other immigrant groups in the Los Angeles metropolitan area. The coalition, which included CARECEN, El Rescate, the Salvadoran consulate, the Casa de la Cultura, the Cámara de Comercio, and grassroots groups, organized demonstrations in the city and sent representatives to Washington. The grassroots organizations in COMUNIDADES have also approached Mexican American political leaders in search of support. However, these inquiries have been rebuffed because Salvadorans lack electoral capacity. As one Salvadoran leader put it, "These refusals have reminded us that we have to use our own political experience to defend ourselves here, as we've done in El Salvador. We can't count on anybody else but ourselves." In pursuing greater political influence in Los Angeles, Salvadorans can draw on many seasoned activists trained in the treacherous political environment of a civil war.

TRANSNATIONAL PRACTICES IN HISTORICAL PERSPECTIVE

Comparing immigration experiences at the turn of the twentieth century with those at the turn of the twenty-first helps clarify how contextual conditions, group composition, and circumstances of migration alter the meanings, reach, and implications of transnational political practices. Five main factors differentiate the historical experiences of European and Latin American immigrants. First, the United States now holds economic, political, and military hegemony in a postcolonial nation-state system permeated by global capitalism. Current migrants arrive from sovereign countries, with established nationalist ideologies and institutions. Most of the earlier wave of migrants either came from colonized territories (for example, Poles, the Irish) or countries in the midst of nation-state consolidation (for example, Italy) or were groups whose sense of identity did not go beyond their own locality (Conzen et al. 1992).[26] For Irish, Polish, and Magyar migrants, for example, migration "came to hold a special place in the political symbolism of the envisaged 'nation'" (Jacobson 1995, 13). In fact, migration was part and parcel of the continuing struggle for national liberation— a struggle that fueled their versions of transnational activism. To prevent migrants from realizing their liberationist ideals, some imperial states of origin in the past century sought to police their overseas populations (Wyman 1993).

In cases like Italy, on the other hand, the state's interests in transatlantic migration were driven by the significant economic and social benefits derived from migration and formed part of the state's efforts to consolidate a unified nation. Accordingly, Italy encouraged temporary migration, remittances, and the promotion of "Italianness" among its overseas population (Caroli 1976).[27] A contemporary politician said that the ultimate interest of the Italian state was "to preserve ever stronger the ties of the mother country with our emigrants in order to facilitate their return" (Caroli 1976, 13).[28] Until recently, Latin American and Caribbean countries maintained a similar stance of exclusive nationalism vis-à-vis their national populations overseas. For the last decade or so, however, these nations have been sponsoring a new type of extraterritorial nationalism among their emigrants, a nationalism that does not promote return to the home country but rather encourages them to become citizens of the receiving society in order to strengthen their position there, remit more money "home," consume national exports, and advocate their state of origin's interests in the United States.

The current global political economy has also resulted in an increased interdependence among nations, a fact that has invested migrants with additional power as potential advocates of their state of origin's interests vis-à-vis the global centers of power where migrants reside. Thus, in contrast with earlier states' practices encouraging return or coercive control, states of origin such as Colombia, the Dominican Republic, and El Salvador are now mostly interested in protecting their citizens abroad and facilitating and promoting their accommodation there (by granting dual citizenship and integrating migrants into the national project). In this way, these states help migrants achieve the most stable conditions possible, and in so doing they guarantee migrants' role as a reliable source of economic and political support for their "homeland."[29] The increased and increasing reach of the state thus also suggests its growing dependence on its overseas citizens.

A second difference separating contemporary conditions from those of the past involves the consolidation of a global governance regime, the universalization of human rights, and the approval of civil rights in the United States. Transnational economic, political, and military institutions (such as the World Bank, the International Monetary Fund, the World Trade Organization, the United Nations, transnational nongovernmental organizations, and transnational military alliances) have transformed the global governance system and enhanced the dominance of the most powerful nation-states, especially the United States. This system regulates and limits the actions of nation-states, especially regarding economic matters, including labor rights and the rights of ethnocultural minorities (see Drainville 1998; Soysal 1994). The universalization of the discourse of human rights also gives contemporary migrants recourse to potential rights that were unavailable to earlier migrants. Because human rights are based not on national membership but on personhood, they can theoretically limit the receiving nation-state's power to legislate against immigrants (see Jacobson 1996). Finally, civil rights legislation in the United States has given migrants legal tools to defend themselves against official and private exclusion and discrimination. The affirmation of these universal and national rights does not make migrants immune from exclusion, but, at a minimum, they provide a legal safety net not available to earlier immigrants.

A third area of difference involves the preexisting relationship between sending countries and the United States. Most of the earlier migrants came from areas and countries that had little contact with the United States, apart from migration itself. Today's migrants come from countries that have been heavily penetrated by the global economic and geopolitical reach of the United States, which has in fact stimulated the immigration in the first place. Most new arrivals know a good deal about the United States— information provided not because they have learned from their forerunners but because American media and interests are well established in the economic, cultural, and political lives of their countries.

Upon arrival, early-twentieth-century immigrants encountered an intolerant society that sought to impose cultural conformity and assimilation. A century of struggles has provided newer immigrants with a less exclusive context of reception, which, despite persistent nativism and xenophobia, definitely provides more room for non-Anglo cultures and far greater legal protection for multiculturalism. This new context is much more amenable to transnational political engagement. However, as the examples of New York City and Los Angeles illustrate, migrants still encounter many obstacles to participation in local politics.

A fourth dimension setting the two periods apart is an increase in the diversity of migrants' ethnic composition at the end of the twentieth century. Contemporary migrants come from many more places, and are far more socially and culturally heterogeneous, than their counterparts of a hundred years ago. At the turn of the past century, only two dozen countries sent a substantial number of people to the United States. Today, the Immigration and Naturalization Service reports more than one hundred countries of origin represented and more than three hundred languages spoken among American residents (U.S. Immigration and Naturalization Service 1994a; Portes and Rumbaut 1991). The majority of newcomers are not from Europe, which provided most of the earlier immigrants. Whereas most earlier European immigrants came from rural areas and small villages, most contemporary immigrants come from midsize cities and large metropolitan regions. Recent ethnographic and quantitative evidence shows that their social, cultural, and political outlooks result in different kinds of transnational practices than those espoused by migrants from rural areas (see Levitt 1999; Roberts, Frank, and Lozano-Asencio 1999; Guarnizo and Portes 2001). According to this evidence, urban migrants tend to have more schooling and to engage in political activity aimed at the national stage, whereas those coming from rural areas tend to focus on their villages of origin. In the aggregate, these differences become significant.

Finally, maintaining transnational ties requires far less time, money, and effort today. The world has been transformed by forces that have "compressed" space and time (Harvey 1989). Just as the steamship and the post office served previous waves of migrants, technological innovations (fax, videos, satellite television, telephone, Internet, electronic money transfers, and so forth) have gone many steps toward allowing migrants to participate in the life of more than one country, even without spatial mobility.[30] Technology is not an autonomous force that alters social relations and power structures by itself. In the end, the significance of contemporary communication and transportation technology lies in the way it is distributed, used, and valued, which in turn rests on the social structures and socially constructed interpretive schemes of a given historical moment.

CONCLUSION

What do these case studies tell us about past and present transnational political practices? Do contemporary immigrants' transnational practices depart significantly from those of previous immigration generations? Clearly transnational social practices were evident in various forms between 1880 and the 1920s. My main question is not whether they existed but rather how they have changed, how they reflect the contexts in which they are embedded, and what theoretical and practical implications they have for politics in sending countries and the United States. My conclusion is that contemporary migrants to the United States and their nations of origin and destination are now embedded in transnational fields of activity that are substantially different from those of the turn of the past century. The cases discussed here show that the types and extent of transnational action vary significantly across national groups. This variation, in turn, is driven by the specific history of each migration process, including the changing composition of the migrant population, the dominant political culture of the country of origin, and the conditions of entry to the United States. On the whole, however, the field of transnational politics is more substantial, and is more heavily institutionalized in sending-country state activities, than was true a century ago.

Evidence from the three contemporary cases and the past century suggests that transnational political activities reflect the reciprocal relationships among U.S. geopolitical interests in the region or country of origin; the country of origin's position in the global political economy; specific features of the locality of reception, such as labor market conditions, interethnic power relations, and local political culture; and the characteristics of the migrant group (social composition, size, naturalization rates, mode of economic incorporation, and level of organization). For the sending states, formalizing and deepening transnational relations with their migrants has an ambiguous impact. On the one hand, it helps legiti-mate existing power structures at both "sending" and "receiving" ends of the transnational field. It recognizes transmigrants as fully lawful "nationals" who have political, civil, and social rights in each state. On the other hand, simultaneous membership in more than one nation-state subverts each state's exclusive jurisdiction. It throws national rights and identities, which are central to the global liberal system of states, into question. Moreover, to the ex-tent that transnationalism undermines the receiving state's control of its "borders" and its ability to determine who is a national and who a "foreigner," it submerges national sovereignty under myriad transnational practices (from above and below) and an unpredict-able whirl of multidirectional ties (from "here" and "there").

Nationalists' fear that transnational political practices will al-legedly be subversive of and deleterious to the nationalist ideal (Jacobson 1996) seem to be unfounded. Transmigrants are not es-caping state control. If anything, transnational practices legitimate the political systems of both the United States (as the country of immigration and equal opportunities) and the countries of origin (as the source of migrants' roots and identity). Transnational polit-ical actors are linked to and identified with national state struc-tures as dual or multiple citizens. In this sense, transnationalism does not undermine nationalism or the nation-state, as some have feared (Appadurai 1996; Jacobson 1996; Kearney 1991; Bhabha 1990; Miyoshi 1993). Nor do they represent a conscious political or economic decision to bypass the control of the state. Instead, one could say that transnational practices are to nationalism what the informal economy is to the formal economy. They are dialec-tically interrelated: if one disappears, so too will the other.

Other analysts have argued that transnationalism represents a grassroots counterhegemonic response to the dominant national project and the domination of capital. This seems to be true only in some cases and at some moments. Transnational practices are potentially, but not necessarily effectively, subversive: formal dual-national membership does not mean substantive dual citizen-ship in the sense of exercising rights and participating in the deci-sionmaking of two nation-states at the same time. As a matter of fact, most dual citizens seem oblivious to the potential power this status has granted them.

Several features of the current situation support this conclusion. Empowerment opportunities tend to be interstitial and often monopolized by an emergent political leadership. In the three cases examined here, leaders come exclusively from a select group of men (entrepreneurs, professionals, and intellectuals) from selected regions in the country of origin. Although most migrants may eventually benefit from their political advances, many cannot afford to participate because they are overworked, spend their time only with close friends and relatives, and cannot afford transnational politics. Put another way, not all immigrants are transmigrants, and not all transmigrants from a particular group engage in the same kinds of transnational practices.

Rather than forming an alternative power structure, transnational political actors are embedded in, and their ultimate goal is almost always to be incorporated into, the traditional power structures of both their countries of origin and the United States. The better-off transmigrant actors strive not for a stateless world but for a special dual or multiple status within existing dominant state regimes. Their activities legitimate existing asymmetrical power relations between the two nations. Being elected to public office in New York or being a dual U.S.-Dominican citizen conveys a higher status and perceived power, for example, than being elected to public office on the island or being a regular Dominican citizen.

Are U.S. political involvement and transnational political practices undertaken by different actors with distinct frames of reference—that of the "settler" versus that of the "sojourner"—as conventional wisdom would predict? Definitely not. Not only are the two forms of political participation not mutually exclusive, in fact they reinforce one another. The institutionalization of transnational political practices through dual citizenship and extraterritorial political representation has generated a complex overlap between local and transnational political interests. Migrants want to live in more than one nation-state, and political and economic actors from both ends of the transnational field want to capture transmigrants' resources and loyalties.

Many other immigrant groups in the United States also have widespread and increasingly formal transnational political practices, including Mexicans (the largest immigrant group in the

United States), Ecuadorans, Peruvians, Haitians, Filipinos, and the anglophone Caribbeans. Transnational political practices are also on the rise among emerging countries from the former Soviet bloc. These practices will undoubtedly affect the incorporation of different migrant groups into the United States polity in a variety of as yet unknown ways, but it is certain that they will play a central role. Some scholars studying local politics in the United States have recognized this point for some time. Ira Katznelson's discussion of politics in Washington Heights points out that in the early 1980s, many of the factors affecting city dwellers, including migration, were beyond their control, in that they "depend[ed] heavily on 'push' factors over which the receiving cities [had] virtually no control." "The state of Puerto Rico and other Caribbean economies," he continues, "obviously have had much more to do with the movement of poor people to New York than any causes that could be controlled in the city have had" (Katznelson 1981, 110). In these times of globalization and transnationalism, the "push" factors that allegedly expel people from their native lands simultaneously "pull" their interests toward their societies of origin once they have left them.

Many challenges confront us as analysts. What the long-term theoretical and practical implication of transnationalism will be for the liberal institutions of national membership (citizenship) and governance (political and social rights and governance structures) is a central question. It seems that contemporary migrants are generating fields of transnational political engagement that have substantial consequences both for their political and social incorporation in the United States and for their countries of origin, as well as for the institution of citizenship itself. This field of study is therefore likely to remain high on the agenda for social scientists and policymakers alike.

NOTES

1. I use the terms "migrant" and "transmigrant" interchangeably. Their meaning begins with, but is not limited to, spatial mobility across national borders. For the present analysis, I define "transnationalism" as the formation of sociocultural, economic, and political fields in-

volving individuals and institutions located in more than one nation-state. This definition delimits transnational action to activities undertaken by a sufficient number of people on a sufficiently regular basis to be considered a social field. At an individual level, transnationalism includes activities that form an integral part of the individual's habitual life.

2. The cultural scholar Homi Bhabha, for example, characterizes the practices of transmigrants as "counter-narratives" that evoke and erase the nation's totalizing boundaries and "disturb those ideological maneuvers through which 'imagined communities' are given essentialist identities" by the state (Bhabha 1990, 300),. The anthropologist Michael Kearney (1991) presents Mixtec migrant farmworkers as having created autonomous spaces in southern California and Oregon in which neither the U.S. state nor the Mexican state exercise control.

3. Irish, Italian, German, and Polish Catholics, the French, the New Dutch, Norwegians, and German Lutherans were strongly and consistently Democratic. English, Scots, Welsh, and Protestant Irish immigrants, on the other hand, were anti-Democratic. In several areas of the country, antisouthern sentiments converged with anti-immigrant, especially anti-Catholic, attitudes and led to the consolidation of the voting against the Democratic Party, which was seen as the party of the South and of the (Catholic and German Lutheran) immigrants (Kleppner 1979, 57–67).

4. Louis Bean (1948) has concluded that migrants' voting behavior was directly related to their ethnic ties to their countries of origin and to the foreign policy orientation of U.S. political parties. Later studies support Bean's conclusion that ethnic allegiances have been a significant factor influencing U.S. foreign policy (Bailey 1958; Gerson 1964).

5. Until the end of the nineteenth century, the United States did not project its aims beyond its own immediate geographic vicinity: its main foreign policy goal was to defend its immediate frontiers. Although the Monroe Doctrine legitimated the expansion of U.S. interests throughout the American continent, it also precluded interference in European affairs. The period between 1890 and 1920 saw an end to this situation. By 1907, the United States had emerged, for all practical purposes, as a world power with a global foreign policy (O'Grady 1967, introduction).

6. Six decades later, in a similar event, the transnational interests of an immigrant group also affected the 1976 presidential elections in which the Republican incumbent was defeated by Democrat Jimmy Carter. The Polish American Political League estimates that Republi-

can president Gerald Ford's comment that eastern European nations were "not dominated" by the Soviet Union cost him up to a million votes in Chicago alone. Recognizing his mistake, Ford immediately contacted the president of the Polish National Alliance to apologize (cited in Jacobson 1995, 228). Nowadays, similar political leverage on domestic and foreign U.S. politics is commanded by various "assimilated" groups.

7. These projects included both quantitative and qualitative data compiled from more than 120 in-depth interviews, three surveys of around four hundred people, and official aggregate and secondary sources (see Guarnizo 1993, 1994, 1997; Portes and Guarnizo 1991).

8. In December 1997, the U.S. Congress passed a bill exempting Salvadoran asylum seekers from automatic deportation, as called for by the 1996 Illegal Immigration Reform and Immigrant Responsibility Act.

9. The greater New York metropolitan area refers to the New York–northern New Jersey–Long Island–Connecticut Consolidated Metropolitan Statistical Area (CMSA), as defined by the Census Bureau. It is the largest CMSA in the country and contained 17.9 million people in 1990 (Alba et al. 1997, 625; U.S. Bureau of the Census 1991).

10. This trend is seen, at least in Los Angeles, as less and less likely to involve whites or as a transitory phenomenon that will "be swept away by the effects of continuing large-scale immigration." Consequently, it is argued, this reversal will yield "increasing levels of separation for Latinos and diminishing levels of mixing" (Clark 1996, 136–37).

11. In 1973, a biracial coalition elected a black mayor, Democrat Tom Bradley, who was subsequently reelected four times. Bradley's victory allowed for the expansion of African Americans' political participation in coalition with white liberals, principally Jews. The twenty-year rule of the liberal, biracial coalition dominated by Mayor Bradley ended in 1993 when a conservative alliance elected Republican Richard Riordan—and subsequently reelected him by a landslide in 1997.

12. This interpretation seems to support a high participation of new South American voters, for they tend to be less Democratic than Dominicans and Puerto Ricans. In effect, Colombian voters have a lower Democratic affiliation (56 percent) and a higher Republican enrollment (23 percent) than Dominicans (71 percent and 11 percent, respectively) and Puerto Ricans (90 percent and 7 percent, respectively) (see Falcón and Hanson-Sánchez 1996, 10). Because Puerto Ricans are ceasing to be the majority among the Latino popu-

lation, "the Democratic Party's hold over the Latino voter will in all likelihood be increasingly challenged in the coming decade" (Falcón and Hanson-Sánchez 1996, 11).

13. In August 1994, the opposition denounced the presidential elections that reelected Joaquín Balaguer for the seventh time as fraudulent. The opposition faced a weakened Balaguer, whose relevance for and support from the United States had evaporated along with the end of the Cold War. International electoral observers and the European and U.S. governments exerted unprecedented pressure on the octogenarian Balaguer to accept defeat and negotiate with the opposition. Opposition parties, taking advantage of strong international leverage, managed to make Balaguer accept several reforms, including the approval of dual citizenship.

14. The participation of a small proportion of Dominican immigrants in drug-related activities in the United States, and their enrichment thereby, sparked a malicious stereotyping of the migrant Dominican population as a whole. Economic success and the lifestyles of better-off migrants came to be equated with drug-related wealth. Moreover, migrants' new cultural identity began to be judged as ostentatious, tasteless, and offensive. Epithets were minted to refer to migrants, such as "Dominicanyork" (a native of New York City as opposed to authentic Dominican), "cadenú" (a person who wears a gold chain, characteristic of drug kingpins and drug peddlers), and "Joe" (an anonymous American-like migrant youngster) (see Guarnizo 1994).

15. Although the United States and Puerto Rico remain the top destinations for Dominican migrants, significant numbers of Dominicans also reside in Spain, Italy, Venezuela, and other European and Caribbean countries.

16. The most recent of these measures, signed in 1991 with the U.S. Treasury Department, gives power to U.S. authorities to investigate migrants' investments on the island.

17. Unlike other U.S. cities, New York City does not require citizenship to vote in school board elections, thus encouraging political participation by immigrants.

18. Evidently, Linares has cast several votes that, though they follow a party line, have been unpopular and perceived as damaging for the Dominican population, such as his vote to authorize the opening of a superstore in Harlem, a decision intensively resisted by African American and Dominican small-business owners and civic activists. Espaillat, on the other hand, is a member of Democrats for Change, a movement within the Democratic Party that is led by African American and Latino leaders seeking greater minority representation and

power in the city, the state, and the party. "We are now the majority, and should have a proportionate representation in the party and government power structure," he emphatically states (Espaillat 1997). In fact, the four district leaders of northern Manhattan are now Dominicans, and three of them belong to Democrats for Change.

19. Dominican political participation has followed a cumulative empowerment process. It has expanded from Washington Heights to other areas in the New York metropolitan region. Political empowerment has put Dominicans in the enviable position of being able to pick, choose, or ignore potential political allies. In areas where the Dominican presence is significant, such as Corona, Elmhurst, and Jackson Heights in the borough of Queens, Dominican leaders are carefully weighing whether to support non-Dominican Latino candidates or to reserve their support for their own candidates.

20. Today, New York houses a representative cross section of Colombian society, including expatriated world-class artists and billionaire industrialists, international drug traffickers and petty drug dealers, underemployed professionals and tenured academics, blue-collar workers and emergent entrepreneurs.

21. This reform was introduced in 1958 by Liberal and Conservative elites after they had been forced into exile by a military dictatorship.

22. The Colombian government's efforts to provide protection and legal assistance to the more than twelve thousand Colombians currently incarcerated for drug-related crimes around the world has produced negative reactions among the migrant population. One informant wondered "why the [Colombian] government has to spend so much money on the criminals that have given us such a bad reputation[.] It should help hardworking Colombians instead."

23. Migrants of upper-class origin, meanwhile, do not mix with "las masas" of Colombians and remain secluded in exclusive areas of the city. The discussion that follows centers on popular political participation and organizing and does not include initiatives taken by upper-class Colombians through organizations such as the Colombian American Association—an organization formed by wealthy investors, industrialists, international traders, and other well-to-do Colombians. For an insightful discussion about racism in Colombia, see Wade 1993.

24. Opposition and left-leaning parties are also commonly led by male middle-class professionals and intellectuals. Although women tend to have more visibility in these parties than in the more mainstream organizations, a man is always at the helm.

25. Both organizations have initiated transnational projects with political

dimensions. El Rescate, in association with COMUNIDADES, sponsored the creation of a community development credit union in Los Angeles—a financial cooperative that will serve Salvadorans in Los Angeles and eventually be linked with a counterpart institution in El Salvador. Also, CARECEN has initiated a pilot program called Learning Across Borders as a vehicle for exchange between students, universities, businesses, and other organizations in Los Angeles and El Salvador. The leaders of CARECEN hope to position the organization as a "transnational broker" by helping to prepare a generation of socially and politically conscious transnational leaders.

26. For example, it was only after they settled in the United States "that East Europeans developed a translocal, national identity as Poles, Ukrainians, Slovaks, Lithuanians, etc." (Conzen et al. 1992, 22).

27. It has been estimated that between 1901 and 1914, Italy received more than $60 million annually from workers living abroad. Such a large amount of money deserved both official recognition and protection because at the local level it supported families left behind, built houses, bought land, and created new or maintained existing business endeavors. At the national level, this money helped balance a trade deficit and maintain a stable economy (Caroli 1973). Moreover, overseas workers' demand for pasta, wine, olive oil, cheeses, and other Italian consumer items stimulated production and trade in times when the national economy was weak and in the process of industrialization.

28. The Italian state's transnational interest was clearly expressed during the lengthy debates in the United States about the enactment of literacy requirements for new entrants, a measure chiefly aimed at excluding Italians. For more than a decade, the Italian Emigration Council, created in 1901, followed these debates very closely. The council was in charge of devising ways to counter the deleterious effects that this measure would bring upon the country. In May 1914, the council passed a resolution establishing schools to prepare people to leave and rapidly trained "emigrants to surmount the obstacles resulting from illiteracy" (*Bolletino dell'emigrazione* (1914), cited in Caroli 1976, 14). Facing increasing restrictionist sentiments in the United States, the Italian state opened hundreds of these schools in southern Italy in 1920 and 1921 (Caroli 1976, 16).

29. For a discussion of this process in the case of Mexico, see Guarnizo 1998; González Gutíerrez 1997; R. Smith 1996. For the case of the Philippines and Haiti, see Basch, Glick Schiller, and Szanton Blanc 1994.

30. This process is not totally controlled by global media corporations

based in the North, however. Thanks to technological innovations, media networks outside the immediate control of global media powers, such as Mexican Televisa, Dominican television networks, and Colombian RCN, are able to broadcast part of their programs beyond their national borders to neighboring nations and their conationals and coethnics abroad. In a more poignant example, in 2000 a Taiwanese financial group launched Space TV Systems, a group of eight digital direct-to-home channels in Chinese, Vietnamese, Japanese, and Korean for Asians in North America and Australia ("School Brief—A World View." In *Economist,* November 29, 1997: 72). These cases demonstrate that the globalization of media can endorse not only the cultural symbols of U.S. culture but also those of the many cultures valued by people who are separated by distance from their places of origin.

REFERENCES

Aguayo, Sergio, and Patricia Weiss Fagen. 1988. *Central Americans in Mexico and the United States.* Washington, D.C.: Hemispheric Migration Project, Center for Immigration Policy and Refugee Assistance, Georgetown University.

Alba, Richard D., Nancy A. Denton, Shu-yin J. Leung, and John R. Logan. 1997. "Neighborhood Change Under Conditions of Mass Immigration: The New York City Region, 1970–1990." *International Migration Review* 20(3): 625–56.

Appadurai, Arjun. 1990. "Disjuncture and Difference in the Global Culture Economy." *Theory, Culture, and Society* 7: 295–310.

———. 1996. *Modernity at Large: Cultural Dimensions of Globalization.* Minneapolis: University of Minnesota Press.

Bailey, Thomas. 1958. *A Diplomatic History of the American People.* 6th ed. New York: Appleton-Century-Crofts.

Basch, Linda, Nina Glick Schiller, and Cristina Szanton Blanc. 1994. *Nations Unbound: Transnational Projects, Postcolonial Predicaments, and the Deterritorialized Nation-State.* Amsterdam: Gordon and Breach.

Bean, Louis H. 1948. *How to Predict Elections.* New York: Alfred A. Knopf.

Betances, Emelio. 1995. *State and Society in the Dominican Republic.* Boulder, Colo.: Westview Press.

Bhabha, Homi K. 1990. "DissemiNation: Time, Narrative, and the Margins of the Modern Nation." In *Nation and Narration,* edited by Homi K. Bhabha. New York: Routledge.

Buell, Frederick. 1994. *National Culture and the New Global System.* Baltimore: Johns Hopkins University Press.

Cambeira, Alan. 1997. *Quisqueya la Bella: The Dominican Republic in Historical and Cultural Perspective.* London: M. E. Sharpe.

Cardona, Ramiro, Carmen Inés Cruz, Juanita Castaño, Elsa M. Chaney, Mary G. Powers, and John J. Macisco Jr. 1980. *El éxodo de colombianos: Un estudio de la corriente migratoria a los Estados Unidos y un intento para propiciar el retorno.* Bogotá, Colombia: Ediciones Tercer Mundo.

Caroli, Betty Boyd. 1973. *Italian Repatriation from the United States, 1900–1914.* New York: Center for Migration Studies.

———. 1976. "The United States, Italy and the Literacy Act." In *Studi Emigrazione* 41: 3–21.

Chinchilla, Norma, Nora Hamilton, and James Loucky. 1993. "Central Americans in Los Angeles: An Immigrant Community in Transition." In *In the Barrios: Latinos and the Underclass Debate,* edited by Joan Moore and Raquel Pinderhughes. New York: Russell Sage Foundation.

Clark, William A. V. 1996. "Residential Patterns: Avoidance, Assimilation, and Succession." In *Ethnic Los Angeles,* edited by Roger Waldinger and Mehdi Bozorgmehr. New York: Russell Sage Foundation.

Clifford, Jim. 1994. "Diasporas." *Cultural Anthropology* 9(2): 302–38.

Conzen, Kathleen Neils, David A. Gerber, Ewa Morawska, George E. Pozzetta, and Rudolph J. Vecoli. 1992. "The Invention of Ethnicity: A Perspective from the U.S.A." *Journal of American Ethnic History* 121: 3–41.

Córdoba, Carlos. 1995. "Central American Migration to San Francisco: One Hundred Years of Building a Community." In *Central Americans in California: Transnational Communities, Economies, and Cultures.* Los Angeles: Center for Multiethnic and Transnational Studies, University of Southern California.

Cury, Jottin. 1995a. "Nacionalismo y emigraciones." *Hoy* (Santo Domingo, Dominican Republic), June 20, 16.

———. 1995b. Paper presented at the XI Conferencia de Seguridad de las Islas-Naciones del Caribe (CINSEC) [Conference on the Security of the Caribbean Isle Nations]. March 23.

Dore, Carlos, Fátima Portorreal, Rafael Durán, Claudia Scholz, and Esther Hernández. 1997. "Transnational Communities: Their Causes and Effects Among Latin American Immigrants in the United States: Informe República Dominicana." Transnational Communities Research Project, Informe Republica Dominicana: Johns Hopkins University and University of California at Davis (March).

Drainville, André C. 1998. "The Fetishism of Global Civil Society: Global

Governance, Transnational Urbanism, and Sustainable Capitalism in the World Economy." In *Transnationalism from Below.* edited by Michael Peter Smith and Luis Eduardo Guarnizo. New Brunswick, N.J.: Transaction Books.

Duff, John B. 1967. "The Italians." In *The Immigrants' Influence on Wilson's Peace Policies,* edited by Joseph P. O'Grady. Lexington, Ky.: University Press of Kentucky.

Espinal, Rosario. 1995. "Flexible Boundaries of Nation-States: Sovereignty and Citizenship in Transition in the Caribbean." Paper presented at the annual meeting of the American Sociological Association. Washington, D.C. (August 19–23).

Falcón, Angelo, and Christopher Hanson-Sánchez. 1996. *Latino Immigrants and Electoral Participation: Puerto Ricans, Dominicans, and South Americans in the New York City Political System.* New York: Institute for Puerto Rican Policy.

Gaceta Oficial. 1994. *Constitución de la República Dominicana.* Santo Domingo, Dominican Republic (August 20).

Galíndez, Jesús de. 1958. *La era de Trujillo: Un estudio casuístico de dictadura hispanoamericana.* Buenos Aires: Editorial Americana.

Georges, Eugenia. 1987. "Distribución de los efectos de la migración internacional sobre una comunidad de la Sierra Occidental." In *La inmigración Dominicana en los Estados Unidos,* edited by José del Castillo and Christopher Mitchel. Santo Domingo, Dominican Republic: Editorial CENAPEC.

———. 1990. *The Making of a Transnational Community: Migration, Development, and Cultural Change in the Dominican Republic.* New York: Columbia University Press.

Gerson, Louis L. 1964. *The Hyphenated in Recent American Politics and Diplomacy.* Lexington, Ky.: University Press of Kansas.

Glick Schiller, Nina. 1996. "Who Are These Guys? A Transnational Reading of the U.S. Immigrant Experience." Paper presented at the Social Science Research Council conference, "Becoming American/American Becoming: International Migration to the United States." New York (January 18).

———. 1999 "Transmigrants and Nation-States: Something Old and Something New in the U.S. Immigrant Experience." In *Handbook of International Migration: The American Experience,* edited by Charles Hirschman, Philip Kasinitz, and Josh DeWind. New York: Russell Sage Foundation.

Glick Schiller, Nina, and Georges Fouron. 1999. "Terrains of Blood and Nation: Haitian Transnational Social Fields." *Ethnic and Racial Studies* 22(2): 340–66.

Glick Schiller, Nina, Linda Basch, and Cristina Blanc-Szanton, eds. 1992.

Towards a Transnational Perspective on Migration: Race, Class, Ethnicity, and Nationalism Reconsidered. New York: New York Academy of Sciences.

Glick Schiller, Nina, Linda Basch, and Cristina Szanton Blanc. 1995. "From Immigrant to Transmigrant: Theorizing Transnational Migration." *Anthropological Quarterly* 681: 48–63.

Goldring, Luin. 1996. "Blurring Borders: Constructing Transnational Community in the Process of U.S.-Mexico Migration." *Research in Community Sociology* 6: 69–104.

González Gutierrez, Carlos. 1997. "Decentralized Diplomacy: The Role of Consular Offices in Mexico's Relations with Its Diaspora." In *Bridging the Border: Transforming Mexico-U.S. Relations,* edited by Rodolfo O. De La Garza and Jesus Velasco. Lanham, Md.: Rowman and Littlefield.

Graham, Pamela M. 1997. "Reimagining the Nation and Defining the District: Dominican Migration and Transnational Politics." In *Caribbean Circuits: New Directions in the Study of Caribbean Migration,* edited by Patricia R. Pessar. Staten Island, N.Y.: Center for Migration Studies.

Grasmuck, Sherri, and Patricia Pessar. 1991. *Between Two Islands.* Berkeley: University of California Press.

———. 1996. "Dominicans in the United States: First- and Second-Generation Settlement, 1960–1990." In *Origins and Destinies: Immigration, Race, and Ethnicity in America,* edited by Sylvia Pedraza and Rubén G. Rumbaut. Belmont, Calif.: Wadsworth Publishing Company.

Grossberg, Lawrence. 1996. "On Postmodernism and Articulation: An Interview with Stuart Hall." In *Stuart Hall: Critical Dialogues in Cultural Studies,* edited by David Morley and Kuan-Hsing Chen. London: Routledge.

Guarnizo, Luis Eduardo. 1993. "One Country in Two: Dominican-Owned Firms in New York and in the Dominican Republic." Ph.D. diss., Johns Hopkins University.

———. 1994. "Los Dominicanyorks: The Making of a Binational Society." *Annals of the American Academy of Social and Political Science* 533: 70–86.

———. 1997. "'Going Home': Class, Gender, and Household Transformation Among Dominican Return Migrants." In *Caribbean Circuits: New Directions in the Study of Caribbean Migration,* edited by Patricia Pessar. Staten Island, N.Y.: Center for Migration Studies.

———. 1998. "The Rise of Transnational Social Formations: Mexican and Dominican State Responses to Transnational Migration." *Political Power and Social Theory* 12: 45–94.

Guarnizo, Luis Eduardo, and Alejandro Portes. 2001. "From Assimilation to Transnationalism: Social Determinants of Transnational Political Action Among Contemporary Migrants." Unpublished paper. University of California, Davis.

Guarnizo, Luis Eduardo, and Arturo Ignacio Sánchez. 1998. "Emigración Colombiana a los Estados Unidos: Trans-territorialización de la participación política y socioeconómica." In *Estados Unidos: Potencia y Prepotencia*, edited by Luis Alberto Restrepo. Bogota: IEPRI, PNUD, Tercer Mundo Editores.

Guarnizo, Luis Eduardo, Arturo Ignacio Sánchez, and Elizabeth M. Roach. 1999. "Mistrust, Fragmented Solidarity, and Transnational Migration: Colombians in New York City and Los Angeles." *Ethnic and Racial Studies* 22(2): 367–96.

Guarnizo, Luis Eduardo, and Michael Peter Smith. 1998. "The Locations of Transnationalism." In *Transnationalism from Below,* edited by Michael Peter Smith and Luis Eduardo Guarnizo. New Brunswick, N.J.: Transaction Books.

Hamilton, Nora, and Norma Chinchilla Stoltz. 1991. "Central American Migration: A Framework for Analysis." *Latin American Research Review* 261: 75–110.

Hannerz, Ulf. 1996. *Transnational Connections.* London: Routledge.

Harvey, David. 1989. *The Condition of Postmodernity: An Inquiry into the Origins of Cultural Change.* Cambridge, Mass.: Basil Blackwell.

Horton, John. 1995. *The Politics of Diversity: Immigration, Resistance, and Change in Monterey Park, California.* Philadelphia: Temple University Press.

Instituto Nacional de Estadística, Geografía, e Informática. 1992. *XI censo general de población y vivienda, 1990.* Aguascalientes, Mexico: INEGI.

Jacobson, David. 1996. *Rights Across Borders: Immigration and the Decline of Citizenship.* Baltimore: Johns Hopkins University Press.

Jacobson, Matthew F. 1995. *Special Sorrows: The Diasporic Imagination of Irish, Polish, and Jewish Immigrants in the United States.* Cambridge, Mass.: Harvard University Press.

Katznelson, Ira. 1981. *City Trenches: Urban Politics and the Patterning of Class in the United States.* New York: Pantheon Books.

Kearney, Michael. 1991. "Borders and Boundaries of State and Self at the End of Empire." *Journal of Historical Sociology* 4(1): 52–74.

Kleppner, Paul. 1979. *The Third Electoral System, 1883–1892: Parties, Voters, and Political Cultures.* Chapel Hill: University of North Carolina Press.

Kyle, David. 1999. "The Otavalo Trade Diaspora: Social Capital and Transnational Entrepreneurship." *Ethnic and Racial Studies* 22(2): 422–46.

Levitt, Peggy. 1997. "Variations in Transnationalism: Lessons from Organizational Experiences in Boston and the Dominican Republic." Working paper, Aspen Institute Non-Profit Sector Fund.

———. 1999. "Towards an Understanding of Transnational Community Forms and Their Impact on Immigrant Incorporation." Paper presented at the Comparative Immigration and Integration Program Writer Workshop (February 19), University of California, San Diego.

Lopez, David, Eric Popkin, and Edward Tellez. 1996. "Central Americans: At the Bottom, Struggling to Get Ahead." In *Ethnic Los Angeles,* edited by Roger Waldinger and Mehdi Bozorgmehr. New York: Russell Sage Foundation.

Lozano, Wilfredo. 1985. *El reformismo dependiente.* Santo Domingo, Dominican Republic: Editora Taller.

Mahler, Sarah J. 1995. *American Dreaming: Immigrant Life on the Margins.* Princeton, N.J.: Princeton University Press.

Martin, John B. 1966. *Overtaken by Events: The Dominican Crisis, from the Fall of Trujillo to the Civil War.* Garden City, N.Y.: Doubleday.

Miyoshi, Masao. 1993. "A Worldless World? From Colonialism to Transnationalism and the Decline of the Nation-State." *Critical Inquiry* 19(4): 726–51.

Mollenkopf, John Hull. 1990. "New York: The Great Anomaly." In *Racial Politics in American Cities,* edited by Rufus Browning, Dale Rogers Marshall, and David Tabb. New York: Longman.

———. 1991. "Political Inequality." In *Dual City: Restructuring New York,* edited by John Hull Mollenkopf and Manuel Castells. New York: Russell Sage Foundation.

Montes Mozo, Segundo, and Juan Jose Garcia Vasquez. 1988. *Salvadoran Migration to the United States: An Exploratory Study.* Washington, D.C.: Hemispheric Migration Project, Center for Immigration Policy and Refugee Assistance, Georgetown University.

O'Grady, Joseph P., ed. 1967. *The Immigrants' Influence on Wilson's Peace Policies.* Lexington, Ky.: University Press of Kentucky.

Peña Salas, Yolanda. 1997. *Las asociaciones colombianas en Nueva York, 1958–1993.* Cali, Colombia: Facultad de Ciencias Sociales, Económicas, y Sociología, Universidad del Valle.

Portes, Alejandro. 1996. "Transnational Communities: Their Emergence and Significance in the Contemporary World System." In *Latin America in the World Economy,* edited by R. P. Korzeniewicz and W. C. Smith. Westport, Conn.: Greenwood Press.

Portes, Alejandro, and Luis E. Guarnizo. 1991. "Tropical Capitalists: U.S.-Bound Immigration and Small-Enterprise Development in the Dominican Republic." In *Migration, Remittances, and Small Business Devel-*

opment: Mexico and Caribbean Basin Countries, edited by Sergio Díaz-Briquets and Sidney Weintraub. Boulder, Colo.: Westview Press.

Portes, Alejandro, Luis Eduardo Guarnizo, and Patricia Landolt. 1999. "The Study of Transnationalism: Pitfalls and Promise of an Emergent Research Field." *Ethnic and Racial Studies* 22(2): 217–37.

Portes, Alejandro, and Rubén Rumbaut. 1991. *Immigrant America: A Portrait.* Berkeley: University of California Press.

Repak, Terry A. 1995. *Waiting on Washington: Central American Workers in the Nation's Capital.* Philadelphia: Temple University Press.

Ríos, Palmira. 1995. "International Migration, Citizenship, and the Emergence of Transnational Public Policies." Paper presented at the annual meeting of the American Ethnological Society. San Juan, Puerto Rico (April 18 to 21).

Roberts, Bryan R., Reanne Frank, and Fernando Lozano-Ascencio. 1999. "Transnational Migrant Communities and Mexican Migration to the U.S." *Ethnic and Racial Studies* 22(2): 238–66.

Rouse, Roger. 1992. "Making Sense of Settlement: Class Transformation, Cultural Struggle, and Transnationalism Among Mexican Migrants in the United States." In *Towards a Transnational Perspective on Migration: Race, Class, Ethnicity, and Nationalism Reconsidered,* edited by Nina Glick Schiller, Linda Basch, and Cristina Blanc-Szanton. New York: New York Academy of Sciences.

Samper Pizano, Ernesto. 1996. "Campaña Colombia para todos." Bogotá, Colombia. Presidencia de la República (May 23).

Sánchez, Arturo Ignacio. 1996. "Colombian Dual Nationality and Immigrant Agency." Paper presented at the Annual Meeting of the American Ethnological Society. San Juan, Puerto Rico (April 18 to 20).

Sassen, Saskia. 1991. *The Global City: New York, London, Tokyo.* Princeton: Princeton University Press.

Sassen-Koob, Saskia. 1979. "Formal and Informal Associations: Dominicans and Colombians in New York." *International Migration Review* 13(2): 314–32.

Smith, Michael Peter. 1994. "Can You Imagine? Transnational Migration and the Globalization of Grassroots Politics." *Social Text* 39: 15–33.

Smith, Robert C. 1994. "Los Ausentes Siempre Presentes: The Imagining, Making, and Politics of Transnational Communities Between the United States and Mexico." Ph.D. diss., Columbia University.

———. 1998. "Reflections on the State, Migration, and the Durability and Newness of Transnational Life: Comparative Insights from the Mexican and Italian Cases." *Soziale Welt* (special issue no. 12). Baden-Baden: Nomos.

Sonenshein, Raphael J. 1993. *Politics in Black and White: Race and Power in Los Angeles*. Princeton, N.J.: Princeton University Press.

Soysal, Yasemin Nuholu. 1994. *Limits of Citizenship: Migrants and Postnational Membership in Europe*. Chicago: University of Chicago Press.

Urrea-Giraldo, Fernando. 1982. *Life Strategies and the Labor Market: Colombians in New York City in the 1970s*. Occasional Paper 34. New York: Center for Latin American and Caribbean Studies, New York University.

U.S. Department of Commerce. U.S. Bureau of the Census. 1991. News Release CB91-100. Washington: U.S. Government Printing Office (March 11).

———. 1993a. *1990 Census of the Population: Persons of Hispanic Origin in the United States*. Washington: U.S. Government Printing Office.

———. 1993b. *1990 Census of the Population: Social and Economic Characteristics: Los Angeles*. Section 1. Washington.

———. 1993c. *1990 Census of the Population: Social and Economic Characteristics: New York*. Section 1. Washington.

U.S. Immigration and Naturalization Service. 1994a. "Estimated Illegal Immigration Population." In *Annual Report*. Washington: U.S. Government Printing Office.

———. 1994b. *Statistical Yearbook of the Immigration and Naturalization Service, 1993*. Washington: Government Printing Office.

Wade, Peter. 1993. *Blackness and Race Mixture: The Dynamics of Racial Identity in Colombia*. Baltimore: Johns Hopkins University Press.

Waldinger, Roger. 1996. *Still the Promised Land? African-Americans and New Immigrants in Postindustrial New York*. Cambridge, Mass.: Harvard University Press.

———. 1998. "Commentary." Paper presented at the International Conference on Nationalism, Transnationalism, and the Crisis of Citizenship. University of California, Davis (April 24 and 25).

Waldinger, Roger, and Mehdi Bozorgmehr. 1996. "The Making of a Multicultural Metropolis." In *Ethnic Los Angeles,* edited by Roger Waldinger and Mehdi Bozorgmehr. New York: Russell Sage Foundation.

World Bank. 1992. *World Development Report, 1992*. Washington, D.C.: World Bank.

Wyman, Mark. 1993. *Round-Trip to America: The Immigrants Return to Europe, 1880–1930*. Ithaca: Cornell University Press.

Zolberg, Aristide, Astri Suhrke, and Sergio Aguayo. 1989. *Escape from Violence: Conflict and the Refugee Crisis in the Developing World*. New York: Oxford University Press.

—— Part IV ——

Immigrants and the American State

—— Chapter 7 ——

Policing Boundaries: Migration, Citizenship, and the State

T. Alexander Aleinikoff

A STATE HAS two sets of boundaries. It has physical bound-aries—the border—and it has political and legal bound-aries—membership. The systems of state regulation of the border and of membership—we generally label the former "immigration policy" and the latter "citizenship and naturalization policy"—are closely related: whom states choose to admit as immigrants in part determines who shall be citizens; and most state immigration re-gimes give special admission preferences to family members of citizens. The legal status bestowed by immigration rules is an im-portant determinant in immigrant integration, playing a significant role in opportunities for work, rights, and social benefits.

Until recently, international migration theory has paid scant attention to the role of states in causing, controlling, and shaping migrant flows. It has focused even less on membership regimes. The importance of these issues has not been lost on historians, who have long examined state migration policy (Higham 1955). Reed Ueda's fine contribution to this volume (chapter 8) shows the increasing interest of historians in citizenship regulation, as well.[1] The recent work of political scientists Keith Fitzgerald (1996), Gary Freeman (1994, 1995), James Hollifield (1992, 2000), Christian Joppke (1998a, 1998b), and Aristide Zolberg (1981, 1999) has begun to suggest theoretical approaches for a field of inquiry that in the past has focused more usually on "segment[s] of social reality within specified time limits in particular countries" (Zolberg 1981, 4). In this chapter I want to help push along the enterprise of investigating the nature and impact of state regulation on both entry and integration of immigrants and membership. Examination of the role of the state requires recognition that the state itself pursues its own interest (with more or less success) and that the concept of "the state" must be disaggregated in order to appreciate the range of federal and nonfederal state actors and the complex ways in which they interact. With respect to the structure of membership, I argue that although constitutional norms play a major role in defining membership, the contours of membership are the subject of much current controversy. It is a debate in which both state and civil society participate, and which ultimately concerns access to both.

STATE POLICIES, MIGRATION, AND INTEGRATION

In their canonical 1985 study, *Latin Journey*, Alejandro Portes and Robert Bach reported that "since the late nineteenth century, the dominant form of international migration has been that of manual labor, and its most consistent direction has been from peripheral regions to regional and world centers" (Portes and Bach 1985, 2). A decade later, Portes reiterated the claim: "Although geopolitical and other considerations have played roles in granting to certain foreign groups access to American territory, the fundamental reason for sustained immigration, at least since the post–Civil War period, has been the labor needs of the economy" (Portes 1994, 634).

This claim might be contested by pointing to large refugee flows to the United States as well as increasing levels of family migration. Many of those popularly described as "refugees," however—those fleeing Cuba, Haiti, El Salvador, and Guatemala, for example—have been motivated by economic considerations. Spouses and children who head north to join wage earners in the United States are also appropriately conceptualized as part of a labor flow.

Viewing migration primarily as a function of "the labor needs of the economy" has significant, although not logically entailed, theoretical implications. Portes and Bach note that "it is . . . not surprising that most theorizing about international migration has focused on the origins, uses, and effects of labor flow" and that although large refugee movements and professional emigration have not been wholly ignored, they have tended to be conceptualized "as variants of the models applied to labor migration" (Portes and Bach 1985, 3). Similarly, in a massive review of the literature on theories on international migration and empirical studies, Douglas Massey and colleagues consider almost exclusively economic models to explain the initiation of migration. A summary sentence from this important study states that "[i]mmigration may begin for a variety of reasons—a desire for individual income gain, an attempt to diversify risks to household income, a program of recruitment to satisfy employer demands for low-wage workers, an international displacement of peasants by market penetration within peripheral regions, or some combination thereof" (Massey et al. 1993, 448). In considering reasons for the perpetuation of migrant flows, the authors analyze network theory and institutional theory. Here too the primary motivation ascribed to migration is economic: migrant networks "increase the likelihood of international movement because they lower the costs and risks of movement and increase the expected net returns to migration" (Massey et al. 1993). The power of the state as such is generally played down. The state is conceptualized either as a "pass-through," manipulated by the powerful economic forces in civil society that truly determine social and economic policy, or as largely unable to affect the migration stream (Massey et al., 450; Massey and Espinosa 1997). The effect of U.S. policy is therefore not to influence the flow but merely to distribute the labels "legal" and "illegal" across the flow.

In more recent work, Massey (1999, 50–51) and Portes (1999, 31–32) have noted that modeling the role of the state must be part of a comprehensive theory of migration. Other scholars, primarily political scientists, have made state policies and structures a central focus of immigration study (Andreas 1998; Fitzgerald 1996; Freeman 1994, 1995; Gimpel and Edwards 1999; Guiraudon and Lahav 2000; Hollifield 2000; LeMay 1994; Schrag 2000; Zolberg 1999). Their work joins historical research on immigration policy and administration (Calavita 1992; Daniels 1962; Pitkin 1975; Salyer 1995; chapter 8, this volume). Once state policy is brought into view, it becomes apparent that economics- or labor-driven models are not sufficient descriptions of migration. Haitian migration to the United States provides a useful example.

Consistent with the labor-based theories, Haitians have for years traveled to Caribbean islands, and more recently to the United States, for the purpose of finding work. Such emigration has peaked, however, in times of political and social turmoil and when U.S. authorities have been perceived as opening the door. Pursuant to an exchange of notes between the Reagan administration and the regime of Jean-Claude "Baby Doc" Duvalier, U.S. Coast Guard cutters began interdicting and returning Haitian boat people in 1981. Although purportedly screening migrants for refugee claims, virtually all interdicted Haitians were returned. The interdiction program substantially reduced boat departures from Haiti and arrivals in Florida. Courts in the United States refused to examine the legality of the program.

Following the coup against the government of Jean-Bertrand Aristide in 1991, large numbers of Haitians again took to the sea. When Coast Guard cutters became overwhelmed, Haitians were taken to Guantánamo Naval Base in Cuba. There they were screened on refugee criteria, and those who were able to demonstrate a "credible fear" of persecution were brought to Florida. Of about thirty thousand Haitians screened, more than ten thousand were permitted to enter the United States. The possibility of entry to the United States increased the boat flow, and Guantánamo was soon overwhelmed. At that point, President George Bush reinstated interdiction and return, and the boat flow quickly ceased.

During the 1992 presidential campaign, candidate Bill Clinton stated his opposition to interdiction. After the election but before the inauguration, reports were received of large numbers of boats being built along the Haitian coast. Clinton announced that interdiction would remain "for the time being," and southern Florida witnessed no major flow of boats in January 1993. In the spring of 1994, the Clinton administration announced that, because of increasing political strife and human rights abuses in Haiti, it would no longer directly return Haitian boat people. Rather, they would be screened aboard a converted U.S. hospital ship moored in Kingston Harbor. Those demonstrating a well-founded fear of persecution would be eligible for entry into the United States; those "screened out" would be returned to Haiti. Again, the chance of U.S. entry sparked an increase in the flow, and the ship was soon overwhelmed with migrants; and again, the United States decided to take Haitians to Guantánamo. This time, however, a decision was made to give Haitians "safe haven" at the naval base; that is, they were neither returned to Haiti nor screened for admission to the United States. The safe haven policy effectively ended the flow of boat people. (In all, almost twenty thousand Haitians received safe haven at Guantánamo). With the restoration of Aristide in September 1994, most of the Haitians at Guantánamo voluntarily returned home. About four thousand remaining Haitians were returned by U.S. authorities in December 1994.

The lessons for theory-builders should be obvious, and at every point the story shows the inadequacy of labor-based analyses. The causes of the flow of migrants were many (economic, political, security, family); the flow was largely determined by U.S. state policy (vis-à-vis both the regime and the boat people); and the flow was not inevitable or uncontrollable (the migrants responded to changes in the home country and in U.S. policy, and they were able to make sophisticated choices about their chances of actually getting to the United States). This narrative underscores the fact that state policies (including state use of force) and legal categories matter—and not peripherally but directly and centrally.[2] States adopt domestic and international policies that make their populations more or less interested and more or less able to leave their jurisdictions, and they make their jurisdictions more or less inviting to foreign populations.

What is crucial here is that movement from Haiti to Florida is not the same as movement from Manhattan to Florida. Borders are constructed and enforced by states that are recognized by the international legal system as having the authority to control the movement of citizens and noncitizens into and out of their territories.[3] Those policies may or may not be coherent, effective, or morally acceptable, but their influence on international migration is apparent.

THE STATE AS ACTOR

In her classic work, *Bringing the State Back In,* Theda Skocpol notes that "states may be viewed as organizations through which official collectivities may pursue distinctive goals, realizing them

more or less effectively given the available state resources in relation to social settings. . . . [Alternatively,] states may be viewed
more macroscopically as configurations of organization and action
that influence the meanings and methods of politics for all groups
and classes in society" (Skocpol 1985, 28). I want to examine both
these claims as they apply to state regulation of immigration and
membership.

States Pursuing State Interests

Immigration policy formation occurs within a complex interbranch and intergovernmental structure that materially influences
outcomes (Fitzgerald 1996, 240). Much of the recent immigration
legislation cannot be adequately explained without a close examination of Congress and the personal agendas of particular members. It is hard to point to outside interests—other than inchoate
"public opinion"—that have pushed for (overly) tough measures
against criminal aliens, restrictions on judicial review, expedited
exclusion at the border, wholesale refashioning of removal procedures, and new detention requirements.[4]

Indeed, other state actors, such as states and executive branch
agencies, are as likely to be influential on the legislation as outside
groups. One curious but significant example is the passage of section 245(i) of the Immigration and Nationality Act, added in 1994.
Generally, persons in a legal temporary status in the United States
can adjust to permanent resident status, if eligible to do so, without making a trip home, whereas aliens living illegally in the
United States who attain a basis for lawful immigration—for example, marriage to a U.S. citizen—generally must go home to receive an immigrant visa at a State Department consular office. Section 245(i) permitted aliens illegally in the United States to adjust
their status to lawful permanent resident in the United States if
they were eligible to do so, provided they paid a penalty of five
times the usual application fee.

Why would Congress adopt a provision that seemed to provide a stimulus to illegal immigration, or at the least seemed to
reward it, at the same time that it professed to be cracking down
on undocumented migration? The answer is twofold. First, section
245(i) saved the State Department considerable resources at a time

when it was closing consular offices overseas; with the new provision, several hundred thousand aliens each year would attain lawful resident status without having to be issued documentation by the department. Second, the penalty money supplied several hundred million dollars a year to Immigration and Naturalization Service (INS) coffers, an amount that therefore did not need to be paid out of general appropriation dollars. This windfall (much of which was applied to the new naturalization program) turned initial INS enforcement concern over the provision into staunch support.[5]

The legislation process tends to be public, and those parts of it that are not are usually accessible to well-connected lobbyists. Administration of the law, however, is far more an intramural affair. It is here that the relatively autonomous state is evident. In an important and unique study, Kitty Calavita has shed light on the development and implementation of an immigration program of significant historical importance, the Bracero Program. Calavita's pathbreaking work examines in minute detail years of internal INS memorandums and looks at the personal histories of federal administrators. In an area of regulation where one might expect nonstate actors to exert maximum influence, Calavita concludes,

> neither the Althusserian structuralist rendition nor the more straightforward instrumentalist account of the state's role in designing and implementing the Bracero Program [is] entirely supported by the historical record. A close look at the immigration agency that shared responsibility for running the Bracero Program reveals a far more complex scenario, and greater inconsistencies and ambiguity of state action, than either of these perspectives can account for. . . . INS policies were not simply a response to the demands of the capitalist class—in this case growers—but were first and foremost the product of the bureaucracy's own institutional needs. Perhaps most important, this study finds a "state" that is rife with internal divisions, as the policy agenda of the Immigration Service collides head-on with the policy goals of other state agencies, most notably the Department of Labor. (Calavita 1992, 4)[6]

Calavita's nuanced study refuses to take sides in the debate between society-centered and state-centered interpretations. Recognizing the role for a "structural" model of the state, she also "bring[s] people back in" by borrowing from "state-centered theorists . . . who insist that the state, and the institutions that make it up, have their own interests and periodically enjoy substantial authority; from [those who recognize] the central role of state managers with distinct state agendas; and from the literature on federal agencies that describes the complex interactions among state institutions and between those institutions and their 'clienteles'" (Calavita 1992, 179).

Close examination of the administrative state discloses a range of state-based variables that influence policymaking (Fitzgerald 1996). These include the desire for larger budgets (and hence the development of new programs that would necessitate larger budgets); the demands of consistency (to withstand outside criticism—witness changes in Haitian and Cuban migrant policies under the Clinton administration); "do-ability" (recognition of the practical constraints—skills, other priorities, shortness of life—on effective implementation); the desire to avoid adverse publicity (no one likes an ugly congressional hearing or a bad headline); concerns about coherence ("if we do this this way, will it affect our ability to do that that way?"); efforts at institution-building and maintenance of morale (professionalism and culture, for example, in the Border Patrol and the asylum corps); and avoidance of lawsuits. The analysis is likely to be untidy; but if one believes that state action has an important role in migration and integration, then such examination will be necessary for a full understanding of that role.

The Intended, Unintended, and Discursive Impacts of State Regulation

The second perspective identified by Skocpol focuses on how state organizations and actions "influence the meanings and methods of politics for all groups and classes in society." These consequences may be intended or unintended, concrete or discursive. Consider, for example, the story of California's Proposition 187. The failure of federal enforcement efforts, combined with racial, nativist, and fiscal concerns, provided impetus to a popular protest that appropriated state power to achieve its goals—that is, the adoption in 1994 of a statewide measure that, among other things, denied benefits to illegal migrants and directed health care professionals and teachers to report undocumented aliens to state and federal authorities. Supporters of the proposition's approach broadened its impact by sponsoring and enacting legislation in Congress that extended similar measures to all states as a matter of federal law.

Opponents of Proposition 187 acted on a number of fronts. They filed lawsuits in California and successfully obtained an injunction from a federal district judge blocking implementation of the proposition on the grounds that it violated the Constitution and conflicted with federal law. Opponents also fought the proposed federal legislation and were partially successful by defeating a provision that would have authorized the exclusion of undocumented children from public schools. The anti-anti-immigrant movement also exercised political power in the 1996 elections, contributing to the Democratic ticket victories in California, Arizona, and Florida. Particularly important was the election of Democrat Gray Davis as governor of California; Davis prevented an eventual Supreme Court decision in the Proposition 187 litigation by settling the case. This is a large story, with complex state and public interactions involving state and federal legislation, the courts, and constitutional discourse. The available governmental structures and forums channeled and influenced the public debate and forms of action.

The Proposition 187 example displays a set of intended consequences: legislation and judicial opinions. The proposition also produced a number of unintended consequences, such as a significant increase in naturalization applications and perhaps a realignment of Hispanic voter allegiances. This is not an isolated case. Unintended consequences of immigration regulation have been startling: from the dramatic shift in immigrants' countries of origin following passage of the Immigration Act of 1965 to the illegal immigration sparked by the ending of the Bracero Program and the 1986 legalization efforts. Indeed, much of the recent legislation can be viewed as a reaction to the unintended consequences of earlier legislation, including the rise in asylum applications following enactment of the 1980 Refugee Act (responsible for administrative reform of the system and the expedited exclusion provisions in legislation enacted 1996) and the creation of a huge market in fraudulent documents following the implementation of employer sanctions (which has produced legislation mandating pilot projects to assist employers in validating the work papers of employees).

Of equal significance to these concrete consequences are the discursive impacts of state regulation. State policies "construct" immigrants and the immigration process in the public mind. Persons arriving in the United States can be labeled "refugees" (Cubans and Russian Jews) or "economic migrants" (Haitians and Dominicans); aliens who enter without inspection may be "illegal" (Mexicans) or "criminals," or they may be "undocumented" or even "potentially documentable" (the view of the Supreme Court in *Plyler v. Doe* [457 U.S. 202 (1982)]). The power to regulate immigration may be described as a core aspect of "state sovereignty" or as a limitation on "fundamental human rights." State actions at the border may be deemed "control" or "facilitation." Membership may be described as based on "residence" or "citizenship." In short, state actors shape public understandings of immigration both in the policies they adopt and in the words they use to describe and justify those policies.

Disaggregating the State

The state, of course, is not monolithic: various state actors pursue various interests for various reasons and with varying degrees of success. The relationships among state actors are both horizontal (the three branches of the federal government, usually placed under the label "separation of powers") and vertical (state and federal regulation, usually placed under the label of "federalism").[7]

On the horizontal level, the federal branches are relatively autonomous in some areas; in others, they share responsibility. The Haitian and Cuban policies demonstrate the former; appropriations and budget are examples of the latter. Interbranch cooperation is likely to be more problematic when different political parties control different branches. Understanding and explaining policy outcomes demands a sophisticated account of "the state."[8]

What I would like to focus particular attention on here is the role of the judiciary as an organ of state power. Scholars tend to see the courts as removed from "the state," as providing a check on policymakers. Yet the courts have played an important, if generally unappreciated, role in the overall structure of our immigration system.[9] Again, this has occurred along both the horizontal and vertical dimensions.

The Constitution nowhere explicitly grants Congress authority to regulate immigration. (Article I, section 8, grants power to adopt "an uniform Rule of Naturalization.") When the Supreme Court considered the issue in upholding the constitutionality of the Chinese exclusion laws in the late nineteenth century, it did so in exceptionally broad terms. It deemed such power inherent in the notion of a sovereign state and declared it virtually immune from judicial review (*Chae Chan Ping v. United States* [130 U.S. 581 (1889)]; Aleinikoff 1989). That view prevails to this day. Although the Court will scrutinize procedures for the removal of aliens, it has yet to invalidate substantive immigration regulations; and it has granted Congress a wide berth in determining the range of federal benefits to be made available to immigrants. As noted by the Court in one important case, "Congress regularly makes rules [for immigrants] that would be unacceptable if applied to citizens" (*Mathews v. Diaz* [426 U.S. 67 (1976)], 80). This lack of constraint has enormous implications for congressional (and executive branch) action, as evidenced by the 1996 welfare legislation that terminates benefits to permanent resident aliens (Personal Responsibility and Work Opportunity Reconciliation Act of 1996) and by discriminatory policies against Haitians and other groups. There is little chance that the courts will intervene in these matters, and the implications for migratory flows and assimilation should be apparent.

On the vertical level, the Supreme Court has established two important fundamental principles: (1) regulation of immigration is an exclusive federal power; and (2) state regulations discriminating against aliens are constitutionally suspect (unless they involve the exclusion of immigrants from political functions of the state). The first principle is the basis upon which a lower federal court enjoined implementation of California's Proposition 187. The second principle means that the states do not have the freedom possessed by Congress to exclude immigrants from public benefits and opportunities, and it provides the basis for the Supreme Court's ruling that the state of Texas could not constitutionally ban undocumented children from the public schools (*Plyler v. Doe*).

Together, the vertical and horizontal dimensions establish a structure of virtually unfettered federal authority to regulate the admission and stay of immigrants and the terms of admission. The power of the states, however, is significantly constrained in certain respects. These structural constitutional rules have had a substantial impact in the public debate and the making of immigration policy. Members of Congress were well aware of the norms when they enacted the Personal Responsibility and Work Opportunity Reconciliation Act of 1996; and the framers of Proposition 187 knew that part of the referendum directly conflicted with Supreme Court doctrine. Constitutional arguments are frequently important rhetorical devices in public debates, and court decisions concretely affect state actions. "Disaggregating" the state should lead scholars to focus attention on the role of the judiciary in the crafting and discourse of immigration policy.[10]

POLICING THE BORDERS OF MEMBERSHIP

I want to apply the preceding discussion to the role of the state in allocating what Michael Walzer has called "the primary good that we distribute to one another": membership (Walzer 1983, 34). The history of citizenship law and policy has been the subject of renewed interest among scholars (Bredbenner 1998; Cott 1998; Haney-López 1996; Smith 1997; chapter 8, this volume); and some recent work by social scientists has focused directly on membership issues, such as immigrants' use of social benefits (Fix and Passel 1994), naturalization practices (Gilbertson and Singer 2000; Bloemraad 1999), and political participation among new citizens (Bass and Casper 1999; DeSipio 1996). Social scientists have generally addressed membership in terms of assimilation and integration, however, examining how (and how well) the migrant makes his or her way in the receiving country. Thus, scholars look at employment and school success, access to and use of state benefits, participation in voluntary organizations and the extent to which home traditions and ways of life are transferred, transformed, or abandoned in the new country of settlement. To be sure, it is recognized that the state builds schools and enrolls students, provides (some degree of) health care, delivers the mail, and raises tax revenues from which it supplies police and fire protection and other public goods. However, the state is seen as playing a distinctly subsidiary role in the integration process,[11] which is generally theorized as occurring in civil society—among family, fellow migrants, and a receiving community that may be either welcoming, passive, or overtly hostile.

In previous sections I have identified three perspectives from which scholarship could profitably examine the state: its impact on migration and integration, its role as a self-interested actor, and its multifaceted nature. Each of these perspectives could be usefully employed in the study of citizenship and its consequences.

Citizenship, Migration, and Integration

Because most states grant immigration preferences to citizens' immediate family members, a state's citizenship regime will have a direct impact on the source and level of immigration. Citizenship at birth can be acquired based either on descent (jus sanguinis) or on place of birth (jus soli). The United States holds to both, as do Canada, Mexico, and a number of other Latin American countries. Many European states have traditionally adopted jus sanguinis citizenship policies. In the United States, jus soli means that children born to temporary visitors and undocumented aliens are citizens of the United States at birth. The Austrian jus sanguinis policy means that the children of lawful permanent immigrants (and their children) are not citizens at birth. Thus, aliens in Austria can obtain citizenship only by way of a naturalization process, which includes a requirement that a naturalizing citizen relinquish citizenship in his or her home country.

The result is that alienage and citizenship are multigenerational issues in Austria and other states that follow jus sanguinis rules; and they occasion complex emotions and calculations about the desirability of obtaining citizenship of the country of one's (and possibly one's parents' and grandparents') residence. In the United States, the naturalization question is an issue only for the first generation; it is not an issue for children born in the United States even to illegal entrants. Furthermore, children born to migrants in the United States routinely acquire two citizenships at birth, and they are under no obligation under U.S. law to elect one or the other.

Because citizenship is the gateway to important social and political rights, it therefore seems likely that differing rules for acquiring full membership in a society will have significant implications
for assimilation and integration. The proposition could be tested
by examining second and third generations in jus soli and jus sanguinis countries.

Naturalization rules ought to have noticeable impacts, as well.
For example, the United States requires naturalizing citizens to re-
nounce other allegiances; Canada, since 1977, has not. Why have
these choices been made, and with what consequences—for naturalization rates, return migration, overall integration? We are witnessing increasing levels of dual citizenship, which permits persons to travel on two (or more) passports and has consequences
for land ownership, inheritance, investment, and political rights.
How have these policies affected return rates, the creation and
maintenance of migrant networks, investment strategies, and
"transnationality"?

Citizenship and the State as Actor

As previously noted, the state is frequently a self-interested partici-
pant in the formation of policy. The recent and intense controversy over naturalization policies provides an apt site for investigation. In 1995, the INS announced a major effort at tackling huge
backlogs in naturalization applications. The reasons for the initiation of the program were numerous, including an oft-stated policy
preference of the INS commissioner, pressure from outside constituencies, internal INS aims at improving service, and goals of
particular INS decisionmakers and field managers (who view naturalization as community affirming and positive for public relations). Republicans charged that the program was an election-year
plot to naturalize likely Democratic voters—an allegation made at
least facially plausible with the disclosure of internal White House
e-mails that appeared to link naturalization and voter registration.
Subsequent congressional investigation revealed weaknesses in
INS processing, including irregularities by outside entities authorized to administered required civics and language examinations
and apparent failure by the INS to ensure that applicants for naturalization undergo fingerprint checks by the Federal Bureau of In-

vestigation. These perceived administrative problems are traceable to long-term neglect of the agency, in terms of both funding and personnel. This is a complex story of core social symbolism ("citizenship"), political posturing, and alleged agency failure (itself based on earlier political judgments) and political interference. It paints a picture of a multifaceted state with different state actors frequently in conflict with one another. The policies are largely state originated, and yet they have tremendous consequences for civil society—intentional (the naturalization of more than 1 million citizens in fiscal year 1996), unintentional (possible effects on elections), and rhetorical (some proclaiming "the death of citizenship" [Geyer 1996]).

A second example regards the requirement that naturalizing citizens swear an oath renouncing all "allegiance and fidelity" to their state of origin. This mandate, present in U.S. law since the first naturalization statute of 1790, purports to prevent dual citizenship for naturalized citizens. The U.S. law, however, is not binding on foreign states; and a number of countries (including Canada, the Dominican Republic, Mexico, and the United Kingdom) continue to recognize the citizenship of their nationals even if they naturalize in the United States. More importantly, neither the INS nor the State Department takes any steps to enforce the renunciation oath—even with respect to states of origin that recognize the renunciation as effectively terminating citizenship in the home country. That is, the federal government does not request that naturalizing citizens relinquish other passports, does not notify the country of origin of the fact of naturalization, does not ask naturalized citizens seeking passports whether they intend to travel on their original passports, and makes no effort to check whether naturalized citizens have exercised any rights of citizenship in their states of origin (such as voting). The policies of nonenforcement mean that the renunciation of prior citizenship has few, if any, consequences—a fact of which most naturalizing citizens are well aware.

Why does the oath go unenforced? The INS views enforcement as difficult and time consuming and basically the responsibility of the State Department. The State Department, however, does not view itself as an enforcement agency and has no staff dedicated to the task. Furthermore, enforcement of the renunciation oath might well cause diplomatic complications with foreign states that do not recognize the oath as effective. It might also raise problems for U.S. citizens who naturalize elsewhere: under U.S. law, a citizen of the United States who takes citizenship in another state does not lose U.S. citizenship unless he or she intends to relinquish it—even if that state has an oath requiring renunciation. The State Department is no doubt concerned that enforcement efforts against naturalized citizens in the United States may lead to reciprocal actions against U.S. citizens overseas. Thus, despite the more than two-centuries-old congressional requirement of renunciation, the interests of the bureaucracy dominate here to render the statutory mandate virtually meaningless.

Citizenship, a Disaggregated State, and the Supreme Court

A third angle of investigation recognizes the various roles that different state actors play. As Reed Ueda's contribution to this volume details, Congress plays the central part in crafting naturalization rules and also sets the terms of membership by legislating which rights and opportunities accompany which concentric circle of belonging. Administrative authorities also play an important role; for instance, they can pursue naturalization as a goal with more or less assiduousness. However, the fundamental membership rules are established by the Constitution and, by implication, by the Supreme Court.

For the nation's first hundred years, the Constitution did not provide an explicit rule for determining U.S. citizenship (Kettner 1978). As is well known, the Fourteenth Amendment's affirmation of jus soli was a direct response to Chief Justice Roger Brooke Taney's opinion in the *Dred Scott* case, holding that free blacks born in the United States were not U.S. citizens. The implications of jus soli have already been described. The Court rendered two decisions of significance in the late nineteenth century. The first (*Elk v. Wilkins* [112 U.S. 94 (1884)]) held that Indians who had left their tribes and affiliated with white society were not, by those facts alone, deemed to be citizens. The second (*United States v. Wong Kim Ark* [169 U.S. 649 (1898)]) held that children born to Chinese immigrants were citizens of the United States at birth, despite the fact that their parents were not eligible to obtain citizenship under the U.S. naturalization law. The latter case provides the basis for the conclusion that children born to undocumented aliens in the United States are citizens. This proposition is currently a matter of political controversy and has been the subject of congressional hearings.

In the latter half of this century, the Court has issued important constitutional judgments on loss of U.S. citizenship. In a line of cases, it has established a rule that U.S. citizenship may be lost only if the citizen expressly intends to relinquish it (*Afroyim v. Rusk* [387 U.S. 253 (1967)]; *Vance v. Terrazas* [444 U.S. 252 (1980)]). These holdings virtually terminate congressional authority to extinguish citizenship. The Court has also adopted procedural rules that make denaturalization of wrongfully naturalized citizens an arduous process for the government (*Schneiderman v. United States* [320 U.S. 118 (1943)]; *Chaunt v. United States* [364 U.S. 350 (1960)]).

These constitutional norms, enunciated by the Supreme Court, provide the framework within which citizenship and naturalization policy must operate. Jus soli cannot be altered without constitutional amendment, nor can the strong rules against loss of U.S. citizenship. These principles are deeply embedded in U.S. political culture and are regularly appealed to in political debate. As such they help shape the "policy space" for congressional and administrative decisionmakers.

THE STRUCTURE OF MEMBERSHIP TODAY

So far, the discussion has been largely heuristic. I have noted ways in which international migration theory might be enriched by taking greater notice of the state policy, state actors, and state rhetoric. The analysis has proceeded from the hardly surprising proposition that the state has a major influence on immigration flows across state borders. I have further suggested that researchers interested in investigating the state role pay greater attention to membership rules as a significant factor in immigration and immigrant integration. As Reed Ueda's essay makes clear, membership policy and immigration policy have been linked from the start in the United States. Congress used naturalization laws early on as the primary device for providing incentives or disincentives to immigration. Today, citizenship decisions continue to have a powerful influence on immigration, because of the preference that the law gives to the entry of family members of citizens, and on immigrant integration, because of the rule that children born in the United States to immigrants are citizens at birth.

The rules regarding citizenship in the United States are among the most generous in the world. The jus soli principle ensures that all persons born in the United States are citizens.[12] The rules for transmitting citizenship to children born overseas to a U.S. citizen were substantially liberalized in the twentieth century, and naturalization requirements are, in the main, not difficult for most immigrants to satisfy.

As I have argued elsewhere (Aleinikoff 1990; 2000, 155–68), a state's citizenship rules may not fully constitute its understanding of membership. Resident immigrants in the United States have traditionally been accorded substantial rights and opportunities that establish a form of membership in the social, economic, and political life of the nation. The Supreme Court has interpreted most of the Constitution's protections of individual rights to apply to *persons*, not citizens. It has also read the Equal Protection Clause to prohibit most state discrimination against permanent resident aliens. Thus the Constitution identifies a circle of membership more inclusive than citizenship—one that protects persons based on their presence in the United States, not their status. This has significance beyond affording aliens the protections of most of the Bill of Rights. It means that immigrants, including undocumented children, have guaranteed access to the primary structure for integration, the public schools.

Congress has filled in additional benefits for noncitizens. Indeed, until enactment of the 1996 welfare law, permanent resident aliens, refugees, and asylees were eligible for most means-tested and non-means-tested federal programs. In effect, the permanent resident circle has overlapped considerably with the citizenship circle.

The central difference in the legal function of citizenship today is that it identifies holders of the franchise. The linkage of voting and citizenship is actually of fairly recent vintage: until the first quarter of the twentieth century, large groups of citizens were in-eligible to vote, and aliens were able to vote in some states. Apparently the presidential election of 1928 was the first in which no alien was eligible to vote (Raskin 1993). Citizenship, of course, brings other rights as well, including the rights to travel on a U.S. passport and to invoke U.S. protection abroad. Citizens also have the right to remain and reenter the United States; they may not be deported or exiled.

Citizenship is a significant subject of current policy discussion. The reasons for this are several, although the appropriate weight to be assigned to each is not clear. First, unprecedented numbers of immigrants, many of whom gained legal status during the legalization programs established by the 1986 Immigration Reform and Control Act, have sought naturalization in recent years. Second, the challenges to state authority posed by globalization and sub-national assertions of autonomy have put citizenship in new light: to the right, emphasizing citizenship is a way to affirm "Americanism" (and undermine multiculturalism) without seeming nativist or racist; to the left, citizenship is seen as potentially supplying an umbrella concept that can hold together an increasingly polyethnic United States. Third, low voter turnouts, general public cynicism about government, and a perceived increase in public incivility have sparked new discussion about the decline of citizenship and proposals for its rebirth. Here the issues are not how one becomes a citizen or what rights follow from that status but rather what it means to be a "good citizen" in a representative democracy.

Yet despite these issues, the U.S. membership regime is un-likely to undergo any major alteration. For example, congressional committees have in recent years examined the issue of whether children born to undocumented parents in the United States should continue to be granted citizenship at birth. It seems clear, however, that proposals for a constitutional amendment changing the rule will not go far, and it is wholly inconceivable that any broad-scale attack on jus soli will either take place or succeed. *Dred Scott* continues to cast a long shadow. Similarly, although extensive criticism has been leveled against INS naturalization procedures, no serious proposal is on the table to change naturalization requirements. The one significant area in which membership principles changed in the 1990s was in the withdrawal of federal means-tested benefits to resident aliens. More recently, however, Congress has restored benefits to some classes of immigrants; and, in any event, states have stepped in to provide aid to many aliens dropped from federal programs. It may well be that the general stability of the U.S. architecture of membership has led researchers to miss its impact in migration and integration processes.

In sum, membership is pervasively regulated by the state (through the Constitution, the Congress, the courts, and the executive branch), and the rights and opportunities defined by various levels of membership have an important impact on immigrants and their integration into American society. The state, through its conduct and its discourse, also influences the debate over membership in society at large. The construction of membership, then, is a joint project of state and society, providing a gateway to each.

CONCLUSION

Theories of international migration would do well to start where migrants start: with the recognition that they are moving across state borders usually according to the rules established by states and that their incorporation into the receiving state (up to and including full membership) will be pervasively regulated by the state. It is not enough to see the central question facing the migrant as "Where can my family and I receive the greatest return on my human and social capital?" Choices to cross borders entail deeper political and cultural questions as well: "How secure will my future be?" (the question of legal status). "How much at home will I feel there?" "Can I speak the language?" "How can I enter the country?" "Can my child be schooled there; can he or she receive medical care?" Migrants do not consider borders, state authorities, or legal rights and opportunities irrelevant, and neither should social scientists.

More than twenty years ago, Aristide Zolberg noted that "the preferences of 'those who send' and 'those who receive' have shaped international migrations to a much greater extent than the preferences of 'those who go'" (1978, 279). We still await the full theoretical development of a state-centered perspective on immigration and membership and the empirical work to support it.

NOTES

1. See also Bredbenner 1998; Cott 1998; Haney López 1996; Smith 1997.
2. Rubén Rumbaut, in commenting on a draft of this paper, has suggested another example: Filipino migration to the United States. Filipinos have constituted the second-largest immigrant group, after Mexicans, for the past several decades. Surely American colonialism, the U.S. military, and Filipino participation in the United States armed forces have played a major role in the formation of the migratory flow.
3. This lack of communication among disciplines is apparently not limited to North American scholars. A paper written for a workshop sponsored by the International Organization for Migration observes that "the scholarly debate on Soviet migration features two conflicting views of the process. Historians and political scientists tend to stress the role of the State in planning and managing these huge movements of peoples, whereas sociologists and geographers believe that no State, not even a totalitarian one, is able to control phenomena on such a scale. These latter underscore that the Soviet Government did not even have a systematic migration policy to accompany the industrialization drive" ("Historical Overview of Migration Movements" 1994).
4. Significant lobbying did occur around several major provisions: weakening sanctions against employers who hire illegal aliens, federal authorization to states to deny public education to undocumented children (the so-called Gallegly amendment), and cuts in legal immigration; see, generally, Gimpel and Edwards 1999.
5. The statutory provision expired in 1998, but was put back in the law for a brief period in 2000 to 2001.
6. For another example of this kind of rich, detailed study, see Hing 1992.
7. See also Guiraudon and Lahav 2000, noting devolution of state decisionmaking upward to intergovernmental institutions, downward to local officials, and outward to private actors (such as airlines and employers). The discussion here ignores important intrabranch differences—for example, differing views among federal departments (such as the Labor Department and the INS on enforcement of employer sanctions) and differing views between the White House and the departments.

8. For detailed studies of the legislative process, see LeMay 1994; Gimpel and Edwards 1999; Schrag 2000.

9. We tend to focus on courts only when they check other branches of government. This misses the crucial role that the judiciary plays in validating state policies by refusing to set them aside; see Black 1969.

10. For a detailed historical study of the interaction of Congress, the executive branch, and the courts in the enforcement of the Chinese exclusion laws, see Salyer 1995.

11. Indeed, the state does not figure in Alba and Nee's (1999) important new work on assimilation.

12. The sole exceptions are children born to foreign diplomats and invading armies, who are not deemed to come within the Fourteenth Amendment's language that children be born "subject to the jurisdiction" of the United States.

REFERENCES

Alba, Richard, and Victor Nee. 1999. "Rethinking Assimilation Theory for a New Era of Immigration." In *The Handbook of International Migration: The American Experience*, edited by Charles Hirschman, Philip Kasinitz, and Josh DeWind. New York: Russell Sage Foundation.

Aleinikoff, T. Alexander. 1989. "Federal Regulation of Aliens and the Constitution." *American Journal of International Law* 83(4): 862–71.

———. 1990. "Citizens, Aliens, Membership, and the Constitution." *Constitutional Commentary.* 7(1): 9–34.

———. 2000. *From Migrants to Citizens: Membership in a Changing World*, edited by T. Alexander Aleinikoff and Douglas Klusmeyer. Washington, D.C.: Carnegie Endowment for International Peace.

Andreas, Peter. 1998. "The Escalation of U.S. Immigration Control in the Post-NAFTA Era." *Political Science Quarterly* 113(4): 591–615.

Bass, Loretta E., and Lynne M. Casper. 1999. "Are There Differences in Registration and Voting Behavior Between Naturalized and Native-Born Americans?" Working Paper 28. Washington: U.S. Census Bureau, Population Division.

Black, Charles L., Jr. 1969. *Structure and Relationship in Constitutional Law.* Baton Rouge: Louisiana State University Press.

Bloemraad, Irene. 1999. "Political Culture, State Institutions, Ethnic Organizations, and Immigrant Naturalization: Lessons Drawn from a Canadian-U.S. Comparison." Paper presented to the Carnegie Endowment for International Peace, roundtable discussion. Washington, D.C (May 14, 1999).

Bredbenner, Candice L. 1998. *A Nationality of Her Own: Woman, Marriage, and the Law of Citizenship*. Berkeley: University of California Press.

Calavita, Kitty. 1992. *Inside the State: The Bracero Program, Immigration, and the INS*. New York: Routledge.

Cott, Nancy F. 1998. "Marriage and Women's Citizenship in the United States, 1830–1934." *American Historical Review* 103(5): 1440–74.

Daniels, Roger. 1962. *The Politics of Prejudice: The Anti-Japanese Movement in California and the Struggle for Japanese Exclusion*. Berkeley: University of California Press.

DeSipio, Louis. 1996. "Making Citizens or Good Citizens? Naturalization as a Predictor of Organizational and Electoral Behavior Among Latino Immigrants." *Hispanic Journal of Behavioral Sciences* 18(2): 194–213.

Fitzgerald, Keith. 1996. *The Face of the Nation: Immigration, the State, and the National Identity*. Stanford: Stanford University Press.

Fix, Michael, and Jeffrey S. Passel. 1994. *Immigration and Immigrants: Setting the Record Straight*. Washington, D.C.: Urban Institute Press.

Freeman, Gary P. 1994. "Can Liberal States Control Unwanted Migration?" *Annals of the American Academy of Political and Social Science* 534: 17–30.

———. 1995. "Modes of Immigration Politics in Liberal Democratic States." *International Migration Review* 29(4): 881–902.

Geyer, Georgie Anne. 1996. *Americans No More: The Death of Citizenship*. New York: Atlantic Monthly Press.

Gilbertson, Greta, and Audrey Singer. 2000. "Naturalization Under Changing Conditions of Membership: Dominican Immigrants in New York City." In *Immigration Research for a New Century: Multidisciplinary Perspectives,* edited by Nancy Foner, Rubén G. Rumbaut, and Steven J. Gold. New York: Russell Sage Foundation.

Gimpel, James G., and James R. Edwards, Jr. 1999. *The Congressional Politics of Immigration Reform*. Needham Heights, Mass: Allyn and Bacon.

Guiraudon, Virginie, and Gallya Lahav. 2000. "A Reappraisal of the State Sovereignty Debate: The Case of Migration Control." *Comparative Political Studies* 33(2): 163–95.

Haney López, Ian F. 1996. *White by Law: The Legal Construction of Race*. New York: New York University Press.

Higham, John. 1955. *Strangers in the Land: Patterns of American Nativism, 1860–1925*. New York: Atheneum.

Hing, Bill Ong. 1992. "The Immigration and Naturalization Service, Community-Based Organizations, and the Legalization Experience: Lessons for the Self-Help Immigration Phenomenon." *Georgetown Immigration Law Journal* 6(3): 413–98.

"Historical Overview of Migration Movements in the CIS and Baltic Region and Their Demographic Consequences." 1994. Paper presented to the International Organization for Migration conference, "Citizenship, Statelessness, and the Status of Aliens in the CIS and Baltic States." Helsinki (December 12 to 15).

Hollifield, James F. 1992. *Immigrants, Markets, and States: The Political Economy of Postwar Europe.* Cambridge, Mass.: Harvard University Press.

———. 2000. "The Politics of International Migration: How Can We 'Bring the State Back In'?" In *Talking Across Disciplines: Migration Theory in Social Science and Law,* edited by Caroline Brettell and James F. Hollifield. New York: Routledge.

Joppke, Christian. 1998a. "Why Liberal States Accept Unwanted Immigration." *World Politics* 50(2): 266–93.

———, ed. 1998b. *Challenge to the Nation-State: Immigration in Western Europe and the United States.* Oxford: Oxford University Press.

Kettner, James H. 1978. *The Development of American Citizenship, 1608–1870.* Chapel Hill: University of North Carolina Press.

LeMay, Michael C. 1994. *Anatomy of a Public Policy: The Reform of Contemporary American Immigration Law.* Westport, Conn.: Praeger.

Massey, Douglas S. 1999. "Why Does Immigration Occur? A Theoretical Synthesis." In *The Handbook of International Migration: The American Experience,* edited by Charles Hirschman, Philip Kasinitz, and Josh DeWind. New York: Russell Sage Foundation.

Massey, Douglas S., Joaquin Arango, Graeme Hugo, Ali Kouaouci, Adela Pellegrino and J. Edward Taylor. 1993. "Theories of International Migration: A Review and Appraisal." *Population and Development Review* 19(3): 431–66.

Massey, Douglas S., and Kristin E. Espinosa. 1997. "What's Driving Mexico-U.S. Migration? A Theoretical, Empirical, and Policy Analysis." *American Journal of Sociology* 102(4): 939–99.

Pitkin, Thomas M. 1975. *Keepers of the Gate: A History of Ellis Island.* New York: New York University Press.

Portes, Alejandro. 1994. "Introduction: Immigration and Its Aftermath." *International Migration Review* 28(4): 632–39.

———. 1999. "Immigration Theory for a New Century: Some Problems and Opportunities." In *The Handbook of International Migration: The American Experience,* edited by Charles Hirschman, Philip Kasinitz, and Josh DeWind. New York: Russell Sage Foundation.

Portes, Alejandro, and Robert L. Bach. 1985. *Latin Journey: Cuban and Mexican Immigrants in the United States.* Berkeley: University of California Press.

Raskin, Jamin B. 1993. "Legal Aliens, Local Citizens: The Historical, Constitutional, and Theoretical Meanings of Alien Suffrage." *University of Pennsylvania Law Review* 141(4): 1391–1470.

Salyer, Lucy E. 1995. *Laws Harsh as Tigers: Chinese Immigrants and the Shaping of Modern Immigration Law.* Chapel Hill: University of North Carolina Press.

Schrag, Philip G. 2000. *Well-Founded Fear: The Congressional Battle to Save Political Asylum in America.* New York: Routledge.

Skocpol, Theda. 1985. "Bringing the State Back In: Strategies of Analysis in Current Research." In *Bringing the State Back In*, edited by Peter B. Evans, Dietrich Rueschemeyer, and Theda Skocpol. Cambridge: Cambridge University Press.

Smith, Rogers M. 1997. *Civic Ideals: Conflicting Visions of Citizenship in U.S. History.* New Haven: Yale University Press.

Walzer, Michael 1983. *Spheres of Justice: A Defense of Pluralism and Equality.* New York: Basic Books.

Zolberg, Aristide R. 1978. "The Patterning of International Migration Policies in a Changing World System." In *Human Migration: Patterns and Policies*, edited by William H. McNeill and Ruth S. Adams. Bloomington: Indiana University Press.

———. 1981. "International Migration in Political Perspective." In *Global Trends in Migration: Theory and Research in International Population Movements*, edited by Mary M. Kritz, Charles B. Keely, and Silvano M. Tomasi. New York: Center for Migration Studies.

———. 1999. "Matters of State: Theorizing Immigration Policy." In *The Handbook of International Migration: The American Experience*, edited by Charles Hirschman, Philip Kasinitz, and Josh DeWind. New York: Russell Sage Foundation.

—— Chapter 8 ——

Historical Patterns of Immigrant Status and Incorporation in the United States

Reed Ueda

THE EVOLUTION AND expansion of central state power has profoundly shaped the pathways that allow immigrants to become permanent settlers and turn newcomers into members of the
host country. The political integration of immigrants has been
deeply affected by a complex and ongoing expansion of regulatory state power involving not only the legislative branch of federal government but also the judiciary and the executive, as Alex
Aleinikoff demonstrates in his legal study (chapter 7 of this volume). What follows is a historical study of the state's management
of immigrant incorporation, which reveals how this governmental
activity sprang from distinctive historical moments and patterns of
events that expressed the relations between government and civil
society, the nation and ethnic minorities, and the concept of national identity.

Immigration provided the "pressure" for the development of
centralized policies shaping the incorporative patterns of the
American polity. During the peak periods of immigration in the
past one hundred years, governmental authorities reacted by creating new administrative and legislative structures to manage
flows into the country and to control the process of positioning

immigrants in civil society. These periods of increased federal activism in immigration policy corresponded to eras during which policymakers began generally to advocate the expansion of centralized state power to reform American society. The project of social reform "fed back" into social policies toward immigrants that functioned as tools for social engineering. Policymakers developed conceptual grids for formatting the population into categorical subgroups that could be labeled and managed as building blocks in the restructuring of American society.

Thus, in a basic way, the efforts by the state in shaping the status and rights of immigrants responded to changing ideas about how the American nation should absorb the ethnic minorities created by large increases in mass immigration. They reflected persistent tensions between individual and collective identity, between civic assimilation and ethnic solidarity, and between the domain of the state and the spheres of civil society.

CONSTITUTIONAL ORIGINS OF IMMIGRANT STATUS AND CITIZENSHIP

In the history of the United States, dependence on mass immigration for development made the creation of policies for politically incorporating immigrants a central issue in nation-building and state-building. The evolution of admissions, citizenship, and antidiscrimination policies for immigrants shaped the categories of status that produced integration into civil society and the political community.

By multiplying ethnic and racial subgroups, immigration challenged the abilities of policymakers to fashion a national citizenship that could unite the variety of ethnic "fragments" into a single national "whole." The role for citizenship came to reflect tensions between what historian John Higham (1993) perceived as two national foundings (Bendix 1977; Marshall 1950).

The first founding occurred as the English colonists arriving in the seventeenth century displaced Native Americans and enslaved blacks. They created a pattern of intergroup relations that supported their dominance. Their descendants would have a presumptive claim to custodial proprietorship of the country (Higham 1993; Morgan 1975; Nash 1974).

The pattern of ethnic and racial relations created by the first founding tended to promote the prescriptive view of a homogeneous American nation that was coextensive with the Anglo-Saxon core. John Jay expressed the idea that American nationality was purely Anglo-Saxon, when he described the new republic as composed of "a people descended from the same ancestors . . . very similar in their manners and customs" (Jay 1961, 38). Alexis de Tocqueville, in *Democracy in America,* provided a parallel description of American nationality as homogeneously Anglo-Saxon. Tocqueville wrote that the United States consisted of "offsets of the same people," a single and culturally unified "Anglo-American" nation "connected with England by their origin, their religion, their language, and partially by their manners" (Tocqueville 1956, 233).

With the coming of the American Revolution, a second founding occurred that expressed the legalistic, contractual, and civic ideals of European enlightenment and republican thought. It provided a new framework for ethnic and racial relations responsive to the unifying power of reason, individual rights, and republican civic voluntarism (Kedourie 1993, 2; Bailyn 1967, 26–30; Handlin and Handlin 1989, 170–73; Wood 1992, 213–22, 233–37, 238–39; Greenfeld 1992, 422–23; Foner 1994, 436; Arieli 1964, 71–73, 83).

The second founding never completely overcame the ethnoracial patterns of the first founding, which continued to have a powerful residual effect. Thus the tension between the two foundings continued to play itself out historically and complicated the capacity of citizenship to unify the multiplying subpopulations of the nation. The charter Anglo-American group formed by descent from English colonizers saw themselves as capable of assimilating Protestant immigrants from Great Britain and northern and western Europe. Many members of this charter group, however, drew the line against the reception of Catholics, Jews, and other non-Protestants from southern and eastern Europe. As the nation expanded geographically, the Anglo-American core group extended their dominance over Native Americans, Hawaiians, Mexicans, Puerto Ricans, and Filipinos (Higham 1975, 3–8). Nevertheless, the principles of the second founding, centering on the legal and ideological allegiance of free persons, shaped an immigrant admissions system that eschewed tests of religion, national origin, and social class. Immigrants from various countries and cultures could be accepted as legal residents (Wood 1969, chapters 1–9; Rahe 1994, 32–34; Kettner 1974, 1976).

In the century after the national founding, when the cosmopolitan ideal underpinned immigration policy, state governments of the Atlantic seaboard primarily controlled the entry of immigrants into the country. Port authorities focused on providing an orderly process of reception and sought to bar only those foreigners who might create social problems and burdens if allowed to enter the country. Denial of admission occurred when an immigrant was deemed to be a likely charity case, to be diseased, or to be socially undesirable. No limitations or ceilings were placed upon the flow of immigration (Hutchinson 1981, 396–404; Taylor 1971, 125–26; Bernard 1980).

After admission, immigrants received uniform legal status as resident aliens. All resident aliens were eligible to convert their status into naturalized citizenship. They would not be an excluded and unincorporated subpopulation, like the guest-worker immigrants in twentieth-century Europe. Furthermore, the United States afforded aliens a status that allowed them to participate immediately in civil society. As aliens, they exercised most of the civil rights possessed by native citizens to pursue employment, housing, educational, and entrepreneurial opportunities.

In defining the architecture of republican civil society, the federal Constitution eschews the British constitutional tradition of dividing civil society into legal corporate orders. In the place of a system of graded status that would constitute civil society, the founders created a legal order based on citizenship, a single and uniform individual status for all members of society (Roche 1949, 6–9; Stephenson 1926, 238). Thus in the American status system, native-born and naturalized citizens possessed the same civil and political rights, except for the opportunity to become president. In its total framework, the American polity configured public space within civil society in such a way that the distance between the native citizen and the immigrant, either as alien or naturalized citizen, remained small or insignificant. This feature of immigrant status tended to promote rapid integration into the structure of civil and political society.

The process of naturalization was open and uncomplicated, making the boundary between alien and citizen porous. Naturalization proceedings involved merely formal and legal tests of the immigrant's achieved rather than ascribed qualities. Naturalized citizenship emanated from the autonomous power of the individual to transfer allegiance from a foreign government to the United States. The individual immigrant controlled the initiation and completion of the naturalization process. The state would set only basic rules of procedure to qualify for naturalization. It would neither organize groups for naturalization nor require immigrants to naturalize. Political parties stepped into the area between the state and the immigrant; in various districts, they often sought to recruit aliens as future citizens and voters. The immigrant, however, ultimately decided how and when naturalization would suit the requirements of his or her life. Naturalization became a reflection of the republican values of personal liberty, rational will, and consent (Kettner 1974).

The United States established the procedural requirements for naturalization through congressional legislation. The federal Constitution of 1787 empowers Congress to "establish an uniform rule of naturalization." This grant of authority was designed to produce a basic national standard consistent with the Constitution's "comity clause," which continued the Article of Confederation's principle of reciprocal interstate citizenship. It also ensured that state governments would not abuse their naturalization powers. Congress's power over naturalization was construed as essentially negative—the authority to set a rule for the removal of the disabilities of alienage, of foreign birth (Roche 1949, 10).

Congress initiated procedural rules for naturalization with the passage of the first federal naturalization law in 1790. An applicant for naturalization had to be a "free white person" who had resided for two years "within the limits and under the jurisdiction of the United States." Fearful of the political support given by aliens to the Jeffersonian Republicans, the Federalists in Congress succeeding in passing a law in 1795 raising the residency requirement for naturalization to five years and further secured a law in 1798 requiring fourteen years' residency. When the Jeffersonian Republicans came into power, they passed a law in 1802 reducing the residency requirement to five years, where it has remained since (Franklin 1906, 48, 70–71; Roche 1949, 1, 10–12; U.S. Department of Labor 1926). The 1802 law laid down other procedural terms for naturalization: an applicant had to be a free white person who had declared the intention to become a citizen at least three years previous to the award of citizenship and had to have been a resident for at least five years in the United States and at least one year in the state in which the petition for citizenship was made. The culminating act of naturalization was the swearing of an oath renouncing allegiance to foreign sovereignty and pledging to uphold the Constitution. The applicant for citizenship could apply in any court of record.

Single alien women were eligible for individual naturalization, but marriage could also lead to citizenship. Congress passed a law in 1855 recognizing that alien women who married American citizens automatically received citizenship. Furthermore, the alien wives of male aliens became citizens as soon as their husbands were naturalized. The road to acquiring American citizenship for married immigrant women deviated from the path for immigrant men. Male aliens autonomously established their citizenship, whereas the tie of marriage possessed an intervening power to determine citizenship for female aliens (Gettys 1934, 111, 113–14).

Because the United States sought to encourage immigration, an open and direct naturalization procedure became a cornerstone of immigration policy. The offer of an easily satisfied and simple naturalization procedure to all newcomers from Europe was an outgrowth of the challenge to feudal and autocratic rule that emerged from the American Revolution. As a nation aggressively seeking to build itself on social movements of mass naturalization, the United States swept away the tradition of enforced national membership found in European states. An anonymous writer to the editor of the *American Weekly Messenger* of Philadelphia in 1813 discussed this distinctive feature of American nation-building: "The Nation that holds out inducements and entitlements to the subjects of other nations, to leave their domicile of nativity and become members of the community so tempting them, will be considered by other political communities as contravening a known and established law of nations" (quoted in Stephenson 1926, 238). The United States was the international leader in elevating and popularizing the principle that individuals should have the opportunity to freely transfer themselves in nationality and political allegiance.

The boundary between citizen and alien was further weakened by the loose and improper handling of naturalization proceedings. During court hearings of applications for naturalization, judges often summarily approved aliens for citizenship in collective groups. Management of fraudulent and illegal naturalizations by political parties seeking new immigrant voters became widespread and notorious. Popular reaction to the corruption of the naturalization process for partisan electoral purposes fueled nativistic movements (Anbinder 1992, 117–22). Without effective federal supervision of naturalization, massive fraudulent naturalizations continued throughout the nineteenth century, especially in local courts of record. In 1886, a judge in New York state was reported to have approved twenty-five hundred certificates of naturalized citizenship in a single day (Mears 1928, 97).[1] Fraudulent naturalizations predictably mounted in number as the dates of political elections approached. In New York City, two judges naturalized over 26,000 individuals in the twenty-three days preceding election day. The aliens were herded into court in "groups" and "platoons" and summarily sworn in en masse as new citizens (Stephenson 1926, 244).

The boundary between citizen and alien was also blurred as most states and territories seeking to lure settlers bestowed generous political, commercial, and property rights upon aliens. States and territories placed little restriction on employment, property holding, and business transactions by aliens. Furthermore, in the nineteenth century, at least twenty-two states and territories granted the right to vote to aliens who merely declared their intention to become citizens. Although alien suffrage was eventually abrogated, it was not until 1928 that the first national election occurred in which no alien in any state possessed the right to vote (Higham 1955, 98; Konvitz 1946, 1).

The demand for immigrants repeatedly prompted organized efforts to pressure Congress to ease the naturalization requirements. In 1824 citizens from New Jersey and New York urged

Congress to relax the probationary laws for naturalization. "Sundry aliens of Louisiana" requested of Congress in the same year that the federal naturalization laws be altered to afford "greater facilities" to foreigners desiring to gain citizenship. "Sundry citizens of New York state" submitted a memorial to the House of Representatives in 1835 asking that no declaration of intention be required and that after two years of residence in the United States aliens should receive all the rights of citizenship. Throughout the nineteenth century, social and political interest groups supported an easy and quick naturalization process. Despite the advocacy for relaxing residency requirements, however, the five-year minimum period of residency stood firm (Higham 1955, 98; Franklin 1906, 170–72, 180).

Some key features of citizenship made available to immigrants remained ambiguous. Before the Civil War, national citizenship was presumed to derive from state citizenship. The states possessed the right to determine whom they recognized as citizens and the rights accorded to them (Roche 1949, 4–5, 12; Kettner 1978, 327, 345–46, 369). The voluntary and ideological form of citizenship embodied in the laws of naturalization also coexisted in a tension with the ascriptive and passive form of birthright citizenship. The latter derived from common law and feudal theory, a status-determining source very different from the republican theory of the revolutionary founders that had given rise to the idea of volitional citizenship. Birthright citizenship could be derived either from birth within the territorial jurisdiction of the United States (the principle of jus soli) or from birth to parents who were members of the national community (the principle of jus sanguinis). State and territorial governments without exception provided birthright citizenship to the children of immigrants (Schuck and Smith 1985, 42–54).

The passage of the Fourteenth Amendment to the Constitution, which politically incorporated emancipated slaves, revised and clarified the general nature of citizenship. It established the essential national character of citizenship, declaring that "all persons born or naturalized in the United States and subject to the jurisdiction thereof, are citizens of the United States and of the state wherein they reside." The Fourteenth Amendment defined birthright citizenship in terms of the jus soli principle of the award of citizenship according to birth within the territory of a sovereign nation (Kettner 1978, 475; Gettys 1934, 8–9).

The "birthright citizenship" clause of the Fourteenth Amendment assured full and permanent political incorporation for the children of immigrants. It thus strengthened the capacity of the nation to absorb immigrants. In immigrant-receiving societies, the disposal of the status of the second generation has been a critical test for the incorporation of an immigrant population into the host nation. The Fourteenth Amendment provided that all descendants of immigrants born within the territory of the United States would automatically gain citizenship equivalent to that of the native born and would be protected from local efforts to derogate their rights of citizenship. It assured that any disabilities of alien status would be limited only to the first generation. The guarantee of birthright citizenship ensured an intergenerational process of political assimilation. Birthright citizenship determined that no immigrant group could be compartmentalized as a permanent alien subpopulation. It meant that as immigrant communities evolved into multigenerational communities, they would be incorporated completely into the political community (Castles 1993).

Until the Civil War, immigration policy revolved around the cosmopolitanism of the ideological founding tradition, but like all policies it existed within a context of societal factors. In the antebellum era, these factors included movements that reflected the pattern of closed diversity associated with the first founding. African Americans were still legally enslaved in southern states, and efforts were being made to import slavery into western territories. The Native Americans of the eastern half of the United States had been reduced through disease and warfare, and those surviving were relocated by force to the trans-Mississippi West. The powerful Know Nothing Party of the early 1850s attempted to pass laws curtailing the easy passage of aliens into citizenship. Obsessed with the danger of a political takeover by Catholic immigrants, the Know Nothing Party presented several petitions to Congress calling for the repeal of all naturalization laws and the exclusion of Roman Catholics from office, but their efforts bore no fruit (Anbinder 1992, 121–22, 137–38). These movements to protect and expand the power of a hegemonic Anglo-Saxon core had not yet affected immigration policy at a national level, but they would, subsequently, with the outbreak of economic and cultural conflicts following the Civil War.

THE RISE OF RESTRICTIONS ON IMMIGRANT STATUS AND INCORPORATION

Changing views about the cohesiveness and stability of American society as it experienced industrial and urban growth precipitated a break from the historic tradition of unrestricted immigration. A second system of immigration control sprang out of a spreading pessimism about the political, cultural, and economic divisions caused by a new mass migration. By midcentury, the arrival of millions of Irish Catholics and Germans made it clear that immigration had become a large-scale social factor that had to be treated as a prime concern of national policy.

The movement toward national immigration policies hinged upon a transformation of government's relationship to immigration. The federal government abruptly entered the domain of regulating immigration after a key U.S. Supreme Court decision in 1875. In *Henderson v. Mayor of New York* [92 U.S. 259 (1875)], the Court declared unconstitutional all existing immigration laws of the seaboard states. Finding that these laws infringed upon the constitutional powers of Congress to regulate foreign commerce, the justices decided that state immigration commissions and port authorities could no longer continue their operation (Hutchinson 1981, 49, 623; Higham 1975, 38; Calavita 1984, 36–37).

Henderson v. Mayor of New York cleared the way for the federal government to take over the field of immigration policymaking. In the decades following Reconstruction, Congress grew increasingly active in immigration policy. Federal lawmakers passed a series of immigration control acts that narrowed the range of admissible immigrants. The nationalization of immigration policy evolved into an instrument for controlling its social impact. As they gained more experience in immigration legislation, lawmakers came to understand that it could serve as a device for social engineering (Higham 1975, 34–37; Hutchinson 1981, 430–33; Daniels 1962, chapter 3; Hing 1993, 19). They sought to admit only those who were deemed assimilable and to exclude those considered burdensome or dangerous to the nation's security. With passage of major immigration acts in 1891 and 1903, Congress determined that admissions would depend on qualitative criteria such as health, moral propriety, law-abidingness, capacity for self-support, and acceptable political beliefs (*Immigration Act of March 3, 1891* [26 Stat. 1084]; *Immigration Act of March 3, 1903* [32 Stat. 1213]). In 1917, Congress added an educational criterion for admission by requiring that immigrants possess basic literacy skills (Bernard 1980, 490–93; Higham 1975, 34–58).

The most profound change in immigration policy during the new era of federally controlled immigration occurred through a shift from admission by individual qualification to admission according to ethnoracial membership. Because lawmakers came to believe in the existence of immutable and homogeneous ethnic groups, they made nationality or country of origin a standard for exclusion or restricted admission. By congressional legislation and international diplomacy, immigrants from Asian countries were first restricted and then excluded altogether. The Quota Acts of 1921 and 1924 provided that immigrants from northern and western Europe would receive large visa quotas, whereas immigrants from southern and eastern Europe received small allotments. The 1924 Quota Act expressly excluded immigrants from Asia as "aliens ineligible for citizenship" (*Immigration Act of May 26, 1924* [43 Stat. 153]; Bernard 1950, 25–26; Divine 1957, 4–9, 17; Hutchinson 1981, 64–84, 430–32, 478–91). Quota discrimination was designed to ensure that the ethnic composition of immigration would not submerge the historic Anglo-Saxon core population, a key nativist goal (Lodge 1891).

Nevertheless, regulatory mechanisms not based on ethnoracial categorization appeared in the Quota Acts and would in subsequent years become the building blocks of new categories of immigrant status. Although Congress made admissible status hinge upon ethnoracial preferences, it also experimented with nonethnic criteria for determining immigrant status. A harbinger of this line of policy developments was the feature of the Immigration Act of 1917 that made certain family relationships exempt from exclusion by illiteracy. According to this statute, any admitted alien could bring in or send for "his father or grandfather over fifty-five years of age, his wife, his mother, his grandmother, or his unmarried or widowed daughter, if otherwise admissible, whether such relative can read or not." This provision assured that illiteracy would not be an obstruction to family reunification.[2]

Furthermore, the Quota Acts, whose restrictive measures have dominated the attention of historians, created a new unrestricted category of legal immigrant status, the "nonquota" class. The non-quota category also expressed the principle of encouraging family reunion by including the wives of American citizens and their unmarried children under the age of twenty-one years. Professors, students, and natives of Western Hemisphere nations were also protected under the nonquota category. Although they supported restrictionist quotas for southern and eastern European countries and exclusion toward Asian nations, lawmakers managed immigration from Western Hemisphere countries as a special case apart from all other foreign influxes. Nationality quotas and yearly admissions ceilings would not apply to them. Seeking to satisfy agricultural and industrial employers in the Southwest, Congress kept a "back door" open to cheap labor from Latin America. Congress introduced a guest-worker program with Mexico in 1943, which lasted until 1965 and resulted in the recruitment of 4.7 million "braceros," or agricultural laborers, under limited-term contracts. This produced a wholly unprecedented category of resident aliens: immigrants who were in the country only to serve as labor and who were excluded from a position within civil society (Ueda 1994, 33–34).

The discriminatory national-origins quota system was a product of historical evolution and contingency. Corporate industries that required cheap labor for manufacturing, mining, construction, and transportation work had formidable leverage with legislators. Leaders of immigrant communities and humanitarian reformers added pressure to keep the gates open to immigrants. This constellation of interest groups thwarted the restrictionist drive of the organized crafts under the leadership of the American Federation of Labor who feared immigrant labor competition, social reformers who regarded immigrants as a dysfunctional force, and a circle of patricians who worried about the loss of Anglo-Saxon dominance. The standoff between pro-immigration and anti-immigration forces in the federal government preserved the nation's open-immigration polices until the end of World War I (Higham 1975, 42–57; Jones 1960, 260–63).

Presidents of the era were unwilling to sanction a literacy test as a qualification for entry. Grover Cleveland vetoed a literacy-test bill passed by Congress in 1896 because he felt it violated the national tradition of free immigration. Senators and representatives voted down literacy-test bills in 1898, 1902, and 1906. When Congress passed literacy-test laws in 1913 and 1915, they were vetoed by Presidents William H. Taft and Woodrow Wilson, respectively. It was not until 1917 that the literacy test passed into law over yet another veto by Wilson.

A minority of representatives dedicated to an immigration policy of openness and nondiscrimination battled into the early 1920s, but they could not avert defeat by the restrictionists. The tide in favor of restriction grew irresistible in nearly every part of the country. World War I played a pivotal role in escalating cultural and political xenophobia. In the early 1920s, annual immigration continued to mount, making nativists fear that the country had reached the limit of its absorptive capacity. A large majority of legislators in Congress were convinced that immigrants were too foreign and too difficult to assimilate. In overwhelming numbers, they voted in 1921 and 1924 to cut immigration drastically.

The waves of immigration from the late nineteenth to the early twentieth century enlarged the number and proportion of resident aliens in American society. From 1890 to 1910, the number of adult male aliens more than doubled, increasing from 1,800,000 to 3,740,000 (U.S. Bureau of the Census 1970, 116). The presence of a large and growing alien population prompted federal and state governments to define alien status and alien rights more clearly. How an immigrant would live as an alien member of civil society or make the transition to citizen became an issue of rising significance.

Lawmakers explored the possibility that certain immigrants be denied political incorporation as naturalized citizens. Federal legislators had begun to use national origin as a means of excluding immigrants in their treatment of Chinese immigration after the Civil War. Directed at international traffic in prostitution, the Page Act of 1875 called for the exclusion of woman immigrants from

China, Japan, and any "oriental" country (Gyory 1998, 71). In a provision of the Chinese Exclusion Act of 1882, which denied entry to laborers from China, Congress decided that the Chinese should be treated as "aliens ineligible for citizenship," immigrants who by their race were denied the right of naturalization. A series of decisions in local and federal courts expanded the legal status of "aliens ineligible for citizenship" to encompass all other immigrants from eastern and southern Asia (Konvitz 1946, 62–66). The permanent Asian alien defined a new legal status in civil society. Through racially restrictive naturalization policy, the state constricted the boundary of American nationality.

In a unique instance, however, the United States offered citizenship to Asians on the basis of the tradition that military service produced qualifications for citizenship. Just after World War I, the federal government made an exception to the rule excluding Asian aliens from naturalized citizenship by giving special recognition to the military service of inhabitants of the Philippines. Congress passed laws in 1918 and 1919 permitting Filipinos who had served in the U.S. armed forces during World War I to apply for naturalized citizenship, although technically Filipinos were not aliens but citizens of a United States territory. A handful of other Asian immigrants applied for U. S. citizenship because of their military service, but were refused (Konvitz 1946, 93–94; Gettys 1934, 69–71).

Although naturalized citizenship was denied to Asian aliens in all other instances, birthright citizenship continued to be made available to the children of immigrants from Asia. The Supreme Court decided in the case of *United States v. Wong Kim Ark* (169 U.S. 649) in 1898 that a child of Chinese immigrants was entitled to American citizenship under the jus soli clause of the Fourteenth Amendment. This decision set a crucial precedent. Even in Asian ethnic communities in which the immigrant generation was deprived of citizenship on grounds of race, their descendants would be incorporated in the citizen community (Smith 1997, 439–43). The Supreme Court's decision found that the constitutional prescription for jus soli birthright citizenship superseded the racial exclusion of the Chinese Exclusion Act (Schuck and Smith 1985, 75–79).

As policymakers of the Progressive Era marginalized Asian immigrants by forming the status category of "aliens ineligible for citizenship," they sought to integrate immigrants from Europe and the Middle East by making them eligible for naturalization as white persons. Although there were disputes, judges interpreted the statute requiring that an applicant for citizenship be a "free white person" to include Jews, Armenians, Turks, and Arabs. Considered "white" with respect to rights to naturalized citizenship, they were therefore qualified by race for naturalization. In this way, naturalization policies during the Progressive Era turned citizenship into a tool for integrating and defining these immigrants as an official white citizenry (Haney Lopez 1996, 26–27; Smith 1997, 446–48; Jacobson 1998, chapter 3; Rundquist 1975, 194–204).

Policymakers also sought to change the relative status of aliens and citizens. State and local governments passed laws that diminished the rights of aliens relative to the rights of citizens. By 1928, all states had abolished alien suffrage. They also excluded aliens from entry to various occupations and professions. States restricted the rights of aliens to the ownership of landed property; states in the Far West prevented aliens ineligible for citizenship (immigrants native to Asian countries) from acquiring or owning agricultural property. These state actions derogating alienage arose from the desire to protect the interests of natives against alien competition and from the feeling that until they had earned their citizenship, immigrants did not deserve the same opportunities as natives (Konvitz 1946, chapters 5–9; Higham 1955, 72–73, 161–62, 214, 300–301; Cleveland 1927).

The opportunities of aliens in the sphere of marriage were affected by a new interpretation of the doctrine that a wife's citizenship depended on her husband's. Since 1855, an alien wife had acquired the citizenship of a U.S.-born or naturalized husband. However, the status of a native-born female citizen who married an alien had never been definitively clarified. In 1907, Congress established a law requiring "that any American woman who marries a foreigner shall take the nationality of her husband" (34 Stat. 228). Henceforward, female citizens who married aliens faced the loss of American citizenship, a situation discouraging the possibility of marriage between male aliens and female citizens. Moreover, two decisions by federal judges established that the

American citizenship a female lost through marriage to a male alien could not be restored through application for naturalization. In *In re Rionda* (164 F 368 [1908]) and *United States v. Cohen* (179 F 834 [1910]), the federal courts found that the general principle that the nationality of the wife was determined by that of her husband precluded her right to individual naturalization. Thus, if a former female citizen who married an alien wished to regain her citizenship, either her husband had to naturalize first or she had to legally separate from him. The dependency of wives on the civil status of husbands was not abolished until 1922 by the Cable Act, which granted independent citizenship for married women. However, this provision did not apply to wives of aliens ineligible for citizenship (Asian-born aliens) until 1931 (Gettys 1934, 123–30; Bradshaw 1944, 24). The Cable Act made female citizenship independent of marital status. Henceforth, alien women could not receive citizenship through their husbands. After the Cable Act was passed, annual naturalizations involving female applicants increasingly approximated the number of males naturalized each year (Ueda 1994, 128).

Popular beliefs and speculative theories that assumed the existence of immutable cultures and homogeneous ethnic stocks made possible organized schemes for the social sorting of immigrant groups. The Progressive Era state fixed the Anglo-Saxon core group at the apex of civil society and created a hierarchy of ethnic and racial minorities under its domination. The legal framework for ethnic sorting began to develop after the Civil War and Reconstruction as American lawmakers attempted to set apart whites, blacks, Asians, and Hispanics according to their characteristics as members of racial and ethnic groups. In the South, local governments created a biracial segregation system that was granted explicit federal approval through the U.S. Supreme Court decision in *Plessy v. Ferguson* (163 U.S. 537) in 1896. In far-western territories and states, multiracial status gradations separated whites, Hispanics, Native Americans, Asians, and Pacific Islanders. The southern and far-western patterns of group status opposed the conception of a polity of different status orders to a polity based on a single political community of individual citizens. The Jim Crow system of racial segregation and disfranchisement confined blacks, including black immigrants from the West Indies and other areas of the Caribbean, to a legally ascribed caste in the South. The ban on naturalization of Asian immigrants combined with local antialien laws to compartmentalize them in an inferior status category (Glazer 1982; Warner 1936; Dollard 1957, chapter 5; McGovney 1911; Wigmore 1894; Gulick 1918; Konvitz 1953, chapter 3; Kansas 1936, 28–33; Moore and Pachon 1976, 33, 49; Romo 1983, 160–61; Bogardus 1930; State of California 1930; Berkhofer 1968, 164–75, 177; Woodward 1966, chapter 3; Cell 1982, chapter 4).

As the United States expanded outside its continental boundaries, legislators attempted to define the position of indigenous peoples in newly acquired territories. The political and civil status of the inhabitants of the Philippines and Puerto Rico, acquired by cession in 1898, posed serious difficulties, because lawmakers and judges believed that these peoples were incapable of exercising citizenship. For example, President William Howard Taft, who had served as the civil governor of the Philippines, argued that an indefinitely long period of tutelage was required before peoples such as the Filipinos would be ready for participation in a republican and democratic polity (Taft 1906, 88–89). Congress denied Puerto Ricans and Filipinos U.S. citizenship by making inhabitants of Puerto Rico "citizens of Puerto Rico" in 1900 and inhabitants of the Philippines "citizens of the Philippine Islands" in 1902. In the Insular Cases of 1901 to 1903, the Supreme Court decided that the inhabitants of the Philippines and Puerto Rico were neither aliens nor U.S. citizens. In 1917, however, Congress passed the Jones Act, which made citizens of Puerto Rico citizens of the United States, as well (Lasch 1958; Cabranes 1979, 49–51; Gettys 1934, 149–55; Ringer 1983, chapter 19).

The status distinctions established by new policies toward Asian immigrants and territorial inhabitants played a key role in the development of racial segmentation. The boundary of racially determined status separated civil society into a fully enfranchised white citizen community and status-derogated groups. Especially, in the southern and far-western regions of the United States, public policies imposed "a color line" depriving a subclass of minorities of equality of opportunity. Popular ideas of the socioeconomic dependency of non-Western peoples, their profound alien cultural life, and their antipathy to modernization were used to justify placing racial minorities on the margins of the central arena of Progressive Era state-building (Handlin 1954, 47; Ringer 1983, 7–11; DeLeon 1983, 8–9; Romo 1983, 94, 127; McEven 1929, 27; Adams 1918, 409; Bannister 1979, 193; Daniels 1962, 49; Frederickson 1981, 189–91).

Among the foreign born in the western United States, the strongest discriminatory controls of public facilities, markets, and institutions were applied to Mexicans, Chinese, and Japanese. Selective school assignments segregated Chinese and Japanese students in California and Mexican students in Texas. In the territory of Hawaii, a dual system of schools based on formal ability in English produced the separation of Asian American students from "haole" (Caucasian) students. Mexican, Chinese, and Japanese residents found their opportunities in the job and housing markets of the far-western states considerably more restricted than those of European immigrants (Fuchs 1961, 275–77; Wollenberg 1976, 38–47, 72–75; Bell 1973, 79; Garcia 1981, 1–9, 110–11, 127, 231, 234; Kansas 1936, 23–24; Heizer and Almquist 1971; Griswold del Castillo 1979, 115–17; tenBroek, Barnhart, and Matson 1954, chapter 1; Bogardus 1930; Montejano 1987, chapters 7–11; Ichihashi 1932, 361–62; Bailey 1934, chapter 2). Many western states passed laws against the intermarriage of Asians and whites. Public policies restricting employment, welfare, residency, and property rights of aliens affected Asians disproportionately.

In addition, because labor unions excluded aliens from membership, Asian and Mexican immigrant workers failed to gain adequate representation in industrial politics. The high proportion of aliens in Asian and Mexican communities exposed these groups to collective disadvantages in an age of growing distance between the status of aliens and that of citizens (Alexander 1931, chapter 3; Kohler 1909; Konvitz 1946, chapters 5–7; MacKenzie 1937, chapter 12; Garcia 1981, 98–99). The pattern of social discrimination against Asians and Mexicans in the western states and territories limited the extent of social inclusion and opportunity available to these immigrants. Nevertheless, this pattern was not as encompassing and confining as the racial caste regime to which southern blacks were subjected (Fuchs 1990, chapter 7).

The traditional domain of American civil society allowed private custom and habit the power to act as effective devices for the social sorting of ethnic groups. The maintenance of boundaries according to the ethnic and racial discrimination practiced by private citizens was made possible by the historic pattern of nonintervention by government in the arenas of individual rights and local communal affairs. The institutions of government permitted private citizens and organizations the right to exclude minority-group members from their spheres of activity and association. Lawmakers and judges approved private discrimination in jobs, housing, and public accommodations and discriminatory selection procedures for admissions to schools and colleges. They tolerated the actions by individual citizens to limit or exclude Catholics, Jews, Asians, Hispanics, and blacks from public accommodations and access to markets for services and assets (Handlin 1964, 26–27).

THE FALL OF RESTRICTION AND THE WORLDWIDE SYSTEM OF INCORPORATION

World War II marked the end of American isolationism and the beginning of a new internationalism that would serve as a pathway toward the globalization of immigration policy. Admissions and naturalization policy were seen as tools for shaping diplomatic relations rather than as instruments for social engineering and ethnic nation-building, as they had in the Progressive Era. Furthermore, the American public began to feel less threatened by the presence of ethnic minorities. After World War II, it became increasingly clear that the descendants of European immigrants had made great strides toward integration within the national culture and socioeconomic structure. In an era of growing confidence over American institutions and the unifying power of American society, the nation's opinion makers and educators began to express a newfound appreciation for ethnic pluralism. Indeed, they began to treat diversity as a touchstone of democracy, a view that would spread to policymakers. Federal legislators began to take a fresh and pragmatic stance toward the existing restrictionist system.

The quota regime of immigration began to retreat before the forces of change from World War II to the beginning of the 1960s, as Congress explored ways to revise admissions and naturalization policies. This trend was galvanized by a new global role for the United States begun by its involvement in World War II and continued during the Cold War. Projection of the image of the United States as a democratic world leader was impaired by an immigration policy that was seen abroad as unfair in its treatment of many nationalities. Legislators pinned hopes for furthering the perception of the United States as a country based on egalitarian internationalism on the reform of admissions and naturalization policy. As Congress passed new legislation that undermined the national-origins quota and exclusion system, immigration law came to reflect the official view that racial and ethnic discrimination in public policy was invalid.

The first step toward a nondiscriminatory policy of immigration occurred with the repeal of the Chinese Exclusion Act in December 1943. At first glance, it represented a small alteration in the fortress of restrictionism: Congress allotted a token quota of 105 annual admissions to members of the Chinese race, with a preference for natives of China. The repeal act marked a historic turning point in the idea of American nationality, however, for it was the first time that the United States had passed domestic legislation that explicitly recognized the right of the Chinese to admissions and to naturalization. Furthermore, it set a precedent for other Asian nations to be given the opportunity to send immigrants to the United States. Indeed, the repeal of Chinese exclusion triggered a chain reaction of legislation that abolished the historic policy of Asian exclusion. In 1946, Asian Indians were permitted a small visa quota, and they, as well as Filipinos, were made eligible for naturalized citizenship (*Act of July 2, 1946*, [60 Stat. 416]). In 1952, Congress passed the omnibus McCarran-Walter Act (*Immigration and Nationality Act of June 27, 1952* [66 Stat. 50]), which, by abrogating all anti-Asian exclusionary provisions in immigration and naturalization policy, culminated a series of initiatives to liberalize controls on Asian immigrants (House 1944b, 1944c, 1945a, 1948; Senate 1944, 1945, 1946a, 1946b).

Parallel in time with the rescinding of Asian exclusionary laws, Congress introduced a wholly new category of legal status for immigrants. In 1948, federal lawmakers passed the Displaced Persons Act, which established for the first time an organized program for the admission of refugees. The Displaced Persons Act was the first in a series of refugee laws that made the United States the world's leader in refugee admissions. Applied at first to refugees fleeing from Communist regimes in war-torn Europe, American refugee policies evolved as products of both Cold War politics and a revival of the historic view of the United States as a sanctuary for the politically oppressed. Refugees were subject to managed residential placement and special support. One out of seven immigrants arriving in the United States from World War II to 1990 were refugees (U.S. Immigration and Naturalization Service 1991, 97; Ueda 1994, 50; Loescher and Scanlan 1986; Rystad 1990, 205–10).

As the Cold War escalated, it became increasingly clear that the principle of discrimination on the basis of national origin was an anomaly in an era of rising globalism and hampered the national interest of the United States as it positioned itself as the leader of the free and democratic world. Although the 1952 McCarran-Walter Immigration Act reaffirmed the discriminatory quota system, it began the process of loosening restriction by providing small token quotas for immigrants from Asian countries, who had been excluded since 1924. The abolition of Asian exclusion stimulated further debate on the need to end discriminatory admissions and citizenship policy on an omnibus scale. The refugee acts of the postwar decades further eroded the quota system by admitting immigrants beyond the quota limits set for their countries of origin.

Consummating this liberalizing movement in immigration policy, Congress enacted a revolutionary new law, the Hart-Celler Immigration Act of 1965, which abolished the national-origins system of discriminatory admissions. The Hart-Celler Act sprang from the progressive momentum of antidiscrimination policy in the wake of World War II. It was closely related in principle to the legislative and judicial efforts to abolish de jure discrimination based on race and ethnicity that also included the Civil Rights Acts of 1964 and 1965, the unprecedented laws designed to abolish racial discrimination in employment and voting against African Americans. The racial egalitarianism of the Hart-Celler Act, however, was not matched by an enthusiasm for promoting immigration from previously excluded areas. Those who voted for its passage did so with the expectation that immigration from Asia and third-world countries would increase very little (Reimers 1983, 1992, 76–77, 85–86).

By 1965, the United States had put into place public policies that enabled the reception and absorption of a worldwide mass immigration. Lawmakers established an admissions policy that included large and flexible admissions categories based on family relationship and occupational matching. The racially restrictive features of naturalization law had been abolished. The priority given to family reunification and economic integration as well as the equalization of opportunity for naturalized citizenship facilitated the development of immigration trends toward the encouragement of permanent settlement. Policymakers and opinion makers invoked the democratic ideology of America's national destiny as an immigration country, and the commitment to a permanent refugee program reasserted the self-image of the United States as an asylum for the politically oppressed. The determinants for the categories of immigrant status were equal visa allotments for each country of origin, a permanent refugee program, preferences for skilled personnel, and preferences and exemptions from per-country visa limits for family members. The nation launched a new movement in public policy to eradicate invidious discrimination based on ethnic origins. The antidiscrimination safeguards of the civil rights movement enlarged the possibilities for the assimilation of immigrants from Latin America, Asia, Africa, and the Caribbean who were racial minorities. The United States produced the conjunction of key elements of legal status conducive to the permanent incorporation of a global immigration within a pluralist democracy.

After 1965, a new era of immigration policy began. It brought about a third system of immigration predicated on a readoption of principles underlying the first system of early-nineteenth-century immigration. It restored acceptance of the central role of immigration in American nationhood and revived the cosmopolitan belief in the capacity of all individuals for membership in the American nation by establishing a nondiscriminatory and worldwide system of admissions. Congress completely replaced the second system of immigration based on "ethnic screening," which had been in force from 1924 to 1965, with an expanded selective system of "family and skill screening" that would operate into the 1990s. Lawmakers abolished discriminatory nationality quotas while embarking on an expansion of the apparatus of selective admissions based on family reunification and occupational needs. The principal legal categories for arriving immigrants centered on family relationships and skill levels that matched the demands of the economy.

In the 1970s and 1980s, the federal government fine-tuned the worldwide system of admission. Immigrant family and occupational networks were allowed to drive annual admissions. The national commitment to refugee admissions was strengthened when the Refugee Act of 1980 established a permanent mechanism for the admission of refugees. Congress passed a major immigration bill in 1990 that renewed the worldwide system of regular and refugee admissions. The pace of federal activity in immigration policy accelerated to keep up with the continuing flow of immigrants into the country (Fuchs 1983; Schuck 1984, 1992; Loescher and Scanlan 1986, 153–55).

Paradoxically, as the country opened its doors wider to an international influx, the flow of illegal immigrants began to mount higher. An estimated 3 million to 4 million illegal aliens resided in the United States in the early 1990s. This unprecedentedly large and growing alien population constituted a problematic new category. These were immigrants who remained out of the reach of political incorporation and therefore inaccessible to government control. Their invisibility in the public sphere made it difficult for political institutions to respond to them. Fearful of detection, illegal aliens avoided contact with government authorities. In an effort to bring the illegal alien population into the domain of civil and political control, Congress passed the *Immigration Reform and Control Act of 1986* (100 Stat. 3359), which afforded illegal immigrants the opportunity to apply for normalization to the status of legal alien (Fuchs 1990, 252–55).

In the 1990s, concern increased among policymakers and the public that mass immigration produced dangerous stresses on the nation's resources. Immigrants added greater pressures to housing, public-health, educational, and other infrastructure systems. They competed against natives in the job market in a time of economic fluctuation and insecurity. A new anti-immigrant mood swept the nation and stimulated interest in policies to reduce the rights and opportunities afforded immigrants. The Presidential Platform Committee of the Republican Party endorsed a proposed constitutional amendment in 1996 that would deny U.S. citizenship to the children of illegal aliens. Congress passed welfare reform legislation that cut off federal welfare benefits to aliens. In 1996, some federal lawmakers indicated they would initiate moderate reductions in yearly admissions. The U.S. Commission on Immigration Reform recommended a 30 percent reduction in the number of immigrants admitted annually.

From World War II until the inauguration of the Great Society, government at the federal and state level assaulted the legal and customary forms of ethnic inequality to sponsor in an unprecedented way conditions for voluntary achievement and association. The purpose of antidiscrimination policies in this era was to galvanize the inclusion and assimilation of ethnic minorities into the patterns of national social life. Its aim was to undo the coercive and confining compartments created out of intolerance toward ethnic and racial differences. The historical tradition of antidiscrimination arising from the Reconstruction amendments for protecting equal rights to opportunity of the individual citizen irrespective of race reached a new culminating point in the mid-1960s. Although it had been aimed primarily at the unequal treatment of African Americans, equal-opportunity antidiscrimination legislation produced ripple effects that affected immigrant minorities, as well.

The statutory and executive sanctions against discrimination toward blacks cast a broad shield of protection that fostered equal treatment of Catholics, Jews, Asians, Hispanics, and other immigrant minorities. Postwar government action against group discrimination expressed the negative liberal imperative to prevent harm to an individual based on national, racial, or religious discrimination. The expansion of the antidiscrimination principle in legislation, jurisprudence, and administrative government undermined the normative use of invidious group identity to determine individual status. By 1965, when the doors were opened to a worldwide multiracial immigration, the antidiscrimination policies of federal, state, and local governments had significantly enlarged the sphere of equal citizenship for immigrants.

After 1965, unprecedented group empowerment efforts en-

couraged the reorganization of civil society into large-scale ethnoracial blocs and the restructuring of public life to accord with
patterns of equitable collective representation. The advocates of
an emergent regulatory state pluralism succeeded in establishing
through legislation, executive action, and judicial decision a de
jure set of classifications for African Americans, Hispanic Americans, Asian and Pacific Americans, and Native Americans as disadvantaged racial minorities. Membership in these ethnoracial
classes established entitlements under state-managed redistributive policies aimed at remediation for historical injuries to group
life, protection from discrimination, collective political power, and
the maintenance of social and cultural diversity.

As such, central state pluralism fostered the political incorporation of immigrants arriving under the worldwide admissions
system according to official groupings as state minorities. The
state's redistributive efforts on the basis of ethnoracial status
groups once more reconfigured the political and civic space for
the incorporation of immigrants. Because legal and social institutions had excluded and limited opportunities to racialized ethnic
minorities throughout the history of the United States and continued to give evidence of reproducing inequality, government policies and programs had to be tailored to ethnoracial categories—as
they had been in the Progressive Era—to break down existing and
deeply rooted patterns of group discrimination.

Aiming at negating unjust discrimination had value as a means
of promoting equality and liberal democracy, but it cut a pathway
in another direction, as well, toward configuring the United States
as a society in which the majoritarian core and ethnic groups were
recompartmentalized. Starting around 1965, a national politics of
ethnic relations based on "race-blind" and integrationist principles
was rapidly abandoned in favor of new public policies based on
an agenda of social regulation. No longer rooted in the negative
liberal principle of nondiscriminatory treatment of individuals,
these new principles derived from a distributionist theory of creating equality of condition as a remedy for setbacks deriving from
historical patterns of discrimination against minority groups, not
minority individuals. The new social regulation of collective ethnic
relations was driven politically by popular mobilizations of racial
minorities and other disfranchised groups, a transformational ide-

ology for expunging social injustices, and the establishment of various federal agencies aimed at protecting and empowering constituencies (Belz 1994, 8–12, 13–22; Brodeur 1985, 143–46; Vogel 1981).

The movement toward regulatory state pluralism that started in the late 1960s encountered a broad shift in the political climate in the 1990s. Influential opinion makers on both the left and the right began to reevaluate the mixed results of affirmative action and to explore other public policies to deal with ethnic inequality. Moreover, interest in pulling away from group preferences gained political advocates. The new insurgency against preferential policies gained popular success particularly in California, where, in 1995, the Board of Regents of the University of California voted to end the utilization of ethnic and racial preferences in student admissions and staff hiring, and, in 1996, voters passed Proposition 209, labeled the California Civil Rights Initiative, to end across-the-board application of ethnic, racial, and gender preferences in the state's public policies. That California—with the most complex ethnoracial policies of any state—began to pull back from group preferences showed that elite and popular forces had brought the nation to a crossroads over the question of whether the state should sponsor group empowerment or the opportunity of individual citizens.

HISTORICAL PATHS AND RESEARCH PERSPECTIVES

The expansion of regulatory state power into the sphere of immigrant-host relations occurred gradually, but two stages of rapid development occurred. The conjunction of immigration and central-government activism in both the Progressive Era and the post-1960s decades produced new ideologies of collective ethnoracial identity. These ideologies shaped the construction of collective ethnoracial categories in legislation, judicial decisions, labor relations, and educational institutions. In the Progressive Era, the state constructed immigration and social policies to institutionalize northern European demographic dominance and ethnoracial inequality as part of a functionalist, modernizing social order. In the post-1960s decades, the state constructed immigration and social policies to institutionalize ethnoracial diversity and minority empowerment.

In the last half of the twentieth century, with the adoption of worldwide admissions and citizenship policies, the United States occupied a position vis-à-vis immigrants at the opposite end from the "guest-host model" of countries, such as Germany and Japan, that limited the incorporation of immigrants by drastically constricting opportunities to move from the guest class to membership in the host nation. Nevertheless, over the span of American national development that led to this point, the extension of federal power into immigrant-host status relations often reflected the interplay of an exclusionary pattern of Anglo-supremacism, derived from the earliest colonial foundings, and an inclusionary pattern of civic nationalism, institutionalized in the constitutional charters of the American revolutionary era.

This interplay was mediated by the changing historical conjunctions of economic expansion, demographic forces, and shifting ideologies of nationhood and ethnicity. It was during the half century following Reconstruction and the post-1960s decades, when the flow of immigration reached its highest amplitudes, that the institutional and legal apparatus to control immigration and the status of immigrants rapidly achieved higher levels of complexity. It was also during these periods that popular reform movements intertwined with renewed efforts by the state to manage the incorporation of immigrants according to an emergent concept of national interest.

Policies for politically incorporating immigrants generally militated against the division of civil society into "hosts" and "guests," with the exceptions of Mexican guest workers and immigrants native to Asian countries in the historical period when they constituted a subpopulation compartmentalized in permanent alienage. The vast majority of immigrants formally received a status as permanent resident aliens and naturalized citizens proximate to or virtually equivalent to the status of U.S.-born citizens.

However, historians have grown increasingly aware of the intellectual history shaping this segmentation of the pool of aliens qualified for naturalization (Yu 2001). Thus, more historical research must be directed at a varied set of judicial decisions occurring from the Civil War to the Progressive Era in which the ethnoracial criteria for qualifying for naturalization were debated and formulated to include all immigrant collective identities except those deemed to be Asian in origin.

The pattern of limited government inherent in American constitutionalism eschewed a fundamental body of law officially identifying or regulating state languages, religions, and separate immigrant minorities. It thus opened up a voluntary public sphere in civil society inclusive of immigrants in which their accommodation, social mobility, and acculturation occurred without centralized state support or management. How immigrants built organizations for mutual benefit and institutions for communal solidarity without state sponsorship should be an area for historians to investigate, particularly by applying concepts of social and cultural capital (Beito 2000).

The exercise of political rights by immigrant citizens in a system of popular participation in mass electoral parties shaped group political mobilization. Although naturalization was an issue of immense importance in the era of the new immigration from southern and eastern Europe, little is known about the people who became new citizens or the timing of their acquisition of citizenship. It is necessary to ask the question "Who became citizens?" and to answer it by identifying the demographic and social characteristics of the naturalized, by locating naturalization in the life courses of immigrants and their family histories (Barkan 1983, 30).

By approaching naturalization as a social process, it may be possible to deepen insight into the motivation of immigrants to pursue naturalization by examining the connections between naturalization and patterns of family migration, occupational careers, residency and transiency, and the dynamics of family formation and evolution (Bloemraad 2000). This research strategy might reveal that naturalization appealed to immigrants not only because it secured the protections of American nationality and complete political and economic rights but also because it permitted rights of personal and family migration in a time of restrictive immigration quotas.

Finally, the growth of state regulatory power that transformed the domain of civil society in which immigrant groups operated is an important historical turning point. Beginning with the New

Deal, federal and state governments expanded rights to public benefits through welfare and relief programs. Immigrants and their families were covered under these economic programs. Historical studies should explore how their inclusion in an expanding safety net of rights to social welfare became an experience of political socialization, shaping a citizenship among immigrants that supported the responsibility of the state to maintain collective security as a social necessity. In this way, immigrants became incorporated as a constituency of a new statism defined by social rights and entitlements (Cohen 1990, 267–89).

NOTES

1. For cases of fraudulent naturalization, see *Federal Digest* (3 FD), section 72, 595–99, and Mears 1928, 97.
2. *Immigration Act of February 5, 1917* (39 Stat. 874), 1st proviso, section 3, continued by *Immigration and Nationality Act of June 27, 1952* (66 Stat. 163), section 212b.

REFERENCES

Adams, Henry. 1918. *The Education of Henry Adams*. Boston: Little, Brown.

Alexander, Norman. 1931. *Rights of Aliens Under the Federal Constitution*. Montpelier, Vt.: Capital City Press.

Anbinder, Tyler. 1992. *Nativism and Slavery: The Northern Know Nothings and the Politics of the 1850s*. New York: Oxford University Press.

Arieli, Yehoshua. 1964. *Individualism and Nationalism in American Ideology*. Cambridge, Mass.: Harvard University Press.

Bailey, Thomas A. 1934. *Theodore Roosevelt and the Japanese-American Crisis*. Stanford: Stanford University Press.

Bailyn, Bernard. 1967. *The Ideological Origins of the American Revolution*. Cambridge, Mass.: Harvard University Press.

Bannister, Robert C. 1979. *Social Darwinism: Science and Myth in Anglo-American Social Thought*. Philadelphia: Temple University Press.

Barkan, Elliott R. 1983. "Whom Shall We Integrate? A Comparative Analysis of the Immigration and Naturalization Trends of Asians Before and After the 1965 Immigration Act (1951–1978)." *Journal of American Ethnic History* 3(1): 29–57.

Beito, David T. 2000. *From Mutual Aid to the Welfare State: Fraternal Societies and Social Services, 1890–1967.* Chapel Hill: University of North Carolina Press.

Bell, Derrick A., Jr. 1973. *Race, Racism, and American Law.* Boston: Little, Brown.

Belz, Herman. 1994. *Equality: A Quarter-Century of Affirmative Action.* New Brunswick, N.J.: Transaction Books.

Bendix, Reinhard. 1977. *Nation-Building and Citizenship: Studies of Our Changing Social Order.* Berkeley: University of California Press.

Berkhofer, Robert F., Jr. 1968. *The White Man's Indian: Images of the American Indian from Columbus to the Present.* New York: Alfred A. Knopf.

Bernard, William S. 1980. "Immigration: History of Policy." In *Harvard Encyclopedia of American Ethnic Groups,* edited by Stephan Thernstrom. Cambridge, Mass.: Harvard University Press.

———, ed. 1950. *American Immigration Policy.* New York: Harper and Sons.

Bloemraad, Irene. 2000. "Citizenship and Immigration: A Current Review." *Journal of International Migration* 1(1): 9–37.

Bogardus, Emory S. 1930. "The Mexican Immigrant and Segregation." *American Journal of Sociology* 36(1): 74–80.

Bradshaw, Cathrine A. 1944. *Americanization Questionnaire.* 8th ed. New York: Noble and Noble.

Brodeur, Paul. 1985. *Restitution: The Land Claims of the Mashpee, Passamaquoddy, and Penobscot Indians of New England.* Boston: Northeastern University Press.

Cabranes, Jose A. 1979. *Citizenship and the American Empire: Notes on the Legislative History of the United States Citizenship of Puerto Ricans.* New Haven: Yale University Press.

Calavita, Kitty. 1984. *U. S. Immigration Law and the Control of Labor, 1820–1924.* New York: Academic Press.

Castles, Stephen. 1993. "Immigration, Citizenship, and the Nation-State: An International Comparison." Paper presented to the Thirty-first Congress of the International Institute of Sociology. University of Paris (June 21–25, 1993).

Cell, John W. 1982. *The Highest Stage of White Supremacy: The Origins of Segregation in South Africa and the American South.* Cambridge: Cambridge University Press.

Cleveland, Frederick A. ca. 1927. *American Citizenship as Distinguished from Alien Status.* New York: Ronald Press.

Cohen, Lizabeth. 1990. *Making a New Deal: Industrial Workers in Chicago, 1919–1939.* New York: Cambridge University Press.

Congressional Globe. 1833–73. 46 vols. Washington, D.C., 1834–73.

Daniels, Roger. 1962. *The Politics of Prejudice: The Anti-Japanese Movement in California and the Struggle for Japanese Exclusion.* Berkeley: University of California Press.

DeLeon, Arnaldo. 1983. *They Called Them Greasers: Anglo Attitudes Toward Mexicans in Texas, 1821–1900.* Austin: University of Texas Press.

Divine, Robert A. 1957. *American Immigration Policy, 1924–1952.* New Haven: Yale University Press.

Dollard, John. 1957. *Caste and Class in a Southern Town.* 3d ed. Garden City, N.Y.: Doubleday.

Foner, Eric. 1994. "The Meaning of Freedom in the Age of Emancipation." *Journal of American History* 81(2): 435–60.

Franklin, Frank George. 1906. *The Legislative History of Naturalization in the United States.* Chicago: University of Chicago Press.

Frederickson, George M. 1981. *White Supremacy: A Comparative Study in American and South African History.* New York: Oxford University Press.

Fuchs, Lawrence H. 1961. *Hawaii Pono: A Social History.* New York: Harcourt, Brace.

———. 1983. "Immigration Reform in 1911 and 1981: The Role of Select Commissions." *Journal of American Ethnic History* 3(1): 58–89.

———. 1990. *The American Kaleidoscope: Race, Ethnicity, and the Civic Culture.* Hanover, N.H.: University Press of New England.

Garcia, Mario T. 1981. *Desert Immigrants: The Mexicans of El Paso, 1880–1920.* New Haven: Yale University Press.

Gettys, Luella. 1934. *The Law of Citizenship in the United States.* Chicago: University of Chicago Press.

Glazer, Nathan. 1982. "The Politics of a Multiethnic Society." In *Ethnic Relations in America,* edited by Lance Liebman. Englewood Cliffs, N.J.: Prentice-Hall.

Greenfeld, Liah. 1992. *Nationalism: Five Roads to Modernity.* Cambridge, Mass.: Harvard University Press.

Griswold del Castillo, Richard. 1979. *The Los Angeles Barrio, 1850–1890: A Social History.* Berkeley: University of California Press.

Gulick, Sidney L. 1918. *American Democracy and Asiatic Citizenship.* New York: Charles Scribner's Sons.

Gyory, Andrew. 1998. *Closing the Gate: Race, Politics, and the Chinese Exclusion Act.* Chapel Hill: University of North Carolina Press.

Handlin, Oscar. 1954. *The American People in the Twentieth Century.* Cambridge, Mass.: Harvard University Press.

———. 1964. *Firebell in the Night: The Crisis in Civil Rights.* Boston: Little, Brown.

Handlin, Oscar, and Lilian Handlin. 1989. *Liberty in Expansion.* Vol. 2, *1760–1850.* New York: Harper and Row.

Haney Lopez, Ian F. 1996. *White by Law: The Legal Construction of Race.* New York: New York University Press.

Heizer, Robert F., and Alan F. Almquist. 1971. *The Other Californians: Prejudice and Discrimination Under Spain, Mexico, and the United States to 1920.* Berkeley: University of California Press.

Higham, John. 1975. *Send These to Me: Jews and Other Immigrants in Urban America.* New York: Atheneum.

———. 1955. *Strangers in the Land: Patterns of American Nativism, 1865–1925.* New Brunswick: Rutgers University Press.

———. 1993. "History of American Immigration: An Overview." Paper presented to the Smithsonian Institution and Federal Judicial Center, "U.S. Immigration: The Land of Promise" seminar. Washington, D.C. (November 2).

Hing, Bill Ong. 1993. *Making and Remaking Asian America Through Immigration Policy, 1850–1990.* Stanford: Stanford University Press.

Hutchinson, E. P. 1981. *Legislative History of American Immigration Policy, 1798–1965.* Philadelphia: University of Pennsylvania Press.

Ichihashi, Yamato. 1932. *Japanese in the United States: A Critical Study of the Problems of the Japanese Immigrants and Their Children.* Stanford: Stanford University Press.

Jacobson, Matthew Frye. 1998. *White by Law: European Immigrants and the Alchemy of Race.* Cambridge, Mass.: Harvard University Press.

Jay, John. 1961. "Federalist No. 2." In *The Federalist Papers.* New York: New American Library.

Jones, Maldwyn Allen. 1960. *American Immigration.* Chicago: University of Chicago Press.

Kansas, Sidney. 1936. *Citizenship of the United States of America.* New York: Washington Publishing.

Kedourie, Elie. 1993. *Nationalism.* 4th ed. Oxford: Blackwell.

Kettner, James H. 1974. "The Development of American Citizenship in the Revolutionary Era: The Idea of Volitional Allegiance." *American Journal of Legal History* 18(3): 208–42.

———. 1976. "Subjects or Citizens? A Note on British Views Respecting the Legal Effects of American Independence." *Virginia Law Review* 62: 945–67.

———. 1978. *The Development of American Citizenship, 1608–1970.* Chapel Hill: University of North Carolina Press.

Kohler, Max J. 1909. "Un-American Character of Race Legislation." *Annals of the American Academy of Political and Social Science* 34: 275–93.

Konvitz, Milton R. 1946. *The Alien and the Asiatic in American Law.* Ithaca, N.Y.: Cornell University Press.

———. 1953. *Civil Rights in Immigration.* Ithaca: Cornell University Press.

Lasch, Christopher. 1958. "The Anti-Imperialists, the Philippines, and the Inequality of Man." *Journal of Southern History* 24(3): 319–31.

Lodge, Henry Cabot. 1891. "The Restriction of Immigration." *North American Review* 152(1): 27–36; reprinted in the *Congressional Record,* vol. 22, part 3, 51st Congress, 2d sess. February 19, 2956–58.

Loescher, Gil, and John A. Scanlan, 1986. *Calculated Kindness: Refugees and America's Half-Open Door.* New York: Free Press.

MacKenzie, Norman. 1937. *The Legal Status of Aliens in Pacific Countries.* London: Oxford University Press.

Marshall, T. H. 1950. *Citizenship and Social Class and Other Essays.* Cambridge: Cambridge University Press.

McEven, William W. 1929. "A Survey of the Mexican in Los Angeles (1910–1914)." Master's thesis, University of Southern California.

McGovney, D. O. 1911. "American Citizenship." *Columbia Law Review* 11: 231–50, 326–47.

Mears, Eliot Grinnell. 1928. *Resident Orientals on the American Pacific Coast: Their Legal and Economic Status.* Chicago: University of Chicago Press.

Montejano, David. 1987. *Anglos and Mexicans in the Making of Texas, 1836–1986.* Austin: University of Texas Press.

Moore, Joan W., and Harry Pachon. 1976. *Mexican Americans.* 2d ed. Englewood Cliffs, N.J.: Prentice-Hall.

Morgan, Edmund S. 1975. *American Slavery, American Freedom: The Ordeal of Colonial Virginia.* New York: W. W. Norton.

Nash, Gary. 1974. *Red, White, and Black: The Peoples of Early America.* Englewood Cliffs, N.J.: Prentice-Hall.

Rahe, Paul A. 1994. *Republics Ancient and Modern.* Vol. 3. Chapel Hill: University of North Carolina Press.

Reimers, David. 1983. "An Unintended Reform: The 1965 Immigration Act and Third World Immigration to the United States." *Journal of American Ethnic History* 3(1): 9–28.

———. 1992. *Still the Golden Door: The Third World Comes to America.* 2d ed. New York: Columbia University Press.

Ringer, Benjamin B. 1983. *"We the People" and Others: Duality and America's Treatment of Its Racial Minorities.* New York: Tavistock.

Roche, John P. 1949. *The Early Development of United States Citizenship.* Ithaca, N.Y.: Cornell University Press.

Romo, Ricardo. 1983. *East Los Angeles: History of a Barrio.* Austin: University of Texas Press.

Rundquist, Paul. 1975. "A Uniform Rule: The Congress and the Courts in American Naturalization." Ph.D. diss., University of Chicago.

Rystad, Goran, ed. 1990. *The Uprooted: Forced Migration as an International Problem in the Post-War Era.* Lund, Sweden: Lund University Press.

Schuck, Peter H. 1984. "The Transformation of Immigration Law." *Columbia Law Review* 84: 1–90.

———. 1992. "The Politics of Rapid Legal Change: Immigration Policy in the 1980s." *Studies in American Political Development* 6(1): 37–92.

Schuck, Peter H., and Rogers M. Smith. 1985. *Citizenship Without Consent: Illegal Aliens in the American Polity.* New Haven: Yale University Press.

Smith, Rogers M. 1997. *Civic Ideals: Conflicting Visions of Citizenship in U.S. History.* New Haven: Yale University Press.

State of California. 1930. *Mexicans in California: Report of Governor C. C. Young's Mexican Fact-Finding Committee.* San Francisco: California Department of Industrial Relations, Agriculture, and Social Welfare (October).

Stephenson, George M. 1926. *A History of American Immigration, 1820–1924.* Boston: Ginn and Company.

Taft, William Howard. 1906. *Four Aspects of Civic Duty.* New York: Charles Scribner's Sons.

Taylor, Philip. 1971. *The Distant Magnet: European Immigration to the U.S.A.* New York: Harper and Row.

tenBroek, Jacobus, Edward N. Barnhart, and Floyd W. Matson. 1954. *Prejudice, War, and the Constitution: Causes and Consequences of the Evacuation of the Japanese Americans in World War II.* Berkeley: University of California Press.

Tocqueville, Alexis de. 1956. *Democracy in America.* Edited by Richard D. Heffner. New York: New American Library.

Ueda, Reed. 1994. *Postwar Immigrant America: A Social History.* New York: St. Martin's Press, Bedford Books.

U.S. Department of Commerce. U.S. Bureau of the Census. 1970. *Historical Statistics of the United States, Colonial Times to 1970.* Washington: U. S. Government Printing Office.

U.S. Department of Labor. 1926. *Historical Sketch of Naturalization in the United States.* Washington: U.S. Government Printing Office.

U. S. House. Committee on Immigration and Naturalization. 1944a. *Au-*

thorizing the Naturalization of Filipinos. 78th Congress, 2d sess. H. Rept. 1940.

———. 1944b. *Naturalization of Filipinos: Hearings on H.R. 2012, H.R. 2776, H.R. 3633, H.R. 4003, H.R. 4229, H.R. 4826.* 78th Cong., 2d sess.

———. 1944c. *To Grant a Quota to Eastern Hemisphere Indians and to Make Them Racially Eligible for Naturalization: Hearings on H.R. 173, H.R. 1584, H.R. 1624, H.R. 1746, H.R. 2256, H.R. 2609.* 79th Cong., 2d sess.

———. 1945a. *Authorizing the Admission into the United States of Persons of Races Indigenous to India, to Make Them Racially Eligible for Naturalization.* 79th Congress, 1st sess. H. Rept. 854.

———. 1945b. *Authorizing the Naturalization of Filipinos.* 79th Congress, 1st sess. H. Rept. 252.

U.S. House. Committee of Conference. 1946. *Agreement on Amendments to a Bill Relating to the Right of Filipinos and East Indians to Become Naturalized Citizens of the United States and to Enter the Country Under Small Quotas.* 79th Congress, 2d sess. H. Rept. 2334.

U.S. House. Subcommittee on Immigration and Naturalization of the Committee on the Judiciary. 1948. *Providing for Equality Under Naturalization and Immigration Law. Hearings on H.R. 5004.* 80th Cong., 2d sess.

U.S. Immigration and Naturalization Service. 1991. *1990 Statistical Yearbook.* Washington: U.S. Government Printing Office.

U.S. Senate. 1944. Subcommittee of the Committee on Immigration. *To Permit the Naturalization of Approximately Three Thousand Natives of India: Hearings on S.R. 1595.* 78th Cong., 2d sess.

———. Committee on Immigration. 1945. *To Permit All People from India Residing in the United States to Be Naturalized: Hearings on S.R. 236.* 79th Cong., 1st sess.

———. 1946a. *Authorizing the Admission into the United States of Persons of Races Indigenous to India, to Make Them Racially Eligible for Naturalization.* 79th Congress, 2d sess. S. Rept. 1440.

———. 1946b. *Authorizing the Naturalization of Filipinos.* 79th Congress, 2d sess. S. Rept. 1439.

Vogel, David. 1981. "The 'New' Social Regulation in Historical and Comparative Perspective." In *Regulation in Perspective,* edited by Thomas K. McCraw. Cambridge, Mass.: Harvard University Press.

Warner, W. Lloyd. 1936. "American Caste and Class." *American Journal of Sociology* 42(2): 234–37.

Wigmore, John H. 1894. "American Naturalization and the Japanese." *American Law Review* 28: 827.

Wollenberg, Charles M. 1976. *All Deliberate Speed: Segregation and Exclusion in California Schools, 1855–1975.* Berkeley: University of California Press.

Wood, Gordon. 1969. *The Creation of the American Republic, 1776–1787.* Chapel Hill: University of North Carolina Press.

———. 1992. *The Radicalism of the American Revolution.* New York: Alfred A. Knopf.

Woodward, C. Vann. 1966. *The Strange Career of Jim Crow.* 2d ed. New York: Oxford University Press.

Yu, Henry. 2001. *Thinking Orientals: Migration, Contact, and Exoticism in Modern America.* New York: Oxford University Press.

—— Part V ——

Immigrants, Schools, and Political Socialization

—— Chapter 9 ——

School for Citizens:
The Politics of Civic Education
from 1790 to 1990

David Tyack

I N A SOCIETY as socially diverse as the United States, it is not
surprising that controversies have erupted from time to time
about the proper nature of civic education in public schools. Such
policy debate has reflected American hopes and fears about the
republic, and it has helped to define and mold what Thomas
Bender calls "the public culture." He notes that continuing contests of diverse groups for "legitimacy and justice" have created
and recreated this public culture and established "our common
life as a people and as a nation." It is essential to understand what
has been excluded from, as well as included in, this public culture, he argues, and why "some groups and some values [have]
been so much—or so little—represented in public life and in
mainstream culture and schooling at any given moment in our
history" (Bender 1989, 201).

This essay explores the history of policy in civic education in
the light of the changing politics of public schooling. It focuses
primarily on the debate about the education of white citizens; the
rules and power relationships that governed citizenship for people of color were complexly and tragically different in ways that
on their own deserve extended analysis. The public schools were
a major arena for debate over what should be the "unum" and
how to deal with the "pluribus." This is a story of millennial hopes

and persistent fears about the destiny of the republic, of cultural differences that fueled political conflict, and of aspirations for cultural autonomy and a search for a common ground of civic values (Anderson 1988; Perlmann 1988; Weiss 1982).

In different eras leaders concerned about the political philosophy of education have addressed several forms of unity and diversity. In the half century following the American Revolution they worried about how to balance liberty and order by instilling uniform republican values through schooling. The diversity that bothered them most was not ethnic or religious but political. They succeeded in establishing a durable set of beliefs about republican education but did not actually create systems of public schools.

In the middle of the nineteenth century, when public education spread rapidly across the nation, common-school crusaders searched for a political and religious common denominator in the training of future citizens. Although some contests over public education revolved around politics and ethnicity, religious controversy proved harder to contain as large numbers of Catholics entered a nation previously Protestant in culture. In the period from 1885 to 1925, as city schools became more bureaucratized and centralized in control, educators became absorbed with the task of assimilating immigrants coming from southeastern Europe (presumed to be "racially" different from those from northwestern Europe), a task that became obsessive during World War I. Many agencies, private and public, joined in this crusade for "Americanization," but zealotry gave the term a bad name for decades to come.

At the middle of the twentieth century, recognizing that hard-edged policies of Americanization stiffened resistance of immigrants to assimilation and fostered conflict between the generations within immigrant communities, policymakers in education praised pluralism and sought to find ways to promote tolerance while at the same time unifying the nation—an "Americans all" strategy. In the civil rights era that followed, movements for social justice appealed at first to the liberal concept that all individuals should have the same rights, but then some activists claimed that redressing group wrongs might require guaranteeing group rights. Culture wars arose over the purpose and character of civic education.

Much has changed in civic education over the past two centuries, but some persistent themes and puzzles weave in and out of these episodes. One is that policy talk has typically been more volatile than practices in the schools (and thus it is easy to exaggerate innovation when focusing on policy). In practice, civic education may have changed only gradually over time; remnants of older ideological versions of patriotic instruction continue, despite decades of criticism and ethnic assertion and agonized rhetoric about the state of the nation. Most of the questions asked of applicants for citizenship today, for example, would have been familiar to my immigrant grandfather when he was naturalized a century ago.

From the Revolution onward, Americans have often been deeply distrustful of governments, especially those that operate at a distance, yet they have entrusted their children's moral and civic education to government schools. Perhaps one answer to this puzzle is that American public education has traditionally been radically decentralized in control. It was not a distant government but one's neighbors who built and bossed the school, especially in the nineteenth century, when the nation was overwhelmingly rural. Another answer may lie in the depth of Americans' commitment to an idea: the notion that civic training in the public school is essential to the survival of the republic and to the preservation of its liberties and order. Such ideas rang out in territorial constitutional conventions in the plains states and in Fourth of July orations in New England.

The line between public and private shaping of civic education has often been hard to trace. At one time or another, an enormous variety of citizen groups have sought to shape the instruction of citizens. In the nineteenth century, as Alexis de Tocqueville insisted, Americans habitually used private voluntary associations to accomplish public purposes, and this was especially true in education. So effective was the Women's Christian Temperance Union in its lobbying of governments that in 1900 temperance instruction was the only subject required in every public school in the nation.

Public programs to Americanize both adults and children attracted a wide swath of reformers and lobbyists of many persuasions. In the period from 1914 to the mid-1920s, a time of intense paranoia about immigrants as potentially dangerous strangers, private associations of industrial leaders and patriotic groups lobbied successfully for laws requiring their own versions of civic orthodoxy in the public schools. Influence went the other way, as well: both federal and state agencies empowered private organizations to assist in a draconian governmental campaign to compel civic and cultural conformity.

Even at the height of this 100 percent Americanism, however, private and public leaders questioned the effectiveness and humanity of hard-edged public programs to eliminate ethnic diversity. From the 1920s onward, private associations have also lobbied for programs designed to celebrate diversity and reduce ethnic prejudice. In the last generation, especially, representatives of many ethnic groups have argued that the "unum" taught in public schools—the standard version of civic education—was entirely too narrow and biased to represent a pluralistic society. They sought governmental sanction for a more diverse conception of democracy, a new kind of cultural citizenship.

Another element of civic education that has persisted from the time of the Revolution is the notion that Americans are made one by one, according to an individualistic paradigm of citizenship. This belief, which owes much to a mentality framed by Protestantism and liberal eighteenth-century political ideology and was later fortified by the popularity of psychology, stresses the individual character of citizens. Such individuals were expected to be loyal to an idealized political order rather than to the primordial claims of kinship or ethnicity or to allegiances of social class and specific religious sects. Schooling was designed to break the hold of the group over the person and to instruct the young in the principles of republican liberty and order and in the responsible individual exercise of their rights and responsibilities. Republican citizens were "free" individuals trained to be uniform in belief and behavior, more culturally alike than different. The institutional structure of schooling has itself remained mostly individualistic in nature, with its pedagogy of recitation, its individual tests and report cards, and its presumed winnowing of the diligent, virtuous, and talented in the competition for life's rewards in adulthood (Olneck 1989; Meyer and Rubinson 1975).

FORMING REPUBLICANS

The idea that the free citizen was the uniform republican becomes somewhat less puzzling if one recalls that the task of balancing liberty and order in the new nation was beset with danger and difficulty. Where along the spectrum from tyranny to anarchy would Americans find the proper synthesis of ordered liberty? A number of leaders in the early American republic believed that republics had historically been as evanescent as fireflies on a summer evening, that monarchical Europe was conspiring to wreck the United States and to draw it into endless wars, that internal disorders and factions were threatening to shatter society, and that a continental nation composed of many states could not long remain republican (Tyack 1966).

A deep foreboding about the future was pervasive, along with an equally deep millennial faith in the destiny of the new nation. Thomas Jefferson wrote in 1811 that "the eyes of the virtuous all over the earth are turned with anxiety on us, as the only depositories of the sacred fire of liberty. . . . Our falling into anarchy would decide forever the destinies of mankind, and seal the political heresy that man is incapable of self-government" (Jefferson 1903, 10: 319). What threatened this experiment was not ethnic or religious diversity—about four-fifths of the population in 1790 was of English descent, and it was overwhelmingly Protestant. Jefferson believed in literacy as a prerequisite for citizenship, but not in English only: a citizen, he wrote, must be able to "read readily in some tongue, native or acquired" (Jefferson 1903). What threatened the nation was diversity (and error) in political principles (Pangle and Pangle 1993, 115; Gleason 1980).

Winning the war and building a new government was only the beginning, said Benjamin Rush, a signer of the Declaration of Independence and an educational theorist. "We have changed our forms of government, but it remains yet to effect a revolution in our principles, opinions, and manners so as to accommodate them to the forms of government we have adopted. This is the most difficult part of the business of the patriots and legislators of our country" (Rush 1951, 388). The schoolmaster and lexicographer Noah Webster agreed and proposed an "association of American patriots for the purpose of forming a national character" (quoted in Warfel 1936, 285; Hansen 1926).

From the beginning of the new nation, a public philosophy of republican education resonated in the speeches of educators and politicians, in territorial and state constitutional debates, and in the textbooks children read in school. The process of admitting new states into the Union illuminates the link between schooling and republican values. From the start, Congress used the national domain to support common schools. In this land-grant common-school system, Congress allotted three times more acreage to elementary schools than to the better-known land-grant colleges.

The U.S. Constitution required Congress to guarantee that new states had "a Republican form of Government." The founding fathers worried about the coherence and stability of a continental nation composed of different states carved from the vast public domain. What assurance could there be that the citizens of those states would share not only a commitment to republican liberties and duties but also an allegiance to the nation based on those principles? As time went by, both the Congress and territorial leaders who wrote constitutions for new states came to agree that public education was an essential feature of a republican government based on the will of the people (Wiebe 1984, 7–20; U.S. House 1878; Browne 1850, 18).

The Founding Fathers believed it important to expose the young to correct political ideas and to shield them from the wrong ones. Europe could be an ideological pesthouse, a source of contagion. George Washington opposed the practice of educating Americans in foreign countries, where they ran the danger of "contracting principles unfavorable to republican government." The "more homogeneous our citizens can be made" in principles, opinions, and manners," the "greater will be our prospect of permanent union" (quoted in Knight 1950, 2: 4, 17; also see 21–22). Jefferson agreed: "the consequences of foreign education are alarming to me as an American" (Jefferson 1950, 8: 636–37). Georgia went so far as to disbar its citizens from civic office for as many years as they had studied abroad, if sent overseas under the age of sixteen.

The "homogeneous" American must study American textbooks, wrote Noah Webster: to use old-world texts "would be to stamp the wrinkles of decrepit age upon the bloom of youth and to plant the seeds of decay in a vigorous constitution" (Webster 1798, 154–55). Webster's pedagogy of civic republicanism was moral as well as cognitive, religious as well as political in inspiration. The young, he thought, should learn the principles of representative and limited government and also should practice republican virtues. The prolific Webster, whose spellers had sold more than 20 million copies by 1829, devised a "Federal Catechism" to teach these proper republican principles to children. The catechism warned of the evils of monarchy, aristocracy, and direct democracy while praising the virtues of the representative republic as embedded in the constitutions of the nation and the individual states. He also inserted a "Moral Catechism" that stressed the virtues of obedience, moderation, truthfulness, frugality, and industry (Elson 1964).

Textbook writers typically used statesmen like George Washington as exemplars of republican character. As soon as the American child "opens his lips," said Webster, "he . . . should lisp the praise of liberty, and . . . illustrious heroes" (Webster 1790, 3: 17–21, 23, 25). Rush agreed with Webster's policy of transforming American statesmen into demigods. Although he had not admired Washington's leadership during the war, Rush thought it wise to tell less than the full truth about the founding fathers: "Let the world admire our patriots and heroes. Their *supposed* talents and virtues . . . will serve the cause of patriotism and of our country" (quoted in Good 1934, 61).

Jefferson, of course, was a passionate advocate of religious and intellectual freedom. He gave to the University of Virginia a charter that proclaimed that it "will be based on the illimitable freedom of the human mind" (Jefferson 1903, 12: 146). He also crusaded for "the diffusion of knowledge among the people" as an instrument of political progress (quoted in Montalto 1982, 144). But diffusion of *what* knowledge? Too many erroneous and dangerous political principles were in circulation. Jefferson was especially concerned about the correct education of future leaders at the University of Virginia. He wanted to expurgate the Tory passages from David Hume's history taught at the university and to prescribe the textbooks used in government. "It is our duty," he wrote, "to guard against the dissemination of [Federalist] principles among our youth, and the diffusion of that poison" (Jefferson 1903, 12: 456). He wanted to make sure that Virginia would be a "seminary" of states' rights principles (Levy 1963, 146).

Benjamin Rush stated in draconian terms the view that the free American was the uniform American. He argued that the best way to "render the mass of the people more homogeneous, and thereby fit them more easily for uniform and peaceable government," was to create schools that inculcated republican principles and attributes of character. "I consider it possible to convert men into republican machines. This must be done, if we expect them to perform their parts properly, in the great machinery of the government of the state" (Rush 1786, 14).

Rush, Webster, Jefferson, and a number of other educational theorists wanted to create schools that were public in finance and control, arranged into a system of lower and higher schools, and devoted above all to producing republican citizens. From the Revolution until Jefferson's death in 1826, however, most American schools remained heterogeneous rather than uniform and systematic, private rather than public, and often served to perpetuate differences of social class, sects, and region rather than inculcating a universalistic republicanism. Nevertheless, the hope that a uniform public education could integrate the polity did not disappear. In the middle of the nineteenth century, during the common-school crusade, the republican ideal vigorously returned, fortified by new anxieties and old claims.

THE COMMON SCHOOL AND
THE COMMON DENOMINATOR

"The great experiment of Republicanism—of the capacity of man for self-government," Horace Mann declaimed on July 4, 1842, "is to be tried anew." It had always failed before "through an inadequacy in the people to enjoy liberty without abusing it" (Mann 1865–68, 4: 345). As Mann, the secretary of the State Board of Education in Massachusetts, looked about at Boston and the nation, he saw riotous mobs and selfish nabobs, votes bought or ignorantly cast, ill-educated citizens serving on juries or in the militia, impoverished children working in factories, and disputes over slavery sounding firebells in the night (Mann 1865–68, 354–56). In Cincinnati at the same time, Mann's fellow common-school reformer Calvin Stowe reminded his colleagues that "unless we educate our immigrants, they will be our ruin," for "to sustain an extended republic like our own, there must be a *national* feeling, a national assimilation." Immigrants can be "grafts which become branches of the parent stock . . . and not like the parasitical mistletoe" (Stowe 1836, 75). In the period from 1830 to 1860, however, when the foreign-born increased faster, proportionately, than at any other time in American history, nativists took a much grimmer view of immigrants than Stowe.

After citing a litany of evils, educational crusaders like Mann could appeal to a Protestant-republican ideology for solutions. God had chosen America as a redeemer nation to prove that humans were capable of self-government and, in the process, to carry out a divine plan. The educated character of the individual was the foundation of public virtue; the good society was an aggregation of such citizens. The common school, a public institution that mixed students from all walks of life, would teach a common denominator of political and moral truths that was nonpartisan and nonsectarian. The quarrels and competition of political parties and religious denominations should stop at the schoolhouse door. Let civic education work its magic (Higham 1974, 13–14; Tyack and Hansot 1982).

All of this was easier said than done. Just how could state common-school advocates and local school trustees find a religiously and politically neutral common denominator? Horace Mann thought he had the answer: Base moral teaching on the Bible, but make no sectarian gloss of scripture. Didn't everyone already believe in the virtues that were embedded in the Massachusetts constitution of 1780 and that the state wanted to have inculcated in the young? Who could object to industry, frugality, benevolence, charity, temperance, patriotism, justice, sobriety, and moderation? Noah Webster's moral catechism stressed similar values, as did the California school reformer John Swett. In his 1885 book for teachers on "school ethics," Swett assumed that all citizens would agree with his textbook list of individual civic virtues: self-knowledge, self-restraint, temperance, honesty, obedience, punctuality, conscientiousness, impartiality, gratitude, friend-

liness, kindness, patience, frankness, seriousness, firmness, clean-
liness, and courtesy (Swett 1885, 21). These lists of virtues would
have been familiar and attractive, for that matter, in 1996 to the
teachers who answered a Public Agenda survey on moral values
in the classroom (Farkas and Johnson 1996).

Mann had a similar solution to the problem of political neu-
trality: In politics, teach only republican principles that are univer-
sally approved "by all sensible and judicious men, all patriots, and
all genuine republicans." If a teacher encountered a politically
"controverted text," Mann advised, "he is either to read it without
comment or remark; or, at most, he is only to say that the passage
is the subject of disputation, and that the schoolroom is neither
the tribunal to adjudicate, nor the forum to discuss it" (quoted in
Cremin 1957, 97). Mann himself, though deeply opposed to slavery, rebuked the principal of a public normal school for taking
students to an abolitionist meeting. That was far too controversial
and could bring ruin to the common school. If, on the other hand,
students could share a moral and political common ground, they
would later be more likely to find peaceful solutions to their disagreements (Cremin 1957, 94–97).

Textbook writers—driven by conscience, custom, and commerce—tried to find the same sort of consensual moral and civic
instruction that Mann advocated. No one captured the common
denominator of civic virtue better than the Reverend William
Holmes McGuffey, whose school readers sold 60 million copies
from 1870 to 1890 and a total of 122 million copies by 1922. The
advertising blurb printed with his fourth reader in 1844 assured
the public that "NO SECTARIAN matter has been admitted into
this work" and "NO SECTIONAL matter" (reflecting on slavery, for
example) appeared (Lindberg 1976; Tyack 1967, 178).

State education officers like Mann and Swett used their positions as bully pulpits to proclaim the importance of civic education through the common school and to suggest school policies.
They had little power, however, to enforce laws or policy. Americans from the time of the Revolution until the end of the nineteenth century tended to distrust strong government and to hobble
the powers of states (Farnham 1963). Citizens were ambivalent
about giving powers to legislators and state school officials and on
occasion even abolished the office of superintendent (this hap-

pened to Henry Barnard and nearly so to Horace Mann). The German immigrant Carl Schurz was fascinated by the voluntary and decentralized character of institution-building in the United States and wrote that "here in America you can see how slightly a people needs to be governed. In fact, the thing that is not named in Europe without a shudder, anarchy, exists here in full bloom" (quoted in Frederickson 1965, 8).

School governance was not quite anarchy, though some of the promoters of state schools thought so. Local trustees made most of the key decisions in most states, at least until the Progressive Era. In the late nineteenth century, local school trustees were the most numerous class of public officials in the world. Then, as now, Americans trusted local officials more than distant government; important questions were often decided by local trustees, not by courts or state officials. Essentially, moral and civic questions were settled by majority rule in most communities. This gave legitimacy, of a sort, but it was hard on minorities, who faced a choice of violating their own consciences by sending their children to common schools or creating separate schools at their own expense (James 1991, 117–47; Blodgett 1893).

CULTURE WARS

Many Americans, especially immigrant Irish Catholics, did not share the worldview of the pietist school reformers or local school trustees. Protestants and Catholics, newcomers and established groups, often talked past one another and sometimes engaged in mortal and sustained conflict that makes today's "culture wars" look like minuets. In 1844 in Philadelphia, for example, the Catholic bishop requested that Catholic children be allowed to use the Douay version of the Bible. Fearing that Catholics were seeking to eject the Protestant Bible from the schools, a nativist mob violently attacked Irish Catholics and burned their houses and churches (Baird 1970; Pierce 1930, 85).

Protestants and Catholics often had quite different views of civic and moral education. Most of the leaders of the common-school movement were white, native born, of Anglo-Saxon descent, and Protestant. As members of the dominant group, the common-school reformers usually did not recognize their own clannishness. They could not understand why their plan to make schools nonsectarian and nonpartisan was not acceptable to all right-thinking people. By contrast, their opponents often regarded this "solution" as a devious or callous power play and sought to have public funds channeled to the schools controlled by Catholics (Kaestle 1983, chapter 7; Tyack, James, and Benavot 1987, part 2).

Protestants and Roman Catholics each identified their different values with the common weal. A Kansas Protestant, reflecting the millenarianism that suffused the common-school movement, exclaimed that "Americanism is Protestantism. . . . Protestantism is Life, is Light, is Civilization, is the spirit of the age. . . . Education with all its adjuncts, is Protestantism" (quoted in Carper 1978, 149). To people like him, the common school was a symbol of patriotism, a means of rooting government in the virtue of free individuals. A Catholic leader expressed a more collective and traditional view that education should train the young to be "docile and respectful to their superiors, open and ingenuous, obedient and submissive to rightful authority, parental or conjugal, civil or ecclesiastical" and to obey "the precepts of the church." In such moral education, the young were to retain the loyalties of kin, sect, and ethnic group as well as to learn a universalistic form of patriotism. Economic survival and advance was more communal than, as in the Protestant Yankee textbook version, the product of individual effort and righteousness (Hecker 1871, 6).

Ethnocultural disputes over moral and civic training in the schools involved language and ethnicity as well as religion. Sometimes they also arose over derogatory stereotypes in textbooks, as when Irish in New York protested vicious slurs. A cartoon by Thomas Nast in 1871 captures the Anglo-Protestant nightmare of an Irish Catholic destruction of true American institutions. The U.S. Public School stands in ruins while flags fly briskly over Tammany Hall. The teacher stands resolutely shielding his pupils, Holy Bible protruding from his coat, while alligators with bishop's miters proceed up the beach to devour terrified children (Nast 1871). Many Catholics despaired of finding any compromise on religion in the schools. By 1890, only about 8 percent of the 676,000 Catholic students attended public schools; by 1920, the proportion had risen only to 12 percent (Cross 1965; Lannie 1968; National Center for Education Statistics 1993).

Language and culture were more negotiable issues than religion in nineteenth-century school politics, though most school leaders preferred the use of English. Some flexibility in linguistic policies seemed warranted, given that a part of the common-school mandate was to attract all children to the public schools, including immigrants. In addition, it was to the self-interest of local school boards to win the support of prosperous groups, like the Germans, who had the political and economic power to create their own schools if they wished. In general, the Democrats were more favorably disposed to cultural pluralism, whether the policies concerned alcohol or language, and they profited from the unpopularity of efforts by Republicans in Massachusetts, Wisconsin, and Illinois to require the use of English only in all schools, public and private (Ulrich 1965).

In some cities Germans pressed for bilingual schools, in others simply the study of German as a special subject. By 1900, there were 231,700 children studying German in elementary grades. In Milwaukee, where even working-class immigrants had achieved political clout, children could attend classes in German, Italian, and Polish, while elsewhere they studied languages like Norwegian, Czech, Spanish, and Dutch (Fishman 1966). In St. Louis in the 1870s, school superintendent William T. Harris saw no conflict between eventual assimilation and the study of German, arguing that ethnic and family traditions "form what may be called the *substance* of the character of each individual, and they cannot be suddenly removed or changed without disastrously weakening the personality" (quoted in City of St. Louis 1875, 114–15). He was arguing, in effect, that there was no reason Germans should not be able to keep their culture while participating as citizens in American political institutions; they would become assimilated more gradually but more also firmly than if their culture were ignored or suppressed.

In Wisconsin, where state laws decreed that all teaching be done in English, a county superintendent said in his annual report that it was better to look the other way when he found that schools were conducting classes in German. After all, he said, the Germans take great interest in education, and if we alienate them they will abandon the public schools. Such toleration for ethnic pluralism would change in the frenzy of World War I. As a result of the anti-German laws and public opinion of that time, the percentage of youth in high school taking German dropped from 24 percent in 1915 to less than 1 percent in 1922 (Jorgenson 1956, 145; Tyack, James, and Benavot 1987, 170–71).

To attract ever growing numbers of children to the common school, educational leaders of the nineteenth century had often been willing to compromise on issues of cultural diversity. Political control of education resided mostly at the local level. Citizens kept federal and state officials on a short leash. In 1890 the average state department of education consisted of two people, including the superintendent, and the U.S. Office of Education had only a handful of employees. Environmentalist assumptions underlay the sort of civic education most common-school crusaders wanted: a good republican was a person who had been taught to think and act correctly. Immigrants could safely be grafted onto the established stock, producing a healthier and more productive tree.

By the turn of the century, however, more and more influential policymakers became willing, even eager, to use the state to regulate education in new and sometimes coercive ways. New kinds of immigrants, they thought, demanded new kinds of schooling. A conclave of educational leaders in 1891 worried aloud about "foreign colonies" of immigrants gathering in the cities. This was seen as a threat to "distinctive Americanism," for the newcomers did not match the older "standard of intelligence and morality" (National Education Association 1891, 295). What would be the solution?

THE "AMERICANIZATION" OF AMERICA

As the twentieth century approached, many policymakers in education began to wonder if the massive numbers of "new immigrants" could ever become good citizens. The pessimists, influenced by racialist theories about the genetic inferiority of southeastern Europeans, low on the scale of "racial" quality, proposed restricting their entry into the country. The optimists saw a long row to hoe: Educating these people to be good citizens would be an arduous task of "Americanization." Doing nothing to assimilate them was unthinkable.

In 1909 one of the new generation of professional educators, Ellwood P. Cubberley, explained that southern and eastern Europeans were of a different breed from their predecessors: "illiterate, docile, lacking in self-reliance and initiative, and not possessing the Anglo-Teutonic conceptions of law, order, and government, their coming has served to dilute tremendously our national stock and to corrupt our civic life." The solution was to break up their settlements and "to implant in their children, insofar as can be done, the Anglo-Saxon conception of righteousness, law and order, and popular government" (Cubberley 1909, 63). His clause "insofar as can be done" echoed the worries of the racialists of the time that perhaps the "new" immigrants were genetically incapable of becoming true Americans. Complicating the task was the resistance to compulsory attendance of some groups, like southern Italians or Poles, who had learned to distrust state schooling in the old country as an imposition by an alien government.

Like other educators who believed it possible to direct social evolution through schooling, however, Cubberley was on the whole optimistic. He melded the new certainty of a "science" of education with the crusading moralism of predecessors like Mann. He believed that the school must take the place of older agents of socialization, "for each year the child is coming to belong more and more to the state and less and less to the parent" (Cubberly 1909, 63). For the school to succeed in its new tasks, compulsory attendance and squads of truant officers were needed; the children of immigrants must be swept into the classroom (Graham 1995).

The new reformers faced two tasks in coping with immigration, then, one political and the other educational. The political fox was in the pedagogical chicken coop: How could the immigrants (first or second generation) who controlled so much of urban education, often through political machines and ethnic politics, produce citizens up to an American standard? Cubberley believed it essential to take education out of the realm of politics, for in the cities the rabble all too often ruled. The state must strengthen the hand of the (Anglo-Saxon) experts who alone could refashion civic education so that it could accomplish the daunting task of Americanization. Educators could then train the young in democracy without having to cope with governance of the schools by riff-raff. There would be education in democracy but not democracy in education.

In New York City, more than half the school staff in 1908 was first- or second-generation immigrants. These veteran educators praised the decentralized ward system of the 1890s that "furnished an Irish Trustee to represent the Irishmen, a German Trustee to represent the Germans, and a Hebrew Trustee to represent the Hebrews" (Tyack 1974, 103). Wait, said one senator during the debate on a charter to centralize control of the city's schools, this is the wrong model. We should put the children of the slums "under the influence of educated, refined, intelligent men and women, so that they will be elevated and lifted out of the swamp into which they were born and brought up" (Tyack 1974, 104). Only if the ethnic ward committees were abolished and the schools put under expert, nonpolitical control would the schools be able to accomplish the herculean task of turning southeastern European children into students who had the civic minds of Anglo-Saxons (Tyack 1974, 103–5).

Taking the schools out of politics was only the beginning of Americanizing urban immigrants. Paula S. Fass notes that reformers of many persuasions at the turn of the century were agreed that there was a "changed context of civic socialization— that is, the manner in which individuals were trained to a responsible American adulthood" (Fass 1989, 16). The common-school crusaders had assumed that a relatively brief exposure to the three Rs and proper textbooks would round out the civic education the child gained in the family, the church, work on the farm or in the shop, and the many other informal sites of socialization.

In the Progressive Era, however, reformers believed that immigrant children did not experience this broader form of moral and civic education. Their parents—often father and mother alike— worked long hours away from the home, typically did not know the English language or American customs well, and found it hard to raise their children consistently either in traditional or American ways. Children had once learned much from work on the farm, John Dewey and Cubberley thought, but factory work was often harsh, unhealthy, and miseducative, both for adults and child laborers. The older informal kinds of political education had atrophied as well. Neither adults nor children gained the familiarity with the republican beliefs, rituals, and practices that had come from everyday discussions around the stove in the country store or from the rituals of politics and Fourth of July oratory (Cubberley 1909; Dewey 1899).

The substitute for this supposedly missing civic socialization of the urban immigrant child was compensatory socialization through the public school. Part of this process would be cognitive instruction with a patriotic message. Learning English, sometimes in special "steamer classes" for immigrants just off the boat, was essential. Educators stepped up the pace and amount of direct instruction in American history and government and required patriotic rituals like recitation of the Pledge of Allegiance, first used in New York in the 1890s, flag rituals, and elaborate celebrations of national holidays (Antin 1912; Tyack and Berkowitz 1977; Shaw 1903; Richman 1905, 113–21).

New kinds of civics texts began appearing. Sarah O'Brien's *English for Foreigners*, aimed mostly at adults but drawing on lessons for children as well, had sections on city, state, and national governments, citizenship, and the American flag (for that lesson students were to copy the sentence "America is another word for opportunity"). Under the lesson on citizenship the students learned that "the United States takes care of all its citizens and gives them many rights. . . . A true citizen pays for his rights by obeying the laws, paying his taxes, and taking his part in protecting the government of the United States. . . . The only way to make good laws is by choosing the right men to make the laws" (O'Brien 1909, 140–41). This was a popular text for naturalization classes, partly because it gave the right answers for the civics test, but it also was a guidebook to the promised land for many immigrants.

Compensatory socialization went well beyond traditional forms of cognitive instruction. Immigrant children, like their parents in adult Americanization classes, learned about proper sanitation and health and "American" styles of eating and dressing. Schools tried to teach mothers to improve the hygiene of their children, prompting one mother to tell her son's teacher that she knew Johnny did not smell like a rose, but that the teacher should "learn him; don't smell him" (Reese 1986, 231). Even recreation was a pedagogical specialty. Nothing should be left to chance in the socialization of immigrants.

One outcome of adapting city schools to immigrant children was the rapid differentiation of the structure of schooling and new choices in programs and courses. Reformers who admired—one might say, glorified—the older forms of socialization by work struggled to create a vocational education that might replace that tradition and at the same time make up for the supposed mental limitations of the newcomer students. Vocational training became a track for "hand-minded" boys, many of them second-generation immigrants, leading to blue-collar jobs. Immigrant girls learned to cook and sew and keep house in the approved "American" fashion. Many immigrant parents and students preferred the commercial tracks, however, that prepared students for white-collar positions (Dooley 1916).

Differentiating the curriculum and developing tests and tracks to screen students undermined the old common-school goal of a uniform education for all. It was generally supposed that performance on IQ tests was a purely individual matter, but when some groups, like southern Italians, did poorly, testers jumped to the conclusion that the Italian "race" was mentally limited. It proved to be but a short step from IQ tests designed to diagnose individual capacities and needs to a newly racialized science of difference (Fass 1989, chapter 2).

NATIVISM TRIUMPHANT

Although they recognized, at least in theory, the principle of a separation of church and state, Americanizers did not believe that there should be a separation of ethnicity and state. Thus the state could not persecute Baptists but could attempt to denationalize German immigrants. There was no bill of rights for cultural diversity. Increasingly, the state reached into the family as well—for example, compelling children to attend school for more and more years (a law often resented by impoverished families and those who had come to regard the state as alien and coercive) (Olneck 1989, 398; Tyack 1993).

Reformers disagreed not so much about the goal of assimilation as about the best means of accomplishing it. Those who pushed 100 percent Americanism urged a sharp-edged intervention: to assimilate such a motley collection of humanity, schools should drive a wedge between students and the parental culture and language, thereby assimilating the second generation, even if it was hard on the first. The humanitarian reformers who knew immigrant families firsthand—teachers and principals, settlement house workers, child labor inspectors, and progressive principals like Angelo Patri, recognized the pain this divisive strategy could bring. They sought to ease cultural conflict between the generations by recognizing the value of the "gifts" that immigrants brought to this country. They sometimes created schools that were health and service centers for whole communities, whose doors were open well into the evening. Some, like the factory inspector Helen M. Todd, recognized that schools could be matched better to the cultural backgrounds of immigrants so that assimilation could be transitional rather than abrupt (Wallace 1994; Todd 1913; Hartmann 1948; Covello 1936).

The outbreak of World War I brought to a boil nativist anxiety about "foreign colonies" and a potential fifth column of unassimilated aliens within the nation. In New York, schoolchildren selling war bonds in the tenements were told to report adults whose loyalty was dubious (Brumberg 1990). "By 1916," writes John F. McClymer, "cultural diversity had come to be defined as a national crisis" (McClymer 1982, 97). That year John Dewey warned about the frenzy for conformity: "Such terms as Irish-American or Hebrew-American or German-American are false terms because they seem to assume something which is already in existence called American, to which the other factor may be externally hitch on. The fact is, the genuine American, the typical American, is himself a hyphenated character" (Dewey 1916, 185).

The Red scare and nativist organizations kept paranoia percolating well into the 1920s. To assist in the patriotic crusade, employers, churches, patriotic associations, and even the Boy Scouts joined forces with the federal Naturalization Bureau and Bureau of Education and state immigration agencies; the distinction between government and the authority it delegated to private groups once again blurred. The Naturalization Bureau developed its own civics text and pressured both school districts and private groups to use it in their Americanization classes. Thus the agency sought to impose a federal curriculum on local schools. Some districts resisted this invasion of local control, others displayed an ecstatic submissiveness. The Naturalization Bureau and the Bureau of Education, however, fought between themselves for jurisdiction over immigrant education. The federal branch of the Americanization campaign produced a tornado of policy talk; how much it changed practice in schools is still an open question (Hill 1919; Connecticut State Board of Education 1920; Higham 1966).

Private groups like the American Legion, the American Bar Association, and the Daughters of the American Revolution pressured dozens of states to pass laws prescribing their own interpretations of orthodox civics, American history, and the Constitution. Whereas in 1903 only one state required the teaching of "citizenship," twenty years later thirty-nine did so. In 1923, forty-three states required the teaching of American history, and twenty-one the Constitution of the United States. The National Security League lobbied to ban the teaching of German and to prescribe superpatriotic instruction. Thanks in part to its efforts, thirty-three states mandated that all teachers pass a test on the Constitution in order to be certified, and loyalty oaths for teachers became increasingly common. By 1923, thirty-five states had enacted legislation that made English the only language of instruction in public schools (Flanders 1925, 62; Tyack, James, and Benavot 1987, chapters 6 and 7).

The campaign to define "American" in a narrow conservative mold and to enforce conformity of thought and behavior among immigrants outraged many ethnic leaders and much of the ethnic press. McClymer has found that despite threats and coercion from employers and various government bodies, only a minority of adult immigrants enrolled in Americanization classes, and those who did rarely completed the courses (McClymer 1982).

BETWEEN THE WARS: TOLERATING PLURALISM

After the war a number of U.S.-born liberals, some of whom had themselves been caught up in the wartime mania for unity, realized that the patriotic binge had produced a civic hangover. "In the eyes of many liberals," Nicholas V. Montalto writes, "the Americanization movement epitomized all that was wrong in the American attitude and policy toward the immigrant: the bankruptcy of racism and chauvinism, the tendency to blame the immigrant for domestic social problems, and the failure of coercion" (Montalto 1982, 144). In 1921, the *Nation* applauded the American Federation of Teachers for its policy statement in favor of cultural pluralism in the schools. Americanization, it declared, did not mean rejecting immigrant cultures in favor of Anglo-Saxonism and praising "the country for qualities which it does not possess" (Wallace 1991, 44; Gerstle 1994).

In reaction to the hard-edged Americanizers, a few writers called for ethnic self-preservation. In 1924, for example, Horace M. Kallen proposed "a democracy of nationalities" in which all groups would enhance "the selfhood which is inalienable in them, and for the realization of which they require 'inalienable' liberty." Kallen thought that culture was "ancestrally determined" rather than an interactive and constantly changing set of practices: "men may change their clothes, their politics, their wives, their religion, their philosophies, to a greater or lesser extent; they cannot change their grandparents" (Kallen 1924, 139, 122, 124). Public schools, he thought, should preserve ethnic "self-realization through the perfection of men according to their kind" (Kallen 1924, 139; for a critique, see Sollors 1986).

As the American Legion called for the coercive "Americanization of America" and Kallen proclaimed the vague goal of total ethnic self-preservation, teachers and social workers and other "street-level bureaucrats" still needed to go about their everyday work with young newcomers. The policies of total ethnic preservation or total assimilation probably did not give these professionals much guidance, nor did they bear much relation to the day-to-day lives of immigrant families, whose cultural practices blended the old and the new in kaleidoscopic ways. The newcomers were enormously heterogeneous in economic class, formal schooling, religion, economic skills, political experience, and cultural and familial patterns. No stereotype of "the immigrant" could capture such diversity, and most of the educators who worked closely with newcomers recognized this fact (Todd 1913, Cohen 1970).

The assimilation of immigrants (or, in a softer version, intergroup relations) became yet another pedagogical specialty. A good proportion of these experts deplored the paranoid ideology and harsh methods of the superpatriots. After laws passed in 1921 and 1924 restricted immigration, educators could go about assimilating the second generation at a less frenetic pace. Social scientists began to portray acculturation and assimilation as a long-term and complex intergenerational process (Daniels 1920; Shiels 1922; Ravage 1919; Weinberg 1977; Smith 1939; Cohen 1990; Montalto 1982).

Many educators were second-generation immigrants who believed that attacks solidified ethnic groups rather than dissolving them. Denigrating the language and cultures of students' parents, they argued, split apart families and created an alienated second generation that was neither foreign nor American. Increasingly these educators argued that a more tolerant, slow-paced approach would produce better results than high-pressure assimilation. They still thought that the public schools should "Americanize" pupils, but they wanted transitional programs that taught tolerance for diversity and preached the doctrine that the United States was a composite of the contributions of many nations (Shiels 1922; Weinberg 1977; Smith 1939; Cohen 1990).

Many schools and other organizations serving immigrants staged pageants, dances, plays, and ethnic feasts that stressed the "gifts" made by immigrants to American society. They celebrated differences while ultimately working toward assimilation. In the 1920s and 1930s, progressive educators experimented with many kinds of cross-cultural learning. Polish pupils in Toledo, Ohio, for example, studied their parents' histories and cultures; students in Neptune, New Jersey, created ethnic family trees and learned the histories of their ancestors; in Santa Barbara, California, pupils prepared exhibits on Chinese art, Scandinavian crafts, and Pacific cultures; and Mexican children in Phoenix, Arizona, attended a class, taught in Spanish, on Mexican history and culture (National Education Association 1942).

The best-articulated version of this early form of pluralism in education was the "intercultural education" movement led by Rachel Davis DuBois, a Quaker and a former teacher. In 1924 she inaugurated in Woodbury High School in southern New Jersey a series of student assemblies on the achievements of different ethnic groups, pioneering a practice that was to become a hallmark of her career. Her work was sufficiently subversive to attract the condemnation of the American Legion. As she expanded her work, she enlisted powerful allies: progressive educators at Columbia's Teachers College, leaders of ethnic organizations, and social scientists concerned with intergroup relations (Montalto 1982; Du-Bois 1935). Although this was a disparate coalition, most of the activists in the intercultural education movement agreed on some basic goals. They wanted to dispel prejudices and stereotypes that might trigger a new burst of nativism and intergroup violence during the hard times of the Great Depression and later the turmoil of World War II. They were concerned about what Louis Adamic (1934) called "thirty million new Americans," the youthful second generation suspended between two worlds, a group described by sociologist Robert Park as "footloose, prowling, and predacious" (quoted in Montalto 1982, 147). They believed that an appreciation for the traditions of the parents would bridge the family gap and help the second generation to find a productive adjustment to American society. They agreed that all Americans, those "on the hill" as well as those "across the tracks," needed better knowledge of one another in order to establish social harmony. By "cultural democracy" they meant fair play for all groups, self-respect, and appreciation for diversity. DuBois and key supporters of the intercultural movement disagreed about an important strategy, however, that has recently become salient once again. She thought that each ethnic group should be studied separately rather than mixed together. Only in this manner, she believed, would children of immigrants and minorities be able to acquire a positive conception of their own groups and thereby cure "the alienation, rootlessness, and emotional disorders afflicting the second generation." Psychic strength would result from strong positive identification with one's ethnic group (quoted in Montalto 1982, 147).

Influential colleagues in the movement dissented, especially members of the Progressive Education Association and many of the social scientists associated with intercultural education. One critic dismissed DuBois's argument about self-esteem as "compensatory idealized tradition," (Montalto 1982, 249) and many were worried that the separate approach would increase, not diminish, group conflict and would solidify ethnic islands. On the eve of

World War II, a time of heightened concern about national unity, two superintendents said that DuBois's curriculum would "arouse in the thinking of so-called minority groups an undesirable emphasis upon their own importance and a determination to insist upon their own rights" (quoted in Montalto 1982, 249). What they wanted was an intercultural strategy that would use psychological methods to preserve civic peace, not mobilize dissidents to secure their rights (for a critique, see Brameld 1945; Goodenough 1975).

Michael Olneck has observed that most educators, hard-line Americanizers and interculturalists alike, distrusted collective ethnic identities. In civics texts and in the writings of the interculturalists, he has identified an underlying ideology of individualism and an ideal of including all people, as individuals, in a greater unity called American society. The cure for group conflict was understanding and appreciation; over time this would result in the inclusion of members of all groups in the mainstream of society as autonomous individuals. Oppression became reduced to stereotyping, and separate ethnic identity was to be dissolved as painlessly as possible (Olneck 1990).

EXPERIENCING SCHOOLING

Policies for educating students in a multicultural society ranged from the 100 percent Americanism of World War I to the "Americans all" version of cultural pluralism of World War II, when it became all right to be a hyphenated American (a Polish-American, for example) if one put the emphasis on the American side of the hyphen. In books of advice to teachers and administrators the trend lines seem fairly straightforward: pluralism comes to be seen less as threat and more as opportunity, and teachers are counseled to make the transition to Americanism less traumatic for all. What is missing from this account of policy, of course, is the hardest part of the story to uncover: how immigrant students (and their families) experienced the system of public education (Gleason 1980, 1992; National Education Association 1942).

Brief forays into two different kinds of evidence provide insight on this matter. One is what textbooks said about immigrants (and what two immigrants said about textbooks). A second is what immigrant students later recalled in their life histories and autobiographical writings. Perhaps the best indication of the ideas to which students were exposed in school—not those they necessarily learned—is to be found in the textbooks used in their classes. In her comprehensive study of high school textbooks in American history during the twentieth century, Micheline Fedyck shows that treatments in high school textbooks of "older immigrants" from northwestern Europe—the Germans, Scotch-Irish, and Irish in particular—were mostly favorable. These people knew and appreciated democracy, quickly became citizens, and were "racially" similar to the nation's Anglo-Saxon stock. By contrast, the "later" immigrants from southeastern Europe were often portrayed in derogatory and often racist terms during the World War I period. They were a bad lot—illiterate, clannish, undemocratic, unintelligent. Many had come here only to make some money at menial jobs and then to return to the old country. Since the Civil War, said one text in 1921, most immigrants "have been from the lower classes . . . and they give much trouble. They are for the most part very ignorant, and having been downtrodden in their old homes, they have no respect for law or government. In fact, many of them would like to see the government of the United States destroyed. How to deal with this undesirable class of immigrants is one of the most serious problems that we have today" (quoted in Fedyck 1980, 109).

"Would it be possible," asked another text, "to absorb the millions of olive-skinned Italians, and swarthy, black-haired Slavs, and dark-eyed Hebrews into the body of the American people?" (quoted in Pierce 1930, 87–88). It may be a perverse tribute to the clannishness of the Anglo-Saxon authors of these textbooks that they did not seem to worry about the effect of such slurs on immigrant students or their families.

Fedyck found in the texts written in the 1930s and 1940s that the American image of southeastern Europeans had been transformed: they were now seen as contributing to trade, literature, art, entertainment, banking, and scientific research. They did the hard work of mines, mills, and construction. They created a whole new American tapestry of customs, crafts, and arts. If they sometimes fell behind in the American march of economic and social progress, it was often because they were treated badly (Fedyck 1980, 110–14).

There are many possible reasons why textbooks took a more friendly view of social pluralism. One text pointed out that the restrictive quotas of the 1920s cut the rate of increase, giving Americans a "breathing space" and a chance to assimilate newcomers in a more humane and gradual fashion: "The 'melting pot' is no longer being filled faster than it can melt, and we now can develop a new and composite race." Ethnic associations protested against negative stereotypes of their groups, and more and more citizens came to see the evil consequences of the obscene doctrine of superior and inferior "races" as practiced by the Nazis. Professional associations like the National Education Association praised an "Americans all" policy of tolerating, indeed celebrating, ethnic differences (this was especially true during World War II) (Fedyck 1980, 114).

It is difficult to assess how immigrant students reacted to the "public truth" taught in these textbooks. Two contrasting views of texts by pupils suggests reactions ranging from the triumph of emancipated citizenship to anger over gratuitous insult. The Jewish immigrant Mary Antin recalled her awe in reading aloud about her "Fellow Citizen," George Washington: "Never had I prayed . . . in such utter reverence and worship as I repeated the simple sentences of my child's story of the patriot. I gazed with adoration at the portraits of George and Martha Washington, till I could see them with my eyes shut" (Antin 1912, 89). Antin would probably have been at home in the Hebrew Institute in New York, where students read the text of the Declaration of Independence in two parallel columns, one English and one Hebrew (Riis 1892, 53–54).

Such direct blending of loyalties did not come so easily to Guadalupe Toro Valdez, a Mexican American in a Texas school in 1919. In history class he and his fellow students were expected to read about and recite the glories of the Texas revolution and the exploits of Sam Houston in defeating Mexican soldiers and grabbing Mexican land. The students rebelled, defacing the pictures of Houston and then tearing the offending pages out of the textbooks. The next day as the teacher called on each one to recite, only to find the same pages missing, she "glanced at her own copy," Valdez recalled. "Watching her, the class was so still you could hear the specks of dust dancing on the sheaf of sunbeams that poured in through a window. Finally, red as a beet, she nodded her head and said, 'Let us take the next chapter for tomorrow. Class is dismissed'" (quoted in Adamic 1939, 243–44).

In reading the life histories of second-generation immigrants I have been impressed by how much they had to say about peers and family and how little to say about what happened in classrooms. The children of immigrants often learned American ways most powerfully not from teachers but from peers intolerant of cultural differences. Over and over again the life stories of newcomers use the word "ridicule" to describe how other children treated them when they were "greenhorns" new to this country. Peers and playmates made fun of their accents, their clothes, their food, their ignorance of American children's ways and games (Smith 1927, 1939; Duncan 1933).

In turn, many of these girls and boys felt ashamed of their parents, or angry because their fathers and mothers did not understand how things worked in America, or rebellious against old-world patterns of authority. The process of assimilation through schooling often involved disengagement from the parental culture, a chance to enter a new life. As an ever larger percentage of American youth graduated from high school (reaching one-half of the age group by 1940), the educational attainment of the children rapidly outstripped that of the parents. Often, however, the family, and even tedious work, was a shelter from the demands of the school, with the strange tasks it imposed. In Chicago in 1909, 412 out of 500 children queried told a factory inspector that they would rather work in a factory than go to school (Todd 1913, 73–74).

Immigrant groups differed widely in their attitudes toward schooling. Some immigrants saw the public school as a gateway to economic opportunity. Others played down education and instead wanted their children to work to contribute to the family's collective long march out of poverty. Ethnic and religious communities built their own institutions—churches, schools, clubs, mutual benefit societies, and political organizations—as a means of mediating structures to ease adaptation to American life while preserving valued traditions. Aspirations and alienation crisscrossed the lives of immigrant families, often muffled amid public discourse about assimilation and cultural pluralism (Todd 1913; Bodnar 1985; Smith 1969; Cohen 1970).

THE LAST GENERATION: POLICY TALK AND PRACTICE IN CIVIC EDUCATION

Public educators have rarely sought to preserve islands of cultural difference. Understanding and appreciation of difference, it was assumed, would eventually dissolve separate ethnic identity and thereby allow all groups to enter the mainstream of American society. Creating citizens one by one, as we have seen, was a liberal political ideal that stretched back to the revolutionary times. Psychology, the dominant discipline in education, reinforced this stress on the individual. The final product of the schools was to be an autonomous, prejudice-free, modernized free agent (Olneck 1990).

In recent years social movements led by African Americans, Latinos, Native Americans, feminists, and other "outsider" groups have altered concepts of cultural citizenship and civic education. This recent politics of pluralism has come more from the grassroots than from the liberal professionals who shaped intercultural education in the past. Although leaders like Martin Luther King Jr. originally appealed to a universalistic ideology of individual rights, over time some activists began to argue that group wrongs (like the laws that suppressed blacks in the caste system) left a legacy that could only be corrected by group rights (like affirmative action).

Courts, legislatures, and local school districts have responded to civil rights movements by adopting policies of desegregation, bilingual education, and ethnic studies. Much of the energy behind "multicultural education" in recent times stems from the demands of activists who have seen that curricular change could go well beyond the inclusion of a few "contributions." Knowledge of how groups have been victimized and a better understanding of their internal histories could mobilize people in groups, not simply as individuals, to achieve social justice. Some also saw ethnic studies and bilingual-bicultural education as a way of preserving the distinctive cultures of groups rather than as a step toward cultural assimilation. The new version of pluralism was explicitly political and challenged not just the traditional civic canon in public schools but also entrenched interests that had sustained racism and nativism. The "culture wars" were not just "academic" (King and Ladson-Billings 1991; Olsen 1988; Lee, Lomotey, and Shujaa 1990; Sleeter and Grant 1987; Banks 1991; Rizvi 1986; Cornbleth and Waugh 1995).

Not surprisingly, this ethnic-centered and social reconstructionist version of civic education has aroused far more controversy, more fear and hope, than earlier forms of intercultural education. Conservative, sometimes nativist, political countermovements have arisen, demanding English-only laws and restricting access of immigrants to schools and other services. A number of more centrist critics have warned that civic education is becoming Balkanized and is neglecting the central American narrative of the "unum" while exaggerating the "pluribus." In the early 1990s, ninety-nine U.S. Senators voted to reject a version of national standards in American history, ostensibly because it failed to be suitably deferential to the Founding Fathers (Theodore Gross, "Classrooms in Chaos," *New York Times,* September 18, 1991, B7; Nunberg 1997; Ravitch 1990).

There is some evidence that today, as in the past, policy talk about civic education—in this case, multiculturalism in the culture wars—has been more volatile than effective in practice. Michael Frisch, a history professor at the University of New York at Buffalo, found that the traditional American heroes were alive and well in the memories of his beginning students. In eight different years from 1975 to 1988 he asked them to write down the names of ten historical figures (through the end of the Civil War) that popped into their minds. They listed, in order of rank, Washington, Lincoln, Jefferson, and a number of other white politicians and military men. The only woman mentioned (ranking fifteenth of the top twenty-four) was Betsy Ross. "If George is the Father of the Country," Frisch comments, "then surely Betsy Ross exists symbolically as the Mother, who gives birth to our collective symbol" (Frisch 1989, 1147; see also Tyack 1999).

Although Frisch's free-association test is just a straw in the wind—we do not really have very good information on what is taught in social studies—another piece of revealing evidence is a survey of public school teachers by Public Agenda in 1996 that asked them what moral and civic lessons were most important. John Swett would have approved of the virtues these teachers applauded and strove to teach: the old values of honesty, responsibility, and industriousness, for example. Supplementing these was tolerance—"respect for others regardless of their racial and ethnic background"—a value endorsed by almost all. The assimilationist ideal of the common school surfaced in their desire to "help new immigrants absorb language and culture as quickly as possible, even if their native language and culture are neglected." Very few wanted to introduce ethnically divisive issues into their classrooms. The survey suggests that the more consensual elements of multiculturalism—like ethnic tolerance—have been layered onto durable strata of more traditional civic education (Farkas and Johnson 1996, 42–43).

Just such a multicultural layering of the new ethnic history on top of a traditional national narrative was what Nathan Glazer and Reed Ueda found when they studied the treatment of ethnic groups in six American history textbooks published in the late 1970s, a time of heightened ethnic assertiveness. They observe that "the major outlines of American historical development, as familiar from the texts of ten, twenty, or forty years ago, still dominate. We will find George Washington and John Adams, Andrew Jackson, Calhoun, Webster and Clay, Abraham Lincoln, Theodore Roosevelt, and Woodrow Wilson as major figures, and the central political story is not ignored, though somewhat reduced." (Glazer and Ueda 1983, 15, 22). There was more social history, they discovered, but pages devoted to ethnic and racial groups accounted for only 5.4 to 11.6 percent of the total. They detected little integration of the older narrative and the new ethnic history beyond celebration of ethnic achievements and a theme of "repeated struggle between victims and [white] oppressors" (Glazer and Ueda 1983, 21; see also Fedyck 1980; Ueda 1995).

A third piece of evidence comes courtesy of the Immigration and Naturalization Service. In 1993 it printed a list of one hundred typical questions (with answers) that applicants for citizenship might be asked as a test of their knowledge of civics. Four questions dealt with George Washington, two with Abraham Lincoln, and one each with Patrick Henry, Francis Scott Key, and Thomas Jefferson. The only figure from the twentieth century added to this pantheon of older heroes was Martin Luther King Jr. Four questions inquired about the Pilgrims and Thanksgiving, thirteen about the Constitution, and four about the symbolism of the American flag. Almost all of the rest of the questions dealt with the structure of government. My grandfather could probably have answered most of the 1993 questions when he became naturalized in 1889. Publicly approved truths for immigrants have not changed much (U.S. Immigration and Naturalization Service 1993, 2211). Evidence drawn from textbooks, students' memories of historical figures, teachers' priorities in civic and moral education, and immigration service's test questions suggests that despite vehement talk about multiculturalism and neo-Americanization, the old icons, values, and practices in civic education have not disappeared. In the midst of current controversies, it is tempting to exaggerate the novelty and vehemence of dissent.

REFLECTIONS

Reflecting on the history of the politics of civic education, political activism seems less worrisome than attempts to pinch the policy talk on educational purposes into a narrow economistic account. David F. Labaree states the issue this way: "The biggest problem facing American schools is not the conflict, contradiction, and compromise that arise from trying to keep a balance among educational goals. Instead, the main threat comes from the growing dominance of the social mobility goal over the others" (Labaree 1997, 73). In a nation that is as socially diverse as the United States, but in which many citizens also aspire to civic unity, conflict over political purposes is healthy, even essential to democracy. In recent years, however, many influential policymakers in education have come to justify education primarily in economic terms, as a consumer good rather than a public good.

Historically, the central rationale of public education has been political: the common school existed primarily to inculcate good citizenship. Some continuities and consensus have existed over time among citizens about what should be taught and how. On

occasion, Americans have discovered common values (visible today, for example, in the Public Agenda survey of teachers and
parents); but conflict has periodically arisen and reinvigorated the
search for democracy. In each of the formative episodes discussed,
disputes tended to focus on political beliefs, religion, harder and
softer ways of assimilating ethnic groups, goals of social justice
sought by social movements, and recently, multiculturalism. As different groups sought to mold the public culture, underlying their
controversies was a conviction that political education mattered to
the whole society.

Today, when education opinion shapers talk about schools,
they rarely have much to say about political purposes. When political commentators talk about political purposes they have little
to say about schools; they may lament "the strange disappearance
of civic America" (Putnam 1996) and exhort citizens to revive a
sense of common civic values, but they rarely have much to say
about public schools, traditionally the main agency of civic socialization (National Commission on Excellence in Education 1983;
Sandel 1996).

So what are schools for? The conventional wisdom now seems
to be that education exists to create human capital that will enable
individuals, and the nation, to succeed in global economic competition. When education becomes a consumer good, why should
schooling not become simply an open market for acquiring cre-
dentials? Vouchers in hand, parents can pick what is best for their
children. In some conservative circles, "government" schools have
become anathema, the word having all the lure of torture and
taxes (Labaree 1997; Wells 1993; Weiler 1982).

Americans have always debated the future of the nation by
discussing how their children should be educated. Public schools
have been the center of this form of political deliberation. They
are everywhere, familiar, still locally controlled in most respects,
and traditionally associated with aspirations to serve the common
good. In short, they are a political resource that has served the
nation well, though in recent years an economic rationale has
eclipsed the political purposes.

Americans now need to negotiate a political philosophy of
public education that attends to cultural diversity as well as political citizenship, that is more generous, tough minded, and pluralistic than in the past. Responsiveness to social diversity is not the

whole task, however. As James March has said, it is also the case that "democratic political systems require a sense of common destiny and identity" (March 1996, 16). In a democracy, a sense of the common good that generates trust among citizens is not a luxury but a necessity. At its best, deliberation about civic education has represented a form of trusteeship that links the past to the future of children yet unborn.

REFERENCES

Adamic, Louis. 1934. "Thirty Million New Americans." *Harper's Monthly Magazine* 169 (November): 684–94.

———. 1939. *From Many Lands.* New York: Harper and Brothers.

Anderson, James D. 1988. *The Education of Blacks in the South, 1860–1935.* Chapel Hill: University of North Carolina Press.

Antin, Mary. 1912. *The Promised Land.* Boston: Houghton Mifflin.

Baird, Robert. 1970. *Religion in America.* 1844. New York: Harper and Row.

Banks, James. 1991. *Teaching Strategies for Ethnic Studies.* Boston: Allyn and Bacon.

Bender, Thomas. 1989. "Public Culture: Inclusion and Synthesis in American History." In *Historical Literacy: The Case for History in American Education,* edited by Paul Gagnon. Boston: Houghton Mifflin.

Blodgett, James H. 1893. *Report on Education in the United States at the Eleventh Census: 1890.* Washington: U.S. Government Printing Office.

Bodnar, John. 1985. *The Transplanted: A History of Immigrants in Urban America.* Bloomington: Indiana University Press.

Brameld, Theodore. 1945. "Intergroup Education in Certain School Systems." *Harvard Educational Review* 15(2): 93–98.

Browne, J. Ross. 1850. *Report of the Debates in the Convention on the Formation of the State Constitution in California in September and October 1848.* Washington: U.S. Government Printing Office.

Brumberg, Stephan F. 1990. "New York City Schools March Off to War: The Nature and Extent of Participation of the City Schools in the Great War, April 1917–June 1918." *Urban Education* 24(4): 440–75.

Carlson, Robert A. 1987. *The Americanization Syndrome: A Quest for Conformity.* London: Croom Helm.

Carper, James. 1978. "A Common Faith for the Common School? Religion and Education in Kansas, 1861–1900." *Mid-America: An Historical Review* 60(3): 149–50.

City of St. Louis. 1875. *School Report.* St. Louis, Mo.: St. Louis City Schools.

Cohen, David K. 1970. "Immigrants and the Schools." *Review of Educational Research* 70(1): 13–26.

Cohen, Ronald D. 1990. *Children of the Mill: Schooling and Society in Gary, Indiana, 1906–1960.* Bloomington: Indiana University Press.

Connecticut State Board of Education. 1920. *Classes for Foreign-Born Adults: Organization and Maintenance.* Hartford.

Continental Congress. 1777–89. *Journals of the Continental Congress, 1777–1789.* Edited by Worthington C. Ford et al. 34 vols. Washington, D.C., 1904–37.

Cornbleth, Catherine, and Dexter Waugh. 1995. *The Great Speckled Bird: Multicultural Politics and Education Policymaking.* New York: St. Martin's Press.

Covello, Leonard. 1936. "A High School and Its Immigrant Community: A Challenge and an Opportunity." *Journal of Educational Sociology* 9(6): 331–46.

Cremin, Lawrence, ed. 1957. *The Republic and the School: Horace Mann on the Education of Free Men.* New York: Teachers College Press.

Cross, Robert D. 1965. "The Origins of the Catholic Parochial Schools in America." *American Benedictine Review* 16(2): 194–209.

Cubberley, Ellwood P. 1909. *Changing Conceptions of Education.* Boston: Houghton Mifflin.

Daniels, John. 1920. *America via the Neighborhood.* New York: Harper and Brothers.

Dewey, John. 1899. *The School and Society.* Chicago: University of Chicago Press.

———. 1916. "Nationalizing Education." *National Education Association Addresses and Proceedings.* Washington, D.C.: National Education Association.

Dooley, William H. 1916. *The Education of the Ne'er-Do-Well.* Boston: Houghton Mifflin.

DuBois, Rachel Davis. 1935. "Our Enemy: The Stereotype." *Progressive Education* 12(3): 146–50.

Duncan, Hannibal G. 1933. *Immigration and Assimilation.* Boston: Ginn and Company.

Elson, Ruth Miller. 1964. *Guardians of Tradition: American Schoolbooks of the Nineteenth Century.* Lincoln, Nebr.: University of Nebraska Press.

Farkas, Steve, and Jean Johnson. 1996. *Given the Circumstances: Teachers Talk About Public Education Today.* New York: Public Agenda Foundation.

Farnham, Wallace D. 1963. "The Weakened Spring of Government: A

Study in Nineteenth-Century American History." *American Historical Review* 68(3): 662–80.

Fass, Paula S. 1989. *Outside In: Minorities and the Transformation of American Education.* New York: Oxford University Press.

———. 1993. "Making and Remaking an Event: The Leopold and Loeb Case in American Culture." *Journal of American History* 80(3): 919–51.

Fedyck, Micheline. 1980. "Conceptions of Citizenship and Nationality in High School Textbooks, 1913–1977." Ph.D. diss., Columbia University.

Fishman, Joshua. 1966. *Language Loyalty in the United States.* The Hague: Mouton.

Flanders, Jesse K. 1925. *Legislative Control of the Elementary Curriculum.* New York: Teachers College Press.

Frederickson, George. 1965. *The Inner Civil War: Northern Intellectuals and the Civil War.* New York: Harper and Row.

Frisch, Michael. 1989. "American History and the Structures of Collective Memory: A Modest Exercise in Empirical Iconography." *Journal of American History* 75(4): 1130–55.

Gerstle, Gary. 1994. "The Protean Character of American Liberalism." *American Historical Review* 99(4): 1043–73.

Glazer, Nathan, and Reed Ueda. 1983. *Ethnic Groups in History Textbooks.* Washington, D.C.: Ethics and Public Policy Center.

Gleason, Philip. 1980. "American Identity and Americanization." In *Harvard Encyclopedia of Ethnic Groups.* edited by Stephan Thernstrom. Cambridge, Mass.: Harvard University Press.

———. 1992. *Speaking of Diversity: Language and Ethnicity in Twentieth-Century America.* Baltimore: Johns Hopkins University Press.

Good, Harry. 1934. *Benjamin Rush and His Services to American Education.* Berne, Ind.: Witness Press.

Goodenough, Ronald K. 1975. "The Progressive Educator, Race, and Ethnicity in the Depression Years: An Overview." *History of Education Quarterly* 15(4): 365–94.

Graham, Patricia Albjerg. 1995. "Assimilation, Adjustment, and Access: An Antiquarian View of American Education." In *Learning from the Past: What History Teaches Us About School Reform,* edited by Diane Ravitch and Maris A. Vinovskis. Baltimore: Johns Hopkins University Press.

Hansen, Allen O. 1926. *Liberalism and American Education in the Eighteenth Century.* New York: Hippocrene Books.

Hartmann, Edward G. 1948. *The Movement to Americanize the Immigrant.* New York: Columbia University Press.

Hecker, Isaac. 1871. "Unification and Education." *Catholic World* 13(73): 1–14.

Higham, John. 1966. *Strangers in the Land: Patterns of American Nativism, 1860–1925.* New York: Atheneum.

———. 1974. "Hanging Together: Divergent Unities in American History." *Journal of American History* 61(1): 5–28.

Hill, Howard C. 1919. "The Americanization Movement." *American Journal of Sociology* 24(6): 609–42.

James, Thomas. 1991. "Rights of Conscience and State School Systems in Nineteenth-Century America." In *Toward a Usable Past: Liberty Under State Constitutions,* edited by Paul Finkelman and Stephen E. Gottlieb. Athens: University of Georgia Press.

Jefferson, Thomas. 1903. *The Writings of Thomas Jefferson.* Edited by Andrew A. Lipscomb and Albert E. Berg. Vols. 10, 12. Washington, D.C.: Thomas Jefferson Memorial Association.

———. 1950. *The Papers of Thomas Jefferson.* Edited by Julian P. Boyd. Vol. 8. Princeton: Princeton University Press.

Jorgenson, Lloyd. 1956. *The Founding of Public Education in Wisconsin.* Madison: State Historical Society of Wisconsin.

Kaestle, Carl F. 1983. *Pillars of the Republic: Common Schools and American Society, 1780–1860.* New York: Hill and Wang.

Kallen, Horace M. 1924. *Culture and Democracy in the United States: Studies in the Group Psychology of the American Peoples.* New York: Boni and Liveright.

King, Joyce Elaine, and Gloria Ladson-Billings. 1991. "Dysconscious Racism and Multicultural Illiteracy: The Distorting of the American Mind." Paper presented at the annual meeting of the American Educational Research Association, Boston, April 1991.

Kirp, David L. 1991. "Textbooks and Tribalism in California." *Public Interest* 104(Summer): 20–36.

Knight, Edgar W., ed. 1950. *A Documentary History of Education in the South Before 1860.* Chapel Hill: University of North Carolina Press.

Labaree, David F. 1997. "Public Goods, Private Goods: The American Struggle over Educational Goals." *American Educational Research Journal* 34(1): 39–81.

Lannie, Vincent P. 1968. *Public Money and Parochial Education: Bishop Hughes, Governor Seward, and the New York School Controversy.* Cleveland: Press of Case Western Reserve University.

Lee, Carol D., Kofi Lomotey, and Mwalimu Shujaa. 1990. "How Shall We Sing Our Sacred Song in a Strange Land? The Dilemma of Double Consciousness and the Complexities of an African-Centered Pedagogy." *Journal of Education* 172(2): 45–61.

Levy, Leonard W. 1963. *Jefferson and Civil Liberties: The Darker Side.* New York: Quadrangle.

Lindberg, Stanley W. 1976. *The Annotated McGuffey: Selections from the McGuffey Eclectic Readers, 1836–1920.* New York: Van Nostrand Reinhold.

Mann, Horace. 1865–68. *Life and Works of Horace Mann.* 4 vols. Boston: Lee and Shepherd.

March, James G. 1996. "Democracy and Schooling: An Institutional Perspective." Unpublished manuscript. Stanford University.

McClymer, John F. 1982. "The Americanization Movement and the Education of the Foreign-Born Adult, 1914–1925." In *American Education and the European Immigrant: 1840–1940,* edited by Bernard J. Weiss. Urbana: University of Illinois Press.

Meyer, John W., and Richard Rubinson. 1975. "Education and Political Development." In *Review of Research in Education,* edited by Fred Kerlinger. Vol 3. Itasca, Ill.: F. E. Peacock.

Montalto, Nicholas V. 1982. "The Intercultural Education Movement, 1924–1941: The Growth of Tolerance as a Form of Intolerance." In *American Education and the European Immigrant, 1840–1940,* edited by Bernard J. Weiss. Urbana, Ill.: University of Illinois Press.

Nast, Thomas. 1871. Cartoon of "The American River Ganges." *Harper's Weekly,* April 1.

National Center for Education Statistics. 1993. *One Hundred Twenty Years of American Education: A Statistical Portrait.* Washington: U.S. Government Printing Office.

National Commission on Excellence in Education. 1983. *A Nation at Risk: The Imperative for Educational Reform.* Washington, D.C.

National Education Association. 1891. *Addresses and Proceedings.* Washington, D.C.: National Education Association.

———. 1942. *Americans All: Studies in Intercultural Education.* Washington, D.C.: NEA Department of Supervisors and Directors of Instruction.

Nunberg, Geoffrey. 1997. "Lingo Jingo: English-Only and the New Nativism." *The American Prospect* 8(33): 40–47.

O'Brien, Sarah. 1909. *English for Foreigners.* Boston: Houghton Mifflin.

Olneck, Michael R. 1989. "Americanization and the Education of Immigrants, 1900–1925: An Analysis of Symbolic Action." *American Journal of Education* 98(August): 398–423.

———. 1990. "The Recurring Dream: Symbolism and Ideology in Intercultural and Multicultural Education." *American Journal of Education* 98(2): 147–74.

Olsen, Laurie. 1988. *Crossing the Schoolhouse Border: Immigrant Students and the California Public Schools.* San Francisco: California Tomorrow.

Pangle, Lorraine Smith, and Thomas L. Pangle. 1993. *The Learning of Liberty: The Educational Ideas of the American Founders.* Lawrence, Kans.: University Press of Kansas.

Perlmann, Joel. 1988. *Ethnic Differences: Schooling and Social Structure Among the Irish, Italians, Jews, and Blacks in an American City, 1880–1935.* New York: Cambridge University Press.

Pierce, Bessie Louise. 1930. *Civic Attitudes in American School Textbooks.* Chicago: University of Chicago Press.

Putnam, Robert D. 1996. "The Strange Disappearance of Civic America." *American Prospect* 7(24): 34–49.

Ravage, Marcus E. 1919. "The Immigrant's Burden." *New Republic* 19 (June): 209–11.

Ravitch, Diane. 1990. "Diversity and Democracy: Multicultural Education in America." *American Educator* 14(Spring): 16–20.

Reese, William J. 1986. *Power and the Promise of School Reform: Grass-Roots Movements During the Progressive Era.* Boston: Routledge and Kegan Paul.

Richman, Julia. 1905. "The Immigrant Child." *National Education Association Addresses and Proceedings.* Washington, D.C.: National Education Association.

Riis, Jacob. 1892. *The Children of the Poor.* New York: Charles Scribner's Sons.

Rizvi, Fazal. 1986. *Ethnicity, Class, and Multicultural Education.* Geelong, Australia: Deakin University Press.

Roberts, Peter. 1920. *The Problem of Americanization.* New York: Macmillan.

Rush, Benjamin. 1786. *A Plan for the Establishment of Public Schools and the Diffusion of Knowledge in Pennsylvania, to Which Are Added Thoughts upon the Mode of Education, Proper in a Republic.* Philadelphia: Thomas Dobson.

———. 1951. *Letters of Benjamin Rush.* Edited by Lyman H. Butterfield. Princeton: Princeton University Press.

Sandel, Michael J. 1996. *Democracy's Discontent: America in Search of a Public Philosophy.* Cambridge, Mass.: Harvard University Press.

Shaw, Adele Marie. 1903. "The True Character of New York Public Schools." *World's Work* 7(December): 4204–21.

Shiels, Albert. 1922. "Education for Citizenship." *National Education Association Addresses and Proceedings.* Washington, D.C.: National Education Association.

Sleeter, Christine E., and Carl A. Grant. 1987. "An Analysis of Multicultural Education in the United States." *Harvard Educational Review* 57(4): 421–44.

Smith, Timothy L. 1969. "Immigrant Social Aspirations and American Education, 1880–1930." *American Quarterly* 21(Fall): 523–43.

Smith, William C. 1927. *The Second Generation Oriental in America.* Honolulu: Institute of Pacific Relations.

———. 1939. *Americans in the Making.* New York: D. Appleton Century.

Sollors, Werner. 1986. "A Critique of Pure Pluralism." In *Reconstructing American Literary History,* edited by Sacvan Berkovitch. Cambridge, Mass.: Harvard University Press.

Stowe, Calvin. 1836. *Transactions of the Fifth Annual Meeting of the Western Literary Institute and College of Professional Teachers.* Cincinnati: Western Literary Institute, Executive Committee.

Swett, John. 1885. *Methods of Teaching: A Hand-book of Principles, Directions, and Working Models for Common-school Teachers.* New York: American Book Company.

Takaki, Ronald. 1989. *Strangers from a Different Shore: A History of Asian Americans.* New York: Penguin.

Todd, Helen M. 1913. "Why Children Work: The Children's Answer." *McClure's Magazine* 40(April): 68–79.

Tyack, David. 1966. "Forming the National Character: Paradox in the Thought of the Revolutionary Generation." *Harvard Educational Review* 36(Winter): 29–41.

———. 1974. *The One Best System: A History of American Urban Education.* Cambridge, Mass.: Harvard University Press.

———. 1993. "Constructing Differences: Historical Perspectives on Schooling and Social Diversity." *Teachers College Record* 95(1): 8–34.

———. 1999. "Preserving the Republic by Educating Republicans." In *Diversity and Its Discontents: Cultural Conflict and Common Ground in Contemporary American Society,* edited by Neill J. Smelser and Jeffrey C. Alexander. Princeton, N.J.: Princeton University Press.

———, ed. 1967. *Turning Points in American Educational History.* Waltham, Mass.: Blaisdell Publishing.

Tyack, David, and Michael Berkowitz. 1977. "The Man Nobody Liked: Toward a Social History of the Truant Officer, 1840–1940." *American Quarterly* 29(1): 321–54.

Tyack, David, and Elisabeth Hansot. 1982. *Managers of Virtue: Public School Leadership in America, 1820–1980.* New York: Basic Books.

Tyack, David, Thomas James, and Aaron Benavot. 1987. *Law and the Shaping of Public Education, 1785–1954.* Madison, Wis.: University of Wisconsin Press.

U.S. House of Representatives. 1878. Committee on Public Lands. *Report on Educational Land Policy* (February 24, 1826). *Barnard's American Journal of Education* 28: 939–44.

U.S. Immigration and Naturalization Service. 1993. *One Hundred Typical Questions*. Washington: U.S. Government Printing Office.

Ueda, Reed. 1995. "Ethnic Diversity and National Identity in Public School Texts." In *Learning from the Past: What History Teaches Us About School Reform*, edited by Diane Ravitch and Maris A. Vinovskis. Baltimore: Johns Hopkins University Press.

Ulrich, Robert. 1965. "The Bennett Law of 1889: Education and Politics in Wisconsin." Ph.D diss., University of Wisconsin.

Wallace, James M. 1991. *Liberal Journalism and American Education, 1914–1941*. New Brunswick: Rutgers University Press.

———. 1994. "Angelo Patri: Immigrant Educator, Storyteller, and Public School Progressive." *Vitae Scholasticae: The Journal of Educational Biography* 13(Fall): 43–63.

Warfel, Harry R. 1936. *Noah Webster: Schoolmaster to America*. New York: Macmillan.

Webster, Noah. 1790. *A Collection of Essays and Fugitive Writings on Moral, Historical, Political, and Literary Subjects*. Boston: I. Thomas and E.T. Andrews.

———. 1798. *The American Spelling Book*. Boston: I. Thomas and E. T. Andrews.

Weiler, Hans N. 1982. "Education, Public Confidence, and the Legitimacy of the Modern State: Do We Have a Crisis?" *Phi Delta Kappan* 64(1): 8–20.

Weinberg, Daniel E. 1977. "The Ethnic Technician and the Foreign-Born: Another Look at Americanization Ideology and Goals." *Societias* 7 (Summer): 209–27.

Weiss, Bernard J., ed. 1982. *American Education and the European Immigrant, 1840–1940*. Urbana, Ill.: University of Illinois Press.

Wells, Amy Stuart. 1993. *Time to Choose: America at the Crossroads of School Choice Policy*. New York: Hill and Wang.

Wiebe, Robert. 1984. *The Opening of American Society: From the Adoption of the Constitution to the Eve of Disunion*. New York: Vintage.

—— Chapter 10 ——

Public Education, Immigrants, and Racialization: The Contemporary Americanization Project

Laurie Olsen

S CHOOLS ARE A crucial site for the incorporation of immigrant students into the fabric of American society. As Robert Bach (1993) has observed, they are a primary public space in which newcomers come into contact with established residents, and it is through the daily course of events in schools that immigrant students learn what it means to be "American." In schools, immigrants learn from their native-born peers and from their teachers about how and where they can fit into American society.

The schools immigrant students encounter are rarely neutral zones for observing and learning about America, however. The public schools of this nation have historically been called upon to play a central role in "Americanizing" and incorporating newcomers. In chapter 9 of this volume, David Tyack discusses the prevalent belief in this nation in earlier eras that civic training in the public schools was essential to the survival of the republic and the preservation of the social order. The notion that schools have an essential role to play still prevails, although it is focused primarily on the teaching of English rather than the teaching of civics. The explicit English-language curriculum is paired with a powerful and implicit, "hidden" curriculum in which schools ac-

371

tively sort students by race and class, offer different opportunities to different students, open some doors and close others based on skin color, class, and mother tongue.[1]

On all of these levels, what goes on in public schools reflects the larger society's responses to increasing immigration and can, especially at times of peak immigration, become a battleground as differing responses to the new immigrants struggle for dominance.[2] Tyack describes a series of controversies that erupted over the history of public schools in the United States related to the incorporation of immigrants, the building of a common civic culture, and social diversity—in one era focused on political beliefs, in another on religion, and so on. This essay presents an ethnographic approach to the same issues by examining the experience of students in one high school, illustrating the contemporary version of these struggles, which is focused on racial identities and language affiliation.

The question of how today's schools shape the process of "becoming American" for immigrant students is a complex one, involving issues of racial and social reproduction through educational institutions and of our society's mixed responses to an unprecedented wave of immigrants. Schools have a tendency to reproduce current social and racial relations, privileging the children of families of a dominant culture, a wealthier class, and whiter skins. They do so (with or without conscious, deliberate intent) by rewarding behaviors, information sets, and ways of speaking that those with more power in the society exhibit and by legitimating those rewards through an ideology of merit.

Immigrants come to the United States from every corner of this globe—representing different cultural groups, different classes, different racial and ethnic groups. No single process of immigrant incorporation is shared across these differences. Rather, the prior education of a wave of immigrants from a particular area, the racial positioning of that immigrant group in the United States, the similarity or disparity between what is valued and rewarded in the United States and the behaviors and values of the immigrant group that is arriving, all shape the process of incorporation, resulted in what Alejandro Portes and Min Zhou call "segmented assimilation," with immigrant groups finding their place in very different sectors of American economic and social life (Portes and Zhou 1993). Little research has been done to show

how these processes become manifested in the day-to-day inter-actions of immigrant students as they learn to become "American" through their schooling.

I attempt to address this deficit here by exploring how daily negotiations of race, class, culture, and language have taken place in one high school faced with a rapid increase in immigrant stu-dents. This study explores the following questions: What do immi-grants learn and construct about what it means to become Ameri-can? What role do the public schools of this nation play in shaping these patterns of incorporation at the turn to the twenty-first cen-tury? How do immigrant students fare in the context of racial sort-ing and class reproduction that they often find in schools? Through this exploration, I hope to encourage historians interested in im-migrant incorporation to similarly probe beyond the formal civic education training designed for immigrants to examine the inter-play of the class structure of schools, the broader contexts of racial positioning and racialization in eras of immigration, and the qual-ity and content of relationships among peers that shape how im-migrants come to learn their place in this nation.

INCREASING IMMIGRATION, SOCIAL AND ECONOMIC STRATIFICATION, AND SEGMENTED ASSIMILATION

These questions are of particular import now because the past two decades have seen a major immigration wave to the United States. During the 1980s, the United States experienced the largest flow of immigrants since the turn of the past century. According to the 1990 U.S. census, there were nearly 20 million foreign-born residents in the United States, more than at any other time in the nation's history. By the 2000 U.S. census, the number stood at over 28 million. Unlike the immigration at the turn of the century, these immigrants are also much more diverse. No longer primarily Europeans, most of this new wave of immigration originates from Asia, the Pacific, Latin America, and the Caribbean.

Although the image of boatloads of eastern Europeans sailing past the Statue of Liberty and arriving at Ellis Island in New York City symbolizes immigration of the turn of the past century, the immigration picture is now quite different. The images in the press and in the public imagination in the 1990s were of people streaming across the Rio Grande and trekking northward into California and Texas. The major ports of entry are now California and the Southwest, and the major destinations are the urban centers of California, Texas, and Florida. This immigration is profoundly altering the demographic composition of the United States—from what had been a predominantly white and English-speaking majority to a population of increasing diversity in race, culture, and language. Most contemporary immigrants are considered "people of color" in the American racial system. These changes are creating a national identity crisis owing both to the racial, language, and class composition of the immigrant wave and the overall tremendous diversity of languages and cultures. As a major public institution, with a historical mission related to the creation of a common civic culture, the schools are once again (as they have been in the past) a focal point of this crisis.

The experience of immigrants becoming incorporated into our culture involves learning their place in our racial system.[3] This racial system is part of a stratification in our nation and political economy that also includes class and language. This stratification is embedded in the institutional relationships and in ideology—and schools play a central role in those processes.[4] For these reasons, schools are crucial sites in which to study our nation as a receiving community shaping the incorporation of immigrants. Because stratification is a product of human interaction, schools are a lived world in which class, language, and racial relations are both reproduced and contested.[5] If the outcome of schooling is differential preparation for a labor market, how do immigrants learn and find their paths? What role does the color of their skin play in this differential preparation?

Immigrant youth face their lessons in what it means to become American within a schooling system that tends to sort by race and class. Like their European immigrant counterparts almost a century earlier, this generation of immigrant youth is greeted by a society that slots them as racially inferior. They face not only the barrier of crossing a national border but also the challenge of negotiating racial barriers to entry into the American mainstream. Complex negotiations are required of these students as they navigate through high school and into American life.

METHODOLOGY

The research reported here is part of an ethnographic study conducted at Madison High School, in Bayview, California, from 1992
to 1994 (the study is fully reported in Olsen 1997).[6] Over the
course of two years, I interviewed students and teachers, watched
them go about the business of schooling, attended meetings, and
read the local media and school site press. Spending an average
of fifteen hours each week at the school, primarily in individual
interviews or observing classrooms and student activity on the
campus, I also focused on a set of in-depth biographies of ten
immigrant students. I "hung out" around the students, shadowing
them throughout their day, sitting in classes, and spending time
with them and their friends at school. In speaking with and observing these students, I explored the following questions: How
did they understand "America"? What does being "American"
mean to them? How were the crossings, borderlands, and terrain
between languages, cultures, and national identities experienced,
shared, and contested? How did they experience and view their
encounters with one another across languages, cultures, and national identities?

I also interviewed six teachers at length, exploring their views
on the social life of the campus and the place immigrant students
took there. Other research activities included examining student
grouping, promotions, and discipline; reviewing curriculum content; and exploring the placement of students and enrollment in
specific gatekeeping courses.

With the assistance of a few teachers and several classrooms
of students, I designed special projects to engage students and
teachers in examining their school and reflecting on matters of
language, race, Americanization, culture, and the demographic
changes in their community. Students in three social studies
classes worked on a three-week unit constructing social maps of
the school. The material from their maps informed my sense of
social and cultural space and were also used to foster discussion
among students about these issues. I also asked teachers and
other students, during interviews, to "map" the social world of the
school. It is these maps that I focus on here.

MADISON HIGH SCHOOL AND ITS COMMUNITY

Madison High School is located in an urban area of northern California. As such, it is affected by a massive shift in California's population. In the past twenty years, the public school enrollment has changed from 75 percent white to 60 percent nonwhite. Today, more than a third of the students have limited English-language ability and come from homes in which English is not the primary spoken language. More than one-fifth of the total enrollment in California were born in another country. In some school districts as many as 85 percent of the students either have limited proficiency in or speak no English.

Madison High School, which enrolls about seventeen hundred students, is a typical American comprehensive high school. Its basic structure, textbooks, classroom organization, and social activities are similar to those one might find in most comprehensive high schools in this country. Yet Madison is undeniably representative of urban California schools in the 1990s, undergoing tremendous change in student population because of the pressures of a powerful new wave of immigration.

The school has changed markedly in the past decade from a primarily white working-class student population to an enrollment that has no single majority ethnic or racial group and speaks sixteen different home languages. Close to one-half of the students come from homes in which English is not the dominant language. Almost one-fourth of the students in the school are designated as "limited English proficient" (LEP). In the past seven years, the number of LEP students in Madison High School has doubled, to more than four hundred. The school does not determine immigrant status as distinct from English proficiency; the "LEP" students range from newly arrived adolescents to teens born in the United States but still not fluent in English. Approximately half of these LEP students are in the sequence of English-as-a-second-language (ESL) classes.

Yet the faculty of the school mirrors an older Bayview. Most are white-skinned, monolingual English speakers, and many were raised in Bayview. Amid rapid changes, it is not only teenagers who are being socialized to a new world; the adults are also encountering forces that are fundamentally changing their community. Teachers are divided, as a group, over whether and how to respond to the immigrants in their midst. Some actively seek professional development and new ways to teach the new population. Others realize something is not working well but have neither the time, the energy, nor the resolve to figure out what to do differently. The community is experiencing considerable resistance to changes that would address the language barriers facing immigrant students and to programs that might deliver on the promise of educational equity. There are rumblings of resentment and anger that any resources in this financially strapped school district should go to "foreigners."

Dialogue among these factions is problematic, at Madison as at many other schools. To admit to not knowing what to do as a teacher is difficult. To name inequality is believed impolite, at best, and divisive in most contexts. To call attention to the differences in student needs, or the differences in opportunities accorded to students of different racial and language groups, is potentially explosive. Those who might be effective advocates for new and more inclusive programs and practices are often silenced or neutralized.

Largely as a result of these struggles and the resistance to change, Madison provides insufficient English-language development and incomplete access to the academic core curriculum. Madison, like most high schools in California, does have an ESL program, but the school needs far more sections than are currently offered.[7] In addition, the school is short on bilingual teachers who help the LEP population in their academic course work while they are learning English more fully.

Madison High offers a few "sheltered" classes taught in English but designed for LEP students; LEP students also take selected electives taught in English, such as physical education or music. Instruction in any language other than English is resisted. When "sheltered" content classes are not available, the school often places LEP students in regular mainstream classes with no special support. In addition, many LEP students receive a shortened schedule of classes—for example, math but no science. They spend the rest of the school day in study halls or in additional classes taught in English where, as the saying goes, they "sink or swim."

The story of Madison High is the story of three seemingly different worlds inhabited by the immigrant newcomers (identified by other students as "the ESL kids"), the "other" students at Madison High (identified by the immigrant students as "Americans"), and the faculty and administration of the school.[8] I discovered these social categories as students and adults became involved in "mapping" the world of the school.[9] Newcomers, "Americans," and teachers inhabit what seem to be three very different worlds, but their maps contest one another's experiences at Madison High. Contradictions between their perspectives and experiences creates a tension that might unseat each group's way of seeing the world. But at Madison, they do not. Only the immigrant newcomers come to see and adopt a new map. The discourse among these versions of "reality" provides a powerful illustration of the silencing and neutralization of what could potentially be a multicultural alternative to a narrow monocultural model of what it means to be American. In the end, the three seemingly contradictory maps work together.

THE MAPPING PROJECT

History teacher Lisa Stern had just finished teaching her classes a unit on prejudice, discrimination, World War II, and the Holocaust. She followed this with a new unit that she and I had designed together to examine how students group themselves in their own school. Assigned to four different cooperative groups, the classes were given the following assignment.

> In this task, you will think about how Madison High students arrange themselves socially. Throughout the school day, students find themselves in many social groups. It is your job to notice what these groups are, describe them, and try to understand why people choose to be part of the groups they are in. Begin by brainstorming the "types" of students there are at Madison. You will then work together to create a large map of the school campus and draw the different groups onto the map to show the class where everyone is. You will also be explaining the map to the rest of the class when you have completed the project. You will each have a paper due describing the different groups and analyzing why the school divides itself the way it does.

Stern teaches social studies both to "sheltered" classes, created specifically for immigrant newcomers, and to regular classes.[10] Although recent immigrants at Madison are separated from U.S.-born schoolmates through the daily program of "sheltered" classes and ESL classes, through the student work on the walls of Stern's classroom they confront each other's presence.

On the day the assignment was due, students came to class with their maps of the high school. The regular sixth-period history students rushed into the classroom and immediately began assembling their maps on the wall. One student looked over and noticed the maps that had been created by the immigrant children in the sheltered class. She whistled and then said loudly, "Jeez, you'd think we were going to a whole different school!" Her comment was a profound foreshadowing of the discussions to come.

CAN I BE AMERICAN AND STILL BE ME?
THE MADISON HIGH OF NEWCOMERS

Lisa Stern's mapping project engaged newcomer students in drawing the "America" they observed; their maps became a backdrop for talking about what they believe it means to be "American." These newcomers have been in the United States anywhere from one day to three years. Initially, they perceive Madison High as inhabited by people of different national and language identities: Americans, Chinese, Vietnamese, and Mexican, Spanish speakers and English speakers, and so on. By adopting a new language they believe they will be bestowed with a new nationality. During this journey to a new nationality, however, they discover that as immigrants from third-world nations, they also need to undergo a baptism into the United States racial scheme, a scheme that often places them at the bottom. As they come to understand their new land, the labels they use to speak of their world—national identity, language, religion—become intertwined with skin color. Skin color, religion, and language seem to be defining characteristics of "being American."

Where groups of students hang out—their proximity to the center or the margins of the campus—seems symbolic of each group's relationship to school life itself. On their maps, most of the immigrant groups draw themselves in clusters on the edges of the campus, close to the Newcomer School across the street, or inside or close to the classrooms in which the sheltered classes are taught.[11] Partly because newcomer students spend half of the school day at the Newcomer School, their view of the other students and school life is truly a view from the margins of the school.

The detailed maps drawn by the newcomers include many categories for immigrant students. In their descriptions, we learn that "Indian girls" eat lunch by a tree on the edge of campus; "Mexican boys that haven't been here too long" are identified by proximity to a fence. Girls and boys are clustered differently: the descriptions often have fine gender distinctions, such as "the Chinese girls' group" or "the Hong Kong group of boys."[12] Repeatedly during discussions of their maps, newcomers spoke of how students cluster by same religion, same language, same culture, and same nationality. In contrast with the detailed descriptions their maps provide about the various clusters of newcomers, immigrant students offered only three social categories for the rest of the campus: Americans, Mexicans, and blacks. "American" was synonymous with "white."

Despite the many categories of immigrant students they discern, newcomers showed themselves, on all the maps, at the edges of the campus. Standing literally on the margins of the Madison High School world, newcomers learn and construct what it means to be American. The persistent question is whether or not the path to being American is truly open to them.

Obstacles on the Path to Becoming American

The children of immigrants have historically always felt the sting of intolerance from their peers about their accents, clothes, food, and cultural differences. It is no different at Madison High. The clearest warning signs to the newcomers that they have made a mistake or are not accepted is hearing the laughter of their "American" peers. Laughter is watched carefully. Is it a joke? Is it just fun? Is it meanness? They sense a nebulous line between the laughter of "having fun" and that of making fun of someone else. Making fun or teasing other students is, of course, a part of life for many teenagers, but the laughter newcomers face is often targeted specifically at their "immigrant-ness"—differences of language, dress, and culture. Carolina, an immigrant who had arrived from Mexico three years earlier, looked back on the experience of having been laughed at and at her relief when it finally stopped.

> Why do native-born laugh at the immigrant students? Mostly I find that immigrant students feel badly about things that the native-born students laugh at. Like the way the immigrant dress, the way they play sports, their language, which are concerned to me. I feel sorry for them because I used to be like them. Right now I am not immigrant. I'm happier. I do look different from what I used to. I learned the American ways and quicker than many other immigrant students. But in one way I don't act American. I don't think it's a good idea to go along with the native born by making fun of other people. And I have seen that situation many, many times. In a larger way, if the native-born people don't like the immigrants, the native born don't give them a job or let them go to school, and how are they going to live? Instead of discriminate of the immigrants, the native should help them out so we all together could heal the world. I think the teachers should be very important because in class they could talk about racism to teach their students not to discriminate, prejudice, or segregate with other races.

The message immigrant students receive from the "Americans" is clearly "stay out of our way if you're going to be different, stay separate in your corner. If you're going to be around us, you better be like us." This message was a deep source of stress and confusion for many of the newcomers in our study, who expressed how sad, nervous, afraid, alone, or confused they felt in adjusting to Madison. Much of their writing about their adjustment centered on racism, discrimination, and the pain of discovering that often people from "your own country" also discriminate against new immigrants. The longer immigrants are in the United States, the more they assimilate to the learned behavior of Americans, which seems to involve excluding and ignoring the newcomers. Such distancing seems particularly important to second-generation immigrants. To become more American means becoming less "other" and going to great efforts to differentiate themselves from the newcomers.

The greatest dilemma immigrant students confront is whether all paths are open to them and how their skin color and language confound the problem of becoming an American. Over and over again, in comments and conversations, newcomers tried to weigh which direction they could and should head when facing the problem of being American. As one Vietnamese boy said,

> People ask me, why can't you be both Vietnamese and American? It just doesn't work because you run into too many contradictions. After a while you realize you can't be both because you start crossing yourself and contradicting yourself and then its like math, when two things contradict each other they cancel each other out and then you are nothing. You are stuck as nothing if you try to be both. So I chose to be Vietnamese. I'm not sure I really could have been American anyway.

This sentiment was echoed by an Iranian girl: "You have to stay on one side or the other. If you try to be in the middle, you are stoned from all sides. You get hurt too easily. There are stones from all sides."

The sense of being caught in the middle, and of the vulnerability of being in the middle, is pervasive. It is made more complex because the "sides" are sometimes defined in terms of nationality, other times in terms of culture, still other times in terms of religion, race, or language. Beset by many pressures to "choose sides"—and with few other immigrant students able to maintain an identity in the "middle"—few newcomers find "the middle" a viable option. Consider the following illustrative quotes: "I mean I'll never be an American. I've got some white friends, but I have a skin barrier with them. And I can't even speak to a lot of my Chinese. . . . Like at my church . . . they all sit around and speak Chinese and I'm just sitting there and can't understand. So I'm not really Chinese, and I'll never be white." "We're from Mexico, and I'm seeing an American guy, and it's the hardest thing not only because he's white but my parents feel I'll lose my racial customs."

As newcomers forge their own paths toward becoming American, they may grow annoyed at those who would hold them back and uncomfortable with being judged when they move in directions that distance them from other newcomers. What might serve at one point as a place of acceptance becomes at another moment a source of torment:

> My cousin embarrasses me so much. She just won't admit that she is here
> in America now. I can't stand the way she keeps talking to me in Manda-
> rin. Sometimes at school she comes up to me and I want to pretend I don't
> even know her because she is just so . . . I don't know . . . like she won't
> talk English. I just try to avoid her. And she tries to tell me that I'm forget-
> ting who I am! All we do is fight now. She is so Chinese I can't stand it.

For these immigrants, to belong seems to involve changing who
they are. They perceive their "American" peers as different and are
often pained by the realization of how much they have to give up
to be accepted by "Americans." "The first for me was just wanting
to speak English, speak English. And I didn't want to speak Arabic
anymore. I didn't want to be laughed [at]. Then the dress. I want
to look so cool, so now I wear short tops. But I don't recognize
me anymore. How American can I get? Do I have to totally change
myself? Sometimes I think, where did I go? Can I ever find me
again?" One thing is quite clear to them, however: it is *they,* not
the "Americans," who have to change. Newcomers just don't always see the full extent of what those changes entail.

English as the Gateway to Becoming American

The struggle to learn English takes center stage in immigrant students' experience as a fundamental requirement for acceptance
and participation in an English-taught curriculum and the "American" social world. Teachers, immigrant students, and native-born
students alike agree on this. Almost the entire school collaborates
in a pattern of pushing newcomers into becoming part of a monolingual English-speaking world. I once asked Mandy, an immigrant from Taiwan, if there were ways in which she felt American.
She answered emphatically, "Of course not! If you do not speak
the English right, you cannot be American." In the initial understanding of newcomers, becoming English speaking is the same as
becoming American.

Learning English here is not easy, however. Most of the English speakers they encounter are not very accepting of accented
and flawed English. Social exclusion of students whose English is
not fluent is prevalent. The affective environment is far from the
"safe" climate that linguist Stephen Krashen (1981) argues is necessary for language acquisition.[13] Every day, immigrant students

are laughed at for their faulty English and teased for their heavy accents. They struggle to find their way and suffer when they do not understand or do not feel free to ask for clarifications of English.

With all the focus on the need for immigrants to learn English, few appear to recognize that the school program mitigates against this goal. Placed in special classes designed to address their lack of English-language proficiency, immigrant students are separated from English-speaking peers. As a result, their opportunity to learn the language naturally and informally, and thereby to become part of the English-speaking world, is severely constrained.

> Sometimes we tried to talk to them to learn more English, some of them helped us, and some just laughed and made fun. Sometimes when an American talk to you and be friendly and be nice, you feel really happy. But most when you walk through a group of American students, you hear them say something or they pick on you or they throw something at you and they do it because they think you don't understand English and speak English. They think we don't understand because we can't understand the words. We understand. They tell us by how they act that they don't want us here. How can we learn English if no one speak it with us? No Americans speak with us. A friend would be best, but it is a puzzle. If you don't speak English you can't have American friend. So how do we learn English?

Immigrants also have almost no opportunities to develop skill or sophistication in their first languages because there is no programmatic support for that task at Madison. Thus many of the students I interviewed described moving from home to school as moving from the world of their native languages to the world of English. It is an abrupt border crossing.[14] "You wouldn't know me at home. I am Mexican there! I speak Spanish all the time. At school I'm American, almost. It mostly comes natural, but there is always a moment each day when I feel confused. Where am I? And my tongue doesn't know which sounds to make, which words to use. Two worlds I live in."

Laughed at for using their mother tongues, and with no support at school for continued development of their home languages, immigrant students not only fail to develop literacy in their native language but even begin to lose it. With that loss, they also weaken ties to their families and homeland cultures.[15] The transnational potential for maintaining relationships and connection with the home nation, possible now in ways it never was for previous generations of immigrants, is cut off by the mere fact of the pressure to abandon home languages as a price of acceptance as American. Nadira, who left Afghanistan at the age of thirteen, found that she was already forgetting her Farsi just three years later. "I used to read when somebody sent a letter. I used to read it but now I can't. I've forgotten! Sometimes my Dad is sad, and he says to me: You have forgotten your own language!"

Concepcion, an immigrant from Mexico just two years earlier, noted, "I sometimes don't have Spanish words anymore for the feelings I have here. And I don't yet have English words for them either. Or I can't find the English words that explain what I know and feel in my Mexican life. The words don't work for me. I have become quiet because I don't have words. I don't even try to use my Spanish at school. I only wait until I know my English."

In addition to receiving insufficient formal training in the English language, immigrant students at Madison are placed in many academic classes that do not address their needs for comprehensible instruction. They regularly express frustration about not being fluent enough in English to participate and comprehend what is happening in these classes. Their native tongue would be the language of choice, particularly as the vehicle of learning difficult academic context, but social constraints—the proximity of English-speaking students and the fear of being overheard and laughed at—keeps them from using it more often. The result is that Madison is a world in which those who are not proficient in English are precluded from full access to the content of their academic courses.

In the classrooms of a few sympathetic teachers at Madison and in the Newcomer School, students appear to appreciate the freedom to use whichever language makes things most comprehensible and also the freedom from harassment. One ESL teacher, Linda O'Malley, groups her students by their first language when they work in small groups. As she explains,

> Misunderstandings are so common because even though they know the English words they want to use, when those same words are spoken by someone else with a heavy accent, they can't hear it. If I really want them to be able to discuss something, it works best when they can speak as fully as possible and understand as much as possible of what one another is saying. It makes it easier for them to share ideas, but also, it is the only place in school where they are allowed to use their [native] language. I

think just to hear their own language, and to feel it is allowed, makes for a different sense of relaxation and "being here" in the classroom.

Unfortunately, this accepting environment is rare at Madison. One day, as immigrant students were working in small groups, an "American" came in bearing a note for the teacher from the principal. On his way back out the door, he said very loudly, "Where am I? Doesn't anyone know how to speak English? Is this some kind of foreign country?!" The class became noticeably silent. When they resumed their conversations, they were subdued, and they spoke only in English.

The discomfort of being "outside," the frustration at not having the words to express themselves, and the shame of being laughed at for using their native tongues, all result in a determination to try to learn English as quickly as possible—to the exclusion of their mother tongues. The transition to being monolingual English speaking is, for most, an uncontested passage in becoming "American."

As they become English speaking, immigrants do participate more and more in the social world of Madison High, but the level of oral English fluency required for social participation is not sufficient for the English literacy required for academic participation. Thus, newcomers become English speakers but not necessarily full participants in the academic system. Is this sufficient for them to be accepted as Americans? With all of the overt focus on English ability as the dividing line between foreigners and Americans, between "them" and "us," it turns out that at Madison High a complex weave of other transitions and changes are expected for true "citizenship." As newcomers face these other transitions, they begin to question their original assumption that if they learn English and work hard, they will make it. They begin to think that to be American is to be English speaking, white skinned, and Christian. They see little tenable ground for having multiple identities or holding on to multiple cultures.

Pressures to Adopt Narrow, Panethnic Identities

As newcomers become aware that fluency in English is not the only requirement for acceptance, they experience pressure to locate themselves on the "racial map" of Madison High. This means figuring out the peculiar meanings of racial categories in the United States—and discovering that some racial categories, such as white or Asian, have a higher status, while others, specifically African American or Latino, have a much lower status, academically and socially. Immigrant students at Madison encounter a limited set of skin-color demarcations—black, white, brown, and yellow—despite the fact that there are also many mixed-race students, and the majority of the immigrants do not fit well into this racial schema. Theoretically, the presence of mixed-race and immigrant students could erode the racial categories of the system. Instead, however, immigrant students find themselves pressured to fit into one of these four categories.

Yet in the amount of concern expressed by newcomers about not understanding where they belong, and their discomfort in making themselves belong, they express a counterdiscourse with respect to the racial categories. They would, in fact, prefer an identity system that acknowledges more complexity, including their national backgrounds—a preference noted in Rubén Rumbaut's (1997) surveys of immigrant students, as well. Holding this counterdiscourse is highly unsettling, however, for being unable to define one's race is, in many ways, not to exist on the social map of the "American" students, on which there are few categories that are not racially explicit. To figure out where one belongs, where one is "supposed to be" or where one chooses to be, is tricky. Is someone a "real Latino" or a "white-washed Mexican"? A "wanna-be black" or a "real" black?

At first, most of the newcomers appeared to resist the process of racialization into broad categories. To them, Americanization into these categories, and the abandonment of hope that others will accept them in their full national, religious, and language identities, is like an annihilation of self. Some choose marginality as a means of resistance. They choose to remain off the social map, to remain "foreign" and not give in to racial categories.

Few of the students I interviewed had been able to maintain this stance for more than two years, however. Their peers, their teachers, and society's inability to see and understand the distinctions in identity that they themselves would make (for example, Guatemalan, as distinct from Mexican) pulled most of them into a pan-national, panethnic racial category of Latino or Asian.[16] New-comers themselves begin to understand the high price of not tak-ing their racial place: as the "American" students' map shows, im-migrants remain largely "invisible" until they find a place on the racial map. The requirement of racial identification is strong for all students—although Chinese students seem most resistant to this pressure and are also the students for whom the implications of their racial place are least restrictive in terms of academic and life path. Although my study of Madison High did not address the role of the community, Rumbaut's (1997) studies have noted how a strong coethnic community helps in maintaining a national iden-tity; in this case, we can only speculate that a strong Chinese com-munity might also play a part in the ability of Chinese students to maintain a national identity.

WE MAKE EACH OTHER RACIAL: THE MADISON HIGH OF THE "AMERICAN" STUDENTS

The world inhabited by the "American" student at Madison High is every bit as intensely involved with "finding one's place" as the immigrant world; however, the discussions are not about being American so much as they are about "race." The maps drawn by these students—who in fact represent a mixed racial group—for Lisa Stern's class were almost wholly racialized: almost every so-cial group was labeled either by a racial identifier or by the cate-gory "mixed race." The descriptions they created for the school overall were largely the standard American ethnic and racial cate-gories (white, black, Latin, Asian, Mexican), appended with great detail about the performative behaviors, activities, and common interests that mark these categories or distinguish subgroups.

> By the portables are the white skaters who hang out in the sun. They dress alike and don't care what others think. No one really pays attention to them. They listen to heavy metal and hang where no one else will bother them. The smokers hang out across the street. It's another kind of white student, bound together by their addiction. Mexicans stay far from the ad-ministration, close to the street, so they can see their friends who drive by and stop for a while. In the middle are black students, a big group who kid around a lot. They seem to know each other from junior high.

These descriptions are rich in aspects of youth culture that are deemed important: the kind of music people listen to, how friendly or unfriendly the group is thought to be, how they dress, how they are thought of by others in terms of being popular or cool—all with racial labels. The only exceptions were two groups related to school activities ("band kids" and "basketball players"). In describing their own "groups," students spoke immediately of their race, although white students often expressed some discomfort in doing so. They mentioned race not casually but rather as a defining aspect of each student group on campus. One student in Lisa Stern's class, Jeff, in a startling echo of Howard Winant's writings (1994) on emerging white consciousness,[17] said, "I never think of myself as white any place but at school. People at Madison think in terms of race all the time. But out in the world, I never have to think of myself as white—only here. And it's starting to affect me out of school, too."

The Quad is the one area of campus identified as the turf of mixed groups. Attached to these groups are terms like "accepting," "don't stand out," and "don't stand for anything." The Quad, a large and crowded area, is architecturally the heart of the campus. Yet the Quad, with its mixed groups of students, actually commanded very little attention as "American" students discussed their maps and described the social world of the school. They did not deny that mixing across races occurs or that there are some social arenas of school life that are "pretty accepting and friendly." What they felt was salient to talk about, however, in describing the dimensions of social life were the separations, the differences of race and ethnicity.

In the classroom discussions about the maps, students argued at length about whether the campus is primarily a mixed campus of friendship groups with a few groups who keep to themselves or, rather, a wholly racialized campus of separate groups, with a few who mix across races. There was enormous tension in the discussion, and clearly heavy investment in how students might chose to characterize their school. Is it divided into racial groups? Is it a mixed and integrated campus? Is it happily diverse? Is it tense and hostile? Is it all of these things? The consensus eventually was that the social life of the school centered around groups isolating themselves by race.

Social capital at Madison High is measured and conferred in terms of racial identity. Crossing the line socially and in the style one adopts (dress, behavior, language) is heavily monitored. Some students do cross lines to have friends of different racial groups; the campus is dotted with mixed-race friendship groups. Unless these friendships are rooted in formal activities such as band or sports teams, however, the friendships are commented on and tempered by a lively discourse among peers: "Sonja's forgetting who she is! That little Latin girl is hanging with the Chinese too much." "It's sad, Hahn used to be really good friends with us. But now she doesn't like to be Vietnamese anymore. Now she thinks she's Mexican." The formal activities appear to provide a rationale for "crossing the line"—while such friendships outside of that formal context seem in need of explanation or defense. Students talk fairly unanimously of the tension caused by the racial dimensions of their choices in friends and in how they dress and the racial appropriateness of those choices.

For African American students, there is little that is as hurtful or as threatening to their sense of identity as being labeled "whitewashed." The term denotes talking white, acting white, wishing you were white, getting good grades or "being in good" with the teachers. To many students, such behavior is an indication of disloyalty or "forgetting who you are." For those students of color who are culturally identified with another nonwhite group, the monitoring term is "wanna-be." This term is used often for both individuals and groups—for example, "those girls who smoke cigarettes and hang out near C Hall are a bunch of Latin wanna-bes." These words have power and evoke issues of loyalty, authenticity, resistance, and fear. Conversely, "finding your place" and "staying with your own group" are generally viewed by students as positive values. "It's racial, pure and simple. There are some kids who mix here, but mostly you stay with your own kind. It's important to know who you are and be true to who you are. Some kids are wanna-bes, looking somewhere else instead of standing by who they are. Me, I'm proud to be Latin."

The rules of interaction at Madison High are quite complicated. Nevertheless, by the time students are juniors and seniors, they have begun to master the art of being friendly with people of racial groups different from their own without appearing to be "wanna-bes" or to reject their own racial identity.

Although their maps focused clearly on race, most of the social maps drawn by the "American" classes simply did not mention the newcomer groups on campus. When the absence of the immigrant students on these maps was mentioned to the regular history class, and comparisons were made between the immigrants' maps and their own maps, the students acknowledged that immigrants should be on the map. "We just didn't think of them," the group said in defense of their maps, and they proceeded to make amendments, adding "ESLers hang out over by the edge of campus near the Newcomer School." The category they used for all newcomers was a single "ESL" label, echoing the truth that newcomers are seen primarily in terms of their lack of English-speaking ability. Absent were the national or language identities that seemed so central to the newcomers. One student remarked that "by E Hall is where ESL kids sit and talk. They don't connect to anyone else. It's their differences that bond them." Noted another, "They hold on to their language. They don't even try to speak English. They don't really have a place here yet." These "American" students may have initially overlooked immigrant students, but when the omission was pointed out to them, they immediately knew where on their maps to fit them. The immigrant students were not so much "invisible" to these students as they were lacking in social importance—"unplaced" until they could speak English. As one young man commented on student life in general at the school, "Ya gotta find your race and take your place"—an exact description of the requirement facing newcomers if they are to become part of the "American map" of the school. For newcomers, learning English is a precursor to learning their racial place.

ADULTS IN THE CROSSROADS:
THE MADISON HIGH SCHOOL OF THE TEACHERS

The school is more than just the context and setting of this drama—it is directly involved in the process as an institution. The nature and shape of the schooling experiences of newcomer and "American" students alike is enacted by adults who are themselves buffeted by massive changes in their community and culture and who play their own role in the places students take, or are encouraged to take, at the school.

As students struggle to find creative solutions in response to the enormous pressures of a society slotting them into cultural, racial, and class roles, teachers grapple with how to teach students with whom they increasingly share neither a community nor national background, culture, or language. As noted earlier, many teachers resist making changes to accommodate the newcomers, though a few newer hires advocate responding to their immigrant students' needs.

Resistance to Change and Restricted Access for Immigrant Students

Despite mandates from above, the majority of the school faculty and administration at Madison fights against making programmatic accommodations to the needs of immigrant students. When a visiting accreditation committee recommended that the school create an ESL department, the veteran faculty dismissed the idea as unnecessarily divisive, feeling it would strip resources from "real" departments. Despite regular offers of training to prepare teachers to work with immigrant students, almost none of the teachers at Madison took the opportunity.

Yet a small group of young faculty members, hired more recently to teach the bilingual and sheltered content courses required by law, have attempted to enact a movement for immigrant inclusion, bilingual education, and educational opportunity for immigrant students. These young teachers seek to "shelter" their newcomer students and advocate for more responsiveness to their needs. They encourage administrators and department chairs to more appropriately place the immigrant students who, in their estimation, can do more advanced work. They take it upon themselves to provide after-school tutoring and find community resources to translate the student handbook into languages their students can understand. Their efforts have resulted in some innovations, but these are contained at the margins of school life. The result is a program that is separate, marginalized, and unable to adequately address barriers to access.

As a result of the resistance, half of the LEP students in the school are not in any classes designed to address their language needs. Those that are appear to be in a system that is separate and still far from offering equal access to the curriculum their English-fluent peers receive. In an attempt to "protect" them from failure in the mainstream—and, not coincidentally, to protect mainstream content-area teachers who do not want them in their classes—the administration keeps limited-English-proficient students out of the mainstream and places them instead in "sheltered" content classes. However, not all teachers assigned to teach sheltered classes at Madison have the training and materials to support such special instructional strategies. Sheltered classes have come at a high price to students who thrive on being "sheltered" from sometimes hostile American peers but pay for the separation in academic and social ways. It is separation, in most cases, without educational benefit.

Such decisions about courses, the school's program, teacher preparation and assignment, resources, materials, and access to information are enmeshed in a daily struggle over how teachers and administrators view their roles in serving immigrant students, addressing matters of culture and language, and ensuring equal access. These have been a source of overt and underlying ideological and political struggles in Bayview as a community. It is a struggle between those who view the answer to diversity as conformity to a single cultural model and a single language and those who view the survival of a multicultural community as dependent on the embrace of differences and rectification of the inequities between groups. These matters are hotly contested by the adults at Madison High.

Students attend classes and interact with peers and teachers, but they have little awareness of the forces that shape where they are placed in the school system. Whether immigrant and "American" students are separated and whether their classes are taught by credentialed teachers deeply affect the kind of access they are given to an education. Who gets needed information about college preparation or about changing a schedule has an effect on which students are prepared for what futures.

An incident occurred in the first few days of my research that echoed throughout the two years I spent at Madison High. At an initial lunch meeting with the principal, I explained why I had chosen Madison. I mentioned the swift and astounding growth of the LEP student population at the school, which at the time represented 24 percent of their students—one in four. The principal seemed surprised. "You must be wrong. The numbers are off. We have a lot of diversity, but it's nowhere near that high. It's more like maybe 12 or 15 percent." I was embarrassed that I had my numbers wrong, but the conversation continued amicably. Later that day, I checked my files and confirmed the figure. I called Maria Rodriguez, the director of the Newcomer School in Bayview and a friend, and told her of the confusion. She exploded: "George should know that. I'm constantly passing along statistics to him, talking to him about the growth of LEP students. It just doesn't register. He refuses to hear it." I came to look back on that first lunch as an early warning of the force with which demographic change is contested and the degree to which the invisibility of immigrant students is perpetuated.

The dimensions of Madison High's diversity, which many faculty remark on proudly, remain unstated and unexplored. The administrators and teachers at Madison consistently view diversity as a mere fact of life, not something to be talked about or addressed directly. Most simply believe that the new population of students does not and should not require them to make any changes in teaching approaches or programs. Despite a state-mandated district plan written to remedy the critical shortage of teachers trained to teach LEP students with limited proficiency in English, few of the new hires and almost none of the veteran teachers have the training to teach those classes.

"Color-Blindness" and Academic Sorting

Adults at Madison view "color-blindness" as a moral position linked to ending prejudice and racism. "I don't see color. All my students are the same to me. I just don't even notice race," explained one teacher. Another told me that "we're really an enlightened school here. We teach here because we like the diversity of our kids. And you know, we don't even notice what race kids are, really. I couldn't tell you how many of this or that I have in my class."

Underlying this color-blindness is a sense of a delicate balance in relations that would be disturbed if differences were acknowledged. Attention to differences, "stirring up trouble" about lack of access, is viewed as highly divisive and explosive. Yet it is attention to the differences in needs, opportunities, and outcomes that is required if the school is to address the basic access issues facing LEP students.

It is not that teachers do not see a divided campus. The salient divisions they speak about in making their own maps of the school are simply not related to race or culture or language. They do not "see" these issues—or, at least, they elect not to speak of them. It is academic distinctions that take prominence in the social maps drawn by teachers, which describe a world that divides students by academic achievement level. There are the "college prep" students, the "regular" students," and the "skills kids."

> I think the fundamental division in our school, maybe even all high schools, is between the academic kids—you know, who are going to college—the skills kids, and the ones who are kind of in the middle. We probably have three different schools going. Maybe you might have to throw in the ESL kids, too. I'm not sure. . . . They don't really fit with the other categories. I'm not sure where they go. Sooner or later, eventually, they become part of the other three.

Teachers explain these distinctions in terms of individual student abilities and motivation. They tend to view the school as offering options to students, who then become responsible for their own choices and behaviors. Anyone willing to work hard, the story goes, could end up in college preparatory classes. The students who are in the skills classes are the ones who do not care about school, who do not try. The students in the top classes, the college prep students, are spoken of as "smart" and "motivated."

I came to understand that this paradigm of a diverse and mixed school in a color-blind system, divided only by virtue of student choice and differential motivation into a hierarchy of academic achievement, holds tremendous power and obscures an entire realm of student experience. Yet stark reality defies it. The very categories teachers use in creating the map of the student world have an obscured racial reality. "Skills" and "college bound" are not race neutral.

The students in the school's advanced placement and college preparatory classes are predominantly Chinese and white, with one or two others. The Chinese seem to find their way there through a combination of hard work on their part, which results in good grades on tests, and stereotyped assumptions on the part of teachers, who reward the quiet, respectful behavior of this immigrant group. Their verbal skills and command of English remain inadequate for participation in class, however. The remedial "skills" classes are almost exclusively black, Mexican or Latino, and Fijian, with a few others thrown in. Thus, the racialization of immigrants at Madison High is not a complete assignment of all immigrant groups to the lower tracks but rather a segmented and differential sorting based on a set of stereotypes and expectations (positive for some groups, negative for others) and peer relations.

It takes deep denial to fail to see the overlap of race and the sorting mechanisms of the school. A look at who graduates, who drops out, and who graduates prepared to go on to a four-year college illustrates an intense racial project at the school.[18] The skin color and language background of a student is closely correlated with the chances of being among those who do cross the stage. At Madison, Latinos and African American students have the slimmest chances of making it through high school.

A Small Group of Teachers Advocate for Immigrant Students

Some faculty members at Madison High draw the map differently; they draw different conclusions and offer a different perspective. These are the young, new hires assigned to teach the courses in English as a second language and the sheltered academic courses for immigrant newcomers. Unfortunately, their perspective, when voiced, appears to be experienced by the others as divisive and naive and by some as just dead wrong.

The growth in the student population in Bayview, precipitated by the most recent baby boom and by immigration, has meant a growth in the teacher force, as well. For about a four-year period, Madison experienced an increase in new hires of mostly young teachers. Joining a cohesive faculty of veteran teachers, the newly hired quickly became a distinct social group among the faculty.

On the first day I spent at Madison High, the principal gave me a list of faculty members who might help me in contacting people to interview. With colored markers he coded the entire list. One color was for teachers who had been at the school for more than five years, another was for new teachers. I did not understand at the time why this was a salient division—although the logic soon became clear.

It is this small group of new teachers who advocate for addressing issues of language and culture. It is not that the school and district do not boast of programs for newcomers. Madison has a formal educational program, the deliberate intervention implemented to "serve" the needs of immigrant and LEP students and meet the letter of the law.[19] The interpretation and implementation of legal mandates, however, is a product of local struggle.

At Madison, there is no leadership voice representing the needs of immigrant and LEP students. The availability of teachers trained to offer either primary-language instruction or sheltered academic-content instruction, in English, to LEP students and the availability of sections and courses for LEP students is a product of the willingness of individual teachers to provide the courses. The reluctance of Madison's teachers to participate in special training programs greatly limits the LEP program. In the context of labor problems in the district, teachers already feel exploited and angry. The suggestion that they have to do something else, something more, to be adequate teachers is hardly welcomed. Many bristle at the suggestion that "we" have put out additional effort for "those" students. If individual teachers do not respond to the offerings of training, there is no mechanism, and no pressure applied, to compel or entice them to do so. Even among those few who have the training, many are unwilling to teach the courses.

Tension exists between the ESL and sheltered-class teachers and the mainstream teachers. Some mainstream content-area faculty feel that the ESL teachers "coddle" the LEP students and thereby hold them back. The ESL and sheltered-class teachers feel that the majority of other faculty are refusing to deal with the academic needs of the LEP students. Within each department, teacher assignment to LEP classes is a highly political issue. Seniority and the ability to negotiate within the faculty hierarchy determines who can avoid being assigned "undesirable" courses, such as teaching LEP students. The immigrants are new to Bayview, outsiders. Among faculty who have been in the school for a while, the LEP students are viewed as the appropriate responsibility for the new "outsider" teachers, the new hires.

The world of the faculty reproduces the programmatic structure that leaves immigrants at the margins of the school society. The splits that have been cocreated between younger and older faculty, and between the ESL and sheltered-content teachers and the mainstream teachers, have muted any voices of advocacy that might speak about changing the school structure to embrace the immigrant newcomers. The young teachers do, however, have a structure of advocacy behind them. Maria Rodriguez, the director of the district's Newcomer School, is always willing to back them up with bilingual educational theory to try to convince the school to buy materials or offer a new course needed for LEP students. Her role in the district as bilingual coordinator also lends her some clout.

When that fails, there is the law. Title VI of the Civil Rights Act, based upon the equal protection clause of the Fourteenth Amendment to the Constitution, bars public schools from denying access to school on the basis of race, national origin, or alienage. The Supreme Court's decision in *Lau v. Nichols* requires schools to take affirmative steps to overcome the language barrier for students with limited proficiency in English.

Maria or the young teachers sometimes have to mention the law to get a response from the administration at the school. For example, when Linda O'Malley discovered that she had two very intelligent students with limited English proficiency in her ESL skills class, she tried to promote them to more accelerated classes. The department chair refused on the basis of the "policy" that LEP students must first finish the skills class before moving to the regular level, and only then to accelerated classes. O'Malley decided to enlist the help of Maria Rodriguez, who called the principal. As O'Malley tells the story,

> Maria had to threaten to take away all of his Title VII funding for LEP students if he didn't do this. She mentioned, for the billionth time, the law about access. And then she mentioned money. That's what it came down

to. She said, "Listen, George, I pay for these students at your school with our EIA–LEP [Economic Impact Aid–Limited English Proficiency] funds and Title VII funds, and if you don't serve them, the money is gone." Two days later, my department chair found me and said, "I've reconsidered and I think you're right. You can go ahead and put both kids into your tenth-grade accelerated class." I was mad. It wasn't right for Eduardo as a twelfth-grader to be put in a tenth-grade class, but it was at least better than staying in a tenth-grade skills class.

The language these teachers use to describe the constant negotiation over meeting students needs is the language of battles and wars—and the law is one powerful weapon they wield.

On some large issues, invoking the law and calling upon Rodriguez has worked. However, such outside support is not sufficient for the daily struggles of these teachers. Their work, as they perceive it, is not just to push the system to be responsive but to be the agents of responsiveness in a system that resists. For example, when the school fails to provide a counselor who addresses the specific needs of immigrant students, the young teachers step in and spend long hours before, during, and after school advising their immigrant students.

On a policy level, whether trying to affect the course offerings or the practice of other faculty, the young faculty lose most battles. Increasingly, they have given up on those levels and concentrate instead on one-to-one work with students. This task requires advocacy, as well, and has propelled them into areas of confusion about what it means to provide guidance at the intersection of cultures and how to push a school that does not want even to acknowledge that the students are there, much less try to respond. Every week, attempts to advocate for their immigrant students bring these teachers into regular confrontations with the understandings, standard practices, and unwritten codes of Madison High.

The formal school program constructed for immigrant students thus institutionalizes a fragmentation of realms and provides only a weak structure of support for students negotiating the process of becoming "American." The comprehensive high schools proceed with the task of creating monolingual English-speaking (but only partially English-literate) students, creating an immigrant class without real access to the full curriculum, while maintaining silence on the racial sorting that their practices perpetuate.

WHAT MADISON HIGH TEACHES US ABOUT THE CONTEMPORARY AMERICANIZATION PROCESS

Together, these three maps create a composite picture of what it means to become American in a contemporary high school. As the maps demonstrate, this composite picture has three salient features: the exclusion and marginalization of immigrant students, the racialization immigrant students confront in finding or forging a social identity, and consignment to limited educational opportunities through academic sorting and segmentation.

Excluding and Marginalizing Immigrant Students

Immigrant students are separated and marginalized on campus, thus giving them little access to their native-born peers, adequate English development, and comprehensible content-area classes. Because of an overall lack of capacity and will to serve them, they are either separated into weakly supported classes where they do not have access to English-speaking peers or are placed in mainstream classes with teachers who are ill prepared to address their needs and with a level of English usage that they cannot fully comprehend. In itself, this separation leads to insufficient development of English language skills and a limited academic curriculum and thereby denies them equal access to an education, as well as keeping many from achieving full literacy in English.

Taking One's Place in the Racial Hierarchy

Immigrant students at Madison, like other students on campus, are pressured to "find their place," but to do so they must first learn English. At first, they assume that learning English is synonymous with becoming American. As they participate more in the social world of the school, however, they discover that they also have to find their place racially. In the process, many feel forced to choose between a "foreign" and an "American" identity. They cease using their mother tongue in public and feel they must trade in their national identities for a racial identity as a condition of acceptance. The middle ground of multicultural identity is intensely uncomfortable, for there is little support for embracing both identities. "Finding a place" usually involves adopting a pan-ethnic racial identity and, for many students, loss or rejection of their home language and culture. Thus becoming American involves taking part in a largely hidden racialization project enacted by the students and supported by the school.

Academic Sorting, Race, and Segmentation

Teachers and other educators participate unconsciously in this racialization project by sorting students academically, failing to take into account the way these academic groupings map onto racial groupings and mirror differential expectations of various racial or ethnic groups. This academic sorting can limit the academic path of some immigrants, especially those with brown or dark skin, while encouraging other immigrants, lighter-skinned and Asian immigrants, to achieve academically. The segmented paths to becoming American become apparent as Chinese students end up in the college preparatory tracks of the school and Mexican and Fijian immigrants end up in the remedial tracks.

Until they learn English and take their places on the racial map of the school, immigrants are largely invisible to other students, and even to teachers; they are grouped together as "ESLers," a categorization that has little status and ignores the distinctions of nation, language, and religion that they make among themselves. Being "invisible" does not mean that immigrant students do not have a place in the social hierarchy, however. In fact, such lack of visibility places them in a no-man's-land of educational opportunity, which is decidedly lacking in power and status. It is immigrants, after all, who must learn to adjust their social maps, to change and adapt to the racialized reality of their school, not their "American" peers or teachers.

Immigrants also pay a high price for acceptance, for the changes they feel they must make involve loss or rejection of their language and culture and embroil them in deep, painful identity crises. Even before they realize the changes they must make, while they are somewhat protected in the less visible status of "ESLers" and find companionship with one another in their separated experience of the school, they lose access to a high-quality education and to sufficient opportunities to learn English. The separation that protects them in some ways also harms many educationally, while at the same time protecting mainstream "American" students and teachers from having to change their monolingual, monocultural mode of being. In large part because of this "invisibility," which maintains the status quo, the opportunity is lost to create a more multicultural alternative to what it means to be American.

One of the most damaging aspects of this racializing and sorting system is that it is largely hidden and denied. Immigrants' belief in individual effort often clouds their ability to see that becoming American involves being racialized. For their part, most teachers "see" how students divide academically, but they view this as a product of choice and effort (and perhaps ability), not as a result of how they and their school unconsciously sort students into different paths by skin color, class, and language. The "American" students see a world divided by race and barely acknowledge the newcomers—yet this map is the closest to acknowledging the racializing process at the school and naming the racial sorting that contributes to different academic outcomes. The school is not a neutral zone in racialization; it plays a role by supporting such "hidden" sorting and by lacking the will or capacity to respond fully to immigrant students' needs. There is also a strong institutional reality to immigrant students' segregation and the implications it has for their ability to succeed academically.

Madison High School is actually a closely knit social system in which conforming to American racial categories and to an American national and English-language identity is necessary to be recognized as part of the fabric of the school world. As noted earlier, despite the initial resistance of some students most eventually adopt racialized, panethnic identities. This system furthermore attempts to enlist students and teachers together in denying the existence of exclusion, racism, and the pain of the loss of native culture and language. It is a silence fed by the fear that to notice and acknowledge the tracking, separation, and losses would be to open doors to trouble. The school and community, in one moment, speak in celebration of cultural diversity, are involved in an intense racial and Americanization process, and deny issues of racial separation, cultural power, and politics.

These aspects of the Americanization process—being separated and invisible until "finding one's race" and the academic position associated with it, losing one's native language and culture, feeling forced to choose between two competing identities—are hardly unique to Madison High School. They reflect the politics of the larger community, which is as impacted by immigration as the school and as conflicted about how to incorporate the newcomers. Madison High, despite its unique personalities and particular demographic mix, also illustrates the daily negotiations that go on within high schools across the nation as they enact a contemporary version of Americanization.

To some degree these patterns mirror the experiences of immigrants in previous generations in the United States—dealing with the ridicule and resultant shame about one's "foreign ways," struggling to learn a new language and culturally acceptable behavior, facing discrimination and exclusion as newcomers. However, the historical context of each era also shapes the ways in which these patterns play out. Our contemporary era is indelibly shaped by the racial conflicts and struggles in the United States and processes of racialization carried out in schools on newcomers and U.S.-born alike. The most recent newcomers have learned that to earn acceptance they must take their place racially and demonstrate their new affiliation as Americans by renouncing their home language.

This contemporary Americanization process provides slots of only partial acceptance for newcomers. As they adopt English as their sole language, they are not given sufficient tools or access to develop the levels of English required for full participation and inclusion. Giving up their native language, many pay a high price in loss of strong family connection and access to their history. Furthermore, abandoning their national identities to become "American" is a one-way journey with a questionable destination, for the places newcomers must take in the racial hierarchy are largely at the bottom. For those students whose race and ethnicity stands them in good stead in the racial hierarchy—Chinese students, in particular—their inevitable participation in the racialized Americanization process may be less detrimental, as they find themselves on a path that allows them to assimilate upward into society. For those from other continents, however, whose skin color is associated with a much lower position, this process often leads to second-class citizenship as they assimilate downward in American society. In either case, the price immigrants pay as they negotiate their identities and relations to their home cultures and languages is often a painful one. As a society, we also pay a high price in discarding the opportunity to develop a more multi-cultural, multilingual, and inclusive definition of what it means to be American.

NOTES

1. Sorting students into different "tracks" to provide varying levels of instruction is one of the most widespread practices in U.S. public schools. It often results in tracking students by race, ethnicity, and class into very different educational and economic futures as some groups are given access to an advanced, higher-order-thinking cur-riculum (in training for college) while others are consigned to a lower-quality curriculum focused on drill and memorization (in training for low-paying service jobs). The rationale for such group-ing is that it is based on ability or achievement. Research has shown that teachers' expectations change based on these groupings, lead-ing to a watering down of the curriculum in the lower tracks. Such labeling begins in the first few years of school and is solidly in place by the time students reach high school (Green and Giffore 1978; Moore and Davenport 1988; Oakes 1985, 1986). Minority, limited-English-proficient, or low-income students are consistently and dra-matically overrepresented in low academic tracks throughout the levels of schooling. White and more affluent students are conversely overrepresented in advanced tracks (Oakes 1985; Slavin 1987; First et al. 1988; Dentzer and Wheelock 1990; Green and Giffore 1978).
2. Historians such as Michael Apple (1982) and David Tyack (1974) have noted that patterns of social change associated with migration and immigration have involved an upsurge in struggles over ideol-ogy (in religious, racial, or cultural terms) and the formal role of the schools, which have created possibilities for new definitions and di-rections.
3. The concept of racialization explicated by Michael Omi and Howard Winant (1986) is central to this analysis. The term rests upon an understanding that "race" has neither a biological nor a natural basis but is rather a social construct constantly being taught, learned, re-

created, and renegotiated through social interactions. The process of the social construction of race is termed "racialization."

4. Traditional reproduction theory is concerned with social class arrangements and the roles of schools in perpetuating those relations from generation to generation by selectively transmitting skills according to which class people are born into and serving to shape individuals' attitudes and identity to fit their class positions (Bourdieu and Passeron 1977; Apple 1979, 1982; Bowles and Gintis 1976). The linking and extension of such theory to other axes of power relations (language relations, cultural relations, racial relations) provides a useful framework for examining the role of schools in creating meaning for immigrants becoming "American." Each of these sets of relations (race, language, and culture) is laden with a long history of social meaning and centuries of relegating people to differential experiences. Examining what occurs within schools in terms of those relations requires an extension of social reproduction theories from social class to systems of racial, language, and cultural relations. The focus should be not simply on the ways in which schools may reproduce such relations but also on how these relations are contested and change, what resistance looks like, and what conditions make resistance more or less tenable.

5. The body of work describing and examining cultural reproduction and resistance with regards to class relations has not focused on the political aspects of resistance and change that are so essential in situating what occurs in schools within a broader societal framework. The concern should be not only with how language, cultural, and racial relations are reproduced and contested within schools but also how the struggle over schools as public institutions responsible for such reproduction occurs. We need to place reproduction and resistance within a historical and political context in order to understand the role of schools and how it changes in particular conditions of demographic shift and political mobilization.

6. For purposes of confidentiality and protection, the names of the city, the school, and the individuals that are the subject of the ethnography have been changed.

7. The number of courses needed was determined by analyzing the annual R-30 Language Census data required by the state of California; this data designates the number of students who have limited proficiency in English and are in need of services. The R-30 also shows the number of students who should have support services but are not in a program designated to meet their needs. Table 10.1, which shows the number of LEP students placed in specially de-

TABLE 10.1 **Enrollment in Limited-English-Proficiency Instruction at Madison High School, from 1992 to 1994**

Number of LEP Students Enrolled in Program	1992 to 1993	1993 to 1994
ESL courses only	153	146
ESL and sheltered content classes	23	19
ESL and sheltered content classes and primary-language instruction	0	0
ESL students not enrolled in LEP instructional program	254	333

Source: California Department of Education 1993, 1994. R-30 Language Census.

signed classes to address the English-language barrier, illustrates the need at Madison High School.

8. I have chosen to use the term "American" throughout this essay to refer to U.S.-born students. Although it is neither an accurate nor a politically preferable term, given that people of the entire North American continent, including immigrant residents, are Americans, it is the term generally used by both students and adults at Madison High to refer to people born in the United States who seem to them to be members of the culture of the United States. Because it is such an important conceptual term in how they view the world, I chose to adopt their terminology here.

9. My exploration of the social maps of Madison High began with a decision to select students for in-depth interviews based on a social map of the school, assuming that a consistent sociological and demographic map would emerge that would direct me to the major student groupings in the school. Social mapping is a technique often employed by social scientists, and I was interested in enlisting students to create their own in Lisa Stern's class. Because Stern taught both "regular" social studies classes and "sheltered" classes for newcomers, we decided that I should do the project in both contexts. Students were asked to write their own analyses of what they had found and present them for class discussion.

10. "Sheltered" instruction is an approach to teaching academic subject matter in English to students with limited English-speaking ability by presenting material in a way that helps overcome the language barrier. Sometimes referred to as "specially designed academic instruction in English" or "content-based ESL," sheltered classes are supposed to cover the same curriculum as regular classes and to be

composed solely of LEP students. Theoretically, sheltered classes use special instructional strategies, including emphasis on extralingual cues (visuals, props) to help the student understand; linguistic modifications (pauses, repetitions, elaboration); interactive lectures with continuous dialogue between teacher and student; and focus on central concepts rather than details. However, not all teachers assigned to sheltered classes at Madison, or most schools in California, have the training and materials to support these special instructional strategies.

11. Newcomer Schools, the first of which was established ten years ago, provide initial assessment, basic levels of ESL instruction, and some bilingual assistance. Recent immigrant students in the high schools in Bayview, including Madison, spend half of the school day at the Newcomer School and half at their own "home-base" high schools. The Newcomer School offers an alternative vision within the Bayview educational community. It is a place where immigrants receive instruction in their primary languages, where relationships between school and family are close, and where there is support for biculturalism.

12. The separation by gender of immigrant youth seemed particularly marked at Madison in comparison with the "hang-out" patterns of nonimmigrant youth. Gender was found to be a particularly salient factor in the incorporation process. The adolescent years are fundamentally about the transition to adulthood, and a key piece of that is the transition into gendered adult roles. Recent literature has found that female immigrant youth experience their adjustment to the United States differently from males. Rumbaut (1994), for example, found significantly lower self-esteem and higher depression rates among female immigrant teens, compared with males, the longer they were in the United States. He also found that while males choose to identify either in terms of their homeland or as Americans, females hold to hyphenated identities, indicating a different sense of bridging two cultures. The young girls in the study at Madison demonstrated the complex interplay between the conflicts of coming of age as immigrants in the United States and bridging the gender expectations of two cultures. Sexuality, marriage possibility and marriageability, and attachment to and participation in schooling are key considerations in determining in which culture a young girl will have a "better" future. Far more than males, they were uncertain about whether they might return to their homeland, whether becoming too American might hurt their "marriageability" to men of their native land. For immigrants of Islamic backgrounds, this involved a particu-

lar conflict related to our culture of romance and their tradition of arranged marriages. Prolonged schooling became an effort to forestall this conflict. The anthropologist Catherine Raissigeuier (1993) studying immigrants of Algerian descent in France, found patterns similar to those I observed among the girls at Madison High.

13. Krashen (1981) has described the conditions under which second-language learning can occur. In addition to comprehensible input—that is, interactive involvement that gives the words meaning—he describes a "low affective filter." The affective filter determines whether a person is able to take advantage of the opportunities to acquire a second language. Stress, fear, and anxiety get in the way of learning. Strong motivation, self-confidence, a sense of safety, and low anxiety are necessary, he claims, for students to begin to use a new language. In situations such as those described at Madison High, where students are afraid to use English for fear of being laughed at or humiliated, the fear acts as a high affective filter and makes the acquisition of English all the more difficult.

14. Patricia Phelan, Ann Davidson, and Hahn Cao (1991) identify five borders that immigrant students must navigate. One is the "linguistic border," which arises when communication between students' worlds is obstructed not because of language difference in itself but because one group regards the other group's language as unacceptable or inferior. This border is created by invalidating students' native language and culture, by the anxiety, depression, apprehension, or fear that blocks an immigrant student's ability to participate, and by the structural limitations that make needed instruction and support unavailable.

15. A national study directed by the linguist Lily Wong Fillmore (1991) documents widespread patterns of language loss among first-generation immigrant youth. As they become English speakers, they abandon their home language. Some immigrant communities, however, do provide their own mechanisms for maintaining the home language and culture. In Bayview, a small number of students attend Saturday schools in their communities that provide native-language instruction (usually mixed with religious or cultural instruction). However, often it is not immigrant children but the next generation, who were raised as monolingual English speakers, who enroll in these schools. Rubén Rumbaut (1994) has found that three-quarters of all immigrant students in his study preferred English and chose to use English over their mother tongue. Mexicans, however, were the exception, with almost half preferring Spanish.

16. Rumbaut (1994) describes a similar kind of phenomenon in his study

of ethnic identities. He found that the foreign born were far more likely to identify by their own national origin, but that proportion drops sharply among the U.S. born. He finds this suggestive of a significant assimilative trend in ethnic self-identification from one generation to the next. The Madison High students in this study illustrate the process and the speed with which it occurs. Rumbaut also found quite different patterns in adoption of panethnic labels, with Asian youth far less likely to adopt the panethnic "Asian" label and Spanish-speaking youth from Latin America more likely to adopt a Latino or Hispanic panethnic label.

17. Howard Winant describes a process of white consciousness as follows: "The shifts brought on by the civil rights movement and the reforms it engendered also had an impact on white racial identity, which was rendered much more problematic than in the days of segregation. Whites had to change their attitudes towards minorities, which meant they had to change their attitudes towards themselves. A desirable feature of this shift was the beginning of racial dualism in whites. On the negative side, whites were threatened by minority gains. They sensed a loss of their majority status. They suddenly noted an identity deficit. Formerly their whiteness, since it constituted the norm, was invisible, transparent, but now in a more racially conscious atmosphere, they felt more visible and more threatened" (Winant 1994, 166).

18. Table 10.2 compares two outcome measures for California high school students by racial or ethnic group: the three-year dropout rate, measuring the loss of students from tenth grade to graduation, and the percentage of graduates from high school who have completed the course requirements for admission to a four-year college.

TABLE 10.2 **Student Outcomes, California High Schools, 1992, by Race or Ethnicity (Percentage)**

Race or Ethnicity	Three-Year Dropout Rate	Completion of College Preparatory Course Sequence
White	10.8	34.2
African American	26.4	27.2
Hispanic	24.6	21.0
Filipino	10.2	43.8
Pacific Islander	16.0	24.9
Asian	9.2	54.5
Native American	19.2	19.3

Source: California Basic Educational Data System 1992.

19. In formal policy, court law, and program design, the educational responsibility of schools is to help immigrants become English speaking and to deliver programs that offer access to the curriculum by addressing the language "barrier." Historically, the mandates to include and to serve immigrant students have emanated from the courts and from the intervention of the federal government.

REFERENCES

Apple, Michael. 1979. *Ideology and Curriculum*. Boston: Routledge.
———. 1982. *Education and Power*. Boston: Routledge.
Bach, Robert. 1993. "Changing Relations: Newcomers and Established Residents in U.S. Communities." Report to the Ford Foundation by the National Board of the Changing Relations Project. New York.
Bourdieu, Pierre, and Jean-Claude Passeron. 1977. *Reproduction in Education, Society, and Culture*. Translated by Richard Nice. London: Sage Publishers.
Bowles, Samuel, and Herbert Gintis. 1976. *Schooling in Capitalist America*. New York: Basic Books.
California Department of Education. 1992. California Basic Educational Data System. Sacramento, Ca.
California Department of Education. 1993 and 1994. R-30 Language Census. Sacramento, Ca.
Dentzer, E., and Wheelock, Anne. 1990. *Locked In/Locked Out: Tracking and Placement Practices in Boston Public Schools*. Boston: Massachusetts Advocacy Center.
Fillmore, Lily Wong. 1991. "When Learning a Second Language Means Losing the First." *Early Childhood Research Quarterly* 6: 332–461.
First, Joan, John B. Kellog, John Wilshire-Carrera, Anne Lewis, and Cheryl A. Almeida. 1988. *New Voices: Immigrant Students in U.S. Public Schools*. Boston: National Coalition of Advocates for Students.
Green, R. L., and R. J. Giffore. 1978. "School Desegregation, Testing, and the Urgent Need for Equity in Education." *Education* 99(1): 16–19.
Krashen, Stephen. 1981. "Bilingual Education and Second-Language Acquisition Theory." In *Schooling and Language-Minority Students: A Theoretical Framework,* edited by California State Department of Education. Los Angeles: Evaluation, Dissemination, and Assessment Center, California State University.
Lollock, Lisa. 2001. "The Foreign-Born Population in the United States:

March 2000." Current Population Reports, P20-534. Washington: U.S. Government Printing Office.

Moore, Donald R., and Susan Davenport. 1988. *The New Improved Sorting Machine*. Chicago: Designs for Change.

Oakes, Jeanne. 1985. *Keeping Track: How Schools Structure Inequality*. New Haven: Yale University Press.

———. 1986. "Keeping Track." Part 1, "The Policy and Practice of Curriculum Inequality." *Phi Delta Kappan* 68(1): 12–17.

Olsen, Laurie. 1997. *Made in America*. New York: New Press.

Omi, Michael, and Howard Winant. 1986. *Racial Formation in the United States: From the 1960s to the 1980s*. New York: Routledge.

Patricia Phelan, Ann Davidson, and Hahn Cao. 1991. "Students' Multiple Worlds: Negotiating the Boundaries of Family, Peer, and School Cultures." Paper presented at the annual meeting of the American Educational Research Association. Chicago (April 1 and 2).

Portes, Alejandro, and Min Zhou. 1993. "The New Second Generation: Segmented Assimilation and Its Variants." *Annals of the American Academy of Political and Social Science* 530: 74–96.

Raissigeuier, Catherine. 1993. *Becoming Women: Becoming Workers*. New York: State University of New York Press.

Rumbaut, Rubén G. 1997. "The Crucible Within: Ethnic Identity, Self-Esteem, and Segmented Assimilation Among Children of Immigrants." *International Migration Review* 28(4): 748–94.

Slavin, R. E. 1987. "Ability Grouping and Its Alternatives: Must We Track?" *American Educator*, 32–48.

Tyack, David. 1974. *The One Best System: A History of American Urban Education*. Cambridge, Mass.: Harvard University Press.

Winant, Howard. 1994. *Racial Conditions: Politics, Theory, Comparisons*. Minneapolis: University of Minnesota Press.

——— Index ———

Numbers in **boldface** indicate figures and tables.

Adamic, Louis, 353
Adams, David, 157
Adams, Truslow, 113
Adamson Act (1916), 47
Addams, Jane, 51, 150
affirmative action, 128–35
AFL (American Federation of Labor), 44–47, 49, 303
African Americans: affirmative action, 128–35; Americanization of, 162–63; assimilation, 119–20; Civil Rights era, 120–28, 312–16; congressional redistricting, 97–98; discrimination against, 14; immigrant distancing from, 9; as involuntary immigrants, 2, 144; liberal universalism, 114–16, 167; limits proscribed on, 146, 159–60; at Madison High School, 390–91; militancy of, 26, 122, 123, 126, 128; north and northwest migration of, 5; origins of immigrant status and, 293–94; political participation, 225–26
Aleinikoff, T. Alexander, 18–19, 25, 27, 292
aliens, resident: early America, 295, 297–98; integration of, 314–15. *See also* naturalization
American Creed. *See* liberal universalism, American Creed of
An American Dilemma: The Negro Problem and Modern Democracy (Gunnar), 114

American Federation of Labor (AFL), 44–47, 49, 303
American Jewish Committee, 126, 127
The American Kaleidoscope (Fuchs), 134
American Revolution and early American era, 21, 294–97, 301–10, 332, 333, 336–38
American Weekly Messenger, 294
Americanization: African Americans, 162–63; melting pot metaphor, 145–51; Native Americans, 152–58. *See also* civic education in public schools, politics of
Americanization, 150
Americanization project at Madison High School, 371–410; academic sorting, 401–4; "American" student experiences, 388–91, 400; community, 376–78; ethnographic high school study methodology, 375; immigration increases, economic stratification and segmented assimilation, 373–75; newcomer student experiences, 379–88, 400; overview, 22–23, 24, 371–73, 400–404; teacher perspective, 391–99
anti-semitism, 117–18, 181, 187
Antin, Mary, 356
Antiterrorism and Effective Death Penalty Act (1996), 79
Aristide, Jean-Bertrand, 270, 271

Asian immigrants: affirmative action, 129–30, 133; discrimination against, 14; exclusion of, 7, 20, 158–60, 164, 302–11, 318–19; female, in Progressive Era, 305–6; political influence of contemporary, 91–92, 94–99; racial identity of, 23, 388, 396; recent, 1; school performance, 388, 396

assimilation: as challenge, 2–3; and ethnicization, 15–16; melting pot metaphor, 126; and preferential treatment, 134–35; segmented, 10, 373–75, 401–4; vs. diversity, 144

Assimilation in American Life (Gordon), 125

Bach, Robert, 268, 371
Bailey, Thomas, 217
Barnard, Henry, 341
Baroni, Geno, 127
Basch, Linda, 195
Becker, Carl, 113
Bender, Thomas, 331
Berger, Thomas, 153
Beyond the Melting Pot (Glazer and Moynihan), 125
birthright *(jus soli)* citizenship, 19, 279, 282, 299–300, 305
blacks. *See* African Americans
Blanc-Szanton, Cristina, 195
border issues. *See* state regulation of border and membership
boss politics. *See* political machines and immigrant culture
Bracero Program, 273, 275, 303
Bradley, Tom, 252*n*11
Brayont, Charles "Boss," 42
"Bread and Roses" strike, 53
Bringing the State Back In (Skocpol), 271–72
Brown, Dee, 153
Brown, H. Rap, 123
Bryan, William Jennings, 46
Bryce, James, 39

Bury My Heart at Wounded Knee (Brown, D.), 153
Bush, George (H.), 270
Butler, Fred, 162–63

Calavita, Kitty, 273
California: Asian exclusion, 158–59, 160; California Civil Rights Initiative, 317; Los Angeles, immigrant political participation in, 224–26, 239–43; policy importance, 89–90; Proposition 187 results, 77, 93–94, 95, 274–75, 277; Proposition 209 results, 95, 317; Salvadoran political participation, 239–43
CARECEN (Central American Resource Center), 239–40, 243
Carlisle Indian School, 155–56
Carmichael, Stokley, 123
Catholicism. *See* religion and churches
Cemka, John, 48
census data, immigrant, 70, 74
Central American Resource Center (CARECEN), 239–40, 243
Chávez, César, 124
children, status of, 284, 299–300, 305
Chinese Exclusion Act (1882), 20, 164, 277, 305, 311
churches. *See* religion and churches
CIO (Congress of Industrial Organizations), 44, 48–49
Cipolla, Luigi, 52
citizenship: current, and future immigration, 279–80; dual, 8, 16, 17, 78, 213, 214, 235, 279; INS activity, 280–82; *jus soli* (birthright), 19, 279, 282, 299–300, 305; and naturalization, 69, 75; origins of , 293–301; Supreme Court rulings on, 282–83. *See also* state regulation of border and membership
civic associations, 12, 34, 50–57, 89–91, 184–85
civic culture, 109–42; affirmative action resulting from, 128–35; "Ameri-

can Creed" era, 110–20; Civil Rights era, 120–28; overview, 13–14, 25, 109–10; transnationalism, 190–91. *See also* racial perspective on immigration

civic education in public schools, politics of, 331–70; "Americanization," 344–48; common school and common denominator, 338–41; culture wars, 341–44; nativism, 348–54; overview, 21–22, 25, 331–34; policy issues, 358–61; reflections on, 361–63; republican formation, 335–38; school experience, 354–58

Civil Rights Act (1964), 120, 312, 398

Civil Rights era: California Civil Rights Initiative, 317; and civic culture, 120–35, 312–16; civic education, 22, 332; European backlash, 124; Hart-Celler Immigration Act (1965), 20, 120, 124, 312; transnationalism, 245; Voting Rights Act (1965), 12, 82, 87, 96–100, 120, 131

Civil War era, 6, 300–301, 304, 307, 318

Cleveland, Grover, 304

Clinton, Bill, 67, 94, 270

Cohen, Lizbeth, 48

Cold War era, 189–90, 312–13, 349–50

Collier, John, 157–58

Columbian migrants, political participation of, 16–18, 218, **219–20**, 221–23, 224, 232–38

Comité del FMLN, 240

Congress: citizenship in early America, 296–99; civic education, 336; ending public benefits for immigrants, 230; exclusionary policies, 304–6; immigration law, 1–2, 7, 19, 272–74, 277, 282–86, 310–17; redistricting, 97–99

Congress of Industrial Organizations (CIO), 44, 48–49

Connolly, James, 43

Constitution and Supreme Court: children of immigrants, 299–300, 305; citizenship in early America, 296–99; civic education, 336; desegregation, 121–22; district deliniation, 99; Fourteenth Amendment, 154, 282–84, 299–300, 398; immigration laws, 9, 277–78, 282–84; naturalization, 161–62; Nineteenth Amendment, 57; origins of citizenship, 293–301

countertradition thesis, American identity, 111–13

criminal behavior and naturalization, 79

crisis years in civic culture. *See* Civil Rights era

Cuban immigrants, 85

Cubberley, Ellwood P., 345–46

cultural issues: Americanization at Madison High School, 373, 374, 380, 389; civic education, politics of, 341–44; multiculturalism, 8–9, 22–23, 134–32, 164–66, 359–60; pluralism, 131–32, 190, 191, 317, 350–54; political culture of immigrants, "new" and "old," 35–39. *See also* civic culture; political machines and immigrant culture

Curley, James, 33

Dahl, Robert, 10

Daley, Richard J., 42

Davis, Gray, 275

Davis, James, 159

Dawes (General Allotment) Act (1887), 154

de la Garza, Rodolfo, 100

Democracy in America (Tocqueville), 294

Democratic party: CIO support, 48–49; citizenship and INS activity, 280; civic education, 343; civil rights movement, 122; Depression-era support, 7; ethnic politics, contemporary, 94, 96; Hispanic political

Democratic party (*continued*)
participation, 226; naturalization
and voting behavior, 67
demographics, 71–73, **72**, 83, 218–24,
219-20
denizens vs. naturalized, 71–77, **72**
Depression era, 4, 7, 58–60, 81, 187–
89, 193
desegregation, 121–22
DeSipio, Louis, 12–13, 15, 24, 60
Dewey, John, 346–47, 349
Dinkins, David, 225
Displaced Persons Act (1948), 311–12
district delineation, congressional, 97–
99
diversity, ethnic and racial, 144, 164–
66
Dole, Bob, 94
Dominican migrants, political participation of, 16–18, 218, **219-20**, 221–
22, 224, 226–32
Dornan, Bob, 67, 82
Dred Scott decision, 282, 285
dual citizenship, 8, 16, 17, 78, 213,
214, 235, 279
DuBois, Rachel Davis, 352–54
DuBois, W. E. B., 164

economic issues: financial impact of
migrants on homeland, 182–86; income and opportunities, 4–5, 6–7;
labor needs, and immigration, 268–
71; segmented assimilation, 373–75,
401–4
education, 8, 20–23, 28. *See also*
under Americanization; civic
education in public schools, politics
of
El Rescate, 239–40, 243
English-as-a-second-language (ESL),
376–78, 385, 391, 392
English for Foreigners (O'Brien),
347
English language and Americanization, 22–23, 371, 383–86, 400–404

equal protection clause, Fourteenth
Amendment, 154, 282–83, 284,
299–300, 398
Equal Rights Amendment, 55, 56
ESL (English-as-a-second-language),
376–78, 391, 392
Espaillat, Adriano, 231, 232
"ethnic group" as term, 129
ethnicity and ethnicization: ethnic politics, 91–100, 217–18; neighborhood character, 6; origins of
immigrant status and citizenship,
293–301; policy changes, 313–20;
transnationalism, 15–16, 26, 179,
195–99, **198**, 246
eugenic exclusion, 144, 147–49
Europeans, northern, as preferred,
317–18, 355
Europeans, southern and eastern:
civic and political involvement,
184–93; civic education, 332, 345,
355–56; discrimination against, 7,
14, 20; eugenics, 147–49; impact on
homeland, 182–86; paths to polity,
34–35, 37–39, 57; as racially distinct, 180–82

families, as immigration basis, 314
Fass, Paula, 24, 346
FBI (Federal Bureau of Investigation),
280–81
Federal Bureau of Investigation (FBI),
280–81
federal government. *See* Congress;
Constitution and Supreme Court
Fedyck, Micheline, 355
female immigration and citizenship:
Asian, 305–6; citizenship in early
America, 297; Columbian politics,
236; exclusionary policies, 304–5;
martial status, 306–7; mutual aid so-
cieties, 52–53; religion and politics,
55–56
Fernández, José, 230, 232
Fernández, Leonel, 17, 229, 230

fertility rates, native born vs. immigrant, 1–2
film, Native American portrayal in, 152–53
financial issues. *See* economic issues
Fitzgerald, Keith, 267
FMLN (Frente Farabundo Martí para la Liberación Nacional), 238–39, 240
Ford, John, 152
Ford Foundation, 127
Fourteenth Amendment, Constitution, 154, 282–84, 299–300, 398
Freeman, Gary, 267
Frente Farabundo Martí para la Liberación Nacional (FMLN), 238–39, 240
Frisch, Michael, 359
Fuchs, Lawrence H., 134
future research, 23–28

gateway cities, 2, 5
gender issues: Americanization at Madison High School, 380, 407*n*12. *See also* female immigration and citizenship
General Allotment (Dawes) Act (1887), 154
Gerstle, Gary, 145
Gilded Age and Progressive Era (1890–1910): civic associations, 50–57; civic education in, 21, 332, 346–47; exclusionary policy, 20, 303–6; melting pot metaphor, 146–47; paths to polity, 38; political machine, 39–43; population impact, 1, 3–4; state regulation, 317–18; transnationalism, 185–86; union activity, 43–50; whites, immigration of, 306
Giuliani, Rudolph W., 225, 226, 232
Glazer, Nathan, 125, 134, 360
Gleason, Philip, 13, 15, 19–20, 22, 25, 143, 167
Glick Schiller, Nina, 195, 215, 217
Gompers, Samuel, 46, 48
Gordon, Milton M., 125, 132

government. *See* Congress; Constitution and Supreme Court
Great Depression era, 4, 7, 58–60, 81, 187–89, 193
Greeley, Andrew, 127
green card replacement, 78
Greenback Labor Party, 45
Greene, Julie, 46
Guarnizo, Luis Eduardo, 16–17, 27

Haitian immigrants, 270–71
Hall, Stuart, 216
Hammerstein, Oscar, 118
Haney López, Ian, 161–62
Hannerz, Ulf, 195–96
Harrington, Michael, 122
Harris, William T., 342
Hart-Celler Immigration Act (1965), 20, 120, 124, 143, 312
Hay Heritage Studies Program Act (1972), 127
Hayduk, Ronald, 84
Higham, John, 293
Hill, Kevin, 85
Hipólito, Mejía, 230, 232
Hispanic immigrants: affirmative action, 128–29; Bracero Program, 273, 275, 303; contemporary, 1, 373–74, 390; dual citizenship, 214; exclusionary policies, 309–10; political influence of contemporary, 91–100; transnationalism, 218–24, 219-20. *See also* political participation of transnational migrants
historical patterns of immigrant status and incorporation, 292–327; constitutional origins of citizenship, 293–301; historical paths and research perspectives, 317–20; overview, 19–20, 25, 292–93; restriction reduction and worldwide system of incorporation, 310–17; restrictions on immigration, 301–10
Hitler, Adolf, 115
Hlinka, Andrej, 187

Holdaway, Jennifer, 84
Hollifield, James, 267
Hollinger, David, 130
homeland. *See* transnationalism
Hoxie, Frederick, 157
Hume, David, 337

identity: countertradition thesis, 111–
13; Native Americans as Americans,
152–58; pressure to adopt racial,
23, 386–91; whiteness, dominance
of, 158–64
illegal immigrants, 78–79, 92, 272–73
Illegal Immigration Reform and Immigration Responsibility Act (1996),
242
immigrants, "new" and "old": comparison of, 3–9; paths to polity, 34–39,
57; political culture, 35–39; population impact, 1; transnational practices, 216–17, 243–47
Immigration Act (1917), 275, 302–3
Immigration and Nationality Act, section 245(i) (1994), 272
Immigration and Naturalization Service (INS): application backlog, 280;
civic education, 360–61; immigrant
tracking, 70, 74; immigration penalty money to, 273; incentives for
naturalization, 77–80; and politics,
67, 78–79
Immigration and Restriction Act
(1924), 20
immigration policy. *See* policy issues
Immigration Reform and Control Act
(1986), 69, 78, 285, 314
In re Rionda, 307
Indian Citizenship Act (1924), 154
Indian Reorganization Act (1934), 157
individualism and civic education,
334
Industrial Workers of the World
(IWW), 44, 49
INS. *See* Immigration and Naturalization Service (INS)

institutions, naturalization in contemporary politics, 86–91
integration, state policies and migration, 268–71
International Typographers' Union, 46
involuntary immigrants, 2, 144
IWW (Industrial Workers of the
World), 44, 49

Janosik, 189
Jasso, Guillermina, 75
Jay, John, 294
Jefferson, Thomas, 335, 336, 337, 338,
359
Jews and anti-semitism, 117–18, 181,
187
Jim Crow laws, 121–24, 307–8
Johnson, Albert, 148–49
Johnson-Reed Immigration Act (1924),
58, 147, 154, 164
Jones-Correa, Michael, 74
Joppke, Christian, 267
Jordan, Barbara, 134
judiciary branch of government, and
immigration laws, 276–78. *See also*
Constitution and Supreme Court
jus soli (birthright) citizenship, 19,
279, 282, 299–300, 305

Kallen, Horace M., 113, 131, 166, 351
Katznelson, Ira, 250
Kazin, Michael, 47
Kearney, Michael, 195
Kennedy, John F., 120, 127
Kennedy, Robert F., 121
Kerner Report, 122
Killian, Lewis M., 119
King, Desmond, 14, 20, 21, 24, 25,
112
King, Martin Luther, Jr., 121–22, 124,
358
Knights of Labor, 44–46, 49
Know-Nothing Party, 161, 300
Kohut, Hans, 193

Labaree, David F., 361
labor needs, and immigration, 268–71
labor unions, 13, 34–35, 43–50
Land Leagues, 51
language: civic education, 22–23; English, and Americanization, 371, 383–86, 400–404; English-as-a-second-language (ESL), 376–78, 385, 391, 392
Latin Journey (Portes and Bach), 268
Latinos. *See* Hispanic immigrants
Laughlin, Harry, 148–49
League of Catholic Women, 55
legal issues: federally-based laws in early America, 301–10; judiciary branch, and immigration laws, 276–78. *See also* Congress; Constitution and Supreme Court; state regulation of border and membership
LEP ("limited English proficient"), 376–77, 393–95, 397–98
Leupp, Francis, 157
Levine, Irving M., 126
liberal universalism, American Creed of: African Americans, 114–16, 167; in civic culture, 110–20; melting pot metaphor, 14, 19–20, 143–44, 146, 165, 167; World War II era, 113, 115–16
"limited English proficient" (LEP), 376–77, 393–95, 397–98
Linares, Guillermo, 231
Lincoln, Abraham, 359, 360
Lipset, Seymour Martin, 165
Little Big Man (film and book), 153
local politics, naturalization encouragement, 82–86, 89
Locke, Alain, 113
Lodge, Henry Cabot, 166
Los Angeles, CA, immigrant political participation in, 224–26, 239–43

machines, political. *See* political machines and immigrant culture

Madison High School study. *See* Americanization project at Madison High School
Malcolm X, 123
Manifest Destiny, 153
Mann, Michael, 153, 338–39, 340, 341
March, James, 363
marital issues and citizenship, 297, 306–7, 309
Massey, Douglas, 269
McCarran-Walter Immigration Act (1952), 311, 312
McCartin, Joseph, 47–48
McClymer, John F., 349, 350
McGuffey, William Holmes, 340
melting pot metaphor, 14, 19–20, 126, 143–51, 164, 165, 167
membership. *See* citizenship; naturalization; state regulation of border and membership
Merton, Robert K., 40
Mexican immigrants, 225, 249–50. *See also* Hispanic immigrants
Mink, Gwendolyn, 45, 46
Minnite, Lorraine, 84
Mollenkopf, John, 84
Monroe Doctrine, 251*n*5
Montagu, Ashley, 129
Montalto, Nicholas V., 351
Montgomery, David, 48
Morawska, Ewa, 15–16, 24, 26
Moreno, Dario, 85
Morton, Samuel George, 154
Moynihan, Daniel P., 125
Mozo, Rafael, 75
multiculturalism, 8–9, 22–23, 134–32, 164–66, 359–60
Murphy, Charles Francis, 41
mutual aid societies, 51–52, 58
Myrdal, Gunnar, 14, 114–15, 116, 117

NAACP (National Association for the Advancement of Colored People), 160, 162
Nast, Thomas, 342

Nation, 351

National Association for the Advancement of Colored People (NAACP), 160, 162

National Association of Manufacturers, 46

National Center for Urban Ethnic Affairs, 127

National Council of Catholic Men, 55

National Latino Immigrant Survey, 70–71, 85

national origin and immigration laws. *See* historical patterns of immigrant status and incorporation

National Project on Ethnic America, 126

National War Labor Board, 48

nationalism vs. transnationalism, 247–50

Native Americans: affirmative action, 129–30; discrimination against, 14; identity, racial perspective on, 152–58; as involuntary immigrants, 2; origins of immigrant status, 293–94, 300; policies excluding, 146

nativism in civic education , politics of, 348–54

naturalization: in early America, 295–301; ethnicization, 26; incentive structure for, 77–80; incentives for, 77–80; political behavior of immigrants, 80–86; rates, **68**, 69, 71–77, **72**; speed of, 71–73, **72**, 78–79; vs. citizenship, 280; "whites-only," 160–62. *See also* Immigration and Naturalization Service (INS); politics, naturalization in contemporary; state regulation of border and membership

Naturalization Act (1790), 160–61

neighborhoods as ethnic political units, 37

New Deal, 7, 26, 59

New York City, NY, Hispanic political participation in, 224–38, 230–38

New York Times Magazines, 113

Newcomer School, Bayview, CA, 391, 394, 398, 407*n*11

newspapers, foreign language, and transnationalism, 185–86

Nineteenth Amendment, Constitution, 57

Nixon, Richard, 121

Novak, Michael, 126, 127

Nuñez, Angel, 231

oath, citizenship, 281

O'Brien, Sarah, 347

O'Connor, Edwin, 33, 41, 42

Olneck, Michael, 354

Olsen, Laurie, 22–23, 24, 28

Olson, David, 84

O'Malley, Linda, 385, 398

O'Neill, Thomas "Tip," 86

Organizacion Salvadorena Americana (OSA), 242

OSA (Organizacion Salvadorena Americana), 242

Ossowski, Stanislaw, 184

The Other America (Harrington), 122

Page Act (1875), 304–5

Palmer, Robert R., 109, 110

Park, Robert, 353

Parkman, Francis, 154

Pastrana, Andrés, 235, 237

Patri, Angelo, 349

Patterson, Orlando, 158

Pawiak, Jozefa, 183

peer perspective, Madison High School study, 379–91

Penn, Arthur, 153

Perlmann, Joel, 181

Personal Responsibility and Work Opportunity Reconciliation Act (PRWORA) (1996), 77, 277–78

Pizano, Ernesto Samper, 234

pluralism, 131–32, 190, 191, 317, 350–54

policy issues: civic education, 358–61; eugenic criteria, 144–45; state regulation of border and membership, 268–71. *See also* state regulation of border and membership

political machines and immigrant culture, 33–66; civic associations, 50–57; electoral breakthroughs, 57–60; labor unions, 43–50; "old" v. "new" immigrants in, 35–39; overview, 7, 9, 11–12, 24, 33–35; voting behavior, 39–43

political participation of transnational migrants, 213–63; behavior of, 184–93; Columbian migrants, 232–38; contexts of reception in New York City and Los Angeles, 224–26; Dominican migrants, 226–32; historical perspective, 243–47; overview, 16–18, 27, 213–15, 247–50; participation of earlier immigrants, 216–18; roots of migration and transnational practices, 218–24, **219-20**; Salvadoran migrants, 238–43; sociological perspectives, 215–16

political parties. *See specific party*

political science, as perspective, 9–11

politics, naturalization in contemporary, 67–108; ethnic politics, 91–100; incentives to naturalize, 77–80; institutions and incorporations, 86–91; naturalization rates, 71–77, **72**; overview, 12–13, 24, 67–69, **68**; political behavior of naturalized, 80–86; political environment structures of naturalized, 86–100; polity integration through, 69–71; voting rights act, 96–100

Polonsky, Abraham, 153

population changes, 1, 3–4, 5

Portes, Alejandro, 75, 268, 269, 372

Powell, Lewis, 130

PPCCE (Programa para la Promoción de las Comunidades Columbiana en el Exterior), 235

Pratt, Richard, 155

press, foreign language, and transnationalism, 185–86

Programa para la Promoción de las Comunidades Columbiana en el Exterior (PPCCE), 235

Protestantism. *See* religion and churches

PRWORA (Personal Responsibility and Work Opportunity Reconciliation Act) (1996), 77, 277–78

public education and schools. *See* civic education in public schools, politics of; education

public policy. *See* policy issues

Quota Acts (1921,1924), 302–3

race vs. "ethnic group" as term, 129

racial perspective on immigration, 143–72; Americanization as melting pot, 145–51; Americanization at Madison High School, 23, 373, 386–91, 394–96, 400–404; anti-semitism, 117–18; civic education, 347–48; contemporary population, 5; diversity and multiculturalism denial, 164–66; eugenic exclusion, 147–49; Japanese-Americans internment, 115–16; Native Americans and identity, 152–58; origins of immigrant status and, 293–94; overview, 14, 23, 24, 25, 143–45, 166–67; policy changes, 313–20; race as defining American characteristic, 9; whiteness as dominance, 158–64. *See also* African Americans

Reconstruction, era of, 301–2, 307, 318

redistricting of congressional districts, 97–99

Refugee Act (1980), 275, 312, 314

religion and churches: Americanization of Native Americans, 155; anti-semitism, 117–18, 181, 187; civic

religion and churches (*continued*)
  education, 332, 334, 341–44, 355; as
  civic support, 53–57; origins of immigrant status and, 294–97, 300; as
  path to polity, 34, 53–56, 58; politics
  in, 54–55; and upward mobility, 5
remigration, 34, 60*n*1
Remington, Frederic, 153
republican formation and the politics
  of civic education, 332, 335–38
Republican party: anti-immigrant
  stance, 315; citizenship and INS activity, 280; civic education, 343; ethnic politics, contemporary, 94, 315;
  Hispanic political participation, 226;
  naturalization and Democratic vote,
  67
research: future needs for, 23–28; historical patterns of immigrant status
  and incorporation, 317–20
resident aliens. *See* aliens, resident
Revolution, American, and early
  American era, 21, 294–97, 301–10,
  332, 333, 336–38
In re Rionda, 307
Riordin, Richard, 252*n*11
Rise of the Unmeltable Ethnics (No-
  vak), 126, 127
Rodriguez, Maria, 394, 398
Rogers, Richard, 118
Rogin, Michael, 153
Roosevelt, Eleanor, 58, 113, 114
Roosevelt, Franklin D., 58, 59, 81, 150,
  157
Rosenzweig, Mark, 75
Ross, Betsy, 359
Ross, Tim, 84
Rumbaut, Rubén, 387–88
Rush, Benjamin, 335, 337, 338

St. John de Crevecoeur, J. Hector, 146
Salter, J. T., 40
Salvadoran migrants, political participation of, 16, 18, 23–224, 218, **219–
  20**, 221, 238–43

Samper, Ernesto, 234
Sánchez, Loretta, 67, 82
Schneirov, Richard, 45
Schurz, Carl, 341
SDS (Students for a Democratic Society), 124
The Searchers (film), 152
second-party system, 36
section 245(i), Immigration and Nationality Act, 272–73
segmented assimilation, 10, 373–75,
  404–4
settlement experiences and naturalization, 74–75
settlement houses, 50–51
The Shame of the Cities (Steffens),
  39
Skerry, Peter, 133
skills, as immigration basis, 314
Skocpol, Theda, 271–72, 274
Smith, Al, 58, 59, 81, 88
Smith, Rogers, 3, 14, 112, 165
Social Security Act, 58
sociodemographics, 71–73, **72**
sociology, as perspective, 9–11
Srole, Leo, 181
State Department, U. S., citizenship
  oath enforcement, 281–82
state regulation of border and membership, 267–91; early American
  laws, 295–301; membership structure, current, 283–86; overview, 18–
  19, 25, 27–28, 267–68, 286; policing
  the borders of membership, 278–
  83; state as actor, 271–78; state policies, migration and integration,
  268–71. *See also* historical patterns
  of immigrant status and incorporation
Steffens, Lincoln, 39
Stern, Lisa, 378–79, 388, 389
Sterne, Evelyn, 11–12, 13, 24, 28, 90
Stewart, James, 152
Storey, Moorfield, 162
student perspective, Madison High
  School study, 379–91

Students for a Democratic Society (SDS), 124
Sumner, Charles, 161–62
Supreme Court. *See* Constitution and Supreme Court
Swett, John, 339, 340, 360

Taft, William Howard, 304, 308
Tammany Hall, 40–41
Taney, Roger Brooke, 282
Teacher perspective, Madison High School study, 391–99
territorial expansion, U. S., and citizenship status, 308–9
Thomas, William, 182
Tocqueville, Alexis de, 294, 333
Todd, Helen M., 349
transnationalism: academic interpretations of, 175–79; benefits of last two significant immigration influx, 193–99; comparison of last two significant immigration influx, 179–93; ethnicization and, 179, 195–99, 198; overview, 15–16, 24, 26–27, 175–79; political participation perspective, 215–16. *See also* political participation of transnational migrants
Trujillo, Rafael Leonidas, 227
Truman, Harry, 118, 119, 165
turn-of-the-century era. *See* Gilded Age and Progressive Era (1890–1910)
Tyack, David, 21, 22, 25, 371–72

Ueda, Reed, 18, 19, 21, 25, 83, 267, 282
undocumented immigrants, 78–79, 92, 272–73
unions, labor, 13, 34–35, 43–50

Valdez, Guadalupe Toro, 356–57
Vecoli, Rudolph J., 125

Vietnam War, 123
voters and voting: contemporary politics, 67–69; immigrant voting rates, 82–86; mobilization of immigrant, 12, 86–91, 98; for "old" and "new" immigrants, 36–37, 38; political machine, 39–43; union activity, 43–44
Voting Rights Act (1965), 12, 82, 87, 96–100, 120, 131

Wagner Act (1935), 48–49, 50, 58
Waldinger, Roger, 181
Wallace, George, 126
Walzer, Michael, 278
Warner, W. Lloyd, 181
Washington, Booker T., 163–64
Washington, George, 336, 337, 356, 359, 360
Washington, Martha, 356
Watergate scandal, 121
Watts riot, 120
Wayne, John, 152
Webster, Noah, 335–37, 338, 339·
whites: backlash of, 126–27; citizenship in early America, 296–97; dominance of, 158–64; Progressive Era immigration, 306
Who Governs? (Dahl), 10
Wilson, James, 154
Wilson, Woodrow, 46, 146, 150, 151, 193, 217, 304
Winant, Howard, 389
Wirth, Louis, 116–17, 118
women. *See* female immigration and citizenship
World War I era: Americanization, 149–51; civic education, 332, 333–34, 349; ethnic politics, 217–18; exclusionary policies, 7, 304–5; melting pot metaphor, 146–47; political activity, 4, 47–48, 57–58; transnationalism, 186–87
World War II era: civic education, 353–54; economic opportunities for,

4–5; liberal universalism, 113, 115–16; pluralism, 310–12, 318; political machines, 41–42; restrictions on immigration, 7; transnationalism, 189

Zhou, Min, 372
Zinn, Howard, 124
Znaniecki, Florian, 182
Zolberg, Aristide, 267, 286
Zunz, Olivier, 3